Fighting Words

THE BOLD AMERICAN JOURNALISTS WHO BROUGHT THE WORLD HOME BETWEEN THE WARS

Nancy F. Cott

BASIC BOOKS
New York

Basic Books
Hachette Book Group
1290 Avenue of the Americas, New York, NY 10104
www.basicbooks.com

Printed in the United States of America

First Edition: March 2020

Published by Basic Books, an imprint of Perseus Books, LLC, a subsidiary of Hachette Book Group, Inc. The Basic Books name and logo is a trademark of the Hachette Book Group.

The Hachette Speakers Bureau provides a wide range of authors for speaking events. To find out more, go to www.hachettespeakersbureau.com or call (866) 376-6591.

The publisher is not responsible for websites (or their content) that are not owned by the publisher.

Print book interior design by Trish Wilkinson.

Library of Congress Cataloging-in-Publication Data
Names: Cott, Nancy F., author.
Title: Fighting words : the bold American journalists who brought the world home between the wars / Nancy F. Cott.
Description: First edition. | New York : Basic Books, 2020. | Includes bibliographical references and index.
Identifiers: LCCN 2019034717 | ISBN 9781541699335 (hardcover) | ISBN 9781541699311 (ebook)
Subjects: LCSH: Foreign correspondents—United States—Biography. | Journalism—United States—History—20th century.
Classification: LCC PN4871 .C75 2020 | DDC 070.922 [B]—dc23
LC record available at https://lccn.loc.gov/2019034717

ISBNs: 978-1-5416-9933-5 (hardcover), 978-1-5416-9931-1 (ebook)

LSC-C

10 9 8 7 6 5 4 3 2 1

to Noah, Fiona, Nellie, and Leo
and their future on a green earth where truth-telling matters

Contents

Maps

Illustrations

Dorothy Thompson, 1920   James Vincent Sheean, 1921

John Gunther, 1922   Rayna Raphaelson, 1923

Passport application photographs, first time traveling abroad.
Source: National Archives and Records Administration.

INTRODUCTION

Dorothy Thompson had no fixed plans when she headed across the Atlantic in 1920. Nor did Vincent Sheean or John Gunther when they soon did the same—nor even Rayna Raphaelson when she crossed the Pacific to China. All were in their twenties, restless, eager to leave the United States for a foreign destination. Traveling independently, each of them started out with breathtaking casualness, unprepared for what might come and how to survive, sure only of needing to earn self-support and wanting "to write."

From such uncertain beginnings each one created a momentous international career in journalism. Writing about distant political urgencies, they alerted fellow Americans to tie their own fates to that of the rest of the world. The impact of intrepid journalists in the decades between the two world wars has never been emphasized, although their reporting and commentary were essential in urging Americans to face global responsibilities in the mid-twentieth century.

Wherever they landed, each of the four met unstable circumstances. The first world war had smashed the international order, and unprecedented military devastation still staggered much of the globe. Nearly ten million soldiers were gone, ten million more disabled with ghastly wounds; uncounted civilians were displaced or dead. Cities lay in ruins in Europe, with national economies blasted. Four empires had been demolished, and the Treaty of Versailles concluding

1

the war set off new conflicts by redrawing international boundaries. Because the United States had suffered comparatively little in the war, emerging with a stable postwar economy and currency, unattached young Americans with little in their pockets could roam cheaply in the early 1920s. Whatever few dollars Americans brought with them would multiply in value across much of Europe and Asia. Even the ocean passage need not cost much, if comfort did not matter.

Young people with some education (though no money), desire for creative work, and curiosity about the global scene might easily gamble on going to live abroad as these four did. They formed part of a larger phenomenon rarely noticed: a surprisingly large proportion of their generation of Americans did go abroad to live and learn for some years between the two world wars. It was not rare. Between a quarter and a third of those in their twenties then—among Americans who would later become notable—lived in a foreign country for more than a year, often far longer, during the interwar decades. "The Spirit of the twenties was everywhere international and cosmopolitan," one of them recalled; "the sign of the moment was Eros, defined by Plato as the soul stirring itself to life and motion." Bringing their experiences home, these travelers (who came from all the regions and races and religions of the United States) influenced American knowledge and politics through the twentieth century. Their numbers and interests went far beyond the famous coterie of literary "expatriates" who lived for some years in France. Worldly exchanges sparked by their generation inspired cultural innovation and social movements, though only in the high arts has their importance been recognized.[1]

The common presumption that Americans in the 1920s were "isolationist" has obscured the extent of foreign travel and residence among the younger generation. It's true that the United States spurned membership in the new League of Nations and restricted immigration severely then, while successive Republican administrations looked to bolster business strength. Nonetheless, "isolationist" is a poor designation for the United States, with its intensifying worldwide financial and commercial commitments, its participation in international conferences and groups (even League of Nations committees), and a foreign policy tellingly concerned with global regions of potential economic advantage.[2]

Journalists were among the most peripatetic of the younger generation who, by exploring foreign perspectives, countered insular policies and provincial attitudes in the United States. Newspaper reporting abroad presented an obvious opportunity for venturers who needed to support themselves, as Dorothy Thompson, James Vincent Sheean, John Gunther, and Rayna Raphaelson did. Print ruled the world media then, and newspapers were ubiquitous in the United States. In the years following the first world war, American newspapers, magazines, and specialized weeklies had more staff abroad than ever before in peacetime. Major American papers had established foreign bureaus in European capitals during the world war; rather than dismantling them in the 1920s, they kept existing bureaus and added others elsewhere. Putting correspondents' eyes on the world made sense. International peace was still fragile, while American commercial interests spanned the globe and more Americans than ever before were traveling abroad. Even though most readers of American newspapers cared far more about local and national matters, owners of major papers sensed an international future and expanded their coverage to far parts of the world.[3]

From anticolonial conflict in northern Africa to China's Nationalist revolution, from Hitler's Berlin to Stalin's Moscow, one or more of the journalists in the chapters to come was on the spot as a witness, sending news of a changing globe. Retracing their paths reanimates the turbulent international era in which they thrived. Their writings ranged like searchlights across rising threats, shaping fellow Americans' awareness of critical trends. In Europe in the 1920s, they watched authoritarian leaders take hold in numerous countries. Fascism, founded by Benito Mussolini, made him prime minister of Italy by 1922 and "Il Duce" not long after; within a decade, looking around Europe, he expressed confidence that "the liberal state is destined to perish." The worldwide depression of the 1930s put capitalism as well as democracy into crisis and created more headway for dictators, including Adolf Hitler. The stakes in alerting American readers to this spreading menace were clear: the future of representative governments and the rule of law, taken for granted by most Americans, was imperiled.

Wide awake to that threat, Dorothy Thompson warily watched it grow. She began her stunning journalistic ascent from Vienna in 1921, leaving her small-town Methodist roots far behind. A modern woman whose marvelous determination made her a foreign correspondent, she was soon promoted to be chief of her newspaper's foreign bureau in Berlin—a post almost unheard of for a woman. Meanwhile she was falling head over heels for a European lover and marrying him. Her bold condemnation of Adolf Hitler in 1932 was among the first to make an impression; it would lead to her being the first American officially ejected from Nazi Germany two years later. She then grew even more influential as a fervent antifascist in her thrice-weekly political column for the *New York Herald Tribune*.

Chicagoan John Gunther was already a newspaperman when he landed in London. Tall and blond, an "Adonis" in one woman's eyes, Gunther debated with himself for years whether he should write fiction instead of journalism. As a foreign correspondent for the *Chicago Daily News*, he roved across the globe, gaining friends and worthy contacts everywhere, until the grip of European politics made the decision for him. By 1930, a promotion put him in Vienna as foreign bureau chief for his newspaper, covering all the surrounding countries where authoritarianism had destroyed parliamentary rule. His subsequent move to book writing so swelled his transatlantic fame that he was credibly dubbed "the world's best-known newsman" before he turned forty.

Deadly upheavals in Palestine in 1929 brought Gunther together with James Vincent Sheean, cementing a friendship between the two. Sheean, who had grown up poor and Catholic in the midwestern sticks, relished daring hazards when he began as a foreign correspondent for the *Chicago Tribune* in Paris in 1923. He barely escaped a court-martial in Spain, fatal capture in North Africa, and drowning in the Mediterranean—experiences of reporting that turned his politics strongly toward anti-imperialism. An individualist and autodidact who read in five languages, Sheean soon chafed at the objectivity expected of reporters. He took up a freelancer's precarious existence as his own political views sharpened, leaving behind a regular salary in order to write as he liked. After becoming a transatlantic celebrity at thirty-five by writing a book on his political learning curve, this self-styled "journeying man" never stopped moving.

Red-haired Rayna Raphaelson turned Sheean's life around in Hankou, China. She was a rebellious Jewish daughter from Chicago with curly hair so flaming red that it stopped people on the street. When the early end of her marriage drove her to China to start her life anew, she did not imagine how she would rise to influence as a journalist for the Chinese revolutionary Nationalists. Her decision to work in political journalism hid latent treacherous consequences—about which Sheean and Dorothy Thompson learned when their paths converged with hers in Moscow, on the tenth anniversary of the Bolshevik Revolution.

All four of them took risks in intimacy as well as in their journalism as they navigated the globe. None of them adhered to conventional sexual standards, much less the expectations of their parents' generation. "People who were in their twenties in the 1920s were amazingly, perhaps unprecedentedly, immoral," Sheean coolly observed; they "created the extreme licentiousness that was the moral characteristic of the age."[4] Their foreign scenarios included ups and downs with spouses and lovers, sexual encounters and affairs that were passionate and meaningful at best, but not always. Their public and private lives entwined. They were rethinking relationships between women and men, as much as between themselves and the world, as much as between peoples and political systems.

In chapters ahead, the political role of these journalists climaxes in the late 1930s. At that point Americans were acrimoniously split between putting "America First" or taking on international responsibilities.

Today, troubling shadows of their era darken the world again. Americans are divided over the nation's role in the world (and much else), making the stability of American democracy appear fragile; authoritarian nationalist leaders in major foreign countries have risen to power, often with popular support, as in Europe in the 1920s and 1930s. Dictatorial states then clamped down on the power of the press, preventing freedom of speech and communication, mounting a formidable challenge to correspondents' aim to use the press to expose tyrannical actions. These techniques have been reprised today, along with shockingly powerful and insidious hazards unique to our digital era. Both then and now the integrity of the press in all its forms is the issue. Despite its distance from us in time, the story told here echoes fearsomely now.

CHAPTER 1

ORIGINAL ROVER BOY

James Vincent Sheean was a child of the twentieth century, born on its cusp in December 1899, in tiny Pana, Illinois. Always "Jimmy" among his friends, he made his name in print as Vincent Sheean, choosing at nineteen to sign an opera review that way, though he later said the name was a "mask" imposed on him by an editor. His doubling went beyond his nom de plume. His early colleagues at the *Chicago Tribune* in Paris could not decide whether he was "nothing but a playboy" or "nothing but a highbrow"—but agreed he was an extraordinary character. In college at the University of Chicago, John Gunther thought Sheean was "bizarre": "He hummed Mozart, wore green pants, spoke better Italian than the Italian professors, read the Talmud, quoted Spinoza, learned German, borrowed money, admired dancing, and wrote a treatise on the Wahabis." By the time Gunther dredged up that memory fifteen years later, the two men were good friends, and Gunther considered Sheean "perhaps the most remarkable American of my generation I know."[1]

Red-haired and blue-eyed, the grandson of four Irish immigrants, Sheean took for granted "the map of Ireland in my face." His small-town Catholic upbringing included attending a parochial school and then public high school. He worked a newspaper-delivery route and other odd jobs in his spare time, as did his four brothers. His father, a traveling salesman and unsteady breadwinner, did not favor Jimmy, but his loving mother, a schoolteacher, happily recited long stretches of Shakespeare, narrative poetry, and Abraham Lincoln's addresses aloud for his pleasure. Never an attentive student in school—nor an athlete, although he grew to be six-foot-two—Sheean was an autodidact whose favorite activity was reading. He read his way through Pana's public library, gulping one author's works whole and then moving along the alphabet to the next, from Austen to Dickens, from Hugo to Twain. He wrote stories, essays, and poems from the age of six and by ten was ghostwriting his older brothers' term papers.[2]

The United States was a land of readers then, with a high and still growing literacy rate and a widespread assumption that reading led to self-improvement and thus to success. Both information and amusement came from the printed page. In Sheean's childhood and adolescence, there was no radio to listen to, certainly no TV; nothing like internet had been envisioned. The silent cinema could be seen in larger towns, but probably not in Pana. Stimulation outside of books arrived live, in lectures, musical and dramatic performances, circuses, political harangues, clerical instruction. From the nuns in his parochial school, Sheean learned to love classical music, and performers on the Chautauqua circuit ignited his lifelong passion for opera.[3]

Omnivorous reading spurred Sheean's imagination to travel far beyond the small town of Pana, preparing him, wittingly or not, for the life he would eventually lead. With remarkable initiative he studied foreign languages so that he could read favorite European authors in the original. A priest recently arrived from Europe who spoke better French than English taught French to Sheean, and a Lutheran pastor helped him with his study of German; he taught himself Italian from a textbook ordered from a Sears, Roebuck catalog and bolstered his ability in conversations with an immigrant fruit merchant. A misfit in his surroundings, Sheean had teenage acquaintances who thought he was a wit and a charmer, but more who found his "talking like a book" difficult to understand.

One exceptional high school teacher, Helen Mills, opened "a door into a world of freedom" for him. Her mentorship signaled that "it was possible to use not only the whole of your wits but the whole of your vocabulary—that vocabulary which, like a miser's hoard, you spent your entire life accumulating and were always afraid to use," he later wrote in autobiographical fiction. She urged Sheean to enter the University of Chicago's scholarship competition for local high school students. Examination in just one subject sufficed—fortunate for him, because his enthusiasms were so skewed toward literature. He finished eighth out of the 289 students taking the test in English literature and won a partial scholarship.[4]

In the fall of 1917 Sheean arrived at the university, "a freshman awed by stone and mortar, seventeen years young." As a would-be writer, he went out for the student newspaper, the *Daily Maroon*, right away, but his dedication was episodic at best. A poor Irish kid from a small town, always suffering "anemia of the pocket-book," as he admitted, he set his eyes on social rather than academic success, becoming a social climber and feeling triumphant making friends among the stars of the undergraduate social scene. Yet he also felt like an impostor. He veered back and forth between smug delight in being accepted by students of wealth and position and disgust with himself for caring. More than once he acknowledged that his "aim of being 'prominent in college'" was "terribly barren"—but it was the golden ring on the merry-go-round that he reached for.[5]

One early episode so burned his memory that he recounted it years later when fascism was marching across Europe. He and his roommate both agreed to pledge a fraternity without knowing that it was a predominantly Jewish house. When a female acquaintance explained to him that it would be socially fatal to associate with Jews, Sheean and his roommate buckled to the widespread prejudice. In the middle of pledge night, they escaped out of an upper-story window of the fraternity house and ran away. He knew the decision was

9

shameful, but it expressed his priorities at the time. Though Sheean blasted the fraternity system as "invented by the demon of social position to plague college men with the corrosive infection of exclusiveness," that did not keep him from joining another one later.[6]

Moving into campus housing after the escape, he lived down the hall from a graduate student named Fred Millett, who became his confidant. Millett called Sheean "ill-balanced" as a freshman—a "prodigy" intellectually, "almost a wreck" physically, and "a chameleon" emotionally. Millett happened to know Sheean's high school teacher Helen Mills and reported to her that Sheean was "brilliant socially": "he can be & usually is, very charming, but his egotism & his heartlessness make him frequently and tho[ugh]tlessly brutal to people who like him."[7]

Sheean was not cut out for standard academic achievement. He chose mostly "snap" courses in literature, never studied, and skipped class almost as often as he attended—scraping through (when he did) by impressing a professor with his French accent or pulling off an acutely intelligent paper. His poems won him election to the Poetry Club, where he met leading lights of Chicago modernism and silently ridiculed other students' pomposity. He cared more about hearing the Chicago opera without paying for a ticket. As a freshman, he volunteered as an usher but could not afford the repeated cost of the starched collars and cuffs that ushers were required to wear. As a sophomore in 1918, until the November end of the world war he was admitted free when wearing his uniform from the Student Army Training Corps, a military preparedness unit required of male college students. Later he became the *Maroon*'s music and theater critic for the free tickets.[8]

When the Student Army Training Corps ended, Sheean did not immediately return to school. Needy and in debt, after first sampling two unendurable jobs he got a part-time position reporting for the Chicago *Herald-Examiner*—a natural for him as an aspiring writer. Newspaper reporting was a lucky-break field and opened doors for creative talent. The long American tradition of creative writers supporting themselves as journalists included Mark Twain, Theodore Dreiser, Willa Cather, Katherine Anne Porter, Alice Dunbar-Nelson, Fannie Hurst, and Jack London, among others. No specific credentials were required to become a reporter—only the drive to do it and ability to write a decent line. Satirist H. L. Mencken "wormed his way in" to writing for the *Baltimore Morning Herald* when he was nineteen, for example, by hanging around the office until he got an assignment. Typical conditions were gritty, the lives of cub reporters unglamorous, and their pay low, but the work offered spectacle, mobility, and the outside chance of influencing masses of people.[9]

Jobs existed everywhere, because newspapers flooded the American landscape. In 1920, approximately twenty-five hundred daily papers were published (in eleven thousand towns), circulating nearly thirty-two million copies every day plus sixteen million copies of Sunday-only editions, while American households numbered under twenty-five million. Today not even thirteen hundred dailies circulate, though the American population has tripled. Then, large cities had four or more dailies, plus Sunday papers, weeklies, monthlies, and innumerable special-interest, foreign-language, and ethnic-group newspapers. Many smaller cities and towns supported both a morning and evening daily, plus less frequent papers. Ninety-five percent of Americans in the 1920s read newspapers, according to a large-scale national study.[10]

When Sheean got his job, Chicago was a newspaper-reading city of 2.7 million inhabitants, where four papers together sold over 1.4 million copies every day. The *Herald-Examiner*'s circulation of three hundred thousand was the smallest. Publishing magnate William Randolph Hearst created the paper in 1918 by merging his Chicago *Examiner* with the *Record-Herald*, adding the newcomer to the growing Hearst chain. Over the previous twenty-five years, competition between Hearst and innovative publisher Joseph Pulitzer (whom Hearst copied) had transformed newspapers into vehicles of entertainment as well as of varied information. Joseph Pulitzer had noticed that masses of readers bought nineteenth-century penny papers for their sensational or sentimental stories, and he applied that approach when he founded the *New York World* in 1883, intending to appeal to a broad working-class public. The *World* investigated and condemned institutional corruption while its "human interest" stories blared melodramatic headlines such as "ALL FOR A WOMAN'S LOVE." Crime, sports, scandal, and violence crowded its pages.

Hearst imitated and went beyond Pulitzer, while buying up newspaper after newspaper. His chain sat on the sensational side of the American newspaper spectrum. One day, for instance, Sheean had to go to Chicago's North Side to look "for the body of a six year old girl who had been diddled with by a low-life sex-hound at the Virginia Hotel and then made away with." Competition between Hearst and Pulitzer led to both adding diversions—puzzles, large drawings, comic strips, opinion pages, household advice, lovelorn columns— that then swept through the industry. By the 1920s, almost every major newspaper carried humor and advice columns, photographs, comics, Sunday rotogravure sections with high-quality half-tone images, and—a new rage—the crossword puzzle.[11]

But Sheean gave little time to the *Herald-Examiner* when he returned to school in the fall of 1919. He was consumed with writing an operetta for the competition run by Blackfriars, a male-only musical comedy club on campus. He and his coauthor won the prize, leading to public performance of the musical in May 1920. Sheean's celebrity made him "deliriously happy," he wrote to Fred Millett, who was no longer on campus. He circulated mostly among people of privilege. "I play around with only two or three girls," he told Millett, all "very nice" and "very wealthy . . . so I am almost in the position of a kept man." For the summer of 1920 he was asked to tutor the seventeen-year-old son of a meatpacking baron. The position put him among the family's rich friends in Lake Forest, Illinois, and then at a dude ranch in the Bighorn Mountains, horseback riding and hobnobbing with Bostonians from Harvard. Staring him in the face, nonetheless, were his "Debts. Debts. Debts. Everywhere debts."[12]

Sheean registered for school in the fall despite having been through "a cyclone of reaction" against his "dawdling, supercilious, superficial life." He stayed because he was in love with his coauthor of the Blackfriars operetta. Though Sheean dallied with women during college, he fell passionately only for men. He could speak openly about this with Fred Millett, his "midnight confessor, guide, philosopher, and friend" in freshman year, because Millett, too, loved men. Millett "played a most important part in the operation of opening my young mind," Sheean said a dozen years later. "It would have happened in any case, but the fact is that Fred B. Millett did it." While still in college Sheean playfully baited the older man, "Some day you can ruin me, if you like—when I'm extremely successful and famous—by divulging all that you know." He was kidding, but speaking the truth. Erotic ties between men were considered a species of moral degeneracy in academia (as elsewhere) and were very, very severely punished. Sheean knew he absolutely had to hide his sensibilities in public. But he took risks. As a senior, he skipped freshman rush at his fraternity while conceding to Millett sardonically, "But then—who knows?—I may meet my Fate. I've met my Fate—Oh, how many times, in the past three years and a half! And still I live."[13]

In letters, Sheean told Millett about one crush after another. One, "a Galahad child," was supposedly irresistible to the whole fraternity—"it's the 'universal disease' in Phi Gam," he reported. Fraternities incubated same-sex eroticism without determining anyone's eventual sexual path. Whether Sheean understood his erotic attraction to men as deeply part of his identity is impossible to determine. He described his crushes—"such a dear fresh young thing" or "the blue-eyed fair-haired innocent"—in the standard literary language of boy-girl romances. Nor did he limit himself to men, apparently: though when one boyfriend "actually wept" because Sheean "went in to a harlot," he promised not to "'screw' as they call it."[14]

A tall, good-looking young man always in need of money, Sheean was not averse to opportunistic encounters. "My head teems with intrigues to get money," he wrote desperately to Millett at one point.

"I'm at the stage, I fancy, where a woman becomes a prostitute."
His vulnerability harbored hazards. One college summer, handed a
newspaper job in Detroit, Sheean soon quarreled "ferociously" with
the man who wanted him there. He explained to Millett, "The man
is my pet aversion. Ugh! . . . I had to live with him—Dieu! Even the
bed we shared. I cannot ask you to believe the horrors of that experience." It was not the first or the last such uneasy connection Sheean
had to finesse.[15]

His feelings about his Blackfriars collaborator differed completely.
Sheean rhapsodized about him, using the rarefied Greek words *hip-
podamus kalos* applied to the idealized youth on Greek red-figure
vases of the fifth century BC. They spent "morning, noon and night"
together for six weeks while working on the operetta, and Sheean
told Millett, "I loved him as devotedly as I have ever loved anybody,
I think. He loves me, too, I believe, for he tells me so in a thousand
mute testimonies of gift and service and act: but his training is all
against it. . . . He abhors demonstrativeness above all else, and he
goes in for the masculine stuff—My boy, you should see me mascu-
linify myself!"[16]

After a year's relationship, the boyfriend shifted his attention to
a girl. Sheean was shattered. "My days are spent in a progressive discovery of the weary, flat, stale and unprofitable uses of this life,"
he told Millett. "I take four courses and loathe them and cut them
and get flunk notices." By then it was December of his senior year,
though he still lacked many credits required for graduation because
he had skipped class so often. The intensity of his own jealousy and
longing terrified him, because the danger of exposure was always
there. "Some day I shall not be able to control, to dissimulate, to
pretend," he forecast direly. "Then there will be a crash. Already a
few people suspect—I mean people of the University's great world,
such as it is." He planned to leave for New York by January, he said:
"The sooner I get away the better." In New York he would "starve in
bliss and forget my Chicago woes."[17]

He was already sunk in despair when he went home to Pana for Christmas. His mother, the one family member he really cherished, had been recurrently ill since the summer. She died on January 21, 1921, deepening his gloom. After her funeral, he returned to Chicago but did not register for school. With empty pockets and no luggage, he went to the Chicago railroad station and boarded a train for New York—escaping his anguish, leaving his provincial past behind. For the long hours of the journey, he slumped in a window seat and stared through the dirty glass. Later he quoted Stéphane Mallarmé's poem, "To flee, to flee far away," to mark the departure, calling it "a kind of epigraph for my youth." Perhaps a coded gesture toward his hidden life, it was also an understated prediction of his next decade of world adventure.[18]

SHEEAN LANDED IN New York City's storied Greenwich Village, where earlier restless upstarts from the Midwest had migrated ten or fifteen years before, to brand the neighborhood a site of cultural and political rebellion. When he arrived in 1921 the Provincetown Players had already dispersed, wartime censorship had quashed the radical magazine the *Masses,* and the Village was attracting sightseers—"becoming an institution," in the wary eyes of a writer who lived there earlier. But rents were relatively cheap and the area's reputation still attracted iconoclasts. Even a brief immersion in the Village announced a breakaway from one's upbringing, a shedding of origins and a reinvention of self.[19]

New York, a city of five million, swarmed with newspapers. Sheean had no need to starve because he found a job right away at the city's newest daily, the *New York Daily News*, the first American tabloid. The *Daily News* had shot out in front of long-established papers in less than two years and was selling over 400,000 copies a day; neither the *New York Times* nor Pulitzer's *World* reached even 350,000. Started by the wealthy owners of the *Chicago Tribune,*

Colonel Robert McCormick and his cousin Joseph Medill Patterson, the *New York Daily News* was modeled on the London *Daily Mirror*, a "half-penny illustrated" with the largest circulation of any newspaper in the world. In 1905, the *Mirror* had inaugurated a new, simple, racy, and photograph-laden format in a newspaper half the size of the standard one—thus twice as easy to read while commuting on subways and trolley cars. The first page was usually entirely pictures, with one startling headline. With one big story in front and not much to read after that, the whole paper could be examined fully in about a half hour.

The tabloid style took Pulitzer's and Hearst's lead toward sensationalism and ran with it, producing a paper limited in content, arresting in presentation, and highly prescriptive in intended reader response. Exaggerated headline fonts and large photographs guided the reader, and because news angles made heroes and villains plain, editorials became unnecessary. The *New York Daily News* demanded little of the reader, while enabling him—and frequently her—to feel completely informed. Though derided as "the servant girl's Bible," the *Daily News* very quickly inspired local imitators and rivals, including Hearst's *Daily Mirror* (almost a carbon copy of the *Daily News*, with even less news) and Bernarr Macfadden's *Evening Graphic* (dubbed by critics the "Porno-Graphic").[20]

Writing for the *Daily News*, Sheean was plunked deep into the seamy details of urban adulteries, divorces, blackmails, and murders. The job bored him, though he was good at it. He handily mastered the required storytelling technique, with the advantage that his youthful looks evoked confidences from the typically female protagonists of the stories he covered. He learned reporters' lingo and gained confidence in his ability to hold his own among journalists. Near the lower Manhattan offices of the *Daily News* and other newspapers, he frequented speakeasies with colleagues, starting the drinking habit that seemed a sine qua non of the reporter's trade. He discovered how common, even fashionable, it was to flout Prohibition (a lesson in itself). The neighborhood called Little Italy was close by, where he ate spaghetti, tried out his Italian, and drank "red ink"—wine disguised in heavy white coffee cups.

He learned more outside his New York job than in it. "I had an immense amount of innocence to lose," he said later, and "the more I found out the more there seemed to be to find out." In Greenwich Village he heard political passions unleashed at the Liberal Club near Polly's Restaurant, a favorite gathering place for radicals, bohemians, and artists. Left-wing ideas were not entirely new to him. During his freshman year, Fred Millett had been a conscientious objector who saw the war "from the proletarian standpoint" and wanted the Allies to support the Bolsheviks. Sheean had occasionally heard lectures by radicals visiting Chicago, such as Rose Pastor Stokes, when she was contesting her conviction under the Espionage Act for her antiwar speeches. In the Village, radical ideas surrounded him. Sheean listened to fervent witnesses of the Bolshevik Revolution. He learned that progressives blamed the Treaty of Versailles that ended the world war for imposing outsize blame on Germany and for augmenting rather than diminishing the British and French empires.[21]

Worldly-wise Louise Bryant made a lasting impression on Sheean. "She's wild and brave and straight, and graceful and lovely to look at . . . an artist . . . a poet and a revolutionary." John Reed had described Bryant in 1915 when he fell in love with her. Dark-haired, blue-eyed, slim, emotionally vivid, she dazzled Sheean six years later. Bryant had left her marriage and mildly freethinking journalism in Portland, Oregon, to go with Reed to Greenwich Village, where she quickly adopted sexual and political radicalism. She was thirty-five when a mutual friend introduced her to Sheean and had just returned from Russia, where she was widowed. John Reed died from typhus in Moscow in October 1920, while attached to the Bolshevik cause, barely a year after his riveting eyewitness account of the Bolshevik Revolution, *Ten Days That Shook the World*, made him famous. Dying in Moscow that way just before his thirty-third birthday made him into a reigning martyr-hero for American radicals. For Sheean, Reed's palpable aura strengthened Bryant's magnetism.[22]

Sheean's attention must have been a welcome diversion for Bryant. She found it "terrible to come back" to the Village apartment that she and Reed had shared—"more terrible than I ever dreamed," she told a friend. A journalist herself while traveling with Reed, Bryant had reported her own eyewitness account of the Bolshevik Revolution in thirty-two syndicated articles, published in over a hundred newspapers. Then she revised the articles into a book, *Six Red Months in Russia*, published before her husband's *Ten Days*. Bryant's engaged political reportage personified a model of journalism utterly different from Sheean's writing for the *Daily News*. Both she and John Reed saw the journalist as a political actor in history, not only a witness to it. After Reed's death, Bryant had stayed in Russia, reporting on postrevolutionary developments for the International News Service (owned by William Randolph Hearst). Her resulting sixteen-part series began appearing in Hearst newspapers in 1921, soon after she met Sheean.[23]

Bryant's use of the power of the press resonated with Sheean, needling him to see journalism as a force for political change. They may have become lovers. Sheean later named "sexual freedom" as one of the "wide range of possibilities" of which he became aware while in New York, without supplying any details. Or he and Bryant were simply friends inclined to flirt. He was probably speaking lightly when he answered a letter of hers, not long after they both left New York for different parts of the world, "No, I shan't get married. I've got into so many extraordinary messes with women in this short month that I don't think I'll ever get married—that is, unless you change your mind and decide to have me . . . and don't you get married to any Turkish pashas or anything like that." He signed that letter, and others to her, with love. Bryant departed for Europe and Turkey, planning to write a new series for the International News Service. For several years afterward she and Sheean stayed in touch, and occasionally met in Paris after she made a surprise marriage to American diplomat William Bullitt in 1923, when pregnant with his child.[24]

Whether they were lovers or not, she was an alluring, accomplished, courageous older woman who blessed him with a new and valuable phase of nurture, turning him away from provincialism and advancing his political acumen. Soon after she left New York, Sheean did too. He applied for a passport in December 1921, saying his purpose was "travel" and "newspaper work also."

AMERICAN TRAVELERS LIKE Sheean were much better off than the hundreds of thousands of refugees and migrants floating in the war's wake. International relations were still scrambled in the war's aftermath. Territorial disputes and internal struggles for power flared in the fledgling nations that the Treaty of Versailles created from the former Austro-Hungarian, German, and Ottoman Empires. The upstart presence of the Bolshevik regime in Russia unleashed an untried political alternative, and the United States, too, emerged unexpectedly as a major potential player on the world stage.[25]

American transatlantic travelers could be intentional, and became more numerous in the 1920s, more diverse, and younger than ever before. Transatlantic communication had improved ever since the 1860s when undersea telegraph cables linked Europe to the United States. In the nineteenth century, typically only wealthy elites took the European Grand Tour, though intellectuals, reformers, artists, and scholars might also travel to reach European teachers or collaborators; commercial purposes also motivated some American businessmen to establish small American "colonies" (as they were called) in major European cities. As telegraphing capability increased, and then when two-way wireless (radio) signals spanned the ocean soon after 1900, the advancing communications revolution seemed to shrink the globe.[26]

American tourists became legion after the world war, dipping into storied European cultural offerings and happily imbibing wine during Prohibition. So many more Americans traveled to Europe—often to see where their husbands, sweethearts, brothers, or sons had fought or died in the war—that the American Express Company began offering travel services, convention arrangements, cruises, and guided tours "to suit practically any pocketbook." Ocean liner companies added cheaper classes of accommodation to lure more travelers, inventing "cabin" class below second class, and then "tourist third," only slightly better than steerage.[27]

Sheean was not a tourist. He wanted to live in France and finish writing a novel he had begun, and he knew that in France's exhausted postwar economy the exchange rate between the dollar and the franc would let him live cheaply. His choice was almost overdetermined because so many Greenwich Village writers were about to do the same. If Paris had long signified cultural grandeur, lavish cuisine, and high fashion, in the 1920s young men like Sheean were drawn by its low cost of living for anyone with dollars. Ernest Hemingway, Sheean's age and likewise a writer-reporter, told his Toronto *Star* readers in 1922 that Paris "in the winter is rainy, cold, beautiful and cheap. It is also noisy, jostling, crowded and cheap. It is anything you want—and cheap." A dollar was worth five francs in 1914, but when Hemingway wrote, it was worth almost twelve. The exchange rate kept mounting until it stabilized at about twenty-five francs to the dollar in the mid-1920s.[28]

Paris after the war became a magnet for creative talent and a crossroads for migrants. When Archibald MacLeish decided to leave his Philadelphia law practice to write poetry instead, he chose to live in Paris because of "the magnificent work being done by people from all over the world and in all the arts." As the inflow from Francophone Africa, Spain, Russia, Central Europe, and elsewhere swelled and diversified the Parisian population, political outcasts and budding anticolonial activists congregated along with avant-garde thinkers and artists from around the world. The absence of segregation and relative racial tolerance in the city attracted many African American sojourners, especially Harlem Renaissance writers. The "elastic" milieu of Paris, a "cosmopolitan world of people of different races and colors," appealed to Jamaican-born writer Claude McKay; he felt comfortable where "radicals, esthetes, painters and writers, pseudo-artists, bohemian tourists—all mixed tolerantly and congenially together."[29]

Parisian sexual tolerance was also a draw. American tourists flocked to the Folies Bergère to see female flesh on display, and sex tourism guidebooks in English pointed out more risqué spots. The sidewalk visibility of commercial sex startled young John Gunther on a visit to Paris in 1925, when a pimp came up close to him "and hissed: 'Come wiz me,' with a frightful leer, 'and I will show you femme avec donkey.'" Gunther acclimated quickly, cheerfully noting three days later that while idling for forty-five minutes near the Cathedral of the Madeleine one evening, he was "accosted by a. Seven pimps. b. One sub-pimp (a dirty postcard vendor) c. Eighteen whores (pretty) d. Six whores (medium) e. One hundred and twenty nine whores (awful) f. One sailor g. Three painted boys."[30]

French ease with extramarital dalliance surprised young Americans more. William Shirer went to Paris a naive college graduate, straight from Coe College in Iowa, and felt "wonderfully carefree in the beautiful, civilized city, released from all the puritan, bourgeois restraints that had stifled a young American at home." He was working as a reporter, on his way up to becoming a successful foreign correspondent, when he fell into a "devouring possessive love" with an older married woman he described as "Parisian to the bone, chic, sophisticated, witty." Deep into their sexual affair, he wanted to marry her, but she would not hear of it. "She teased me about being so bourgeois and so foolish," he recalled. "'Why spoil so great a love by marriage?'" she asked him. "'Now we are two free spirits. It is the only way to be in love.'"[31]

Unlike the United States, England, and Germany, France did not criminalize sex between men, and harbored a long, if pornographic, tradition recognizing sex between women. That enticed a number of creative Americans, including writer Djuna Barnes, who dropped Brooklyn journalism and opted for more ambitious modernism once she saw Paris. Janet Flanner likewise migrated there when she fell in love with a woman; within a few years she became the Parisian columnist for the newly founded *New Yorker*. Virgil Thomson, later music critic and composer, first appreciated Parisian sexual largesse when he lived there as a Harvard student on a fellowship in 1922. His roommate then was Eugene McCown, a friend from high school in Kansas City who was supporting himself playing the piano in the wee hours at Le Boeuf sur le Toit, a chic and noisy bar. With wry pleasure Thomson described the bar's habitués as "English upper-class bohemians, wealthy Americans, French aristocrats, lesbian novelists from Roumania, Spanish princes, fashionable pederasts, modern literary and musical figures, pale and precious young men, and distinguished diplomats towing bright-eyed youths." Thomson moved to Paris more permanently a few years later, when he felt stifled in his musical career and constrained in his sex life in the United States. Berlin was more notorious for easy sex with boys, he knew, but Berlin was also full of hustlers capable of blackmail. Thomson wanted a life in music, and counted Parisian discretion as important as its freedoms. "Everybody knew what everybody else was up to" in Paris, Thomson later said. "But you did not talk about it."[32]

If Sheean was drawn to Paris for its sexual reputation at all, the city also appealed as a hub of international journalism, where the major American dailies had foreign bureaus. Scores of American periodicals kept Paris offices. Aspiring American writers arrived with hopes like Sheean's that they could live cheaply, earn a bit as journalists, and still find time for their own writing. A later estimate concluded that almost 70 percent of the three to four thousand American writers, artists, and intellectuals in Paris in the 1920s earned "a considerable part of their income" from newspaper work or allied journalistic and publishing endeavors.[33]

Thinking ahead to supporting himself, Sheean carried with him a letter from the city editor of the *New York Daily News*, affirming his bona fides as a reporter and introducing him to the editors of the Paris-based European edition of the *Chicago Tribune*. Fortunately for Sheean, the two newspapers were both owned by the same publisher. During the world war, Colonel Robert McCormick (he was always called "Colonel") established an overseas edition of his Chicago paper so that American soldiers in France could read US news in their own language. (A few years later, he and his cousin founded the *New York Daily News*.) Though McCormick became stolidly isolationist in his own politics, he kept the Paris-based European edition going after the war. His European edition competed with the well-established and higher-status Paris *Herald*, published by the New York *Herald* since 1887. Both of these papers catered to American tourists and had a curiously local rather than cosmopolitan flavor. Their original reporting covered Parisian events and news of Americans' transatlantic comings and goings. The news of the world and of the United States in both papers was republished from the home paper in Chicago or New York.

Both the *Tribune* and the *Herald* in Paris held out lifelines to impoverished American writers living in Paris. Each had a distinct aura, in the eyes of those who vied for jobs there. The *Herald* was staid, respectable, proud of itself, and its large and commodious offices overlooked the city markets of Les Halles. The *Tribune* did not take itself as seriously. It was more literary and satirical, partly because of booziness among the staff, many of them Montparnasse denizens such as Harold Stearns, Eugene Jolas, Waverly Root, Elliott Paul, and Henry Miller. The *Tribune*'s office was "a single, dingy room on the upper floor of a building on the rue Lamartine" when Irene Kuhn worked there in 1921, she recalled. "There were no desks, merely scarred, battered plank tables to support the decrepit typewriters, of which there were never enough to go around. Rickety chairs, a Telex machine, a few telephones, and a half dozen or so naked lightbulbs dangling from a painted-tin ceiling completed the décor." A bistro operated in the courtyard immediately below, from which the often raucous staff hauled up buckets of beer via a rope. Kuhn, as society and fashion reporter—the only woman on a ten-member staff— spent her days roaming the grand hotels to find tidbits for a column called Americans in Paris. She was twenty-two and loved her job.[34]

Sheean did not take advantage of his letter of introduction right away. When he arrived early in 1922, hardly believing he was really there, he first wandered Parisian avenues and byways in wonder and delight, visiting landmarks he knew from novels, stopping in cafés and museums, and observing people. Then he left. To perfect his French, he found a place to board in the home of a retired couple in the northern countryside. Sequestering himself there for a few months, he spoke and heard only French while writing his novel (in English).

Afterward he could not resist visiting Italy, where he stayed for a while in Venice to improve his Italian and enjoy the watery city's beauty. He boarded cheaply in the palazzo of a corrupt baron who ran an illicit gambling hall and needed a paying tenant for cover. There he saw the alarmingly lawless ways of the blackshirted Fascisti, loyal followers of Benito Mussolini. They seemed to him a "rabble army," "half-grown boys from the gutter." Noticing that the baron paid them protection money, he found out that they extorted payments not only from the baron but also from many businesses, legitimate or not, and would smash the windows of any who did not cooperate. When he left Venice, Sheean stopped in Rome to absorb its ancient grandeur. On his departure he saw the blackshirts again, crowding into Rome's railroad station with banners and loud songs, heading for a Fascist congress in Naples. Little did he imagine that barely a week later, at the end of October 1922, Mussolini would lead his minions in a March on Rome and be anointed Italy's prime minister.[35]

Paris then lured Sheean back. When he showed up at the office of the *Chicago Tribune* with his letter of introduction, Henry ("Hank") Wales, second in command there, took him on as an assistant. Sheean was hired not only to write local news for the paper's European edition—the position that American would-be writers in Paris typically sought—but also to assist Wales in reporting French news for the *Chicago Tribune* published in the United States. Language abilities made Sheean stand out from the job-seeking crowd;

he had been reading newspapers in three languages since he arrived in France. Foreign correspondents' methods at that time began with reading the local newspapers and deciding which stories to follow up. The chief of the *Chicago Tribune*'s foreign bureau in Berlin, for example, said that he and his assistant scanned forty German newspapers daily. Language fluency was a must.[36]

Though Hank Wales (called "a tough man to work for—mean, suspicious, and a bit of a bully" by William Shirer, who served under him a bit later) was not easy to please, Sheean must have impressed him. Within five months Sheean became a full-fledged foreign correspondent for the *Chicago Tribune*, with a beat centering on French politics. The *Tribune* was expanding and syndicating its foreign news service in the 1920s, trying to beat the reputation of its local rival, the *Chicago Daily News*. Syndication meant that other newspapers could subscribe to the *Tribune*'s foreign service and publish its correspondents' special reports in their own pages. For the correspondent, it meant wider recognition when bylined articles were published nationwide.[37]

Sheean cannot have been immune to the aura surrounding the foreign correspondent. Ever since H. M. Stanley of the *New York Herald* published his immortal line—"Dr. Livingstone, I presume?"—upon finding the missing doctor deep in Africa, the foreign correspondent had become a figure of recognizable flair, not only reporting but making the news. Profit-seeking publishers egged on their correspondents to faraway adventures, expecting these accounts to attract more readers and thus more advertising revenue. Newspapers put bylines on foreign news more consistently than on domestic news, lending individuality to the correspondent. During the world war, the celebrated exploits of war correspondents catapulted great expectations into young people's dreams. Scrappy Milly Bennett, for example, becoming a cub reporter in San Francisco in 1917, fantasized her exciting future: "A newspaperwoman would tear around the world. A war here. A coronation there. A flood, a famine, a revolution or two. All in the day's work."[38]

The *Chicago Tribune* had boasted some of the most daring war correspondents. One, "headline hunter" Floyd Gibbons, was editor in chief of the paper's European edition and also chief of the paper's foreign service in Paris (Wales's superior) when Sheean was hired. Gibbons was "the quintessential foreign correspondent, a handsome man with a huge sense of adventure, unlimited daring, and great personal courage," in Irene Kuhn's eyes. Gibbons had tempted fate in 1917—before the United States entered the war, but after Germany's unrestricted submarine warfare had led to severing diplomatic relations—by embarking across the Atlantic on the Cunard liner *Laconia*. The *Laconia* was hit by a torpedo and sank in little more than a half hour. Gibbons had planned for such an emergency by packing a life vest, and after spending a tense night in a lifeboat, he landed in Liverpool and immediately cabled a dramatic scoop about the experience to Chicago. The *Tribune* gave his story a huge banner headline, and it was published all across the nation (through syndication). Gibbons was less lucky when he covered the German engagement of American Marines and French troops at Belleau Wood. Machine-gun fire blew out his eyeball. He was treated as a war hero when he returned home, and the white eyepatch he wore to hide his disfigurement became his trademark ever after.[39]

Sheean did not face war, but postwar peace on the continent was fragile. Major controversies arose in the wake of the war. Sheean began to think for himself politically as his work plunged him into these fracases among European nations. He confronted heads of states and their spokesmen directly and felt that in his role as a reporter he was more than an observer. He wielded a power larger than his young unknown self: "The power of the press," he thought, "enabled such fragments of humanity as myself to exert . . . a kind of suffrage, at least in opinion, so that the course of events was never wholly regulated by the desire or machinations of the powerful." From the first, he saw his reporting as a "political job."[40]

Sheean began writing political news when what was called the "crisis over the Ruhr" reached a new level of impasse. The crisis arose

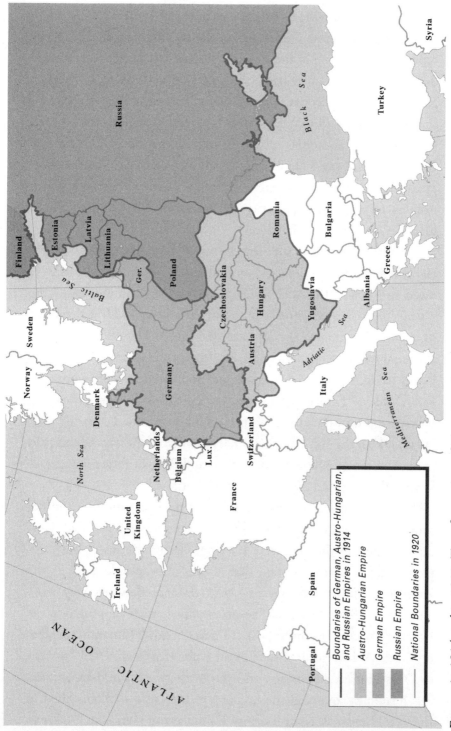

Europe in 1914 and in 1920: Transformations of Three Empires

from punitive provisions of the peace treaty signed at Versailles, which blamed Germany for causing the war and required it to pay reparations to several of the victorious Allies, to compensate for their losses. The Allied victory had ended the German empire. In its ashes arose the smaller Weimar Republic (so called because the new constitution was signed in that city). The Treaty of Versailles gave selected border regions and cities of the former German empire to France, Belgium, Denmark, Poland, and Czechoslovakia, or to international guardianship, and also severely restricted Germany's rebuilding of military force, requiring too that the east bank of the Rhine River in Germany remain demilitarized.[41]

Because France had suffered the most destruction by far, especially in its industrial capacity, more than half of all reparations were owed to France. The Weimar Republic's weak economy made the reparations schedule unrealistic, however, and in 1922, it defaulted on paying the money, timber, and coal due to France. In response, France showed no flexibility and, joining with Belgium, sent military forces to occupy the rich mining and industrial area of Germany's Ruhr Valley. The occupiers took over the railroads there, intending to keep and transport the coal that would be mined. To stymie that, Weimar kept the German coalminers away from their work and paid them a minimal dole instead. French and Belgian forces began collecting aboveground coal in lieu of reparations.[42]

By the time Sheean began reporting on the issue, one after another proposal for ending the French-Belgian occupation had failed. German workers in the area were starving, German industry was crippled, and Weimar's inflation was hitting unbelievable levels as the government printed money to pay the miners. Between May 1923 and March 1924, dozens of Sheean's bylined articles appeared in the *Chicago Tribune*, beginning with "France Sends Ultimatum to Allies on Ruhr." When rioting began in the Ruhr area late in 1923, he went to Dusseldorf, a major city, and stayed there until mid-December. His headlines conveyed the urgency of the crisis—"Blood Shed in Ruhr as Hunger Renews Rioting"; "France and Germany Dicker to

Restore Ruhr Railroads"; "Ruhr Magnates Agree to Reopen Mines and Mills"; "Rescued Ruhr Starving Still as Nations Row."[43]

Now mired in the "pesthouse" of Europe, Sheean had to replace his haloed romantic views of France with rueful realism. The aging French prime minister Raymond Poincaré became his bête noire. Sheean saw Poincaré as a leader deformed by venomous hate for the power next door. "If I lived to be a thousand I could never forget the sound of his maniac shriek as he pronounced the word *Allemagne* [Germany]," Sheean wrote later. "The whole curse of Europe was in it." He had no sympathy for Poincaré's long memory, which stretched back to France's defeat by Germany in the Franco-Prussian War, nor did he fully grasp the old man's dread of German resurgence along its long common border with France.[44]

International meetings contributed to Sheean's newly critical appraisals. He went to Lausanne, Switzerland, in June 1923, for a great-power conference intended to set new national borders in lands formerly in the Ottoman Empire (also ended by Allied victory). The self-interested calculations of the ministers of Britain and France there repulsed him. He saw both of them "squirming and dodging" to protect their imperial possessions, each jockeying for favor with the new Turkish leader, Mustapha Kemal (later called Ataturk). Nor did the fledgling League of Nations inspire Sheean's confidence. Its high ideals proved no match for Mussolini's international aggressions in 1923 and 1924, he saw. Hard realities triumphed as the great powers met behind closed doors to work a deal with Italy, rather than submitting the dispute to the League Assembly. Sheean concluded that the League was already in its death throes, impotent to solve actual international conflict.[45]

As Sheean shuttled from Paris to Lausanne and Geneva, then to Essen, Dusseldorf, and Brussels and back to Paris, his political education accelerated. In March 1924, he went to Madrid, where he had a hair-raising brush with Spanish authorities. He was there to report on the political progress of the new dictator, General Primo de Rivera, who had dissolved the Spanish parliament and seized autocratic power the previous September. Sheean hired a Spanish assistant and began exploring, but bronchitis laid him low. While lying sick in bed, he was served with an arrest warrant signed by His Majesty King Alfonso XIII. What followed would have been farcical had it not been so dangerous. Sheean was put under military arrest and headed for a court-martial, all because of a telegram he had sent to Louise Bryant in Paris to congratulate her upon the birth of a daughter. Spanish authorities had bizarrely misinterpreted the telegram to suggest that Sheean was trying to manipulate the Spanish currency. They had been trailing Sheean since he arrived: opening his letters, tapping his telephone, intercepting his telegrams to his office. His Spanish assistant confessed to being a government spy.

Sheean immediately appealed to the American *chargé d'affaires* in Madrid, Hallett Johnson. Johnson did not believe Sheean's story until a cablegram from US Secretary of State Charles Evans Hughes arrived, ordering him to act quickly, because the State Department had received word that Sheean was in danger of being shot. The State Department's source exaggerated, but Johnson jumped into action. He arranged an official visit to Primo de Rivera and took Sheean along. When the dictator claimed smugly that there were "no spies in Spain," Johnson and Sheean brought forward the shamefaced assistant to tell the truth. Sheean was rapidly released.[46]

By May 1924, Sheean was in London, where implementation of the Dawes Plan proposed by the United States was being discussed. Under this plan, US loans enabled the Weimar Republic to pay the reparations owed (at a negotiated lower rate); with that boost, the European powers could then pay their war debts to the United States. The reparations acrimony lessened—but new crises soon arose. Sheean went to Rome in June to assess the mysterious murder (by Fascists) of a Socialist deputy named Matteotti. The "Matteotti affair" marked the emergence in Italy of the Fascist dictatorship as a total state, in Sheean's view—a state "constructed so as to expunge all opposition automatically the moment it appeared."[47]

AFTER LITTLE MORE than a year covering postwar European controversies, Sheean had become a seasoned reporter. He wowed Jay Allen, who joined the *Tribune* staff then and thought Sheean "fabulous," sophisticated "beyond words!"—"the original Rover Boy." Sheean's whirlwind of political reporting had jaded as well as educated him. Fed up with the ways of European diplomacy, he had lost whatever faith he had in European political leaders' words.[48] Repulsed and disheartened by European ploys, Sheean looked across the Mediterranean. In the Rif mountains at the craggy northwestern edge of Africa, an insurgency against Spain was taking place. Could an army of indigenous Riffian fighters succeed in routing imperial power? Sheean was determined to find out.

CHAPTER 2

BLUE-EYED TORNADO

D OROTHY THOMPSON WAS twenty-seven, her adolescence well behind her, when she crossed the Atlantic in 1920. Arriving in Europe ushered her into a second youth. "In her late twenties she seemed nineteen," German playwright Carl Zuckmayer thought after meeting her in Berlin a few years later. "She was marvelously healthy; her face always looked as if she had just been running in a stiff sea or mountain breeze; and her bright, clear eyes flashed and glowed with eagerness and enthusiasm." Thompson trusted her intuition and acted on her own strong will when she took the risk of going abroad without money or connections. She applied for a loan to underpin her journey, telling the bank that she would support herself abroad "through correspondence for American newspapers," though she had no prior experience as a journalist. She did not get the loan, but she did fulfill her promise about her future.[1]

Scores of promising young men like Jimmy Sheean arrived in Europe and looked for newspaper jobs, while few women tried it, and those who flourished were singular. Amid tough competition, Thompson soared like a helium balloon over others filled only with air. "When I wanted to come abroad, and leave a good job," she insisted to a good friend a year later, "and to embark without money upon a profession for which I was quite untrained, all my friends thought me mad, but the 'inner voice' told me this was the thing to do, and I must do it, and always I was lighthearted and happy."[2] She was not always lighthearted and happy that first year, in fact, but she was not downed by hurdles, either. Determination, ambition, and her "inner voice" thrust her ahead where those less bold would have cowered.

THOMPSON'S STICK-TO-ITIVENESS STEMMED partly from knowing she would have to support herself. She had grown up in upstate New York, the older daughter of a Methodist preacher born in England. The family moved from parsonage to parsonage, wherever a congregation would hire her father, almost every other year. Though they lived sparely, often in habitations without an indoor toilet, Thompson remembered her early childhood as carefree. Her loving and unworldly father radiated kindness, and she learned the household arts early from a mother she adored. An omnivorous reader, she knew early on that she wanted to be a writer. When she was naughty, her father's punishment was requiring her to memorize poems or psalms. Long into adulthood her head overflowed with a store of literature that she could quote at will.

Her mother died when Thompson was eight—a devastating loss. She was made more miserable by not getting along with the woman her father courted and then married three years later. The tension made her adolescence stressful. Fortunately, the family hit upon the solution of sending her to live in Chicago with doting aunts, her father's sisters—one a widow and one unmarried. Relatively well-off, the aunts could afford to dress her more fashionably and to enroll her in a private high school incorporating two years of college. She played girls' basketball and joined the debate team—the only girl to do so. Thompson then attended Syracuse University for junior and senior year, gratis, because the school waived tuition for the children of Methodist ministers. During summers she took what jobs she could get, working in a candy factory or as a waitress. Later she said she never thought about marrying but only about how she would earn a living.[3]

Once she graduated in 1914, her own sense of justice made her feel obligated to help support her younger siblings through college. She found work she believed in, as an organizer for the New York state woman suffrage movement, a cause that challenged her ingenuity and gave her good practice for on-the-spot public speaking to indifferent or hostile male audiences. Mainstream women's organizations were all in favor of women voting by then, but only men could make it happen, and a majority were not convinced. The New York suffrage referendum that she was working toward failed in 1915, as did similar referenda in Pennsylvania, Massachusetts, and New Jersey. The movement plowed on, engaging glittering New York socialites as well as working-class women. A second referendum in New York in 1917 triumphed, and her job was over.[4]

The United States had entered the world war by then, and Thompson, eager to go overseas, applied to do aid work. Turned down, she instead wrote copy for an ad agency, but disliked the work. In 1918 she moved to Cincinnati to become publicity director for a pilot project of the National Social Unit Organization, a group trying to bring philanthropists together with social workers to aid the urban poor. When the Cincinnati project closed the next year, she moved to New York City to the national office.

There, she fell in love for the first time—with a married man, the forty-year-old leader of the Social Unit. Though he returned her feelings he also loved his wife, and the situation tied him in knots. Thompson treasured for a long time her recollection of his declaration of feelings, "so sensitively made, with such an overwhelming sense of the things mental and spiritual involved." Their relationship, never physical, continued unconsummated for almost a year. She had no prior sexual experience, and this relationship woke her up to sexual desire. Her desperate and unfulfilled yearning made her impatient to turn in a new direction.[5]

The "agony of inexpression" in her love affair sent her across the Atlantic, she told a friend later; that "was what drove me abroad, and keeps me here." Thompson felt free to leave once her younger sister graduated from college. Europe exerted an irresistible magnetism on her; she hoped also to reach Russia, where the Bolshevik regime had given women equal voting rights and promised a new and more equalitarian society. With the ballast of her puny savings of $150, and no friends or contacts abroad, she willfully imagined making her way as a single woman amid foreigners.[6]

Her one crucial support was a friend whose company she prized. She made the transatlantic journey together with Barbara De Porte, the daughter of Russian Jewish immigrants, a Cornell University graduate with a sharp mind and left-wing political beliefs. Thompson had known hardly any Jews or Catholics while she was growing up, but she and De Porte bonded as coworkers in the suffrage campaign. As they planned their departure, De Porte was also eager to see Russia but made London their first destination. She was going to an International Zionist Conference there, to meet up with her sweetheart, Meir Grossman, a Russian-born Zionist. Presumably through De Porte's connections, Thompson included in her passport application a letter from the Zionist Organization of America affirming that she was a member of the American delegation to the conference.[7]

They departed on June 19, 1920, traveling with an all-male group of Zionists on an unusually slow boat. On board twelve days, Thompson enjoyed flirting with the most attractive men, while absorbing a compressed education on the contestation between Zionists and Arabs in Palestine. Upon arriving in London she and De Porte went to the International News Service (INS)—the Hearst press agency, which relied heavily on freelance writers—and wangled assignments to report on the Zionist conference. Proud of what she had recently learned, Thompson wrote to a friend at home, "if I keep on I think I shall perhaps become the leading Gentile authority on Judaism." Maybe she was kidding. She felt "a very real admiration for this extraordinary race" while retaining the commonplace assumption that Jews were a group apart.[8]

Energy characterized her every move as Thompson reinvented herself as a journalist. She had no resources but her talents, cleverness, courage, and perhaps most importantly her insistent belief in herself. Five-foot-six, with determined gray-blue eyes, even features, pearly skin, and her dark hair bobbed short in the style of the modern woman, she radiated a fresh-faced, girlish appeal. She cared about how she looked and dressed accordingly. In London—"a marvelous city," she thought, she and De Porte rented a small room together. Thompson concentrated on finding topics to write about and firing off articles to any outlet that might buy, including the INS, the *Christian Science Monitor*, and the *London Star*. She met people through her writing and made new contacts and new friends.[9]

Within six weeks she tripped into her first big break. Dashing to Ireland to look up her father's Irish relatives, she managed to interview the Sinn Féin leader, Irish Nationalist Terence MacSwiney, who had just been arrested by the British authorities for sedition. He protested with a hunger strike, but the British convicted and imprisoned him anyway. MacSwiney continued fasting in prison. Forty days later he died, and Thompson was the last journalist to have interviewed him. She had to be clued in to the value of her notes by the INS news chief, but once she learned the context she wrote a unique story. It won her press credentials from the INS, which meant a reporter's access wherever she went.[10]

In September, Thompson and De Porte moved to France. While her romantic sensibilities warmed to the beauty of Paris, Thompson buckled down to improve her inadequate French and to find angles for political stories. She investigated topics such as France's colonial trade, English imperialism, the fortunes of new Poland, and labor syndicalism, but significant writing commissions rarely came her way. The only income she could count on was writing penny-a-line publicity for the American Red Cross, hundreds of whose workers were present in battered postwar Europe.

Casting about for alternatives, and having in mind the bohemian model of life in the Latin Quarter, she considered writing a novel. She imagined a self-searching project, tracing a "year in the love-life" of a "self-conscious sophisticated young woman." "I want her to face problems free from artificial repressions, conventions or traditions," to discover "what repressions, traditions or instincts hold," Thompson jotted down. Marriage seemed out of the question to her then because she wanted to be free to pursue her aims. Yet she felt the strength of an "instinct" toward marriage "even in the most emancipated woman." The apparent incompatibility of a woman's independence and marriage seemed a "tragedy" to her.[11]

Her precarious economic condition worried her. Could she support herself abroad? When an American labor organizer, a friend of De Porte, urged both women to go with him to Italy to report on labor conflicts there, they did. Many hundreds of thousands of Italian unionized workers in autos, metals, and railroads staged a wave of factory occupations in the fall of 1920, continuing production but shutting out their bosses, intending the factories to be worker-controlled. Thompson reached Rome, she told a friend, with "letters to people who were able to get me into occupied factories and get me audiences with all the labor people." Her contacts (through De Porte's friend) were remarkable: "we've met everyone who is concerned in the present revolutionary situation—that is to say everyone on the labor side." The labor stories took her to Florence, Genoa, Milan, Venice, and Rome. Thompson judged Italy "indescribably lovely—memorable . . . the most beautiful country imaginable." But it was a "land of wretched women" that made her feel "certainly more of a feminist than ever!"[12]

Her surprising claim—since she almost never used the word "feminist"—was spurred, apparently, by Italian men's assessment of every woman as potential sexual prey. She expected to be approached as an individual and a journalist, but "Every man in Italy is first interested in you as a woman!" she expostulated to her diary. She had been fending off men wherever she went. A "sweet" Czechoslovakian journalist in London wanted to marry her, for instance, and a "very serious" American journalist in Paris suddenly made "violent love" to her after his intriguing job offer left her cold. Italy was different: sexual come-ons there aroused her. "The only thing I miss in Italy is a lover," she told a friend. "To be twenty-seven and loverless in Italy is a crime against God and man." She said this in jest, but a heavy-breathing episode in Milan almost made her succumb. As she stood in a dark room very close to "the piratical leader of the Seamen's Federation," Giuseppe Giulietti, he urged her to stay with him for two or three days, because he desired her so. She found him "terribly handsome"—a tall man with smashingly white teeth and locks of black hair falling over his forehead—the possessor of "a joie de vivre which is irresistible." Though she was "simply flaming," she tore herself away. Later she half-regretted it. Her virgin condition began to feel like a burden.[13]

Then De Porte hurled a bombshell: she was to marry her London beau, Meir Grossman. No news could have been more unwelcome. Thompson never expected she would lose her precious companion so soon. She went to London for the wedding in November, of course. Upon returning to Paris, she felt lonely. Others were finding love and getting married—not only Barbara but also her own younger sister Peggy married happily that year.

Worried about her future, Thompson was overcome by self-doubt, a rare thing for her. She wanted to stay in Europe but had not secured any steady work. Under the perpetually gray skies of Paris in early December, she sagged into "melancholy aloneness." She felt she was getting nowhere. "I wonder if I shall be able to stick out the winter!" she wrote in her diary. "Oh, I wish that I were either more talented or less intelligent." Writing publicity for the American Red Cross for a pittance felt insupportable. She cataloged her own flaws, calling herself vain, fond of praise, often untruthful, and a snob. She did not even like her few Paris acquaintances.[14]

Where others might have sunk in despair, Thompson was too strong-willed to abandon her course. She chased away her uncharacteristic despondency, bucking herself up with a tough-minded philosophy of living. "I believe that being happy doesn't count," she wrote to a close friend who was having boyfriend troubles. "My dear, only fools and cows are happy. No intelligent human being is happy. There are moments of release, moments of bliss. Thank God for them, but don't hope to keep them, because it is the eternal measure of things that you shouldn't." She advised decisively, "Happiness doesn't matter. Getting somewhere does. I don't mean achievement as it may be measured by the world, but the achievement that you yourself feel—getting on somewhere in your own character. That, and being free, are the only things that count."[15]

Was she honest with herself in these stark rules? She was a zestful and gregarious person who loved to eat, drink, smoke, dance, joke, argue. She sought to look attractive and to have fun. Of course happiness mattered to her. But she felt that pursuing the worthwhile aims she believed in sat at the core of her identity as a vital human being. Not to strive in that way would mean perishing altogether. Conservatives at that time condemned attitudes like hers, accusing "modern" women of wreaking harms to society with their own self-ishness, but Thompson breezily ignored such pressures.[16]

Soon she was marching on. "I am happy here," she affirmed two months later. "I like my work. . . . I am free. I can go where I choose." She reminded herself that she felt "more at home spiritually" in England and Europe, where life had "much more harmonious proportions" than in the United States. "I have been awfully fed up on America for a long time. It is very materialistic and very strenuous and its idealism is a little too cold and puritanical to fit my temperament and philosophy," she wrote, reinforcing her determination to stay abroad. Remaining in Paris, she began exploring its international population. Because of postwar migrations Paris was larger in the 1920s than ever before (or since). Almost one-sixth of its three million inhabitants were resident foreigners, including a large population of Russian émigrés who had fled the Bolshevik regime.[17]

Thompson became acquainted with a Russian baroness, the refugee wife of an anti-Bolshevik leader, and wrote a feature article about her, earning a tidy sum when the *Philadelphia Public Ledger* bought the piece. More importantly, Thompson's article impressed veteran newspaperman Paul Scott Mowrer, head of European news coverage for the *Chicago Daily News*. Mowrer, a Midwesterner, got his start as a local reporter in Chicago and then earned his stripes as a war correspondent. He invited Thompson to his home for dinner with him and his wife and they discussed Thompson's prospects. Mowrer advised her to leave Paris, where so many Americans jostled for newspaper positions. She should find a stake elsewhere, he suggested.[18]

She agreed. She wanted her own city, and she chose Vienna. She had been "profoundly moved" by the city's pathos when she had stopped there briefly in November 1920. "Everybody is so miserable, and everybody is so brave! Everybody is hungry," she wrote to a friend about it. Once a resplendent metropolis, Vienna that winter was a crumbling mass of rubble and weeds. Before the war it had been a commercial entrepôt, a dazzling cultural mecca with legendary cafés and magnificent music halls, as well as the administrative and financial center of the multiethnic Austro-Hungarian Empire encompassing fifty-two million people. After the Treaty of Versailles, Vienna perched at the eastern edge of the small republic of Austria, the weakest of the new nations carved from the former empire, surrounded by rivalrous neighbors Czechoslovakia, Hungary, and Yugoslavia. The very viability of Austria was questionable. It was "a mutilated trunk that bled from every vein," native son Stefan Zweig wrote in horror. The country was harrowed by war debt and runaway postwar inflation. Refugees, ex-soldiers, and ruthless profiteers roamed Vienna's grand avenues. Economist Joseph Schumpeter, also a child of Vienna, compared Austria to "a patient who has had practically all his organs injured by an explosive catastrophe. Such

Austria and Surrounding New Nations Created from the Austro-Hungarian Empire

Adapted from Helmut Gruber, Red Vienna *(New York: Oxford University Press, 1991), and Eve Blau,* The Architecture of Red Vienna *(Cambridge, MA: MIT Press, 1999).*

a patient cannot simply come to the physician and ask for a pill to make him well."[19]

If Thompson feared starting from scratch in a ruined city of two million people, she left no trace of it. Before leaving Paris, she went to see the European chief of the *Philadelphia Public Ledger*, which was just then building up its foreign reporting, hoping to rival major New York and Chicago newspapers. She cited her Russian baroness story and boldly asked him to give her a salaried post in Vienna. He refused. But he gave her press credentials and agreed to pay her at a per word rate for any articles she wrote that he accepted for publication. Because the paper paid in American dollars, she knew she could survive: the mounting inflation in the Austrian krone made Vienna very cheap for anyone with foreign currency. She soon wrote about the inflation-induced buying panic: Austrians were "spending money frantically and recklessly, knowing that prices are rising hourly and fearing that the supply of all goods soon will be exhausted and the valueless crown can buy nothing further abroad."[20]

Thompson arrived in 1921 just as Vienna was reinventing itself. The needy population had elected the first Socialist government of any European capital, and municipal authorities set about reviving trade unions, building affordable housing, providing education and health care. Forty percent of the labor force in the city was female, most wives were employed, and Austrian women had had equal voting rights since 1918. Thompson warmed to the newborn revolutionary zeal of "Red Vienna" and rented a proletarian apartment. Under the housing authority's controls, a person living alone could not have both a hot bath and a kitchen. She chose the bath, gaining use of a kitchen by befriending her near neighbors and offering them English lessons in exchange. She worked hard to improve the German she had learned in college and soon flowed with conversation, although her grammar and usage were sketchy, with errors that her German friend Carl Zuckmayer found "enormously funny."[21]

The city's cultural reawakening excited her. Even with Baroque marble facades pockmarked by bullets, Vienna's grandeur of scale remained; musicians' practicing could be heard from open windows, and theater ushers resumed wearing splendid gold-braided costumes. When contemporary music was played for the first time at a Vienna music festival in July 1921, Thompson was there. The city's inhabitants were known for a disarmingly mellow outlook, dwelling on present enjoyment of life. "The situation is desperate, but not serious," conveyed the Viennese attitude—which Thompson relished.[22]

She set to work. A favorite coffeehouse served as her office. Full of chatter and clatter of drinks served *mit schlag*, coffeehouses were the heart of Viennese social life, where friends and lovers met, black marketeers sold their varied wares, spies plotted, prostitutes found johns, and—most important for a journalist—numerous newspapers were available, each in its own rattan holder. "For the price of a coffee you have a whole library at your disposal," she knew, a godsend for someone in her position. Amid "satin-brocaded walls, deep divans, onyx-topped tables, great windows curtained in gold-colored silk," in her admiring words, she could take a bentwood chair or leather banquette, drink coffee, and remain as long as she liked, reading local and foreign newspapers, writing, chain-smoking cigarettes (as was her habit), perhaps conducting interviews.[23] Story after story flew to the *Philadelphia Public Ledger* from her ideas and her research as she took up topics from high politics to coffeehouse gossip to rubble removal in the broken city.

She went often to Budapest, four hours on the fast train, to find stories from Central Europe and to write publicity on the side for Captain James Pedlow, the commissioner of the American Red Cross in Hungary. Pedlow soon introduced her to the urbane Hungarian who was the *Manchester Guardian*'s correspondent for Budapest and Vienna, Marcel Fodor. Only a few years older than Thompson, Fodor was a political liberal and an experienced newspaperman who knew more about the politics of Central Europe than any other English-speaking person. He and Thompson immediately clicked and began spending a great deal of time together. Fodor "*wanted* to marry me," Thompson told a new writer friend, Rose Wilder Lane, "but got over it wonderfully, and relaxed into the friendliest and most humorous acceptance of his lot." After marrying a Hungarian woman the next year, Fodor remained an extraordinarily generous mentor to Thompson, enabling her to rise to the demands of reporting in Central Europe. She gratefully credited him with making her career there possible. Fodor later similarly helped both John Gunther and William Shirer, who said of him, "I have never known a man and especially a journalist, who gave so much of himself and his knowledge to others." All three Americans felt immensely indebted to Fodor and became his close friends.[24]

A tip from Fodor allowed Thompson to engineer a journalistic coup her first year in Vienna. The former Habsburg emperor, who had also been king of Hungary, had hidden himself and his wife in a castle outside Budapest after an aborted attempt to regain the Hungarian throne. Every journalist in Europe was dying to talk to the royal couple and no one could get access. Thompson concocted an astonishing ruse in which she enlisted Captain Pedlow, who was going to check on the health of the pregnant empress. Thompson masqueraded as a nurse in order to accompany Pedlow to the hideaway. Pedlow balked at first, saying, "What do you think I am?" but when she nudged him, "I think you are an Irishman with a sense of adventure," he took the bait. As Pedlow spoke with the royal pair, Thompson, behind a curtain, took furious notes. She also spoke directly with the empress. The ingenious scoop confirmed her mettle as a journalist.[25]

By the spring of 1922 the *Public Ledger* made Thompson a salaried correspondent at $50 a week (about $700 in today's dollars). It was less than her earnings on a per word basis for her slew of publishable stories, but a distinct step up in status. As a correspondent rather than an accredited freelancer, she could feel she was an equal among the international press corps who congregated in Vienna coffeehouses almost every day. In her new position as Vienna-based correspondent for Central Europe, Thompson was to cover Albania, Czechoslovakia, Hungary, Romania, Bulgaria, Yugoslavia, Turkey, and Greece as well as Austria. "Nine countries over an enormous territory, every one of them with a different history and problems," she was proud to recall. "I had no assistance, not even a secretary." She relied on wide-ranging reading plus the reporting of stringers elsewhere who cleared their work through Vienna.[26]

VIENNA BEGAN TO return to life economically by 1922, and Thompson's career rose in tandem. She made the most of every opening, ignoring hurdles that would have halted ordinary souls. Central Europe was knotty territory, alive with alarming threats to parliamentary governments: monarchists, communists, nationalists who saw Jews as a source of evil, irredentists who wanted former territory back.

Italy's Fascists were nearby. "No Dove-Nest on Danube: Austria Bankrupt, Hungary Flirting with Fascism, Moslem Shadow Looms over Balkans" headlined one of her articles. When the prime minister of Bulgaria was decapitated in a brutal coup, Thompson reported him "butchered." Yet she could report Austrian optimism sprouting by August 1923, once a $113 million loan from the League of Nations helped to set the economy upright. Vienna was again awash with musicians and artists. Thompson enthusiastically tracked plays and concerts enlivening the city and intellectual trends percolating in cafés.[27]

Private gatherings brought her new friends. Always outgoing, Thompson became a favorite of philanthropist Eugenie Schwarzwald, an older woman whose dinner salons stimulated interchange among a heady mix of politicians, performers, businessmen, students, and artists. Thompson flourished under "Genia's" gentle guidance and got to know contemporaries such as painter Oskar Kokoschka and composer Arnold Schoenberg. The sheer vitality of her presence opened doors for her. More than one man remembered her youthful vivacity, her "intellectual incandescence," and a "physical radiance that goes beyond being physical." Her friend Zuckmayer said, "Dorothy took time; despite all her professional work she took time to live, to be a woman and a human being," chiming in with others who marveled that she had none of the personality drawbacks of the stereotyped "career woman."[28] (Seeing her as an exception, they did not revise their generalizations about the category.)

Always thinking of herself as a professional, Thompson ruled out using feminine wiles in her work, and no male colleague accused her of using sex appeal to get ahead. Nonetheless, she turned being a woman into advantage more than once, including her ingenious ploy with the Habsburg emperor and empress. Another story from her early years put her in Czechoslovakia without ready funds, desperate to send an urgent scoop to Vienna. At the telegraph office, the Czech clerk refused to send her message "collect" to her newspaper, as she requested. Ever imaginative and plucky, she scribbled a (fake) note in German addressed to the Czech foreign minister, writing very familiarly as if he were her lover, suggesting that the recalcitrant clerk be fired. The clerk must have read German, for after looking at the note, he sent her story through. Thompson's feminine warmth also made her a brilliantly successful interviewer of political and celebrity figures alike. Tomáš Masaryk, a principal founder of Czechoslovakia, spoke with her for five hours straight, and almost the whole interview reached newsprint.[29]

The American newspaper industry had made room for women reporters to enter because the reading audience was at least half female. By the same token, women on staff were usually consigned to fashion, society gossip, or women's pages. But nervy women such as Thompson pressed hard to move beyond such confinement. They made their way into daily beats, investigative stories, news services, editorial positions, and even foreign capitals—though the last was the least likely. Thompson stood out. At a time when most newspapermen presumed that a female colleague would be a nuisance, those who worked in Central Europe genuinely respected Thompson's work and liked her as a good friend. They regarded her as a woman and a professional at the same time.[30]

Thompson denied that she faced any special hurdles or discriminations as a woman in a field that was almost all male. When *The Nation* magazine asked her to write about her career in 1926, she responded sharply: "There seems to me to be nothing extraordinary or of significance in the fact that a woman should be a foreign newspaper correspondent." Piqued at *The Nation* (a left-leaning political magazine), she wrote that it was "a disservice and an anachronism" to play up women as such, rather like "the specious feminism of the women's magazines" celebrating any woman for being first in her field. Women ought not to highlight their gender in their jobs, Thompson wrote, but simply forge ahead, because stressing women's singularity or solidarity was outdated. Younger women looking for meaningful careers echoed her. Martha Gellhorn, for example, an aspiring journalist fifteen years younger than Thompson, wrote approvingly in 1930 that the woman who represented Denmark in the League of Nations would never "make an issue of herself as a woman" despite being a first, because she was "a human being, living in the twentieth century, with certain obligations and certain abilities."[31]

In contrast, Thompson thought of herself as all woman in her love life. She fell for Josef Bard as if a thunderbolt hit her. She was in Budapest in 1921, having tea with Marcel Fodor, when she noticed Bard. Her heart jumped. Fodor introduced them. Bard, a Hungarian intellectual and writer—and in Thompson's eyes a gorgeous hunk of a man—was the lover she had been looking for. She happily let him seduce her. "Delirious with love" (in her own later words), she ended her virginity with passionate satisfaction. Born of a Jewish father and a harrying Protestant mother, Bard had trained as a lawyer in Hungary, but did not want to practice there because he hoped to leave. He had been educated at the Sorbonne and was a charming conversationalist, amusing and considerate and especially tender with Thompson. He was also vain and somewhat pretentious about his philosophical and intellectual distinction as he occupied himself writing a tome he called "The Mind of Europe."[32]

While Thompson lived in Vienna and Bard in Budapest, their romance was perfect. Every two weeks or so they would get together for a weekend to luxuriate in each other's bodies and company, going to the mountains, or a lakeside, or enjoying the theater and social life in Vienna. Bard said he loved her. Right away, he wanted to marry her. Thompson loved him intensely and was very happy—but torn. Her usually decisive inner voice was muted. When he pressed her to marry, she hung back.

She knew marriage would inevitably constrain her. She adored Bard, and loved that he loved her, but passion for her work and her independence coursed through her as fiercely as her passion for him. "I hold the cup of my happiness tremblingly in my hands and fear that any moment it may spill," she wrote to her favorite mentor from suffrage days, looking for advice. "Sexual love is possessive.

Dorothy Thompson's second passport application photo, 1922.
Source: National Archives and Records Administration.
Thompson lost her first passport and had to get another while she was in Europe. Her picture here, so different from the staid image of her first passport application, suggests how much she had changed in two years abroad.

Sexual love is a bar to freedom," she knew. "I want so to be free," she explained to Rose Wilder Lane. "I know if I marry I'll never take risks again in the same way. I'll never start off across the world with nothing in my pocket and be able to say, 'Well, it's my *own* life, isn't it? And if I *do* starve??'" For quite a while she temporized. Then, thinking she would lose him if she continued to refuse, she gave in. They married in April 1923. As a couple, they gained the right to a full apartment in Vienna, a boon she appreciated.[33]

She did not mind supporting Bard on her salary; he was her creative genius, a would-be philosopher. In a strange pairing with her professional ambition, she believed that she would find her womanly fulfillment by loving a man whose deep creativity she would nourish.

But she bitterly resented Bard's sexual betrayal, once she discovered it. He seduced women right and left, including Thompson's friends, during their marriage. Louis Untermeyer, an American writer living in Europe and friendly with Bard, thought of him as "a devastating charmer . . . the irresistible embodiment of the romantically susceptible and ever-ready lover."[34]

She found out early in 1926. Even more distressing than Bard's rampant infidelity—which she might have forgiven if the sex was casual—was her wounded pride on finding out that he had told her friends he did not love her. The couple had moved from Vienna to Berlin by then, because Thompson was promoted in 1925 to head the Berlin bureau for the recently merged foreign service of the *Philadelphia Public Ledger* and *New York Post*. It was a major, coveted position. John Gunther later dubbed Thompson a "Blue-Eyed Tornado" for conquering journalism in Central Europe so swiftly. Only two other American newspaperwomen had status near Thompson's—Sigrid Schultz, who held the Central Europe desk for the *Chicago Tribune*, and Anne Hare McCormick, foreign news analyst for the *New York Times*.[35]

Freewheeling, gender-bending Berlin, capital of Weimar Germany, was bursting with wild intellectual energy and sensational nightlife when Thompson and Bard moved there. By 1925, the German economy had recovered considerably from postwar hyperinflation because of Dawes Plan fixes. Thompson warmed to the city's cosmopolitan scene and felt at home with its passion for political discussion. Her acquaintances multiplied because she divided a duplex apartment, much too large for her and Bard, with Edgar Mowrer and his wife, Lillian, and their daughter. (Edgar, a renowned foreign correspondent, was the younger brother of Paul Scott Mowrer, who had advised Thompson to leave Paris.) They all became very good friends. Thompson could telephone them and say, "Do come on up, I have a jolly crowd here," and vice versa. Lillian Mowrer was an accomplished Englishwoman who appreciated living in Weimar Germany because "a woman could do what she liked," in her view.

Dorothy Thompson and Josef Bard on a mountain hike, 1923.
Source: Dorothy Thompson Papers, Special Collections Research Center, Syracuse University Libraries.

No field or profession was barred to women; more women sat in the Reichstag than in any other nation's parliament, circumstances that Thompson appreciated, too.[36]

Bard, however, said he hated Berlin. He began to spend his time in London and objected that Thompson cared more for her work than for him. She heard his complaints as underhanded insults. A fear that had haunted her at the start—"this man will let me down; I shall break my heart over this"—came true. Why had he insisted on marrying her? Perhaps it was because she could support him. Perhaps he thought that her American citizenship would help him exit Hungary for good. In fact, their marriage imperiled her American citizenship. The US immigration law of 1907 declared that American women who married foreigners assumed the nationality of their husbands. Thompson lamented "this damned law" in 1921. The Cable Act of 1922 overturned that proviso, but her marriage still put certain constraints on her citizenship—which she simply ignored.[37]

Though Bard's insincerity and faithlessness tortured her, for almost a year she hoped to repair their marriage. Then, in December 1926, Bard told her that he was truly in love with the young London heiress-turned-artist Eileen Agar. Thompson exploded. "You have done me every wrong a man may do a woman and every wrong one human being may do another," she accused him. Her fury was operatic. Miserable, looking for comfort, she had a one-night stand with one-eyed Floyd Gibbons, the "headline hunter," who was passing through Berlin. Her impulsive infidelity incensed Bard, who now felt justified in walking out. He told others that he had to escape because Thompson's bossy domination was stifling him.[38]

Six weeks after Bard left, Thompson was a wreck. "I am done for," she told her friend Rose. She had been spilling torrents of words on pages addressed to him (most of them not sent), calling him a Judas, a cad, a rotter, as she tried to recast her experience and assuage her pain. "I loved Josef with all of me, and was so proud, so proud. . . . But I haven't any life, because he has gone." It crushed her *amour propre* as well as her heart to have discovered that all the while she believed in his love, "he plotted to undo me." How could she have so misjudged! She lost confidence in herself. "I am afraid. . . . and I have never been afraid of anything in the world before," she admitted to Rose. "I shall never get over it." Only her work brought her back to herself, even as she went through the motions mechanically at first. "I work very hard and am grateful to have learned the discipline of work," she told Bard in March 1927.[39]

As that troubled spring bloomed in Berlin, Thompson was depressed. She saw only a "senseless circularness" in the office, a "feeling of eternal repetition." She viewed her work as "an elevated drudgery," redeemed only by its service to Bard, who represented the lost beauty she had really sought. Because he had deserted her, she felt she had "no life . . . only a profession," and it was one she "always hated," she told him (surely for effect, to pierce his conscience). She felt she must change her life, that her efficiency in interviewing and reporting was a "curious mask," hiding the passionate person she really was.[40]

Her inner rage spurred her to think about changing her professional life. Writing to Bard from Geneva, where she was covering the World Economic Conference the first week of May, she said she might look for a job reporting on the League of Nations because it would be "incredibly easy." Nonetheless, her "striving, energetic, ascending mind" that had alienated Bard kept going willy-nilly, contemplating a book she might write titled "The Forming Face of Germany." From her post in Berlin, she would analyze the tensions besetting the Weimar Republic. The idea that it might fall to a Nazi Party was not within her forecast (or anyone else's) in 1927, but her knowledge and foresight led her to sketch a chapter that would include Hitler's presence in Bavaria "with his young werewolfs and steel-helmet." Other chapters would cover the weakness of German parliamentarianism, the rising youth movement, newly prosperous industrialists, German foreign policy toward Russia and England, and the competing pulls of Europeanization and Americanization.[41]

She sprang out of her depression within a few weeks. By pure determination, she decided that Josef was beyond her grasp and she was "out of love" with him. She even wrote a sonnet to celebrate her release. She filed for the divorce Bard demanded and resumed living in Berlin alone. Still, she felt broken. Her "inner pain" was immeasurable, she told him, and she meant it when she wrote, "what it cost me to get this divorce . . . made me a completely different person." Although she took it very hard, divorce was hardly rare among her set. Lifelong marriages were more the exception than the rule among correspondents who were on the move in the 1920s and 1930s; the same was true of related networks of journalists, authors, editors, and publishers in New York City.[42]

The divorce came through on her thirty-fourth birthday, July 9, 1927. The day before, she had met the famous American novelist

Sinclair Lewis, who was visiting Berlin. A correspondent friend brought him to the German foreign minister's weekly press tea and introduced him to Thompson there. Finding Lewis somewhat amusing, she invited him to a dinner party she was having at home the next evening, her birthday. Lewis behaved unremarkably at dinner, but stayed after other guests left. He and Thompson had been talking for hours when—to her utter shock—he asked her to marry him. "I don't even know you, Mr. Lewis," she protested.[43]

His impact on her nonetheless went deep. She described him in a letter to Bard right away as "a very curious and demonic person, hard-drinking, hard-thinking, blasphemous, possessed, I often think, of a devil." Lewis was tall, slender, and ungainly; his long legs "seemed to have forgotten where to stop," in Thompson's words. She later recalled her first sight of his "narrow, ravaged face, roughened, red, and scarred . . . reddish but almost colorless eyebrows above round, cavernously set, remarkably brilliant eyes, transparent as aquamarines and in them a strange, shy, imploring look . . . the face of a man who had walked through flame throwers." She felt compassion for him. "My instantaneous reaction was, God, what a lonely, unhappy, helpless man! Somebody must love and take care of him!"[44]

Lewis at forty-two was the most successful American fiction writer alive. *Main Street*, *Babbitt*, and *Arrowsmith*, all published between 1920 and 1925, had brought him immense renown. His critical puncturing of the American dream in *Main Street* and *Babbitt* hit a nerve and created long-lasting character types of midwestern Americana. A huge audience relished the satiric realism with which he skewered American boosterism and provincial small-mindedness. He was offered the Pulitzer Prize in 1925 for *Arrowsmith* and turned it down, saying "all prizes are dangerous." His next novel, *Elmer Gantry* (1926), slammed the hypocrisies of American fundamentalist Protestantism so effectively that he became notorious; he was so decried by pulpit-pounders that he fled to Europe to escape.

When in good form, Lewis was a droll, impishly word-playing companion and a hilarious critic as well as a superb inventor of fictions. His playfulness enchanted the young John Hersey, who became Lewis's research assistant one summer. Hersey remembered how Lewis would not simply tell a story but would "jump up . . . and become the people in the story, switching from side to side as he conversed with himself in the telling. His improvisations were uncanny."[45]

Everywhere Thompson went in the next few days and weeks, Lewis wooed her. Even in the most inappropriate public as well as private settings, he appealed to her, "Dorothy, marry me." He left out, at first, the detail that he already had a wife and was trying to end that marriage. Dorothy was the only woman who could make him happy, he insisted. Overwhelmed by the force of his personality, she felt rejuvenated by his extraordinarily earnest attention. Yet she was fearful—and distrusted herself. Bard had wounded her so grievously that she doubted that she could ever be a successful wife.

The lengths to which Lewis went in pressing his suit amazed her. A week after they met, political riots broke out in Vienna and she prepared to fly there from Berlin. Commercial passenger flights had just begun; earlier that year, Charles Lindbergh had flown solo across the Atlantic, landing in Paris to a waiting crowd's cheers. Thompson took to air travel immediately. She rhapsodized over "the sudden starts at early dawn, the silvery plane rising into a rosy sky, the long flights over massive clouds . . . like a vast arctic sea." When she went to the airfield at dawn for her Vienna flight, Lewis followed her, continuing to beg. She said she would consider marriage if he would take the flight with her and write a few articles about the riot for her newspaper. He did both—conquering his fear, since it was his first flight.[46]

Lewis's pleading so affected Thompson that she agreed to go on a hiking vacation in England with him, in August. Hiking was Lewis's favorite recreation. "He could walk hard and fast, uphill and downhill, or he could suddenly throw himself on a grassy bank at the edge of a ditch and count the cows in a field and make up some insane but very funny story about them," Jimmy Sheean remembered. "His mind was never so blazingly active and irresistible in its ceaseless pyrotechnic; he was never gentler, kinder or more understanding."[47]

The walking trip—"truly halcyon days of tramping"—was a turning point in Thompson's feelings about Lewis. "I am in love, thank God, again," Thompson told her friend Rose. Her energy and hopes resumed. To Bard, she wrote melodramatically of Lewis: "He has saved my life. I know that if he had not come, I would have died." Her feeling for Lewis was not the "vast, monstrous, absurd, terrible love" she had had for Bard, giving her whole self with abandon, imagining flesh bonded with flesh. "I shall never, ever, care for anyone, as I loved you," she told Bard, needling him.[48] She continued writing to Bard—intending less to wound him (although she did wish to, at first) than to retain her dignity by maintaining a friendship with him and Eileen Agar.

No jolt of sexual electricity urged her on this second time. On the surface Lewis was far from attractive. It was his talk that drew Thompson in. (Upon first meeting Lewis, John Hersey "would have sworn that he was hideously ugly until he started to talk, when his face suddenly turned on, like a delicate, brilliant lamp.") Master of reams of literature that he could recite—or gamely parody—at the snap of a finger, Lewis had a prodigious imagination. He "could no more stop telling stories than he could stop his hair growing," Carl Van Doren once said. The stories he spun with Thompson had to do with their imagined future, starting not with "once upon a time" but with "I've often thought I would . . . " or "When we grow up, let's . . . " Thompson exulted in his storytelling genius.[49]

She came to think of Lewis as a kindred soul and called him by his childhood name, Hal, though his friends called him Red. His phenomenal talents promised Thompson the creative marriage she idealized. She clung to that conception despite it being so at odds with her desire to be independent. "One is willing to be swallowed up by a man, if in his brain and heart one is transmuted into something 'rich and strange,' something better than one could be of oneself," she mused in her diary two months after she and Lewis met. The "fertilizing and re-fertilizing of the other's personality is the real creative end of marriage." Thompson was prone to making such pronouncements in her private writings. "The real woman . . . looks for the man to whom she can be life, rest, energy, strength, whom she can fertilize with her own spirit." She concluded only, "Anyway I love Hal and belong to him."[50]

She was taking a huge risk. Her friends warned her against Sinclair Lewis. He was an incurable alcoholic, driven by unnamed buried wounds. The truth stared Thompson in the face when she arrived to pick him up for a dinner date, just a week after her diary musings. She found him sodden, unable to move. He murmured despairingly, "God, I'm lit again, darling." She wept "like a child, sobbed, half in rage at him, half despair"—but he was so gone in alcoholic haze he did not hear. Later that evening, Ramon Guthrie, a good friend of Lewis who was in Berlin, told Thompson that he thought "honestly" that Lewis had only "about one chance in ten" of surviving and that she was that chance.[51]

Her urge to save him flooded over her doubts. Within three days he returned to being the person that Thompson adored, full of plans for writing, for starting new businesses, for buying a house in the country. When they were spinning plans together, she "forgot the bogey" and thought, "He is altogether adorable." But then there was a "dreadful" night soon after—an endless awful night that showed her how terrifying—and pathetic—his drinking was, "his body like rank weeds," his eyes "fishy, dead," "like red moons," his thickened voice whimpering to her "I cannot ruin your life. . . . I will go away. . . . You must never have anything to do with me again." She refused. She felt tied to him already. "Don't think that you can just walk off and free me of you. Wherever you go I will be with you in you, and you with me, in me," she replied. In the morning, "his whole body quivering, he said miserably, 'Sweet, sweet, I know it's giving up spirits or giving up you. And I can't give up spirits.'" With her "heart dissolved," Thompson saw, too, that they should separate if he did not change his ways, but she told him she refused to let that happen.[52]

Even while Lewis monopolized her emotions, Thompson could not resist the pull of politics. Stark in the midst of her diary musings about him, she jotted down, "Hindenburg made a damn fool speech." Eighty-year-old Paul von Hindenburg, a war hero and current president of the Weimar Republic, had repudiated the Versailles treaty clause that declared Germany's guilt for the world war. Thompson sensed political reaction taking hold in Weimar and whipped off an article to that effect for *The Nation* magazine.[53] Her mind was also jumping ahead to a unique assignment: she was soon going to Soviet Russia to see the Moscow celebration of the tenth anniversary of the Bolshevik Revolution, and then to stay much longer to write a series of articles assessing the accomplishments of a decade of Communist rule. The prospect electrified her. Though she hated to leave Lewis behind, she never considered not taking the opportunity.

THOMPSON HAD BEEN in Europe for seven years. Her persistence there had washed away her upstate New York provincialism. She spoke German with great confidence; French less so, but enough to think she was getting along. She had fallen in and out of love lightly many times and seriously twice—had had a lover, married him, been betrayed, been divorced, and attracted a phenomenal new lover. With astounding energy and discipline, she had gained extensive knowledge of European politics and a keen ability to discern probable implications in political moves. Other foreign correspondents who lived in or passed through Vienna or Berlin accepted her as one of the best of them. Her lively personality also had brought her vast numbers of friends and useful contacts. Her skills at reading people were generally very good (though Bard was a killing exception).

In Bard's betrayal, Thompson had come painfully face-to-face with the "tragedy" she named abstractly years earlier—the seeming impossibility for a woman to have a freely chosen work life and marry happily too. Falling in love with Sinclair Lewis made her newly optimistic. When Bard, to exonerate himself, wrote her that "the problem of the woman who works is a great one," Thompson did not disagree. Instead, she responded cheekily that the only greater problem was "the woman who doesn't work." She closed their exchange with a dash of triumph: "I still believe that it's possible to find the person with whom one can live, and work, and build up a life together. I think, indeed, that I <u>have</u> found him."[54] The next years would put her assumptions about Sinclair Lewis to a fiery trial—and even more so, her assumptions about Germany.

CHAPTER 3

LUCKIEST
YOUNG UPSTART

IN THE FALL of 1924, John Gunther could no longer resist his impulse to go abroad. He was an aspiring novelist and, like Jimmy Sheean, thought living in Europe would benefit his writing. Chicago had been his home all twenty-three years of his life. He had a job as a reporter for the *Chicago Daily News*, and a girlfriend he adored, but was frustrated with both. Though the hometown paper gave him supportive colleagues and a steady salary, he had more ambitious literary aims. His girlfriend kept him on the string but was bafflingly aloof—not rejecting him, but refusing to commit herself. He imagined that his absence and the worldly sophistication he would gain while abroad might make her see that she loved him after all.

Several years later he laughed about his sense of himself then, when he "told everybody I wanted to starve in London in the accepted literary fashion." "Absurd!" he reflected. In that offhand way, he began a global odyssey that would make his name a household word.[1]

GUNTHER WAS BROUGHT up on the lower edge of Chicago's German Protestant middle class. His mother, a strong believer in education and self-improvement (rather like Sheean's mother), shaped his early outlook. She found her pleasures in literature and art, and home-schooled John and his younger sister till high school. Shy and socially awkward through his adolescence, with no interest in sports, he recalled being a "bookworm from about the age of four," especially enchanted by the Greek mythology his mother read to him. In his parents' unhappy marriage he took his mother's side. "I was my mother's son," he later reflected. He felt grateful for her decision to acquire teaching credentials and go to work as a schoolteacher when his father's income as a traveling salesman slipped precipitously. John was about ten then. With some hyperbole, he later described his father as "a robust ne-er-do-well, vain, sanguine and gregarious, who weighed almost 300 pounds and smoked, when he could afford it, 30 cigars a day."

When John graduated high school in 1918, his father opposed him going to college, expecting him instead to get a job and help support the family. To persuade his father to let him enroll at the University of Chicago, where he had a partial scholarship, Gunther promised to major in chemistry—a suitably vocational choice—and live at home. That won the day. While Sheean, a year ahead, succumbed to the draw of the Greeks dominating university social life, no fraternity tapped Gunther.

Then, in his second year, modern literature hit him "like a burst of skyrockets." Reading innovative American writers such as Sherwood Anderson, Theodore Dreiser, Carl Sandburg, and Robert Frost, he "was inflamed by them as by a case of malaria," he later said. James Branch Cabell's ironic and somewhat erotic fantasy *Jurgen* (1919) rocked his literary world. Finding friends at college who shared his literary passions, the shy Gunther came into his own. Easy to look at—six feet tall, with thick blond hair and blue eyes, a long nose in an oval face, and eyeglasses—he began to impress people with his intelligence. Before long he dropped the chemistry major, began reviewing books for the college newspaper, the *Daily Maroon*, and in his senior year carved a niche for himself as its first literary editor. Gunther met Sheean, probably through the *Maroon*, but they were not college friends.[2]

Chicago was thick with would-be writers then, and many of them earned their pay as newspaper reporters. The book review pages in all the major papers buzzed with the city's literary energy. Satirist and critic H. L. Mencken, editor of *The Smart Set: A Magazine of Cleverness*, called Chicago "the literary capital of the United States" because its residents got excited about books the way urbanites elsewhere followed baseball or politics. In that environment, Gunther was not only smitten with literature but also enterprising about it. As the *Maroon*'s literary editor, he solicited publishers to send him copies of their new books, promising to review them in a weekly column. Once he launched his Literary Leaders column, he invited midwestern newspapers to carry it, for a fee. Three took the bait. He was re-creating the model of syndication in miniature. Gunther's opinionated reviews caught Mencken's eye, and when Mencken asked him to write an essay about the university for *The Smart Set*, Gunther happily obliged.[3]

The literary editor of the *Chicago Daily News*, Harry Hansen—a former war reporter in Europe who had come back to Chicago to write fiction—also noticed Gunther's reviews and became a generous mentor. The *News* office was a literary hotbed. Henry Justin Smith, the news editor and a fiction writer himself, hired reporters who were novelists and poets at heart, regarding the newspaper "as a daily novel written by a score of Balzacs," in the words of Ben Hecht, who was on the staff, as was poet Carl Sandburg. Hecht—later a novelist, playwright, screenwriter, and author of the now-classic newspaper play *The Front Page*—recalled of that time, "I worked in Chicago, but I lived, a little madly, between book covers."[4]

The news staff spent long Saturday lunches arguing over books at Schlogl's, a German restaurant near their office, inviting authors visiting Chicago to join them. These lunches became legendary, the equivalent in Chicago to the Algonquin Round Table in New York. As the host, Harry Hansen saw Gunther, still an undergraduate, as a "critical spokesman for the youngest generation," and invited him to join.[5] Gunther's presence at Schlogl's shaped him as a writer and linked him to contacts in journalism and literature that benefited him for years.

Gunther graduated from the university in 1922 with honors in English and a Phi Beta Kappa key. Chasing dreams of the Europe he had read about in novels, he worked his way across the ocean on a cattle boat for a summer lark on the continent with college friends. Though this brief taste whet his appetite for more, he came back to Chicago to take up the job offered him, unsurprisingly, by the *Chicago Daily News*. He not only had to support himself but felt obligated to contribute to the support of his mother and sister.

Gunther gained a second education in the newsroom of the second-largest-selling paper in Chicago. The *News* had been founded in 1875 as an evening daily that cost only a penny, vying for a broad reading public against the *Chicago Tribune*, a morning paper that cost a nickel. It succeeded (forcing the *Tribune* to lower its price, among other things), and the two papers remained constant rivals. In the grimy *News* office, with sagging floorboards and dust-caked windows overlooking the elevated train tracks, Gunther was "pitched head first into a world of hijackers, 4-11 fires, riots, conventions, Rotary clubs, tough police captains, and Al Capone." He thrived there, though his job was grueling. Since scoops were the gold standard, he had to chase breaking news, but he much preferred to write feature articles with no urgent deadline. The news editor, seeing where Gunther's strengths lay, sometimes indulged him. As a result, his work won inclusion in *Best News Stories of 1923* and *Best News Stories of 1924*.[6]

After two years Gunther was restless. His job was fine, but it was stifling his own writing; he wanted to finish writing a novel he had partially drafted. The elusiveness of his beautiful and clever sweetheart, Helen Hahn, also frustrated him terribly; she stayed interested in him but continually dodged any firmer pledge. Her family had moved in across the street from Gunther's in 1920, and in 1924, recommended by Hansen and Gunther, she became crossword puzzle editor at the *News*, hired when the rage for crossword puzzles made every major newspaper add one.[7] As he contemplated living abroad for at least six months, Gunther did not mean to give Hahn up but to make her long for him. He hoped his adventures and accomplishments abroad would impress her and make her want him back for good.

His grand plan required getting the *Chicago Daily News* to transfer him to its foreign bureau in London. (Moving to Paris made no sense because he did not know French.) The *News*, disappointingly, did not cooperate. Its foreign service was top-notch, employing more than a hundred correspondents around the world in the 1920s. At the beginning of the Spanish-American War in 1898, its publisher had decided to cover foreign news more fully, and began dispatching the paper's own correspondents abroad to report. At that time, most American newspapers relied on local stringers on site. The reputation of the *News* in foreign correspondence grew from that point on; other papers did not catch up until war broke out in Europe in 1914.[8]

Gunther's request to transfer to London was turned down because he lacked experience. He tried again a while later and got the same answer. Then, buoyed by self-confident optimism, he simply quit. He determined that he would find work in London as best he could, save his money, and then move to a cheaper location on the continent to finish his novel.

London especially tempted Gunther because the writers he most admired lived there. His favorites, such as Aldous Huxley and Michael Arlen, were setting new fictional standards of frankness about sex. Huxley's satiric novels of the early 1920s toyed with conventional sexual morality, and Arlen's *The Green Hat* (1924) became an international sensation, a best seller in numerous languages, because of its sexually free heroine. These and other contemporary novels, most shockingly *La Garconne* (1922) in France and *Flaming Youth* (1923) in the United States, indelibly linked the modern woman to her open expression of sexual desire.[9]

Gunther was excited about such writing despite having been "a terrible innocent right up to about 20," sexually ignorant in almost all ways, in his own recollection a decade later. "For a time I thought you screwed only once for each child," he mused at his own bafflement. Until well into his college years his upbringing had kept him insulated from the sexual revolution coursing through his generation. "How shocked I was, meeting a pretty girl . . . at Roy's," he remembered, "when he told me, 'First time I met her, I had my hand up her leg in 20 minutes.' And it was simply unbelievable that he had screwed her. She seemed so nice!—we grow quickly. Within a week I was trying to screw her myself." Gunther slid easily into the new standards once he encountered them but still took it for granted that no "nice" girl would indulge in sex outside marriage. Worshiping his sweetheart Helen Hahn, he assumed—erroneously, as he discovered much later—that she was a virgin and so did not press her on sex.[10]

He left Chicago in the fall of 1924, telling Hahn he would return in a year, and traveled first to New York City, center of American publishing. There he signed with literary agent Carl Brandt, whom he would use as the conduit for placing freelance articles that he intended to write for American magazines. In three weeks' time— courtesy of his Chicago colleagues—he met with an astounding number of helpful contacts. He spoke with publishers and editors who gave him letters of introduction to scores of London editors, newspapermen, and trendy writers. A bit later he marveled that he could not remember "what on earth did I do and say in N.Y. to keel over all the big birds" whose letters gave him excellent entrée in London. Such letters of introduction were the coin of the realm of writers' global circuitry.[11]

Gunther made the most of his ocean passage. Having learned that Edward, Prince of Wales, whose every move grabbed transatlantic attention, would be traveling on the same ship, Gunther parlayed his knowledge into a commission from the United Press to capture news about the prince en route. What if the royal personage slipped on deck? Or—eligible bachelor that he was—cast his eye on a pretty young woman? By wiring from the boat, Gunther could scoop all the reporters waiting at London's port of Southampton. He persuaded the United Press to upgrade his steerage ticket, since the prince himself was traveling first class. Gunther's trip was, thus, far pleasanter—though to his chagrin, the purser and captain foiled his plan by closely censoring wireless transmissions to protect Edward's privacy. Gunther got the jump on nothing. But in his six days on board, he observed English upper-class habits and made friends with several travelers who eased his adjustment into London life.[12]

Once he arrived, Gunther booked into a cheap hotel and set out to find a job. He began with the several press associations—also called wire services by the 1920s. These were agencies that aggregated news from numerous reporters and syndicated the resulting articles to any newspaper that would pay to subscribe to the service. Agence Havas in France had pioneered the model in 1835, and the Associated Press (AP) in the United States and Reuters in Britain copied it within fifteen years. Competing American newspaper owners founded the United Press (UP) and the International News Service (INS) early in the twentieth century.[13]

Gunther's inquiries brought only middling results. Reuters and the AP both turned him down flat, saying that jobs were extremely scarce. At the United Press office, he got the more encouraging news that they expected a vacancy within three weeks. To buck himself up, he stopped by the National Gallery of Art for a refreshing look at beautiful paintings, and then nonchalantly took himself to one of the best tailors in Savile Row—a street synonymous with men's clothing of the highest quality—where he ordered two suits, an overcoat, and various accessories, charging them to an account to be paid in the future. "I decided to burn my bridges and stick my chin high," he reported to Helen Hahn. He loved to spend money, whether he had it or not. His bravado worked like a charm. Returning to his hotel, sodden from the rain and tired from hours of pounding the London pavement, he discovered that a call had come in for him from the London office of the *Chicago Daily News*.

Rushing to the office late in the day, Gunther learned that Hal O'Flaherty, London correspondent for the *News* and executive head of its foreign service, was taking a three-week vacation and needed an assistant. O'Flaherty was a veteran of the Chicago office, a University of Chicago alumnus ten years older than Gunther. He had heard that Gunther was in town. The two men met, discovered acquaintances in common, and soon chatted like old friends. O'Flaherty thought Gunther would do as his assistant for three weeks and hinted at longer-term possibilities.

Gunther was elated. Barely twenty-four hours after landing, he had an exciting job with the *News* in London, despite having been turned down earlier. (His Chicago bosses were furious to learn of O'Flaherty's independent action.) He went straight to the classic British eatery Simpson's-in-the-Strand to celebrate, treating himself to roast beef, nut brown ale, and a Scotch. To his mother and sister at home he wrote, "It's really an outrage, most of my friends say. Here I come to London to write a book and starve in a garret in the accepted literary fashion; lo and behold, jobs are hurled at me and I <u>have</u> to work. Besides London is expensive and you know my habits." Sinclair Lewis, who passed through London a few days later and invited Gunther for tea (probably having met him at Schlogl's), pronounced him the "luckiest young upstart he'd ever met."[14]

All this Gunther reported gleefully to Helen Hahn. To amuse and impress her and keep her on the hook, he jotted his observations, pleasures, aims, and conquests into a daily log, which he mailed to her weekly. It was part of his lifelong habit of self-documentation. Imagining Hahn as his audience, he probed his intentions, accomplishments, worries, and failings, constructing an implicit narrative of himself just as he would write fictional narratives. At home he had consulted Hahn all the time, eager to hear her reactions even if she deflated his wild visions. In London he terribly missed their conversations. He sent her his writing and worried about her judgments of it. "Somehow I can't keep it all to myself," he told her. He loved having an attractive woman as a sounding board. He did not presume that his judgment was keener than Hahn's simply because he was a man. Nor did he see intelligence and sexual attractiveness in a woman at odds. He praised Hahn as "the wisest person I've ever known" and "the most beautiful," seeing nothing contradictory in his compliments.[15]

He told Hahn of his "strange, tremendous love" for London. He hung a big city map on his wall and took long exploratory walks after work. The city cast a spell on him—even the fog that "floated over the city . . . a mellow grey mist, wafted down the old streets and around the gloomy grey buildings like a celestial caress." "You should see the lights twinkle along the Thames embankment at dusk from Waterloo bridge," he wrote home after a month, "or the patrol of a lamp-lighter along the velvet midnight streets, or the clean sweep of Oxford street bisecting the city, or the strange glamour of Piccadilly Circus and Leicester Square at night, or the towers of Parliament silhouetted in sharp mezzotint against the gloom of Whitehall, or the bookstalls along Charing Cross and Tottenham court road, or the surging human flood of Trafalgar Square." With delight he called the changing of the guard at Buckingham Palace "England's state ballet." He found the British Museum appallingly depressing but liked the Tate Museum and the National Gallery, went to plays and opera for entertainment, and sidestepped the "swarms" of prostitutes near Mayfair and Hyde Park, who looked "dull and dowdy." He observed men's waxed mustaches with fascination and no envy, drank port, loved afternoon tea, and remarked on British locutions such as "Stick No Posters" for "Post No Bills" and the admonition over the sink in the men's room at the British Museum: "This basin is for casual ablutions only." He was amused to find himself "the only man in London with tortoise shell spectacles."[16]

GUNTHER'S YOUTHFUL GENIALITY and good looks made it easy for people to like him. He had in mind to interview British authors for a series of publishable word portraits of them, and an inordinate number of noted writers took him up on the offer. Before three weeks had passed, he met writers W. L. George (a "brilliant conversationalist" and "a broken man"), Michael Arlen (a "spoiled child," taking an "assiduously naughty and delicately fastidious pose"), Siegfried Sassoon ("the most perfect imaginable idealization of the young soldier-poet"), and others. Cass Canfield, an American son of privilege and a youthful world wanderer who had retraced Marco Polo's global route on foot for fun, asked Gunther to lunch. Canfield had recently bought interest in the New York publishing house of Harper & Brothers and was managing its London office. Their lunch (initiated by Canfield's New York superiors) began a long and fruitful relationship between the two.[17]

As Gunther wrestled with the demands of his newspaper job, he had very little time for these literary portraits or his half-drafted novel. His employment windfall came with a steep learning curve. O'Flaherty approved him using several hours of his working day on a crash course of reading in British and European politics. Much of his time was also occupied with the basic work of any foreign correspondent, reading the local newspapers to see what news to pursue and write up for American readers. This was no small task in London, a newspaper-rich city more than three times the size of Chicago. Chicago had four major daily papers. The London morning dailies included the "Times, Telegraph, Post, Mail, News, Express, Herald, Westminster Gazette, Manchester Guardian, Chronicle, Mirror, Sketch, Financial Times, and Globe," every one of the fourteen "well known, well established," Gunther recounted to Hahn. Evenings brought additionally the "News, Standard, Star, Observer, Sunday Times, News of the World, Weekly Dispatch, Sunday Herald, People, Referee, and Circuit." Besides, there were important weeklies: the "Sphere, Universe, Sketch, Tatler, Punch, Illustrated London News, New Statesman, Saturday Review, Times, Spectator, Nation, Athenaeum, and Truth."[18]

Gunther found it "killingly funny" that only three of the London morning papers placed the major news on the front page. Most of them used page one for advertisements, including want ads; the news followed in an order that made no sense to him. To his eye, these papers seemed to "exercise no selection of news whatever and simply start at the front columns of the paper and fill up with whatever comes along. When the paper is full, the staff goes home." He had heard that when war was declared in 1914, the London *Times* carried the information on page seven, the usual place for foreign dispatches.[19]

Because he was only twenty-three, Gunther took for granted a revolution in newspaper format that had progressed more rapidly in Chicago than in London. He was unaware that American newspapers not long before had looked like these old-fashioned London papers, with ads on the front page and little prioritization of news by page order or column placement. Standard newspapers revised their formats in the early twentieth century, becoming more directive and designing the front page as a textual map of a fast-changing social world. The new format responded to the phenomenal expansion of news enabled by modern communication technologies. Steering readers' quick comprehension, modern format placed the most important items on the front page, with headline size as an added guide, and less pressing items farther back or in their own sections. Coming fully into place in the 1920s and 1930s, modern newspaper format gave readers the shape of their social and political world as soon as they glanced at the paper. Tabloid format pursued similar aims with simplification and exaggeration.[20]

When Gunther's three weeks at the *News* ended, he reluctantly accepted a job with the United Press (UP). He would have preferred to resume his own writing, but Hal O'Flaherty insisted in no uncertain terms that if he "ever expect[ed] to do cosmopolitan journalism," he would be crazy to pass up the training and discipline he would get at the UP. Gunther hesitated. Should he burnish his credentials as a newspaperman so as to build a reliable career, or bypass that—and a salary—on a risky shot at fame and fortune as a great novelist? For the present, he was young, he had not been in London very long, and he thought he could do some of both.[21]

At his desk at the UP, Gunther received incoming stories and routed them as quickly as possible to the newspapers subscribing to the press service. These newspaper subscribers spanned the world, and not all of them subscribed in the same way. Some wanted only important breaking news, others a larger panoply of foreign articles. The news articles arrived into the UP office via telegraph over cable lines, still the quickest and most efficient way to transmit text internationally. Wireless radio transmission in 1924 was weak and unreliable over long distances. All urgent stories were cabled, and because telegraph services charged per word, reporters invented shortcuts—conglomerating several words into one—to reduce expenses. Thus "cablese," the lingua franca of foreign correspondence, was born.[22]

Gunther had already encountered cablese at the *News*. When a foreign correspondent sent a story in cablese, it was translated into prose and given a headline by someone on the receiving end. That was why Gunther told Helen Hahn not to bother criticizing his prose in any of his bylined articles from Europe. Anything he wrote had to "be skeletonized into unintelligible cablese and sent in that fashion. Then in Chicago, it's rewritten." The "easy" example of cablese he gave her happened to deal with the Ruhr crisis that Jimmy Sheean was just then reporting for the *Chicago Tribune*: "Miller Herriot Ruhrwarding exparis handfirst investigation Germfinance Germcon Germpol subdawes stop Herriot overhanded Parbudget reichwards upset Frgovt upfollowing consent deputies satisfaction Francewide." These twenty-three words of cablese became a short article under Webb Miller's byline, reporting that "Premier Edouard Herriot is hurrying to the Ruhr to gain firsthand information for Paris concerning German finance, German economics, and German politics. M. Herriot on his arrival handed over the Paris budget to representatives of the Reich. The budget was set up by the French government following consent of the Chamber of Deputies and following the widely expressed approval of the French people."[23]

At the UP Gunther was expected to master reading cablese into English and vice versa as fast as normal reading. It was his job to decode the incoming stories and decide which subscribing newspapers to send them to, depending on how important the story was.

Similarly, if local reporters handed him their articles in prose, Gunther had to turn those into cablese to send them abroad. He had to send breaking news "INSTANTANEOUSLY, with proper routing, proper directions, and proper wordage, to Japan, South America, Spain, Central Europe, or all at once," he wrote to Hahn. A thousand papers around the world subscribed to receive breaking news from the UP. "Think what happens if I make a mistake!" he worried.[24]

The job ran him ragged. It felt like "a three-ring circus, firing from all fronts at the same time," he said, his jumbled metaphor suggesting its toll. Overnight shifts left him exhausted, but he proved himself highly competent. His boss, recognizing his talent with people, did not keep him on the desk all the time but sent him out occasionally on assignments, including interviewing a broad range of political leaders. Gunther succeeded in interviewing both the recently defeated Labor prime minister Ramsay MacDonald and the newly reigning Conservative prime minister Stanley Baldwin in the same week. It was "the damned most amazing stunt . . . ever whangled out of London by an American newspaper man," Gunther bragged to Hahn.[25]

Beyond his UP job, Gunther nourished his literary side in an intoxicating friendship with the outspoken feminist writer Rebecca West. Only one week after he arrived in London, the two saw each other at a celebrated "Red Dinner," where the anarchist Emma Goldman expressed her disillusion with Bolshevik Russia. He was covering the event for the *News*, and West was there because she was a friend of Goldman. Gunther was thrilled that she remembered him from her American speaking tour the previous year, when he had interviewed her in Chicago.

West was a transatlantic celebrity for her convention-defying personal life as well as for her fiction and her acerbic political and literary commentary. Born Cicily Fairfield in 1892, she had made a name for herself literally and figuratively before she was twenty. She took the name of Ibsen's passionate tragic heroine in *Rosmersholm* in place of her own when she was writing in the feminist journal *The*

Freewoman in the 1910s. At nineteen, she became the lover of the inimitably versatile H. G. Wells, a married man more than twice her age. She bore his son in 1914 and continued a hot-and-cold relationship with him for ten years, deserting him in 1924 not long before she and Gunther re-met.[26]

Six weeks after their initial reacquaintance, West sent Gunther a coy note, out of the blue, saying that she had officially appointed herself "mother, grandmother, aunt, sister, and all other discreet female relatives" to take care of him in London. He called her instantly, and she invited him for a dinner tête-à-tête at her flat a few days later. Her wittiness, casual elegance, and literary gossip beguiled Gunther completely. She was "pretty as a picture" and "disconcertingly brilliant in conversation," he thought, though he felt "a little afraid of her." West's repartee was famous: she was dubbed "Bernard Shaw in skirts," "one of the most scintillating conversationalists of our time." She flirted by regaling Gunther with stories of other men and surprising him with delicious barbs about well-known writers. When he offered his solemn judgment that Edna St. Vincent Millay was the "finest creative artist in America," for instance, West did not disagree, but calmly commented, "as soon as I saw that Millay girl I knew . . . she is a bitch."[27]

They saw each other often in the early months of 1925. He thought she had "the best brain I've ever known. And such hatred of cant, and such scorn of presumptuous fools, and such delightful humor at herself, and such fine, ready generosity." West critiqued and sponsored Gunther as a fiction writer. She invited him to dinner parties and introduced him to literary figures. When she told him that his half-drafted novel was awful, he threw the draft into the fire, but her heady attention made his already outsize ambition bloom. For West, the earnest attentiveness of Gunther—strapping and handsome, almost ten years her junior—offered a welcome respite from Wells, who was hounding her to return, and from their hard-to-handle ten-year-old son Anthony, "H.G.'s brat," as she referred to him, shocking Gunther. West was half in love with the head of England's largest publishing empire, Lord Max Beaverbrook, who was (like Wells) short in stature, quixotic, imperious, and unfaithful.[28] Gunther made no demands, and he fairly seethed with eager educability, a combination of intelligence and energy that led literary men to warm to him, too. He was adorably willing to absorb what West had to offer.

DESPITE THE FRISSON of West's friendship, by early spring of 1925 Gunther dreamed of getting away from the UP. He had been saving half of his salary since he arrived, planning to build up sufficient funds to quit regular work and move to a remote and cheap location where he would write a more mature novel. In March he got word of a perfect job on the horizon. Hal O'Flaherty, who championed him, had succeeded in pressing the higher-ups at the *News* to hire Gunther as a regular correspondent. With an offer in hand to start work for the *News* in July, Gunther decided to take April, May, and June for his writing break. He left the UP. A friend from Chicago, Leonard Weil, was ready to join his travels.[29]

In April he and Weil and two other friends went to Paris. Gunther was again captivated, as on his postcollege trip. "The chestnuts are just blooming in the Champs Elysees and the scent, the dim shrouded trees, the mystery and majesty of that long promenade, are wonderful, wonderful," he exulted. "The pink lights streaking down the Champs Elysees like fire opals on a long swinging chain. . . . The miraculous thing is, of course, that it is all true—you are seeing it, and it isn't a dream." The low prices in Paris compared to London astonished him—"you can eat breakfast for three pennies, lunch for a quarter, and dine magnificently on 75 cents." Looking for the cheapest hotel, they unwittingly took rooms in a Montmartre brothel—at sixty cents a night. After discovering their mistake, they decided to stay, anyway. A riotous week ensued, and then Gunther and Weil traveled south, stopping at a Mediterranean resort where Weil's wealthy parents were vacationing.[30]

They were headed for the small Mediterranean island of Por-querolles. It fulfilled Gunther's vision of a beautiful and cheap place to write, and he buckled down. Within three weeks he wrote sixty-five thousand words of a novel, well on its way to completion. When a telegram from the *News* in late May called him back to Paris much earlier than planned, he took the new schedule in stride. The paper wanted him to begin filling in sequentially for *News* correspondents who would be taking three-week summer breaks. He was pleased with himself after being abroad for six months.[31] The question mark on his ambition doubled—would he be a fiction writer, sidelining newspaper work as a day job when needed, or the other way around?

Now Gunther was placed in the Paris office of the *News*, where he struggled to browse through thirty French newspapers every morn-ing. That was quite an uphill climb, even though he had dutifully studied French an hour a day for five months. Fortunately, Weil stayed in town for a while, and another Chicago pal, Jerome Frank (later a New Dealer and judge), was also there briefly, for some light-hearted diversion. Weil introduced Gunther to an American friend of his, Frances Fineman, who joined them several evenings. Fineman at twenty-eight was footloose. A petite gamine with a tousled blonde bob, she had just spent four months in Leningrad and Moscow, en-thralled with the new society and enthusiastic about its innovative theater. She hoped to find a job related to theater in Paris or Lon-don. She had the wit and intelligence that Gunther appreciated in women, and he was impressed that she had gone to Russia on her own, and stayed so long.[32]

After Weil and Frank left Paris, Gunther looked up Fineman, who shepherded him to a party hosted by the British novelist Ford Madox Ford. Ford's weekly bashes were legendary for their flow-ing liquor and live music, drawing in American literary and artistic sojourners abroad. Gunther found the party "pretty ghastly." He poked fun at Ford, who as former editor of *Transatlantic Review* had been "England's most promising young man for about forty years." He decided he loathed "the whole expatriate gang," except for "a boy named Ernest Hemingway . . . the most personable youngster I've met in France. . . . He can think straight and he can write English."[33] At that time, Hemingway, Gunther, and Sheean shared the same profile as would-be writers from the Midwest in their mid-twenties, living abroad, earning their bread as newspaper reporters—though a year later when Hemingway's *The Sun Also Rises* was published, his reputation leaped ahead.

On June 3, 1925, Gunther received a letter from Helen Hahn telling him she was engaged to another man. Gunther's world collapsed. He reeled—but quickly recovered, insisting he was not anguished. Frances Fineman was there to fill the void. "I am perhaps a little bit in love with this Frances child," he soon thought, being cautious, aware that he might be rebounding from Hahn's devastating news. He liked this "small corn-colored-haired creature." Her small stature contrasted appealingly to Gunther's height. She was "fun," he decided.[34]

Fineman's background differed from Gunther's, yet their international ventures and writerly aspirations provided common ground. She was born to Russian Jewish immigrant parents in New York City in 1897. Her beautiful mother had chafed in an unhappy marriage, dallied with lovers, and then ran away with one to Galveston, Texas, about 1910, taking adolescent Frances with them. In high school in Galveston, Frances excelled academically though her home life was stormy. She endured a troubled relationship with her mother, worshipped memories of her real father, and resented her stepfather, possibly for sexual abuse, though the evidence is uncertain.[35]

Her college years were lengthier than usual. In January 1916 she entered Barnard College of Columbia University, in her father's city, New York. As her third semester ended in the spring of 1917, she was told to leave. The Barnard dean disapproved of Fineman's friends in the journalism school, though the delicate phrasing in college records obscured details. Without formally expelling Fineman, the dean told her not to return to Barnard; she also made it hard for Fineman to transfer elsewhere, by planting doubts in the minds of deans at other schools where Fineman applied. Fineman's fate may have been tied to the antiwar protests on the Columbia campus that spring, when the United States entered the world war. She was not among the students the university prosecuted for protesting (in what became a civil liberties cause célèbre), but she was the secretary-treasurer of the Socialist Club at Barnard, when the Socialist Party opposed US entry into the war. She was also friendly with one of the two faculty members fired by the university for their antiwar views, comparative literature instructor Henry Wadsworth Longfellow Dana (called Harry), a Harvard PhD of distinguished New England lineage whose enthusiasm for Russian modernist theater may have contributed to Fineman's interest.[36]

Forced out of Barnard, Fineman spent a year repairing her reputation by returning to Galveston and doing war-related work. She was then admitted to Rice Institute (now Rice University) in Houston. After one year at Rice, she transferred to Radcliffe College of Harvard University. There she resumed her creative writing and also her friendship with Harry Dana, who was living nearby in Cambridge. During her college years, she studied foreign languages, history, and politics and wrote short stories and plays, imagining going into theater or journalism. When Radcliffe refused to give her credit for her courses at Barnard and Rice, she sought and gained readmission to Barnard, where she received her Bachelor of Arts in 1921. After college, Fineman scrabbled around in New York for a few years, taking whatever jobs she could get, as a waitress, a factory worker, a cashier, an organizer of community theater, a secretary. She was psychoanalyzed, a mark of her uneasy mind and her intentional modernity. When she went to Russia in 1924–1925, it was in part to look up a long-lost aunt but also because she was eager to see communist society. Once there, she felt she was "a simpler and happier person," because there "everything is joined with everything else," a "complex intellectual life . . . combined with the simplest material life."[37]

Willful and talented, Fineman wrote creative fiction peopled by "New Woman" characters who sought important work and relished adventure in sexual relationships, as she did herself. Her characters were skeptical about marriage and open-minded about their destinies, as were many educated and sophisticated young women in the 1920s. It was "a nonsequitur to say that simply because a woman paints, writes, builds bridges, or any thing else that man alone has been accustomed to doing, she therefore becomes less womanly," she wrote in the early 1920s. "Does it lessen a man's sex activity to do these things? Neither will it a woman's. It seems to, at present, because always the problem of choice is put before the woman, all sex or all work, as tho[ugh] sex & work—for her—were mutually incompatible." She saw self-expression in sex and in work as equally essential and complementary.[38]

When young women of Fineman's generation and type—educated, mobile, modern, disrespectful of conventional morality—embraced sexual freedom, they imagined having sex with men without becoming pregnant. That was risky, but not unreasonable in the 1920s, because both condoms for men and diaphragms for women were available to those who knew about and could afford them. Birth control was illegal virtually everywhere in the United States, but two transformative court decisions in 1918 undercut that fact. The US Army's crisis over venereal disease during the world war led to condoms becoming widely purchasable, not for contraception (supposedly) but for men's protection from venereal disease. Second, because of birth control reformer Margaret Sanger's law-defying efforts and subsequent defenses in court, physicians could legally prescribe diaphragms for married women (or women who presented themselves as married). Still, only women who had the physician access, the money, and the mind-set to get and use a diaphragm did so. Condoms were used far more commonly than diaphragms were; men could buy them everywhere, not only in drugstores but also at hotels and gas stations and from shoeshine men. But condoms were only indifferently reliable in the 1920s and relatively expensive. Withdrawal (coitus interruptus) remained the most widely practiced way to avoid pregnancy, for rich or poor—especially poor—despite its unreliability.[39]

Abortion was a likely choice when withdrawal, unreliable condoms, or postcoital douching (which many women trusted) failed to prevent pregnancy. Fineman was sexually experienced when she met Gunther and had had at least one abortion. She and women like her saw abortion as distasteful and unfortunate (as well as illegal) but nonetheless a necessary fact of life. Doctors were aware of how widespread it was. Getting an abortion required courage and cash and the friendship networks to locate a decent practitioner, but there were decent practitioners in major cities in the 1920s. For women who could find all of those, abortion worked.[40]

Fineman and Gunther probably began a sexual relationship in mid-June 1925. Both were in London—where Gunther's job moved him for three weeks after his three weeks in Paris—though they did not stay in the same place for long. Fineman returned to New York very soon to begin working as a press agent for a well-known theatrical producer who had brought the Moscow Art Theater to the United States on tour. John signed a letter to her, "I'm yours, utterly and maybe forever yours, John." The "maybe" was important, though they wrote passionate letters for months. Missed opportunities and mutual blame led them to break up at the end of 1925, but Gunther nevertheless wrote to Fineman, "If you think I don't wake up in the middle of the night, sweating blood at thought of you, with my heart in my throat and my soul in my boots, damn you, DAMN you, you're crazy."[41]

When Gunther was in London, Rebecca West was eager to see him again. They too became lovers once he told her of his shock, despondency, and sense of new freedom after Helen Hahn's break with him. Part of West's freethinking feminism was taking up lovers as she liked, and she certainly liked John Gunther. Because he no longer consistently lived in London but moved where the *News* wanted him, he and West arranged to meet each other here and there, in Paris or on the Riviera when she vacationed with her son.[42] West became his guide to sexual experience as she had been his guide in the literary world. She cut his provincial moorings, much as worldly-wise, sexually emancipated Louise Bryant had done for Jimmy Sheean in New York. Each of these midwestern boys—who grew up indebted to attentive mothers for intellectual stimulation and loving care— had the luck and the charm to attract a new kind of nurture from a fascinating older woman.

Both West and Gunther seemed to accept from the beginning that their sexual relationship, though exciting and meaningful, would not last forever. She was dallying, and for Gunther, West's sexual past was not what he envisioned in his life partner. In his sole recovered love letter to her, he savored "the day in Antibes when you had more of me than anyone ever had had before." But he went on to say, in his usual self-examining way, "it's curious—I've never been a good lover to you—oh yes—never. I can't tell why. But I know it's true. I suppose it is because I want to save for myself some final & eventual illusion of myself—why have everything now?—what hell it would be—not to be able to dream."[43] Despite his gain in sophistication, Gunther's conventional moral underpinnings made him imagine his true love as a sexually inexperienced woman, not someone with West's history, titillating as her history was. He also had in mind his intense, stormy, on-again off-again love affair with Frances Fineman.

Meanwhile, the *News* kept Gunther very busy, having put him in a correspondent position as "swing man" or "roving second man" under the renowned correspondent and bureau head Paul Scott Mowrer, the same man who had helpfully advised Dorothy Thompson. Gunther got a raise, and was based in Paris with Mowrer, but moved around often to fill in for correspondents elsewhere when they took leaves of absence. Mowrer also sent him to cover sudden political outbreaks. For example, when France used massive force in 1926 to put down an anticolonial revolt by the Druze people in Syria (then controlled by France under a League of Nations mandate), Gunther went there to report on it.[44]

He was constantly on the go. Only someone young, determined, and vigorous could do the job effectively, and to these qualities Gunther added his extraordinary ability to write rapidly and on the fly.

Mowrer recognized how good Gunther was at conveying the atmosphere and mood of a place, and when sending him out to report on political news, he usually let him "prowl around for a week or two" to pick up scents and write a feature with no immediate deadline. These lengthier stories were mailed rather than cabled to Chicago (thus dubbed "mailers"). When Gunther was dispatched to Spain to follow up rumors about dictator Primo de Rivera, for example, he also wrote a feature on Madrid as a "City of Contrasts," describing the city's cuspidors, traffic lights, bookshops, desserts, beggars' and waiters' habits. At home in Paris he typically wrote political and diplomatic news but might cover the fashion industry's latest styles when nothing else was pressing. Because he was dispatched to almost every country in Europe and the Levant at one time or another in the 1920s, he eventually wrote six- to seven-thousand-word mailers on situations in Egypt, Syria, Transjordan, Sweden, Poland, the Caucasus, the Soviet Union, Greece, Albania, Romania, Turkey, Czechoslovakia, Bulgaria, Hungary, and Austria.[45]

He was rising as a correspondent, yet somehow found the hours to complete his novel, titled *The Red Pavilion*. It traced the intertwined lives and loves of a group of young friends in Chicago, and though Gunther insisted there was "almost no autobiography in it," the main characters bore a recognizable likeness to him and Helen Hahn. The maverick publisher Martin Secker published it in Britain in June 1926 (and went bankrupt not long after). Harper & Brothers published an American edition six months later, courtesy of Cass Canfield, who had become an editor in the New York office. The novel was banned in Boston for its sexual references, along with many others, including Sinclair Lewis's *Elmer Gantry*. Both English and American reviewers noticed the sexual frankness; they commonly thought the novel was clever and gracefully written, but several thought it derivative of Aldous Huxley.

Rebecca West told Gunther that she liked *The Red Pavilion* more than Hemingway's *The Sun Also Rises*. He did not know till years later how she talked up the novel at dinner parties and among book critics in London and New York, lending it buzz. By the end of 1926 West fell in love with someone else and she and Gunther were no longer lovers. Nonetheless she insisted to him, "I do want you to say you'll come back to me and be my nice sweet friend you've always been. I truly love you, John, and I'm enormously grateful to you for all the dearness you've shown me." They remained lifelong friends.[46]

Frances Fineman cushioned any letdown he felt, for she resuscitated their relationship through letters and took up the role Helen Hahn had played as audience for his self-narration. "I _have_ had a time!" Gunther wrote to her in the fall of 1926, listing his recent jaunts for the _News_. "New York, London, Paris, Marseilles, Port Said, Cairo, Kantera, Haifa, Beirut, Damascus, Jaffa, Jerusalem, Cairo, Alexandria, Marseilles, Paris, Rome, Naples, Venice, Florence, Milan, Rome, Antibes, Paris—now London again." Still, he felt mired in the "old business of compromise between hogging the cable page of the CDN and thus earning a living, and my somewhat fantastic desire to write some littrachoor." He could not decide.[47]

On November 2, 1926, the second anniversary of his arrival in London, he looked back. The two years felt like two centuries. He had seen a great deal of Europe and the Near East, and secured the job he wanted, which brought him a regular salary and earned enough to make his mother and sister comfortable also; he had published a novel, got past a love affair that had "throttled" him for three years, and even learned a new language passably. To Fineman he totted this up with a note of self-deprecation: "I've lost some of my old prejudices and illusions and gained some new ones. . . . I know a little more than I did, I think, about most things, and perhaps have lost that damned crass juvenile obtuseness which once so nicely distinguished me. (Perhaps though it still does.) I have an infinitely healthier and more capable body. I have begun to know my limitations. I have made a great many valuable friends. And (bless us) I have been an idiot in seventeen countries instead of just one." He subtly

conveyed his indecision about her, as well as about his career, in adding, "I'm still trying to find out where the devil I am in this world,
and why, and for whom, and what I am going to do about it."[48]

LATE IN 1926, Fineman and Gunther were again together in London. She then returned to New York, but quite suddenly they met
in Rome in March 1927 and got married—possibly because of a
pregnancy soon ended.[49] They established a home in Paris, Gunther's
base for the *News*. Though their marriage was rocky at first, his frequent travel gave both of them a lot of freedom and they could appreciate one another in long letters. Their temperamental differences
were extreme—Gunther genial and openhanded, Fineman brilliant
and impatient—but temperamental differences can complement as
well as divide.

Gunther's job during the 1920s offered vast opportunities for
political education. He had to look hard at many nations and cul-
tures, many political systems and their methods. Perhaps it was the
very plethora of politics he witnessed that kept him politically pli-
able beyond his foundational American belief in liberal democracy.
European power politics in the 1920s did not arouse his political
emotions the way they did Sheean's. Aware of his own political in-
determinacy, Gunther described himself as "one of those queer birds
who always sees both sides of everything."[50] Though his attitude was
well suited to being a reporter, as he circulated among journalists
with keener political judgments he worried whether he measured up.
In years ahead, menacing political changes in Europe would repeatedly test his outlook.

CHAPTER 4

THE FREEST MAN ON
ANY NEWSPAPER

WITH HIS BLUE eyes and his height, Vincent Sheean could not avoid sticking out among the Arabs whose mule caravan he was joining, but he wanted to make himself as inconspicuous as he could. He shaved his head, put on a turban, and donned the local garb, a rough brown homespun garment called a *jellaba*—so short on him that it revealed his city-white legs. To be taken for an Arab was impossible; still, he hoped to escape notice on his mission to interview Abd el-Krim, leader of the rebellion against Spain taking place in the Rif, the mountainous African terrain north of Morocco. During a year of European reporting, Sheean had become repulsed by British and French doggedness in hanging on to their colonial possessions despite the Versailles principle of national self-determination. Anti-imperialist activists living in Paris may have egged on his critical views; radicals from Francophone Africa, the Caribbean, and Asia who lived there championed the Rif insurgency, making it a rallying point for their own budding nationalisms.[1]

The Rif had been made a Spanish protectorate in 1912 as a result of complex bargaining among Spain, France, and Britain, all three imperial powers with interests in North Africa. Now resistance by the Riffians, an ethnically distinctive Muslim people dwelling there, threatened to topple Spanish rule. Their leader Abd el-Krim intended to establish an autonomous political region—a modern Islamic state. He had raised an army so effective that it had crushed nearly ten thousand Spanish troops in one devastating battle in 1921.

By the time Sheean fixed his attention on the issue in September 1924, Riffian fighters had taken over most of the territory. The Spanish retained control only around Melilla at the eastern end of the protectorate and in the towns of Ceuta and Tetouan at the western end. Riffian success put France on edge, as well as Spain: France's African empire in Morocco began at the southern border of the Rif, and the line between Spanish and French territory existed only so far as troops actively reinforced it. In the shadowy area of the border lived Arab residents whose loyalties could easily sway toward the Riffians.[2]

AFTER SHEEAN WROTE an initial article from Paris on Riffian success in pushing sixty thousand Spanish troops back to Tetouan, the *Tribune* assigned him to follow up the story with inquiries in Spain.[3] He went to Madrid in November 1924 but found officials there closemouthed. The dictator General Primo de Rivera had just taken charge of the campaign, setting up his headquarters in Tetouan and boasting that he would conquer the Rif. He declared an impassable "Primo de Rivera line" along the narrow strip of land that Spain still controlled. Sheean had nothing but scorn for the dictator, after his terrifying erroneous arrest in Spain earlier that year, but he decided that he must speak to Primo de Rivera himself in Tetouan. Sheean sailed from southern Spain in December. As soon as he landed in the city of Tangier, an international zone at the northwestern edge of the Rif, his pulse quickened. Street hawkers jabbered at him in Arabic, and conflicting rumors about the Rif flew about their crowded stalls. He could see that the beach was calm, with British and French ships floating nearby, but he heard the boom of guns coming from the direction of the mountains. He made his way forty miles by car to the coastal city of Tetouan and interviewed General Primo de Rivera,

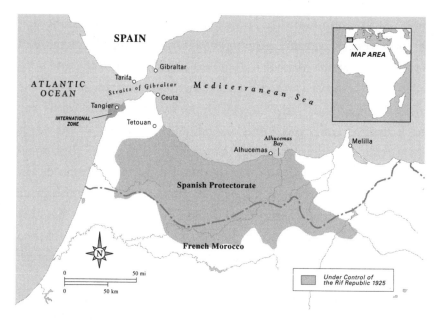

The Spanish Protectorate in the Rif, Northern Africa, 1925
Adapted from Sebastian Balfour, Deadly Embrace: Morocco and the Road to the Spanish Civil War *(New York: Oxford University Press, 2002).*

who admitted that he was withdrawing his forces temporarily over the winter. Spanish troops were lying low behind the Primo de Rivera line and waiting until spring to start a new offensive. Sheean saw this as an admission of defeat for the time being.[4]

Infinitely curious about the rebels, Sheean then decided that he must speak to the Rif leader, Abd el-Krim. It would be a risky enterprise, entirely different from the many interviews he had done with European leaders. He had a great deal of latitude in the way he conducted himself as a foreign correspondent, and easily got approval from the *Tribune* to venture into the Rif. "The foreign correspondent is without doubt the freest man on any newspaper," Sheean's older colleague George Seldes said, making the claim in a wry critique of American newspaper publishers: "The owners of the papers are ignorant about Europe and careless."[5] Perhaps. In any case, the *Tribune* would pay for Sheean's self-set mission. By starting his journey from the area still held by the Spanish, Sheean could reach Abd el-Krim fairly easily. John Gunther's boss Paul Scott Mowrer had done that in September. Gunther recounted admiringly that Mowrer had "tramped down to Morocco, disguised himself as an Arab, and with a boy and a camel worked through the Spanish lines, reached the army of the Riffs, stayed 15 days with the Riff sultan, worked his way back again in really precarious danger, and then filed 10,000 words on it from Gibraltar, scooping the world for the *News*." But when Sheean asked for permission to enter the Rif that way, Primo de Rivera refused, saying it was impossible. There were no Spanish posts along the way, no communication, and besides, said the haughty general, it would be "'against the new policy. We have established the Line. It is a blockade and you cannot very well ask us to break our own blockade.'"[6]

Sheean formulated a daredevil plan: he would approach the Rif from the south, a longer and far more arduous route, crossing French lines as well as Spanish. He had found out that Arab agents of Abd el-Krim crept stealthily through French Morocco, carrying goods and arms to the Riffians by mule and camel caravan, without French forces cracking down. Joining one of these caravans would mean entering "a world in which the European was not only a rarity, but an enemy," he knew. It would be no simple matter to find a caravan leader he could trust not to rob him or abandon or kill him on the way. "Your life isn't worth a *sou* once you get beyond the French outposts," a French official warned him, declaring flatly that border tribes between the French outposts and the Rif "think nothing of robbing and killing." Nonetheless, the same official suggested one Arab agent Sheean might possibly trust.[7]

The challenge excited Sheean more than it scared him. He would face danger, but a spine-tingling story could result. The *Chicago Tribune* assumed that reporters' "personal adventures" boosted newspaper sales, and encouraged them. That very year, the *Tribune* had sent Floyd Gibbons on a unique assignment, inspired by the way women swooned over screen idol Rudolph Valentino in *The Sheik*. At the *Tribune*'s bidding, Gibbons traveled across the Sahara Desert

An invented sketch of Vincent Sheean as he looked going into the Rif, 1925.
Source: Vincent Sheean, An American among the Riffi *(New York: Century Co., 1926).*

to obtain a "true picture" of Arab sheiks' appeal for "Anglo-Saxon and American women." After spending immense sums to equip a camel caravan to travel two thousand miles, in heat so hellish that his company nearly expired from lack of water, Gibbons reported that he had nowhere seen the "dashing, handsome, love-making sheik made famous" in the movies.[8]

In Tangier Sheean struck a bargain with a caravan leader and a guide who knew some English. He then shaved his head, wound the turban around it, and slipped on the *jellaba*, pulling its cowl over his head. Setting out in darkness, the caravan traveled through an embattled landscape, vulnerable to Spanish air raids, roving Arab bands, and attacks by the French. Sheean bumped along astride a bony mule, his long legs dragging. Or to save his buttocks he walked, like the rest of the party. The arid terrain was blazing hot during the day and freezing cold at night. The travelers' beds were ditches or flat stones. Sheean soon was filthy, exhausted, and crawling with lice.

He managed to survive the double-dealing of his thieving guide, who tricked him out of all his money and disappeared. Then he faced a worse roadblock. When the caravan stopped to rest at the settlement of the Metalsa, Arab allies of the Riffians, its headmen pulled off Sheean's cowl, stared at his face, and began interrogating him. Sheean's explanations of his purpose, poorly translated by their interpreter, meant nothing to his captors. They had never heard of the United States—nor ever seen a newspaper. They moved Sheean into a dank cave teeming with vermin and imprisoned him there under constant guard. Interrogation followed interrogation, to no avail. And then, nothing.

Endless days went by. Only the surreptitious kindness of a scribe, who brought him a little food, kept him alive. Sheean retained a shred of hope, in that he had earlier sent a courier to Abd el-Krim to ask permission for the interview. That saved him. The courier finally appeared, bearing the desired precious note from "the sultan of the Rif," as Abd el-Krim was called by his loyalists, and transformed the attitude of the Metalsa. Two of them guided Sheean the rest of the way. It took several more days by mule, over three mountain ridges, to reach the Rif capital of Ajdir close to the Mediterranean coast.

Sheean was relieved and utterly grateful to have arrived. He was fed, housed well, and cordially treated by Abd el-Krim's closest councilors, educated men who appeared to be thoughtful and determined strategists. They answered Sheean's questions about their army, their tactics, their gun runners. Sheean would soon write that "the picture of savage Riffian tribes fighting fanatically under barbarous chiefs" was a fiction concocted by Europeans. The Riffian army numbered under twenty-five thousand (far below Spanish strength) and fought almost wholly as guerillas, making the most of their knowledge of their home terrain by ambushing and sniping at the enemy. With those tactics—and no cavalry, antiaircraft missiles,

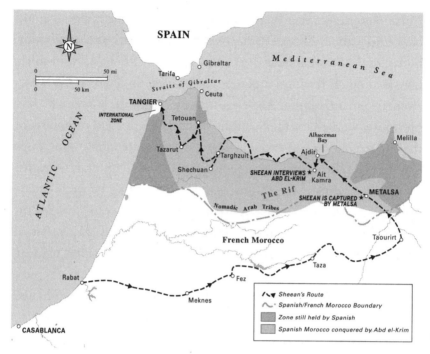

Sheean's route on his first trip to Abd el-Krim, Winter 1924–1925
Adapted from Vincent Sheean, "The Robin Hood of the Rif," Asia, November 1925, 970.

airplanes, or bombs—they had forced the Spanish into seeming submission. France and Spain claimed that Germany or Russia must have been helping the Riffians, but Sheean saw no trace of foreign advisers or capital.

Sheean gladly accepted all this information. Then he was stopped short by the refusal of his interlocutors to take him to the headquarters of their "Sultan," several miles away. Abd el-Krim had resented earlier misrepresentations in the European press and apparently expected no better from Sheean. Desperate to avoid the thwarting of his purpose in enduring the whole trip, Sheean pressed his case for ten days. He finally broke through the councilors' resistance by writing down the questions he would ask.

Delivered into Abd el-Krim's company, Sheean had to conduct his interview through an interpreter, for Abd el-Krim spoke in the local

Riffian language rather than his fluent Spanish, which Sheean could have understood. Sheean came away full of respect and admiration for the man and what he had accomplished. Far from the "wild chieftain, leading his fanatical mountain tribesmen" in jihad, as the Western press portrayed him, Abd el-Krim was a dignified lawyer who had previously worked for the Spanish. By declaring for the autonomy of the Rif region, he had brought together disparate ethnic subgroups as allies. His administrative organization and military draft—headed by his European-trained brother, the commanding general—made up the vertebrae of a modern Islamic state, in Sheean's judgment. Sheean warmed to the Riffians, likening their faith in their eventual triumph—"the characteristic faith of a small, devout nation fighting on its own soil"—to that of the Irish. The fact that the Riffians were typically fair-skinned and that a few were blue-eyed and red-haired also led him to feel almost a racial kinship with them.[9]

Sheean's return journey to Tangier was nothing like his earlier ordeal. Abd el-Krim supplied a gentlemanly Riffian soldier as a guide. As they traveled through Rif territory on a much shorter westward route, Sheean counted hundreds, perhaps thousands, of putrefying bodies lying on the roads—grisly evidence of Spanish troops killed in their retreat from the Rif advance. He reported that, to refute the Spanish claim of having lost only fifteen soldiers. When the time came to traverse the blockade at the Primo de Rivera line, Sheean passed through alongside hundreds of Arab fighting men and as many peasants, their donkeys and mules laden with goods. De Rivera's claim that it was impassable seemed a joke.[10]

Having been incommunicado for two months, Sheean arrived in Tangier and contacted his Paris office. His colleagues were stunned to hear from him. They had figured him dead. Sheean's five lengthy articles describing his findings about the Riffian cause soon appeared in the *Chicago Tribune* (and elsewhere through syndication). He clarified that Abd el-Krim sought no conflict with France and wanted only independent national sovereignty for the Rif and the departure of Spanish forces. The *Chicago Tribune*'s unpredictable and politically conservative owner, Colonel Robert McCormick, happened to be in Paris when Sheean returned there, and wined and dined him to celebrate his unique reporting.

Just a few weeks later, Sheean was sacked. His colleague Jay Allen thought he was fired "for being too good," suggesting that Sheean's superior was jealous of his success. Sheean himself wryly stated the cause as "a disagreement between my immediate superior and myself over the length of time I had stayed out to dinner." Any deeper reasons remained hidden.[11] This sudden dismissal at the height of his triumph deflated Sheean. For a few days he walked around disoriented and alarmed about losing his salary, small as it was.

Then he realized he felt relieved. Being booted out of a regular correspondent's job meant greater freedom to speak his mind. Sheean took it for granted that a correspondent should be strictly objective. That standard in newspaper journalism was actually quite recent, superseding an earlier practice in which the press was admittedly partisan. The professional ethics requiring separation of "fact" from "opinion" was part of the press's larger adaptation to modern times, a series of developments that included the founding of schools of journalism. A chorus of criticisms of the press for misguiding the public, arising at the turn of the century and recurring in the 1920s, propelled the turn.[12]

The professional ethics of objectivity had been getting in Sheean's way. As a freelance journalist he would no longer have to profess a disinterestedness he did not feel. At twenty-five he decided on that route, though it risked poverty. He would rely on the fruits of his pen without any institutional support, in order to express his opinions freely. He chose his own journeys: whenever a world event grabbed his interest, he went there, so long as an outlet would pay him to write about it. His keenness for reporting on far parts of the globe did not disappear. He continued to be so peripatetic that he never had a permanent home until the last decade of his life. Instead, he moved around, renting or borrowing places to live in Europe, Britain, and the United States.

ALL SHEEAN NEEDED to set himself in motion again that spring of 1925 was the casual suggestion that he should write a book about the Rif. "I was one of those dangerous characters who will write a book at the drop of a hat," he noted flippantly, "and besides, as all young reporters know, there is no surer way to get rich." He sped to New York at a very favorable time in the publishing industry. The American reading public was growing fast: high school education was a growing norm, and there was widespread belief that self-improvement through reading advanced entrepreneurial success. Publishers could take risks with new authors, print small editions, and still make a profit. "Suddenly it seemed that everybody you knew was living on publishers' advances," another writer recalled.[13] Sheean intended to do just that.

Though Sheean disliked the fevered pace of New York City, his sweltering summer there produced good results. The Century Company offered to publish his book on the Rif, the sober *Atlantic Monthly* published his political analysis of "Abd El Krim and the War in Africa" in August, and a friend introduced him to the editors of the monthly magazine called *Asia*, who wanted to pay him generously to serialize his Rif story. Magazines, too, were multiplying in the 1920s. *Asia* belonged to a rising genre of niche magazines for particular interest groups. The magazine, tempting racial zealots, touted Sheean's forthcoming series as "one of the best pictures of this Moroccan phase of the revolt of Asia and Africa against the white man."[14]

In the Rif, meanwhile, the balance of power was shifting drastically. When Abd el-Krim's forces resumed fighting in the late spring of 1925, Arab groups in French Morocco began to join with them, riveting the attention of France. Where Spain had been lackluster in defending its interests, France, with a disciplined military and a large African empire to defend, was avid. French colonial forces were on the ground by May, though their usual battle strategies were not effective against Riffian sniping from hidden crevices in the hills. The

French could not use their greatest weapon—air power—because Spain refused access to the air space over the protectorate.

For many weeks the French parliament wrangled over how to win the Rif war, an expensive and divisive prospect when the French budget was strapped. By early summer, the French prime minister managed to get the appropriations he sought to extend the war. Paris and Madrid began to confer and collaborate. French bombers were allowed to enter Spanish air space to attack Riffian redoubts, while Spain planned an amphibious assault on the Rif citadel at Ajdir from Alhucemas Bay. Rumors flew that France and Spain wanted to make peace on terms close to Abd el-Krim's hopes—but Abd el-Krim held out. France broke its budget to fund the war and on August 1 assigned Marshal Henri Philippe Pétain, hero of the Battle of Verdun in the world war, to head the campaign. (Fifteen years later, when France fell to Nazi Germany, Pétain would lead the collaborationist Vichy regime.) It was later revealed that the French added 325,000 troops to Spain's 140,000 and had 400,000 in reserve. By mid-August of 1925, French military power bid fair to crush the rebels into oblivion.[15]

The Rif had become a global story. Following the developments from New York, Sheean boiled with impatience and rage, feeling sure that Western journalists were writing the news from solely European informants. When he learned that the North American Newspaper Alliance had been looking for him, wanting to commission him to spend two months in the Rif, Sheean jumped at the chance. Leading newspapers in the United States had set up this alliance—called by its acronym, NANA—to dispatch special correspondents to cover extraordinary events in greater depth than staff correspondents could.[16]

Sheean arrived in Tangier by the end of August. The pressure on the Rif rebels seemed fatal. To reach Abd el-Krim this time, Sheean knew he would have to enter an active war zone, but he was determined. He located a caravan of Riffians (rather than Arabs) to take him, and having learned from his earlier experience, he devised a plan that he hoped would speed publication of his reporting. He gave the British telegraph office in Tangier his signature and said that if couriers arrived with scrawled notes bearing the same signature, the telegraph office should transmit these directly to NANA's London office, to be paid on receipt. His improbable plan worked well, despite the iffy runners he had to employ along the way.[17]

The military blockade preventing entry to the Rif was no longer a fiction. Searchlights raked the area, and machine guns pounded out fire as Sheean's caravan approached. Sheean's companions instructed him to get through the line of fire by waiting for the searchlight to pass, then crawling or running as fast as possible before hitting the ground again to wait, and then run or crawl again. Only "the egotism and reckless of the wild Irish" kept him going for four hours of frantic dodging.[18] He was terrified. But he and the whole party made it through without injury, and after a rest, they continued, managing to escape Spanish air raids. Sheean's Riffian guide then decided to go on ahead. He left Sheean overnight with a smuggler who had attached himself to their group and who called Sheean a "Christian dog" once the guide departed. As darkness fell, the smuggler sharpened a very long knife he had been brandishing. Sheean's mortal terror took over his rational brain and he ran away as soon as the smuggler fell asleep.

He slept in a field that night. The next morning, he found his way to the Riffian headquarters by bargaining for guidance in broken Spanish and Arabic as other travelers came along. The Riffian commander in chief there, Abd el-Krim's brother, seemed calm, despite the fierce Spanish and French bombs and tank assaults. Though he blamed France for the ferocity of the fighting and wished a neutral power would intervene to speed peace, he seemed confident that the Riffians would win in the long run. "We are fighting for our existence, for our right to live in peace and liberty," unlike France, which had no such compelling urgency, he told Sheean.

After a week's rest Sheean trekked another seven days over three rocky ridges to reach Abd el-Krim's field headquarters, set high above the half-moon shoreline of Alhucemas Bay. Colonel Francisco

Franco (later the generalissimo of the fascist Spanish Nationalists) had launched the amphibious landing there two weeks before, using eight thousand troops of the fearsome Tercio, the Spanish Foreign Legion. Riffian fighters were counterattacking from caves and crannies in the crags rising from the shore. While under intensive gunfire on land, and bombardment from the air, the Riffian leader spoke with Sheean for hours in the ready Spanish he had previously withheld. The two men were dangerously exposed on their high promontory, looking down at the shore. When planes appeared above, Abd el-Krim simply ducked into a cave—Sheean close at his heels.[19]

Abd el-Krim's steady devotion to the goal of independence seemed ever more heroic to Sheean. Abd el-Krim at that point wanted peace, but not at the sacrifice of autonomy for the Rif. Every article Sheean wrote poked holes in French and Spanish claims and stressed the capacity and endurance of the Riffian resistance, saying that Riffian forces could wage war for another year. He sent at least eighteen unique dispatches, which appeared in papers that subscribed to NANA. When Spanish and French sources celebrated taking the Rif capital of Ajdir, Sheean minimized it, calling it a "manufactured victory," because the Riffians had evacuated Ajdir weeks before.[20]

Sheean struck out for the southern front of the war when he left Abd el-Krim, traveling with a Moroccan Arab and his mule. They made only halting progress, having almost nothing to eat, and Sheean was soon hungry, filthy, and lice-ridden. Then he was felled by the shuddering chills and blast-furnace fevers of malaria. His companion fled. Delirious with fever much of the time, with guns booming around him, Sheean stumbled on bleeding feet for almost two weeks, thinking he was getting somewhere while fearing that "the disaster that was overwhelming the Rif" was about to take him, too. He had reached a village and was dozing feverishly on a pile of rags when he thought he heard an American voice speaking in the pidgin-French of Morocco. Hardly trusting that he wasn't hallucinating, in French he asked the man wearing a ragged French uniform, "Are you French?" The answer came back in French, "I am American."[21]

It was twenty-year-old Wesley Williams, an African American from San Francisco who had joined the French Foreign Legion on a romantic impulse, then deserted. Now he was building roads for the Riffians. Recognizing Sheean's malaria symptoms, Williams took pity on him and helped him through the worst of his illness, bringing him food, even sitting on him on top of a pile of rugs, to keep him warm and tamp his shaking limbs during a blast of his chills. Recovering from the worst of it, Sheean was doubly lucky to meet up next with a fearless Italian antifascist, Alfredo Morea, a twenty-eight-year-old deputy in the Italian parliament who had come to the Rif as a journalist for the newspaper *Voce Repubblicana*. Morea literally dragged Sheean through the Spanish blockade lines and then protected him during an ambush, possibly his most life-threatening passage yet.[22]

Even before Sheean emerged from the Rif late in November 1925, his articles for NANA appeared in the American press (because of his courier setup) and then were picked up and translated in the European press. His reporting of the Riffian point of view got outsize attention because all other correspondents used only French or Spanish sources. He even carried the insurgents' peace terms to French authorities in Rabat, Morocco. He had made himself into a sought-after "war correspondent," and barely escaped death doing so.[23]

No peace was achieved that fall. Sheean blamed the imperial powers for the failure to settle, because the gap between what the Riffians wanted and what the Europeans were willing to concede did not seem large to him. Abd el-Krim surrendered in May 1926, after six more months of fighting. French authorities exiled him and his family to the French island of Réunion in the Indian Ocean, but sporadic Riffian resistance persisted, and the war did not end officially until July 1927.[24]

The prominence Sheean gained for his reporting did not lessen his bitterness about the war's outcome. His headstrong ventures into the Rif had deepened his anti-imperialist leanings into solid convictions. More firmly than ever, he felt that "imperialism was

murderous and hypocritical." His fervor focused on European imperialism; never did he mention (or, it seems, reflect upon) the United
States as an imperial power in its hemisphere.[25] Nonetheless, he had
put his finger on the indigenous nationalisms that would roil the
globe and disassemble the remains of European empires in the next
several decades.

PARIS WAS EXCEPTIONALLY cold and sunless, even seeing snow, that
winter of 1925–1926 when Sheean returned. He escaped to the
Mediterranean island of Corsica, meaning to put the debacle in the
Rif behind him and to write a new novel. His book *An American
among the Riffi* would be published in 1926, and he wanted to return
to fiction. His half-finished earlier novel had been stolen the previous
year in Paris. He had let a down-and-out young journalist stay in his
room, and the fellow absconded with everything portable, including
the manuscript and Sheean's clothing. To get the police working on
the robbery, Sheean contacted the erudite, high-born, and influential
French political journalist Pierre Lacretelle, hoping that Lacretelle's
word would help in getting the crime solved. (It did not.) Lacretelle
wrote for the *Journal des Debats*, a respected conservative paper, and
Sheean and he had met when both were covering the Lausanne Conference in 1923. That they remained in touch was notable, because
Lacretelle was known to seek sex with men; it suggests that Sheean
may have worked through networks of men whose sexual interests
brought them together, to advance himself.[26]

As spring budded, Sheean noticed in a French newspaper that
a new shah was about to be crowned in Persia (as Westerners then
called Iran). Sheean saw a story, or really two stories, there. Reza
Khan, a military man, had earlier forced his way into becoming
war minister and then prime minister of Persia. His ascension in
April 1926 to the Peacock Throne, symbol of the Persian monar-
chy, would complete his takeover in a picturesque exercise of power.
Sheean imagined *Asia* magazine might be interested in that. Second,

although most Americans were unaware, an American economist and oil expert, Dr. Arthur C. Millspaugh, had been in Tehran for four years with the title of Administrator-General of the Finances of Persia. Millspaugh's office had complete control over the purse strings of Persia, including the collection of taxes and disbursement of all state revenues. His post had no formal link to the United States, but he had previously worked for the US Department of State and remained well connected. The United States had approved the Persian government employing Millspaugh as an independent financial expert who would restructure the helter-skelter Persian finances. Reza Khan had accepted this intervention in order to smooth the way for continued investment in his country by Western nations. The arrangement was an example of US "dollar diplomacy": future American loans would be dependent on the success of Millspaugh's mission.[27]

Speeding to New York to check with *Asia* and to find a publisher for a potential book on Persia, Sheean struck gold on the terrain of coincidences. The president of the Century Company, publisher of *An American among the Riffi*, had a very strong interest in Persia, and Sheean's proposal to write about the changes wrought by Reza Khan appealed to him. *Asia* magazine also wanted to feature the new shah, and welcomed an article on the American financial mission.[28] Thus Sheean was set for a destination halfway around the world, his trip paid for (though not lavishly), with commitments in hand for a prospective book and articles.

The only problem was timing. The shah's coronation would take place in three weeks—barely enough time, if one were lucky, to reach Tehran. Sheean met a maddening setback when he returned to Paris and applied for the visa he needed to cross Syria, where France was trying to quell an anticolonial revolt. Officials delayed and delayed his visa, apparently because they knew of Sheean's role in the Rif. Deciding he must move on without the visa, he went south by train to Marseilles, thence by creaky boat across the Mediterranean to the port of Alexandria, Egypt, and from there coastwise to Cairo. After another week of delay by French officialdom in Cairo, he secured his

Syrian transit visa. For the last legs of his trip, from Beirut to Baghdad and to Tehran, he booked passage in a caravan of two Cadillacs owned by Australians who made a business of ferrying strangers across the desert. They reached Baghdad on the day before the coronation. Tehran was still five days of dusty driving away. He would miss the main event.[29]

Sheean stayed on course, reached Tehran, and as soon as possible went to present his letters of introduction to Dr. Millspaugh. American journalists were a rare species in Persia, and Millspaugh welcomed Sheean warmly. Straightaway, Millspaugh insisted that Sheean should abandon the shabby hotel he had booked and stay at the home of Tom Pearson, a young American who headed the Civil Service section of the financial mission. Pearson readily agreed, making Sheean his companion and shepherding him to elaborate festivities following the coronation. At diplomatic ceremonies, champagne receptions, dinners, and parties with extravagant food, drink, music, dancing, and fireworks, Sheean observed the Tehrani elite—elite men, that is. The few women he saw were the wives and daughters of foreign diplomatic personnel because Persian women were secluded.[30]

Millspaugh and Pearson brought Sheean to meet the shah, the crown prince, and the head of the Anglo-Persian Oil Company; they called on the prime minister, cabinet members, and diplomatic corps of numerous countries. Sheean knew that his exposure was superficial and selective, and that deeper knowledge of the lives of ordinary Persians would require more than a short stay. Nevertheless, he quickly wrote *The New Persia*, offering some observations on Persian culture and landscape while dwelling on geopolitical issues. Before the world war, the Russian Empire and Great Britain had both established spheres of influence in Persia, essentially dividing the country north and south, and rivaling each other for superior power. Britain still retained a presence in Persia so strong that it seemed almost a governing role. The Bolsheviks, on the other hand, formally disavowed the privileges that imperial Russia had held and pledged openhanded friendship to Persia.

Sheean made numerous visits to the Russian diplomatic legation, still the largest in Tehran despite revolutionary transformation in its diplomacy. Chatting with resident Bolsheviks strengthened his understanding of their approach, and he went so far as to communicate by letter with Georgy Chicherin, the Soviet foreign minister, to make sure he understood Soviet policy. Sheean was drawn to the anti-imperialism of the Bolsheviks, whose Leninist theory presumed that all colonized peoples shared an interest in throwing off the imperial yoke. But he criticized both Soviet Russia and Britain in his book. Britain exerted its force via the ubiquity and power of the Anglo-Persian Oil Company and additional commercial entities answerable to the British government. The Soviet government had renounced imperial privileges, but when Sheean traveled in Persia he noticed Soviet agents practicing "peaceful penetration," encouraging Persian malcontents and circulating false rumors likely to disrupt the ongoing regime. He saw "very little difference" on the ground between Bolshevik methods and those of Czarist Russia.[31]

Sheean's conversations with Soviet personnel educated his outlook by opening his eyes to a gap between Leninist principles and Soviet practice. His visits to the British legation opened new pathways in his life with more far-reaching consequences. The British counselor in residence was Harold Nicolson, who had arrived six months earlier. An Oxford graduate, Nicolson at forty had a decade of distinguished diplomatic service behind him. He spoke Farsi, the Persian language, like a native, because he had spent his early childhood in Tehran when his diplomat father, Baron Carnock, was posted there.

Nicolson was a British snob and an imperialist, though an irreverent one—and a prolific wordsmith besides, who had written four well-reviewed literary studies and a novel in the previous five years while carrying out his diplomatic role. Nicolson's marriage to the tempestuous writer Vita Sackville-West encouraged his literary bent and sustained his emotional life. They were a devoted couple. Often apart because of Nicolson's diplomatic career, they wrote to each other at least once a day, and sometimes oftener. Sackville-West had remained at home in England with the couple's two sons when Nicolson went to Tehran. The separation was painful for both of them and she had recently come for a two-month visit, concluding with the shah's coronation. Nicolson was melancholy about her departure at the time Sheean arrived.[32]

When Tom Pearson brought Sheean to meet Nicolson, Sackville-West was gone, but Nicolson was not alone. His London friend and lover Raymond Mortimer was there on an extended visit. Whether Sheean knew in advance that he would find Harold Nicolson at the British legation in Tehran is unknowable, but Sheean did know about Nicolson's sexual habits. Pierre Lacretelle had told Sheean of having a two-week affair with Nicolson a dozen years earlier. Both Nicolson and his wife were sexually drawn to their own sex and did not hide their sexual "muddles" from each other. At that time Vita Sackville-West was deeply involved with Virginia Woolf, who modeled *Orlando* on her.[33]

Soon after the three men met, Sheean signaled to Nicolson what he knew, by singing a private song that Pierre Lacretelle had taught him. "You could have knocked me over with a feather," Nicolson wrote to his wife, flabbergasted at the young American's revelation. Nicolson recalled his two-week fling with Lacretelle as idyllic, but it meant nothing next to his deep relationship with Mortimer, a three-year intimacy extraordinarily meaningful for both of them and the foundation of a deep and lasting friendship.[34]

Nicolson thought of himself as a manly man and rued any lapses in virility as he defined it. Discretion was crucial in his diplomatic career. He was a devoted husband and father, while his sexual habits were (in his biographer's words) an "open secret to a closed circle." He was very far from identifying as a homosexual or a gay man in anything like current understanding, and scorned the effeminate sort of man he called a *tapette*. In his view, his desire for sex with men was simply a private "vice," something a man might indulge in for "fun" without it undermining his sense of manliness or his identity as a husband. When his older son had an affair with another boy at college, for example, Nicolson regarded it without concern, writing to his wife, "Ben can have all the fun he wants if he is quiet about it and does not dress like a *tapette*." Vita Sackville-West likewise saw nothing reprehensible in same-sex desire, though she found obvious male effeminacy—such as her cousin Eddy Sackville-West's "mincing in black velvet"—repellent and decadent.[35]

Mortimer, thirty-one when Sheean met him, was an agile intellectual and something of a sybarite. He had enough independent wealth to do as he liked (unlike Nicolson, who needed an income to support his family in suitable style). Both men had studied at Balliol College, Oxford, but Nicolson graduated, whereas Mortimer left after two years. In the 1920s Mortimer was an eclectic essayist, book reviewer, art critic, and sometime writer of fiction. He favored French authors such as André Gide (the French Symbolist who defended same-sex love in his 1924 book *Corydon*), playwright Jean Cocteau, Cocteau's lover Raymond Radiguet, and René Crevel, who was thrown out of the Surrealist group for his sexual involvements with men. In the magazines *Vanity Fair* (New York) and *Vogue* (London), Mortimer wrote in the voice of a modern and arguably queer literary iconoclast with cosmopolitan avant-garde tastes.[36]

Mortimer and his friends in London adopted the sexual iconoclasm of the Bloomsbury group, their elders by about fifteen years. Ten years before the world war, Lytton Strachey, John Maynard Keynes, Roger Fry, Duncan Grant, Vanessa Bell, and Virginia Woolf dabbled in sexual love with both sexes as they mocked both religion and custom. The men had gone to the University of Cambridge together and joked about their frequent sexual affairs as "the higher sodomy." It was a "sexual merry-go-round" before and during the world war years, in the words of Keynes's biographer: "friends became lovers and then went back to being friends." Though "gross indecency" between men was a crime in England, punishable by up to two years in prison, the Bloomsbury friends lived by their own rules—and got away with it, privileged by their upper-middle-class status and individualist genius.[37]

In the mid-1920s, a binary division had not yet solidified between two kinds of individuals named "homosexuals" and "heterosexuals" for their sexual desires. Both words were just starting to come into general use in English, and same-sex desire was not at all uniformly understood either in social science or popular culture. Gender self-presentation—whether a man looked and acted manly, a woman, feminine—mattered far more in public judgments. But as popular culture in the 1920s increasingly put sexual appeal and desire at the center of the self, desire for one's own sex became graspable as a queer erotic variant. Still, a man's transgressive desires for his own sex were usually assumed to be manifest in effeminacy like that of the "painted boys" who approached John Gunther in Paris or the rent-boys who wore rouge and powder to advertise themselves in Berlin.[38]

In the company of Nicolson and Mortimer, Sheean could see sexual love between men as a habit of witty, highly educated, urbane, superior masculine beings. Nicolson assessed Sheean coolly as "rather too jazz," but Mortimer was immediately attracted to him, describing him in a letter to his close friend Eddy Sackville-West as "a twenty-six-year old who has already won a great reputation for his daring as a correspondent, crawling through the French lines to see the Riff and so on. He is pleasant, more naïf than serious, and above all, to my taste, most good-looking, tall, with bright eyes, a long firm, face." At a grand party they went to the evening after they met, Nicolson noticed that Mortimer "was making up in scandalous fashion to the American journalist."[39]

Sheean got along very well with Raymond Mortimer. They shared a number of interests in literature and the arts; both were playful as well as keenly intellectual. Sheean attached himself to Mortimer and Nicolson as they went to parties, teas, lunches, and other jaunts. When Mortimer decided to join Sheean on his planned excursions to investigate the Persian cities of Isfahan and Shiraz, Nicolson graciously lent his car, his chauffeur, and a servant and arranged for British diplomatic personnel to host their stays. Nicolson's generosity was a great advantage to Sheean, who not only had Mortimer's companionship but also traveled in unaccustomed fine style at little expense.[40]

Once they returned to Tehran, Mortimer had no trouble persuading Sheean to join him in an intended month-long tour of Russia. The two men took off from Tehran for Baku before dawn on July 4, 1926, the only two passengers in a small German-made airplane. Their travel concentrated on sightseeing and the arts, for Mortimer had no political purpose in mind and Sheean, too, "shied off political implications on that first visit to Moscow with the nervousness of a suspicious colt," he later wrote.[41]

Whether the relationship between Sheean and Mortimer became sexually intimate on their trip, or ever, is uncertain. Later, in print, Sheean described his friend blandly, calling him "clever, dark, inquisitive, interested in everything"—but he addressed Mortimer as "Angel-face," sending him "love and kisses," in letters just after leaving Persia. Mortimer returned the fondness, telling Eddy Sackville-West that Sheean was "one of the most endearing human beings I have ever met."[42] Whatever the whole truth, their time together in Persia began a solid friendship that shaped Sheean's life significantly. Sheean also remained in touch with Nicolson, whose political and class connections were more valuable than those of Mortimer.

When Sheean returned to Paris, Mortimer put him in touch with Eugene McCown, Virgil Thomson's former roommate, now trying to make his way as a painter. Sheean found McCown seductive, confiding to Mortimer, "I adore your little boy-friend Gene." McCown's recent affair with the tormented French writer René Crevel had led Crevel to write an intensely personal novel, *La Mort Difficile* (1926). The novel's narrator-protagonist, representing Crevel, tortured himself about his sexuality, while his inconstant lover—McCown—did not. During November and December of 1926, McCown and Sheean were frequent companions, regarded as a couple by some friends, though Sheean was well aware of McCown's promiscuity. McCown led him down some risqué byways of Paris, such as the notoriously sketchy rue de Lappe near the Bastille. (A sex tourism guidebook for

Americans pointed out the rue de Lappe as a "long dark lane" packed with dance halls, where men "dance, not alone with their girls but 'man with man,'" and warned that the "Rue de Lapp Lothario" was "a bad boy.")[43] Meeting McCown's friends among American and French writers in Paris, including Robert McAlmon, Kay Boyle, Glenway Wescott, Janet Flanner, Jean Cocteau, and André Gide, widened Sheean's circle of acquaintances. But his relationship with McCown was brief and it ended definitively. "Making an effort to see Eugene would be like digging up a dead body to look at it," Sheean told Mortimer three years later.[44]

Sheean's friendship with Raymond Mortimer was very different. It ripened over time. Mortimer lived in London in Gordon Place, the very epicenter of the Bloomsbury group. Sheean relished his repeated opportunities to stay with Mortimer, going to his parties and getting to know his friends. On visits, Sheean met the Bloomsbury originals. Anticipating being introduced to Virginia Woolf in 1927, he felt "all agog at the idea of meeting her," because he considered her "the one novelist of unquestionable genius now writing in English." Mortimer's friendship ushered him into a sexually cosmopolitan London subculture of men who were open about sex with other men, whether or not they also had sex with women. Eddy Sackville-West—Vita's cousin, whose "mincing" she deplored and whose inheritance of the centuries-old family house, Knole, she greatly resented—became fond of Sheean and invited him to stay often at Knole, a medieval palace of hundreds of rooms holding rare treasures.[45]

Sheean slid easily into Mortimer's sexually iconoclastic social circle, taking sexual freedom as his modern birthright, as did other "advanced" young people of his generation. In a novel he wrote a few years later, his fictional protagonist (a twenty-something who was a world traveler) guiltlessly enjoyed a sexual relationship with an older woman in Paris, fending off his older sister's disapproval: "Here I am, an able-bodied male, footloose and fancy free. Is there any reason on earth why I shouldn't do as I please if I find a similarly disengaged female who is willing? There's no harm done to anybody."[46]

The novel was autobiographical in several respects, but not so far that Sheean could portray his character in an erotic relationship with another man. Sheean never referred to same-sex relationships in his published writing, except in declaring his whole generation's sexual divergence from the past. "My generation had practically no moral sense as that term had hitherto been understood," he wrote of Paris and London in the 1920s. "Promiscuity between the sexes, homosexuality, miscegenation and every variety of sexual diversion known to the most learned of German professors could have been studied with ease in the Paris café, night club, theatre or semi-fashionable house." Including himself in his generation's ethics, he went on, "I am in this, as in other respects, an *enfant du siècle*. . . . We may like it or not (I like it, at least in preference to bourgeois respectability); but the fact is that the people who were in their twenties in the 1920's were amazingly, perhaps unprecedentedly, immoral."[47] His frolics with McCown and with Mortimer's London crowd must have been in mind as he wrote.

Sheean kept his sexual options open in his youth, fell in and out of love casually and often, and enjoyed nonmarital sex—that much can be said with certainty. Whether he had a sexual relationship with Louise Bryant or any other woman in the 1920s remains unknown. In 1929, hearing that Eddy Sackville-West might be falling for him, he stressed his own fickleness to Mortimer. "Being in love with me is a dreadful waste of time," he said. "My instability is not only in my character and emotions, but in the life I lead, so that you literally can't be sure where I am in any sense at all." Both men and women found him appealing only because of the "very impossibility of the situation," he told Mortimer. Without meaning to brag, he continued, "several people have hypnotized themselves into thinking they are in love with me. Among these is a young lady who intends to marry me in the spring, and a young man who intends to spend several years with me next summer." He confessed to Mortimer his current crush on artist Duncan Grant, a central Bloomsbury figure who had uncountable sexual relationships with both men and women.

("Anyone could fall in love with Duncan if he wanted to," John Maynard Keynes wrote during his lengthy affair with Grant.)[48]

Five months later Sheean told John Gunther he was engaged to be married—although nothing came of the supposed engagement. Was his remark a convenient way to present himself to Gunther, who knew nothing about Sheean's escapades with men? Such rumors helped to allay suspicions about a single man. Mortimer, for example, allowed gossip to float in 1927 that he was engaged to marry a woman friend.[49] There were many reasons for a man to seek the benefits of marriage, regardless of his sexual attraction to men, as the successful marriage of Harold Nicolson and Vita Sackville-West showed.

SHEEAN'S PERSIAN VENTURE looked on the surface to be one of his least remarkable: he gained no major political insights from its politics or culture. He published a few articles and a book, but they were quickly forgotten. Yet from another angle, his experiences in Persia signaled a tension that would pulse within him as he moved around the globe. The legations of the two diplomatic rivals, Russia and Great Britain, sparked two conflicting impulses of his that would soon war in his mind and heart. His conversation with Bolsheviks at the Russian legation bolstered his turn toward the left, because of Soviet support for anti-imperialism. From it he gained a broader awareness of Soviet Communist practices than from reading Marx or Lenin. Though he was not avidly seeking to absorb those lessons at the time, what he learned would shape his consciousness of world inequality. On the other hand, the friendships he formed at the British legation nourished a countervailing impulse of his, to avoid politics and accept the world as it was—even with Britain and other imperial powers on top—and find intellectual stimulation in sophisticated company. Sheean's stay in Tehran brought him new like-minded companions in Mortimer and Nicolson, and led him to admire the values of the Bloomsbury fraction—their rationality, their ease, their irreligion, their intellectual riches, and their sexual unconventionality, too.

When Sheean looked back on the many sites that had influenced him in the 1920s, he said that the "most potent" were in England. He meant Knole, the inherited home of Eddy Sackville-West: Knole's hundreds of ghostly rooms, its dark winding passages, its great banquet hall, its tapestries and portraits summed up England's poetic and romantic appeal for him.[50] He meant Gordon Place, emblem of Bloomsbury self-made rules and heady indulgences. His next circuit—beyond Paris and London, beyond the Rif and Persia—all the way to China, would heighten the tension between the magnetism of these pleasant circles and his impulse to stake a claim on repairing the world's ills.

CHAPTER 5

WITH HER WHOLE HEART

W HEN RAYNA SIMONS Raphaelson crossed the Pacific in 1923, she had fixed her mind on living in China. She joined the same impulsive enterprise of global venturing as Dorothy Thompson, Vincent Sheean, and John Gunther, seeking freedom, mobility, and new stimulation when she left home. Her venture was all the more courageous—or foolhardy—because China was foreign in ways that Europe was not, and almost twice as far away from American shores. Though she had no newspaper background, she was optimistic, just as Dorothy Thompson had been when she started out, that there were newspaper jobs to be had and she would get one.[1]

Feeling she was at an impasse in her life, Rayna Raphaelson wanted to start anew; she was as ready as the other three to take risks with her future. She pinned her hopes on her second-class ticket from Vancouver to Shanghai. "I'm scared inside although I'm going anyway," she acknowledged as she departed. "I go to China as a very ridiculous Childe Harolde." Thus she likened her quest to that of Byron's prototypical romantic hero, whose grand tour traced his self-development along the course of his exotic travels. Her upper-middle-class upbringing in a Jewish family in Chicago did not prevent her from being independent-minded, though the warmth in her hazel-brown eyes, mischievous smile, and frequent laugh sometimes disguised her seriousness. Everyone who knew her identified her most by her red-gold curly hair—"a flaming aureole, with sun and brightness in it," in the words of a college friend—so eye-arresting it could stop traffic on a public street. Friends likened her whole personality to a flame, a blaze.[2]

Her choice of China was a mystery. Where literature inspired Thompson, Sheean, and Gunther to dream of Europe, Raphaelson's imagination was not fired by familiarity with the literature of China. Nor did she go with revolutionary hopes or partisan intentions. Some American women of her generation dedicated themselves to China as Christian missionaries, but she was born a Jew, and anyway, she was secular.

What sent her? She revealed something of her motivation when she urged her close friend Rebecca Hourwich Reyher to accompany her. Trying to persuade, she told Reyher that China contained "the biggest struggle that is taking place in all the world"; "the future of Europe or America are simple compared to it." Going there would mean witnessing a historic transition, seeing "the most significant— and, incidentally, the most dramatic—problems of civilization being fought through . . . at their most interesting stage." Both women needed to support themselves and she assured her friend, "We will get jobs . . . the demand for intelligent English-speaking women in the Orient is almost inconceivable." Reyher disappointed her by saying no.[3] Rayna Raphaelson went to China alone. Once she took up residence there, she made choices she certainly had not anticipated in advance.

BORN IN 1894, Rayna DaCosta Simons chafed against her parents' conventional restrictions as she grew up, yet she knew they loved her and felt grateful for their support. She did well in school, and her parents urged her to stay nearby for college, at the University of Chicago. After enrolling there, she transferred to the University of Illinois at Champaign-Urbana to be with her boyfriend Samson Raphaelson.

She and "Raph" shared aspirations to write, and both of them worked for campus publications, while she gave more attention to academic study than he did and won a Phi Beta Kappa key, concentrating in philosophy and sociology. The economics classes she took in her senior year with the left-liberal economist Paul Douglas made an outsize impression, strengthening her concern about social injustice.[4]

One of Rayna's close college friends at the University of Illinois in 1915–1916 was Dorothy Day, a Socialist then, and much later the ascetic founder of the Catholic Worker Movement. Day could not afford to continue at the university and moved to Greenwich Village, where she worked for the radical monthly called the *Masses*. When Rayna visited her there during the summer of 1917, the two friends, both opponents to US entry into the world war, had fun with the raucous *Masses* crowd. They hosted potluck parties in Day's borrowed flat, picnicked along the Palisades, or took the ferry to Staten Island to lie on the sand. Rayna's generosity and intensity made an indelible impression on Day, who recalled, "Whatever she did she did with her *whole heart*." Rayna enjoyed the *Masses* crowd, but criticized their politics as emotionally driven. "I am too prone to see the faults of the cause I am associated with. I can always argue against myself better than I can with myself," she reflected on the episode in a letter to her younger sister.[5]

She married Raph at her parents' home—despite her parents' lack of enthusiasm for him—on New Year's Day, 1918, after both graduated. Though Rayna adopted her husband's surname she rejected the conventional model of marriage. She shared with Dorothy Thompson the "New Woman" outlook in their generation and expected to be economically independent, seeing herself as an individual equal to Raph, with her own aims. It was a novel stake; the vanguard of young women who tried this in the 1920s outlined a path to the future, even though most had a hard time achieving what they hoped.[6]

Neither one of the couple had clear employment aims as they took up residence in Chicago. Rayna took one meaningless job after another; Raph tried to write short stories while working for pay in advertising and then magazine editing. A year after they married, they thirsted for travel. Raph wanted to go to Japan, but more realistically (given their finances) they decided to travel across the country, to San Diego. On the train in March 1920, they happened to meet the American poet Witter Bynner on his way to China, who read them some of the Chinese poetry he was translating.[7] The encounter may have planted a seed in Rayna's mind.

Their San Diego plan fell away once they got to the San Francisco area and were seduced by the beauty of Mill Valley, north of the city in the wooded foothills of Mount Tamalpais. They stayed there. In nearby Berkeley, Rayna found a close friend in Helen Freeland, who was part of a convivial and learned circle around the cultural anthropologist Alfred Kroeber at the University of California. Rayna also got to know a wisecracking reporter for the San Francisco *Daily News*, Milly Bennett, who lived in Mill Valley and commuted by ferry to her job. Raph found a friend who liked to discuss writing in William (Bill) Prohme, reporter and editorial manager of the *San Francisco Examiner*.[8]

Despite their long relationship, Rayna's and Raph's expectations of each other as husband and wife clashed. For the academic year of 1920–1921, they separated to take up opportunities in different places. Berkeley so appealed to Rayna that she enrolled in graduate courses at the University of California, while Raph returned to the University of Illinois for a position as a writing instructor. He asked Bill Prohme to check on Rayna now and then, and Prohme obliged. "Charming dinner companion, is your wife," he wrote to Raph that fall, "a most remarkable girl." Rayna barely remembered those occasions, though Prohme seemed smitten, appreciating her mind and also her looks. "You should see your wife since her hair is bobbed," he wrote to Raph. "In the light, her face seems positively haloed in that wondrous reddish-golden reflection of her abundant hair."[9]

The couple did not get along any better when Rayna, aiming "to try to patch up some sort of relationship," came back to Chicago in

Rayna Simons and Samson Raphaelson, 1920.
Source: Private collection, Joel Raphaelson.

1921. Raph remained in Urbana, and Rayna saw him only episod-
ically; she lived in her parents' home while taking summer graduate courses in philosophy at the University of Chicago. In class she
formed a new friendship with New Yorker Rebecca Hourwich Reyher, whose unconventionality and secular Jewishness—and currently
rocky marriage, too—closely paralleled Rayna's. Reyher worked as a
paid organizer for the National Woman's Party, the militant group
that campaigned for equal rights after the vote was won. A modern
feminist, Reyher dismissed Raph as "a little shrimp in both brains and
looks compared to Rayna. He regards himself as the 'doer,' the 'man
of the house,' all that sort of he-man, red-blooded male stuff. His
egotism completely breaks down Rayna. He disregards her time, her
interests, calmly takes for granted that she lives for him alone." Both
women found a mentor in the broadminded liberal minister Edward

Scribner Ames, a philosophy professor and ideal father figure, more understanding and less judgmental than Rayna's own father. Ames had studied with John Dewey and embraced a pragmatic approach to God and doctrine. Rayna felt she could talk about "everything under the sun" with him.[10]

As the Raphaelson marriage skidded further downhill, Raph moved to New York on his own. By June 1922, their breakup appeared inevitable. Visiting Raph in New York, Rayna explained to Dr. Ames, "Raph honestly feels that he could do better work and be in many ways more happy and contented if I weren't here. And of course you know I haven't a passionate desire to stay and we both feel that maybe I should leave. So I'm going to go. For good, this time." She immediately added that she was "flirting extravagantly with plans to go to China or Java or Russia or any place that is far away and not America." She knew that American missionaries had established schools in China and hoped that Ames might have connections who would help her find a position teaching English. She wondered if such a school would hire a Jew. Should she lie about her religion? She insisted that her impulse was "not insane romanticism." She had thought about leaving the United States for "a long time," she told him, wanting to move abroad because she felt "dead inside."[11]

As she returned to Chicago for more graduate work—and she and Raph moved toward formal divorce—she began to think of a PhD in philosophy as a promising path to a solid professional career. Several professors encouraged her. Then a remark from Ames stopped her short. "<u>Divorced Jewish women</u> . . . are not wanted in universities," she learned from him; there was "little hope" that she would obtain an academic position, though Ames maintained that a PhD could be useful in other respects. In a letter to Reyher she despaired, "What's the use of working to be a scholar if the scholars don't want me?" In "the one place where I had not anticipated discouragement . . . I got it in large hunks."[12]

By the fall of 1922, Rayna felt that she had to restart her life on an entirely different footing. Already "completely empty inside" because of Dr. Ames's revelation, she fell into despondency once her divorce came through in September. Losing Raph shook her more than she anticipated. Although divorce was no longer rare, it carried a stigma in all but the most sophisticated circles. Marriage as a social institution and personal commitment was simply not supposed to end that way. Raph had been so present in her life—all through college and five years of marriage—that the divorce unmoored her. Like Dorothy Thompson, Rayna experienced her divorce as a personal failure.[13]

Styling herself "Miss Rayna Raphaelson" rather than return to her birth name of Simons, she traveled westward in December of 1922, seeking solace in the Bay Area, where she knew she would find Helen Freeland and other lively friends. She had written ahead to Bill Prohme, seeking his help in securing a newspaper job in San Francisco. Though he tried to oblige and was attentive when she arrived, her job hunt was difficult. She found no steady job, and though she sold an article or two, she had borrowed to get there and stayed in debt.[14]

Early in 1923 she began focusing on China. She sent out letters, wanting to arrange a "definite newspaper connection" before she departed. That goal escaped her, but she remained firm about going. She did not say why China gripped her so. Perhaps the eminent philosopher John Dewey, whose philosophical work she certainly read, influenced her. Dewey traveled to China out of curiosity in 1919 and landed in the midst of a powerful student uprising so fascinating and impressive that he stayed more than a year. His views of China's transformative changes were published in 1920 and got further play in magazines in the early 1920s. "To say that life in China is exciting is to put it fairly," Dewey wrote. "We are witnessing the birth of a nation, and birth always comes hard."[15]

If Dewey's philosophical eminence encouraged Rayna to take his views to heart, the political news from China, which she could read in the *San Francisco Chronicle*, may also have urged her on. An era of new possibility began at the time she decided to go. In January 1923, Sun Yat-sen struck a deal for his Nationalist Party, the Guomindang, to receive support from the Bolsheviks' new Communist International (the Comintern).[16] Though he and other Chinese Nationalist revolutionaries had ended the reign of the Qing Dynasty in 1911, the ineffectiveness of China's central government since then had enabled regional strongmen, called warlords, to take hold of various sections of the vast country. Warlords raised their own armies, forced revenue from the populations they ruled, and battled with one another to extend control. Sun Yat-sen and the Nationalists, struggling to remake China into a unified constitutional republic, knew by the early 1920s that the Guomindang needed outside help to achieve its goal.

The pact Sun made brought generous Comintern funding and Russian military advisers and generals, who would train Chinese recruits in a new military academy in Whampoa, near Guangzhou (then called Canton), the southern coastal city where the Guomindang was based. At the same time that the Comintern aided the Guomindang, it funded the recently founded Chinese Communist Party (CCP) at a lower level, surprisingly. The agreement created a united front, in effect: the CCP and the Guomindang remained separate and distinct, but Communists as individuals could join and work with the Guomindang. Though advantageous to the Guomindang, the alliance proved fractious from the beginning.[17]

Both the Guomindang and the CCP aimed to unify China by defeating the warlords. Both also wanted to end the long-standing "unequal treaties" that held China's sovereignty in thrall to foreign powers. During the long Qing era, Britain, France, the United States, Japan, Czarist Russia, and other powers had used military force to achieve treaties giving them tremendously advantageous trading positions in China. With Britain in the lead, these powers had obtained territorial and economic concessions in many coastal and river cities (called the "treaty ports"), where they collected major taxes and customs duties, in effect controlling much of China's economic infrastructure and depriving China itself of revenue. Foreign troops and gunboats were standard presences at the treaty ports—humiliating signs of subjugation, casting China into a semicolonial position in the eyes of Chinese Nationalists and Communists. In a significant gesture, the Bolsheviks gave up Czarist Russia's rights and privileges in China (as in Persia) shortly after they took power.[18]

However much Rayna knew or did not know about these developments, she applied for a passport in mid-April, with Bill Prohme vouching for her US citizenship, and bought a second-class ticket to Shanghai on the *Empress of Russia*, departing from Vancouver on May 17, 1923. She knew that second-class cabins, tiny rooms without private baths below deck, were "at best a little shabby and galling to the spirit," but that was all she could afford.[19]

Two matters close to her heart then interrupted her plans and she changed her ticket for a departure in June. First, Helen Freeland begged Rayna not to leave before she came back from a trip that had kept her away longer than expected. Rayna had been living in Helen's Berkeley apartment and could not refuse her friend. The second matter went deeper and was more confusing. Rayna fell "quite madly in love," as she told Rebecca Reyher, with someone she had "never expected to fall in love with"—Bill Prohme. When he made his feelings for her clear, she resisted at first, feeling emotionally unprepared. Self-doubt about falling in love so quickly after her divorce assailed her—was she "not at all the independent, self-sufficient creature" she had prided herself on becoming?[20]

Prohme was six years older than Rayna, tall and blond, with blue eyes behind his eyeglasses. He had been a newspaperman in California since 1915. A son of German Protestant parents in New York, he was well-read, politically on the left, and interested in China. Milly Bennett knew Bill as a fellow reporter in San Francisco and admired many of his qualities: "a very methodical guy" and "a conscientious and excellent reporter," she said of him, a newspaper editor's dream because "his copy was always well written and on the desk before deadline." Bill was "a man of slow, phlegmatic humor, very honest, very forthright," with a "solemn" look on his face. But Bennett (who had a sharp tongue) hated the attitude of intellectual superiority she saw in Bill. "He was as prim as an old maid and as arbitrary as a

Jesuit," in her view, turning an "annihilating" contempt on anyone who disagreed with him. Bennett said almost the opposite about Rayna: "By nature she was determined, forceful, and egotistical, but she had a quick, charming way of switching too rancorous a debate, too acrid an argument, into a whimsical, lighthearted channel."[21]

Bill shared Rayna's interest in China and did not discourage her from going in 1923. He said he wanted to follow her as soon as his money constraints let up. He had been married and divorced and was obligated to support his ex-wife and their eight-year-old son; additionally, he had a tubercular infection that waxed and waned, compromising his health. A recent stay in a TB sanitarium had used up all his savings. Leaving his job while continuing his child support payments would be hard for him to manage financially, unless he had a worthwhile job lined up in China.[22]

In June she departed, alone. "I'm a bit frightened—really!" she dashed in a note to Rebecca Reyher the morning of her departure. She had rebooked to leave from San Francisco on the *Tenyu Maro*, a Japanese boat, though the tourist bureau and steamship office warned her against it, saying, "White women cannot go on these Japanese boats, particularly alone." Traveling second class, she would have Japanese and Chinese for company rather than whites, they said. The prospect did not daunt her at all, though it alerted her to white supremacist attitudes that she would come to find hateful in Asia. On board, she liked mixing casually with Asian passengers and paid close attention to the reform thinking of a young Chinese man who spoke English.[23]

Summer heat and humidity greeted her when she disembarked in Shanghai, China's most important Pacific port. Shanghai was economically critical because it was near the mouth of the mighty Yangtze River, which served as a water highway across China from east to west. Of course it was a treaty port. Foreign powers had wrested away large areas of property along Shanghai's Huangpu River, a tributary leading into the Yangtze, and in these so-called concession areas, France, Britain, the United States, and Japan held sovereignty. European-style granite buildings, luxurious shops, and imposing Christian churches lined major streets. The concessions had their own ruling councils, their own police, and their own taxes and customs duties. The foreign citizens enjoyed extraterritoriality, meaning that they were subject only to their home country's laws, not to Chinese regulation or prosecution. They socialized in elegant clubs, bet on ponies at the racecourse, and hired Chinese laborers and servants at a pittance when they held cocktail parties and tea dances. Nightlife was always hopping. Rayna saw "cabarets, cafés, motor cars, a street of shops that rivals New York." The acreage of the concessions dwarfed the old Chinese city, where small one-story houses and shops lined narrow meandering alleyways called *hutongs*. Chinese residents of Shanghai spread out well beyond the old city and lived in the concession areas, too, though the foreigners did not welcome them.[24]

Several English-language newspapers served British and American residents in Shanghai. Starting to look for a job, Rayna decided right away that the main American newspaper "out-Hearsts Hearst at his worst." Glaring evidence of foreign exploitation of Chinese labor, resources, and trade distressed her as she continued her search. The city's shoddy glamour (especially the plentiful low-life entertainment for men) repulsed her. Shanghai was "a phony," Milly Bennett agreed when she got there later, "an alluring, crapulous, degraded phony."[25]

Though jobs were within Rayna's reach in Shanghai, she moved on very soon to Beijing, nearly seven hundred miles north. Formally the national capital where foreign consulates were located, Beijing was actually ruled by whichever warlord had conquered it most recently. It was still a walled city, with ancient ceremonial gates and inner and outer rings of walls—so thick that a sunset stroll along the walls' flat tops was a warm evening's entertainment. Grander buildings, such as government offices and a half dozen universities, also had elaborate entry gates. Most of the population lived in *hutongs*, where the decorative facades of small shops and artisan enterprises alternated with small lodgings. Teahouses, bathhouses, restaurants, hotels, and theaters were sprinkled about. Peddlers carrying their wares on their heads or backs sang out, as did petty food vendors hawking snacks. Rickshaw men shouted and pulled their two-wheeled open passenger carts everywhere. The hireling soldiers of warlords also marched through. Beggars lodged themselves in small, dusty streets near grand ancient buildings, such as the Forbidden City (the palace complex of the Ming and Qing dynasties) and the magnificently circular Temple of Heaven. Only the larger avenues were paved, but streetcars, modern factories, and telephone service also operated in Beijing.[26]

Soon after arriving in September 1923, Rayna jotted a note to Reyher saying, "I'm not a bit disappointed. I'm going to find what I wanted here in China and I think, Rebecca, I'm going to be happy." Strange street noises and smells assailed her. China was "as unsanitary a country as can be imagined," she conceded. She had been told that Chinese food could be "poison" for Americans. She missed Bill Prohme and Helen Freeland and worried when Bill cabled her about the devastating fire that burned half of Berkeley that month. But she liked her new life so much that she regretted she had not come a year earlier.

Shaking off her "dead" mood, she felt ready to dig in. After a bout of whooping cough, she went into a job-hunting frenzy and pieced together various employments: part-time secretary to the dean of the Peking Union Medical College, private tutoring of English, and a bit of writing for San Francisco newspapers. On the dresser in her rented room, she put photographs of Helen and Rebecca in her double picture frame, where her own and Raph's photographs had once been.[27]

The very strangeness of China allowed her to reinvent herself. That she was a Jew—a woman—a divorcée—mattered little in comparison to the larger fact that she was a white Western stranger whose life in China was a blank slate. By December, her address was in a *hutong*. She was trying to learn Chinese and was "crazy about" Chinese food, which was not at all like the greasy fare she had eaten in San Francisco's Chinatown. For exercise, she rode a Mongolian pony every morning from six thirty to eight, wearing boys' knickers and Raph's hat. She was working in a teacher-training school for women and was eager to pay her father back the $800 she had borrowed, but the school was government-run and the warlord government in Beijing was not delivering teachers' pay. Still, she was thrilled with the opportunity to counter the "humiliating" status of Chinese women by training them to be teachers. "I am the world's great destroyer," she reported cheerily to Dr. Ames. Teaching debating and English conversation to the equivalent of college seniors, she encouraged "them to bring up all sorts of ideas—the modern woman, industry, scientific method, Chinese home life, western art—everything. And I always present the opposite side of the question."[28]

RAYNA HAD BEEN in Beijing about three months when Helen Freeland sent the alarming news that Bill Prohme had disappeared. Rayna dropped everything she was doing. Sixteen days on the *Empress of Asia* from Shanghai brought her to Vancouver, and she arrived in San Francisco by the middle of January 1924. From one shred of information gained from a friend of Bill, she managed to trace his path. She found him in El Paso, Texas, stricken with severe bronchitis. The Berkeley fire he had cabled her about earlier had burned his house and everything in it to the ground. Then his ex-wife made unpleasant new demands, he came down with a high fever, and three leads on possible jobs in China fell through. Depressed and ill, he had fled to Mexico.[29]

Bill's needs brought out Rayna's gallantry—what Milly Bennett called her "Galahad quality." She nursed him back to health, and then they began living together, without marrying, though they let others assume they were married. Rayna's unconventionality went only so far in sexual adventure, and she had no lovers but Raph and then Bill. She was still "thoroughly, completely interested in China" and intended to return there. Bill shared her goal, but they were dead broke and in debt, so they moved gradually to build up funds. From El Paso they went to Los Angeles, where Bill secured a newspaper job on a friend's recommendation and then a higher-paying job as a publicity agent. Rayna found hack work. It was a grind, and in November 1924, they moved to Honolulu, where Bill's reputation enabled him to get a newspaper job right away.[30]

Hawaii felt like paradise to them because of its extraordinary natural beauty. Rayna rediscovered her Mill Valley friend Milly Bennett there with her husband, Mike Mitchell, both writing for the Honolulu *Advertiser*. She was greatly troubled by attitudes of white supremacy she saw in Hawaii, however, and wrote a critical essay about it, published in a small midwestern journal, in which she emphasized white men's hypocrisy in refusing to acknowledge any race problem while lording it over Japanese and Hawaiian Polynesians. Not wanting to take Bill's surname, she signed the article Rayna Raphaelson, and did the same in a small colorful book called *The Kamehameha Highway: 80 Miles of Romance*, in which she related what older men told her of the islanders' myths and legends.[31]

Despite Honolulu's lures, Bill and Rayna left in six months. Inching their way closer to China, they moved to Tokyo when Bill received an offer in the spring of 1925 to become editor of the *Japan Times*, an English-language newspaper. Bill arranged for Rayna to write a humor column three times a week—a challenge for her—plus Sunday features paid on space rates. Bit by bit she was building her experience as a journalist.

Their stay in Tokyo was short, but it left a scar on their relationship. Rayna became pregnant and wanted to have the baby. Bill was opposed. He had bitter feelings about fatherhood because of his feelings about his ex-wife and their son. His job editing the *Japan Times* was demanding and ill-paid, and his tuberculosis had recurred, feeding his pessimism about supporting another child. As Rayna went through the "unsavory" and "really difficult" hunt for an abortionist, her relationship with Bill hit a low. A doctor in Tokyo performed the procedure decently but it was painful, and he kept her for ten days afterward in a room that felt like a "ghastly little cell." Referring to the experience as "the slaughter house," she said she had not "been able to banish [it] from my mind." In a letter (to Raph, with whom she kept in touch), she interjected without context, "Since I didn't have a baby, I've become pathologically attached to my dog."[32]

Toward the end of 1925 Bill learned of a job offer in Beijing (then Peking), at the *Peking Leader*, an English-language paper. It had been nearly two years since they began working their way west from LA to Honolulu to Tokyo. Though Rayna knew the *Peking Leader* job offered "scarcely enough to live on," they jumped at the chance. They probably had kept abreast of the political protests developing in China. On May 30, 1925, police in the International Settlement in Shanghai (which combined the British and US concession areas) had opened fire on students who were protesting the shooting of a Chinese millworker by Japanese factory guards. The police action killed a dozen demonstrators and seriously wounded many more. The International Settlement authorities also massed thirteen hundred Marines to patrol the streets, and responded harshly to further demonstrations and strikes, arresting and jailing many Chinese and causing scores more deaths and injuries. Both Guomindang and CCP organizers used the episode to mobilize workers and students, drawing many new members into both parties and boosting Chinese popular rage at the unequal treaties. As political protests spread to twenty-eight cities, the major foreign powers beefed up their military forces in and near China.[33]

If Rayna and Bill did not follow this news while they were in Japan, they would have learned it quickly once they arrived in Beijing. They found a house where the rent was miniscule by American standards. The house was cold and damp in the winter when they arrived, but they saw rosebushes bloom around their Chinese gate in the spring, with snapdragons and nasturtiums on either side, and at the back were willow trees, iris, and marigolds.[34] Delighted to be living there, they both were terribly set back when Bill's tuberculosis became so severe that it put him in bed.

Rayna then took over Bill's job as editor of the *Peking Leader*—but she found it insupportable. She described the situation as "the most goshdarned awful thing that any human being ever stood up under," and she quit. The paper's owner, a reputedly liberal American with missionary connections, cared only about impressing "men at the political and social top," in Rayna's estimation, and treated most Chinese as inferiors. His attitude of white supremacy was the same she had found reprehensible in Honolulu. She was learning fast that few American residents in China shared her own open-minded approach to the Chinese.[35]

Her disheartening experience on the job was one of several reasons their early months in Beijing were difficult. Their money worries mounted as Bill lay in bed. He felt unmanned by the situation and was also cranky about household disorder. While she had to find a new job, Rayna ran their household, uncomfortably overseeing the necessary four or five Chinese servants with whom she could hardly communicate. It was "impossible to cook for oneself or clean or shop; the whole technique of life is different and almost impossible to learn," she explained to Helen. Exhausted, she felt like a "grub-worm." Bill's "neat orderly Germanness" depressed her. She found his needs cloying and worried that they were poorly matched, though she responded appropriately. The quick burst of gaiety that she wished for to lighten the load was not something Bill could provide—unlike Raph, who, for all his faults, tickled her fun-loving side.[36]

Only the gathering momentum in Chinese nationalism raised her spirits. In December 1925, Rayna had gone to a press conference to hear the Guomindang activist Eugene Chen. Chen had recently escaped from imprisonment by the Manchurian warlord Zhang Zuolin, who intended to crush Chen's Nationalist newspaper, the *Peking People's Tribune*. Born to Chinese parents in the British West Indies, Chen spoke English as his first language. Having grown up hostile to British imperialism, he migrated to China in his thirties during the 1911 revolution, and founded a pro-Guomindang newspaper—and then another and another, every time his enemies quashed one. Chen became Sun Yat-sen's private secretary and a Guomindang leader-in-waiting by the mid-1920s.

Rayna invited Chen to tea after the press conference and landed an unanticipated job that excited her.[37] Chen planned to flee south to evade Zhang Zuolin (who wanted him dead) and needed someone to carry on the *Peking People's Tribune*. Rayna, eager to help, had the American privilege of extraterritoriality, meaning that Chinese authorities could not touch her. When Chen asked her to take the job she welcomed the opportunity. Her support for the Chinese Nationalists came less from preformed ideological convictions, it seems, than from her observations of life and labor in China. Rayna allied herself with the Guomindang's struggle at a time when the party, strengthened by two years of military support and funds from the Comintern, was consolidating its hold on the southern city of Guangzhou (then called Canton). Although its founding hero Sun Yat-sen died in March 1925, the party carried on via a complex system of governing councils, with Sun's protégé Wang Jingwei at the helm of the most important councils.[38]

Attaining the "definite newspaper connection" in China she had hoped for, Rayna knew it was a political connection. She would be presenting news to advance the Guomindang. Her work began in late January 1926. Chinese translators on staff relayed to her what was being reported in dozens of Chinese newspapers; then she decided what she would write up for the English version of the *Peking People's Tribune*, which was only four pages. (The Chinese version was eight.) Unlike foreign correspondents in Europe who similarly began with the local press, she did not follow up with her own independent reporting. She was a news aggregator, pleased that she could use her own judgment to "pick and choose and play up or throw in the wastebasket." Chen continued to write the editorials, from Guangzhou.[39]

When Bill got back on his feet, in June, Chen hired him to set up the Nationalist News Agency, a wire service, to send news of Chinese political developments abroad. Most international reporting was biased against the Guomindang's organizing because it threatened the privileges of foreign powers. Bill saw the influential British-run paper called the *North China Daily News*, relied upon by many foreign journalists, as especially culpable—prone to exaggerate the Guomindang's destructive intents toward foreigners and to call any bold action the work of Bolsheviks.[40] He was happy to spread internationally what he saw as a more accurate view, more favorable to the Guomindang.

IN JULY OF 1926 the Guomindang began a long-planned military drive called the Northern Expedition, moving northward from Guangzhou to conquer warlords' territories and unify the country. To carry on the campaign, Guomindang troops banded together with Communist troops and the armies of certain cooperative warlords to create a National Revolutionary Army—though friction within the alliance surfaced even before the armies moved. The commander in chief of the composite army was Chiang Kai-shek, a Guomindang officer and previous head of the Whampoa Military Academy built with Comintern aid and Russian military advice. Chiang had developed overt hostility to the Guomindang's Russian advisers and to Communists in the alliance, believing they were conspiring against his rise to political leadership. The immediate dissension in 1926 was resolved by negotiation, but an incipient rupture was widening between the Guomindang's left wing, unruffled about allying with Communists, and a more conservative wing of civil and military leaders who supported Chiang, opposed cooperation with Communist colleagues, and did not want Russian advisers.

Whether or not Rayna knew of this early fracture—there is no evidence that she did know—she became raptly attentive to the Northern Expedition. As the several corps of the army swept through southern provinces of China with stunning success, Rayna felt "too excited to sleep."[41] Political organizing accompanied the armies, generating local protests against the unequal treaties and against the long hours and harsh conditions imposed by foreign-owned factories. Chinese workers began pouring into unions, agitating for higher pay and decrying their employers' coercive tactics. Strikes mounted. Peasants who were organized (mostly by the Communist Party) into agrarian units wreaked sporadic violence on tyrannical landowners.

By September 1926, the National Revolutionary Army had triumphed through southern China up to the Yangtze River. Strike waves, boycotts of foreign concession areas, and mass protests against foreign imperialism accompanied the army's successes. The Guomindang declared Guangzhou to be China's national capital rather than Beijing, which was still in Zhang Zuolin's grip.[42]

Rayna was holding her breath until she and Bill would move south. Eugene Chen wanted her to bring the *People's Tribune* to Guangzhou and publish it there. Before they could leave Beijing, they needed to find someone to carry on the Nationalist News Agency. It was a hard position to fill. Who might understand their aims, yet not be endangered by Zhang Zuolin? Somehow, Rayna learned that Milly Bennett had moved to Shanghai. Bennett had left Honolulu quite downhearted at the smashup of her marriage—a casualty of her own independent ways. Rayna and Bill invited her to Beijing and proposed the position to her. Having no better option, she very reluctantly accepted. As an American unknown in Beijing, she would avoid immediate danger, but she had no political convictions and was anxious about hiding the press operation from Zhang Zuolin's notice.[43]

To reach Guangzhou from Beijing, Rayna and Bill traveled nine hundred miles overland to Shanghai and then another thousand miles by sea. Arriving in late October 1926, Rayna found Guangzhou "a million times more interesting" than Beijing. The Guomindang hub buzzed with political electricity. She marveled at the unique cityscape, "absolutely airless and flat," exceedingly crowded and appallingly dirty, its streets (except for some new thoroughfares) so narrow even rickshaws could not pass. Her open arms could span their width. The Pearl River flowing through the city was equally crowded, with hundreds of thousands of people living in sampans, junks, and powerboats, so densely packed together that no water could be seen. She was fascinated by everything "open to the eye. Women fixing dinners in the streets, peddlers cutting fish, butchers, fruit merchants, weaving, a thousand kinds of shops, long pieces of cloth being dyed, washing clothes, and of course all the eating, nursing and latrine operations that are always open in China." She thought it would be "great fun prowling" if she could find the time.[44]

Her job was demanding. She judged the existing Guomindang newspaper in English a "howling propaganda rag" and intended to replace it with a creditable *Canton Gazette* of eight pages. As she patched together selected news from Chinese newspapers, she tried to present it as "first-hand, hot-off-the-griddle authoritative news of the big events." She and Bill were also sending mail stories and foreign cables to international readers, explaining the Nationalists' point of view. Although they had barely settled in Guangzhou, Eugene Chen dispatched Bill to Hankou (then Hankow), an industrial city on the Yangtze. The Guomindang, triumphant about the Northern Expedition's progress, was moving its capital from Guangzhou to Hankou and Bill was to establish a wire service and "Nationalist Information Bureau" there. With high hopes, he ordered presses and linotype from New York.[45]

For several weeks Rayna had only her dog for company in the cold, rat-infested, barnlike room in Guangzhou where she lived and produced the *Canton Gazette*. She found Bill's absence a relief. Though she loved him, she had been finding his constant presence oppressive. She rued the "difficulty of two people trying to live in too close a harmony. Suddenly you find there is only closeness and no harmony. Then the closeness becomes a horror almost at times." Wasn't conventional marriage "an insane system," she protested to Helen Freeland. "People were never intended for constant adjustment to <u>anyone</u>." She vowed to "make a stab at least for a room of my own"—two years before Virginia Woolf would write an essay on that theme.[46]

Soon Rayna was bound for Hankou, too, going coastwise first to Shanghai, where she heard nothing but "calamitous talk" from

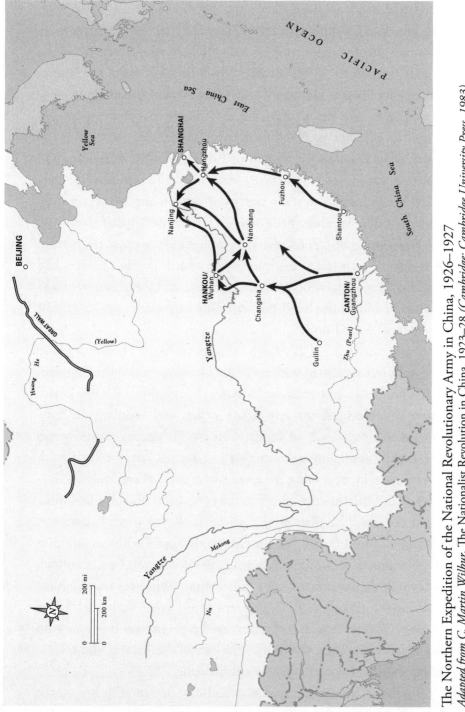

The Northern Expedition of the National Revolutionary Army in China, 1926–1927
Adapted from C. Martin Wilbur, The Nationalist Revolution in China, 1923–28 (Cambridge: Cambridge University Press, 1983).
The black arrows show the routes of various army corps moving from the south of China toward the Yangtze River.

foreigners, who assumed the worst of the Northern Expedition and imagined an imminent attack. Gunboats of the foreign powers crowded threateningly in Shanghai's harbor, while French sailors, British Tommies, and US Marines patrolled the edges of the foreign settlements. Britain sent more cruisers and infantry battalions every week. Rayna felt like a pariah on the British boat that grudgingly agreed to take her to Hankou, five hundred miles west along the Yangtze, amid a floating armory of British, French, American, and Japanese warships. One of three closely sited river cities collectively called Wuhan, Hankou was a treaty port and an important commercial and industrial node, because it sat where two smaller rivers met the Yangtze, enabling raw materials brought along those rivers from inland to be transferred eastward or westward. Foreign powers had grabbed large concession areas in Hankou, and the shipping docks of foreign companies lined the waterway below a broad waterfront avenue called the Bund.[47]

On February 1, 1927, Rayna disembarked in Hankou, whose city walls were splashed with revolutionary posters denouncing warlords and foreign imperialists. As soon as the National Revolutionary Army had captured the city, labor strikes and spontaneous antiforeign actions surged. In January, an irate Chinese crowd overran the British concession and occupied it. Eugene Chen averted British intervention by beginning tense talks with the British minister. Successfully negotiating the return of the concession property to China, Chen became "the man of the hour," in Rayna's words. She was pleased also to find Bill "getting his stride again" with his work on the Nationalist Information Bureau. Besides sending news abroad, the two of them operated as an information source for non-Chinese journalists in Hankou. Bill's frequent brusqueness with questioners made Rayna hover near to "make sure he doesn't snub people who might be useful." She would play the part of the "tactful, diplomatic fixer" and "smile sweetly to take off the sting."[48]

While the Northern Expedition had made splendid progress, the Guomindang was increasingly split. Mutual hostility between the left wing and the conservatives in the party was growing as their strategies diverged. Chen was among the left-wing leaders, along with Soong Ching-ling, Sun Yat-sen's widow (much esteemed by the party), and the Soviet adviser Mikhail Borodin, the original Comintern emissary who had planned the buildup of the Guomindang's military effectiveness, and stayed in China afterward. Tall, pipe-smoking, deliberate in speech, with an impressively drooping dark mustache, Borodin in his forties was a learned and reflective Communist intellectual very comfortable speaking English, the language he, Madame Sun, and Chen used together. After being persecuted for his radical activity as a young man in the czar's Russia, Borodin had fled to the United States, where he spent the years between 1906 and 1918, married a Russian-born woman, and conducted a school in Chicago teaching English to immigrants. He then returned to Russia to join the Bolshevik effort.[49]

Rayna's and Bill's political education had taken place within this left-wing group. Like their Chinese colleagues, they saw alliance with Communists in the struggle as true to Sun Yat-sen's intentions. The conservative wing of the Guomindang, however, and Chiang Kai-shek, increasingly saw the Hankou leadership, Chinese Communists, and Borodin as enemies. The Communist project of revolutionary incitement of workers and farmers alarmed conservative Nationalists, who wanted to end the alliance and send Borodin back to Russia. Chinese generals heading several corps of the National Revolutionary Army, growing numbers of civil leaders in the Guomindang, and Chiang saw things the same way. Even though the left-wing leadership in Hankou attempted to meet the conservatives halfway by trying to tamp down agrarian and labor militancy, the political rift widened. The split took heated and even murderous form in the provinces, labor unions, social organizations, and other interest groups.[50]

Because of this searing internal conflict, Rayna found that starting up the *People's Tribune* in Hankou was "the hardest of all" the editing jobs she had done for the Guomindang, and "the most exacting," she wrote to Helen Freeland. It required delicate planning because of "many conflicting views to be synthesized in some way, much careful manipulation and skirting" of controversial matters. In crafting the paper's initial editorial statement, Rayna worked in concert with Soong Ching-ling, who was her own age, having been much younger than Sun Yat-sen when she became his second wife. A delicately beautiful woman educated in the United States, Madame Sun looked fragile but held a firm view of her deceased husband's intentions and stayed staunchly loyal to the Hankou left wing. In the statement, the *People's Tribune* put its editorial policy under four headings: it would be "pro-Nationalist"; "anti-imperialist (not anti-foreign)"; favor "efforts being made to improve labor conditions in this region"; and do "all in our power to foster the feminist movement in China." The fourth initiative came not from Rayna, whose feminism was formless, but from Madame Sun, who intended to set up an institute for Chinese women's political education. She asked Rayna to help, and Rayna agreed, though she felt that writing a feminist curriculum or speeches stretched her capabilities.[51]

The *People's Tribune* launched on March 12, 1927, the date a tribute to Sun Yat-sen, who had died two years before on March 12. In producing the paper, Rayna relied on Mikhail Borodin's directives. He impressed Rayna "as a mind, a personality, a social force," more than anyone she had met in a long time. In her eyes, he was "the biggest man in China," the only one who saw "the whole movement here in big historic terms," who had "the power of throwing on his searchlight and making things stand out in bold relief, so the irrelevant disappears."[52] She consulted with him every evening, welcoming his opinions as dependable reference points. Borodin was conveniently staying in the same up-to-date Western-style building where Rayna and Bill found a comfortable apartment.

The National Revolutionary Army reached Shanghai in March. In concert with militant workers' movements organized by Communists, the army triumphed over the city and occupied it—without touching the foreign settlements at all, relieving those residents'

Rayna and Bill Prohme with Chinese colleagues in Hankou.
Source: Milly Bennett Papers, Photo File, Envelope H, Hoover Institution Archive.
Milly Bennett, wearing a hat, stands next to Rayna, and Jack Chen, a teenage son of Eugene Chen who drew political cartoons for the *People's Tribune*, stands next to Bill. The others are unidentified; Rayna's beloved dog is in front.

Bill Prohme in China.
Source: Milly Bennett Papers, Photo File, Envelope I, Hoover Institution Archive.

anxieties for the moment. An army corps then moved to Nanjing, a city about two hundred miles west along the Yangtze. There, "outrages" occurred. Uniformed Chinese soldiers attacked and looted the British, American, and Japanese consulates and the homes of foreign nationals, killing at least six foreigners, including one American. American destroyers and a British cruiser then shelled in a circle around Standard Oil employees' residences so that about fifty of their citizens could escape, killing at least twenty Chinese. Britain and the United States threatened further retaliatory actions.[53]

The question of culpability for the Nanjing "outrages" aggravated the internecine struggle within the Guomindang. Chiang Kai-shek denied that his troops in the National Revolutionary Army were responsible. He pinned the blame on Communists, deserters, or warlords' troops wearing false uniforms. His blame of Communists took fire among others, including representatives of foreign powers. Some Guomindang officers echoed Chiang's call to "purify" the Guomindang by eliminating any Communist presence.

On April 11 and 12, 1927, Chiang and generals allied with him took decisive action in Shanghai. Their forces, aided by underworld gangs they hired, attacked the militant labor unions in which Communists had organized many hundreds of thousands of workers. They shut union headquarters, seized unions' arms supplies, and killed hundreds of people. Thousands more fled. Chiang soon had all Communists purged from the Guomindang (not infrequently by murder) and disarmed them in every city where his supporters could accomplish it. Emergency meetings of party councils aimed at conciliating the two sides, but secret meetings, betrayals, mass arrests, and murders had more force. The several corps of the National Revolutionary Army split apart, with Chiang's side gaining the larger number of generals and their troops. Chiang determined to establish his Guomindang capital at Nanjing instead of Hankou.[54]

In Hankou, rumors of further betrayals and defections circulated daily, roiling the city's atmosphere of international revolt. Notices of mass meetings were plastered all over; long parades of little boys marched through the streets every day with desperate gaiety, holding banners proclaiming "Down with militarism—down with foreign imperialism—long live the Chinese revolution—long live the world revolution." When the radical American journalist Anna Louise Strong arrived in China, a Berlin newspaperman friend advised her not to "waste time" seeing Chiang's Nanjing, saying, "It will not live. . . . Hankow will live; if not the men, at least the idea that is alive there . . . that which is behind all revolutions—sudden hope of long submerged masses." Strong was one of dozens of American correspondents in Hankou that April and May. They came from the Associated Press, United Press, and International News Service, the Hearst newspapers, the *New York Times*, the *New York Herald Tribune*, the *New York World*, the *Chicago Tribune*, the *Christian Science Monitor*, the *New York Evening Post*, along with more from around the world.[55]

Jimmy Sheean was one of them. As a special correspondent for the North American Newspaper Alliance (NANA), he arrived in Shanghai later than he hoped, the day after Chiang's forces crushed the radical workers there. He moved to Nanjing after ten days, had an interview with Chiang, and saw the destruction wreaked by the "outrages." He realized he was too late to witness a revolution in its prime. The revolutionary Nationalist movement had "completely collapsed already," he told Raymond Mortimer in a letter. "That traitor Chiang Kai-shek ruined it," Sheean wrote, and "only the discredited remnants of it at Hankou and Nanjing" remained. As he saw it, the Guomindang now amounted only to "three or four utterly disreputable factions."[56]

Sheean headed to Hankou. To his surprise, other journalists advised him to reach the left-wing leaders through an American known as Rayna, recognizable by her flaming hair. Henry Misselwitz of the *New York Times* described her as a wild Bolshevik "spitfire" when he took Sheean to meet her. "Everybody that's got anything to do with this government is a Red, whether they admit it or not," Misselwitz warned. Sheean, with no compunctions about "Reds," did a doubletake when introduced to Rayna. He heard a "very American" voice—and saw "the kind of girl I had known all my life." To take her as a revolutionary seemed as improbable to him as believing that "cousin Cecilia, with whom I grew up, had suddenly turned into a Red." He soon appreciated how central she was among the Hankou leaders and began stopping by her office often, to get the latest news.[57]

Hankou was a "Red" city in the eyes of the world. Being connected to the leadership there, both Rayna and Bill were assumed to be "Red," by foreigners. Bill was furious that news media in the United States and England referred to him as a Communist. He told his friend Lewis Gannett, an associate editor at *The Nation* magazine to whom he sent China news, that he would sue for libel "if times were normal"; but he was well aware that "the 'communist' stuff is worldwide. It's part of the campaign against the Nationalist Movement." Rayna was incredulous that American missionaries and businessmen in Hankou stepped "around me on the sidewalk as though I were a leper, think[ing] I am a trained revolutionist with a bomb in each pocket!" She told this to Randall Gould, the United Press correspondent in Hankou, who knew her from San Francisco and sympathized with her views.[58]

To counter the exaggerated pronouncements of other Western reports, Bill Prohme wanted to keep the Nationalist News Agency "neutral" regarding the split between Hankou and Chiang's conservative allies. He stuck to "plain news . . . on matters in which the 'split' doesn't figure at all," he told Gannett, "hoping that the split will be bridged efforts eventually and then, if I shall have kept the news agency neutral, the work may go on." Likewise, Rayna had to take pains editing the paper, given that the *People's Tribune* was supposed to be the English mouthpiece of the Guomindang as a whole. Their work found a champion in Anna Louise Strong, who judged that Bill's and Rayna's dispatches sent to the United States were highly effective in supporting "the liberal opposition" that "prevented armed intervention" in China after the Nanjing episode.[59]

Milly Bennett soon came to Hankou to assist Rayna with the *People's Tribune*. The risky outpost in Beijing closed, but not before warlord Zhang Zuolin arrested Bennett and threw her in jail. The American consul in Beijing, who should have jumped to the cause, rescued her only reluctantly, so wary was he of stirring Zhang's wrath. Bennett moved in with Rayna when she arrived in Hankou, while Bill Prohme was away investigating the causes and effects of the "outrages."[60]

That May, a heat wave raised the temperature in Hankou's humid subtropical climate to 105. The banks of the Yangtze became red dust. On the waterfront Bund, the sturdy buildings of foreign commercial interests towered blankly, because the revolution had stopped up industry and trade. Sundown brought no relief. No breeze stirred; the only movement in the trees was the cicadas chirping. No matter how tired the two women were from the daily stress of the newspaper, they distracted themselves and friends in a makeshift salon, welcoming visiting labor delegates and journalists, including Strong and Sheean, to the apartment. They had "jolly times" there, Randall Gould remembered, listening to records, singing, arguing, and joking. To cool down enough to sleep, Rayna and Milly improvised a routine that involved soaking a bedsheet in the bathtub, winding it around the body like a cocoon, and then, with the fan whirling at top speed, diving into bed under the mosquito-netting. Bill, a killjoy, howled against their "lunatic" method when he returned to Hankou and prohibited it, certain that the women were inviting pneumonia.[61]

Some evenings, many of the same people collected in Borodin's apartment for classical music and inspiring conversation. Borodin's quiet certainty as the revolution spiraled downward appeared "singularly noble" to Jimmy Sheean. When Anna Louise Strong sought his counsel about the left wing's desperate situation, Borodin answered calmly, emphasizing that the Chinese revolution was in an early phase and would take time. Because of China's size—"one fourth of all earth's people," he reminded Strong—the Chinese revolution would be "the biggest thing in the world, . . . many times bigger"

Rayna and her dog in China.
Source: Milly Bennett Papers, Photo File, Envelope H, Hoover Institution Archive.

than the Bolshevik Revolution in Russia. "It will take long," he said, and "will kill more than one Borodin before it is through."[62]

Confusion and danger grew as the Guomindang military campaign, though no longer unified, continued to try to capture territory from warlords. Additional generals teamed with Chiang Kai-shek and battled not only enemy warlords but also the corps loyal to Hankou. Thousands upon thousands of the troops clinging to Hankou were wounded, unable to serve. The Hankou economy ground to a standstill and the Hankou government's paper money inflated into worthlessness.

In July, a meeting of the Guomindang's central council voted to sever the party from Communists, with only Madame Sun and Eugene Chen dissenting. Men who a few weeks earlier had promised to stand with the Hankou dissidents reversed course. Army generals dismissed their Russian military advisers and threw them out of China. On July 2, 1927, Sheean jotted in his daybook: "The government here is doomed. It will fall soon, any day. God knows what will happen to Rayna." He left Hankou three days later, headed for Beijing.[63]

SOON ALL RAYNA's close colleagues had to flee or hide. The revolution had "slumped into a cat and dog fight between various militarists," and civil leaders "knuckled under" and followed their lead, eliminating Communist-leaning leaders by gruesome means, Rayna wrote to Helen Freeland; conservatives made Borodin into an "arch villain" who must be "plotting to usurp the Guomindang control and replace it by communists." Borodin was the first to leave, his whereabouts kept hidden as he traveled overland by car to Moscow with a few others.[64]

Madame Sun did not fold quietly. She wrote a courageous statement disavowing Chiang Kai-shek's policies, which Rayna planned to print in the July 14 issue of the *People's Tribune*. Madame Sun then disappeared from Hankou, going to her residence in the French concession in Shanghai. Bill, greatly admiring Madame Sun's courage, sent her statement to all the correspondents he knew, "by wireless to Vladivostok, and thence to Moscow, Berlin, London, New York." He urged Lewis Gannett to print it in *The Nation*, where it was published in the issue of September 21, 1927. The several Chinese newspapers that carried her statement were immediately closed down.[65]

Rayna and Bill resigned their positions with the *People's Tribune* on July 31, one day after the new Guomindang propaganda minister told Eugene Chen that the newspaper must be "reorganized" without them. In a letter of resignation, they expressed pain and regret at leaving, saying they "could not honestly follow the present tendencies" in the party, which seemed to them "to defeat the revolutionary cause." To Helen, Rayna admitted that the betrayals and turnabouts within the party had disillusioned her. She felt "sick with knowledge of the capacity within the human race for treachery and rottenness." Her feelings vacillated wildly. Two days later she wrote to Raph—with whom she had been keeping in touch the whole time—that "the past two years have been lived so rapidly & with so much satisfaction in them that, in spite of the present collapse of the revolution here, I am on top of the world."[66]

Leaving Hankou, Rayna joined Madame Sun in her residence in Shanghai's French concession. Bill initially remained in Hankou at Eugene Chen's request, and then moved to a hotel in Shanghai. All three were under surveillance—their movements tracked, their mail opened—by the Criminal Investigation Department (CID), a detective agency mostly serving British imperial interests. Rayna's awareness of being followed made her especially tense, but the CID staff was on duty only from ten in the morning to eight thirty at night and was so inept that much of its reporting was wrong, even amusingly so.

She and Madame Sun were able to sneak out at 3:30 a.m. on August 22 to a sampan waiting for them. The sampan delivered them to a Soviet merchant ship bound for Vladivostok. Eugene Chen (who had escaped Hankou in disguise) was aboard, along with his two daughters. They were all heading to Moscow, where the tenth anniversary of the Bolshevik Revolution would be celebrated in November. Bill did not go, because Chen had assigned him to remain in Shanghai as a liaison for those who were departing. Though the separation distressed Bill and Rayna, they accepted it.

As they departed, Rayna summed up for her younger sister, "The past six months have surely been the most exacting, stupendous, and maturing months I have ever lived. . . . I've seen a big historic movement closely from the inside, and have become intimately associated with it, probably for a lifetime." She believed that "an underground organization as strong as ever—but much more bitter" had been salvaged "out of the murder and the wreck" and "there will be a recovery." What that pattern meant for her and Bill was the question. "What we will do or where we will go in the interim, I do not know."[67] Only Moscow would tell.

CHAPTER 6

MOSCOW PASSAGE

JIMMY SHEEAN HAD no idea where Rayna was, as he went north from Hankou intending to interview two infamous warlords. Traveling through territory where three Chinese armies were fighting each other and outlaws were taking advantage of the chaos, the trains were agonizingly "slow, filthy, crammed with soldiers, indescribably hot," he recalled. But he faced no danger; the "belching, spitting, stinking passengers" treated him courteously. Making his way to Beijing and remaining there for much of the summer of 1927, he read outrageous rumors about Rayna and Borodin and their colleagues, and imagined grim possibilities. Late in August he saw a newspaper report that Madame Sun and Eugene Chen were on their way to Moscow. He was intending to return to Europe—writing to Louise Bryant that "China's terribly depressing"—by way of Harbin and Moscow himself.[1]

Sheean did not know that Rayna was traveling to Vladivostok by ship and from there on the Trans-Siberian Railway (in a special car) to Moscow. He did not know that he would find her there, or anything about her state of mind or future plans. Nor could he have foreseen that Dorothy Thompson, whom he had met casually in Berlin the year before, would also arrive in Moscow, to write a series of articles for her newspaper. The celebration of the tenth anniversary of the Bolshevik Revolution would bring all three together—none of them, however, having any inkling of the fate that would soon overtake Rayna.

THE TEN-DAY RAIL journey from Vladivostok to Moscow kept Rayna busy working as publicist for Eugene Chen and Madame Sun. She composed greetings for the Chinese party to deliver in Moscow and lengthy biographical sketches of Mme. Sun and Eugene Chen to be used once they arrived; she also handled "long strings of questions" about the Chinese situation, put to her by reporters from the Russian newspaper *Pravda*, who accompanied the Chinese party on the train. Chen and Madame Sun gave Rayna the impression that the future held new work for her on behalf of the Chinese revolution, perhaps again under Borodin, even though the revolutionary organization would have to work underground. To her sister, Rayna wrote that she was excited about entering Soviet Russia "under auspices that will make it possible to stay and work there."[2] Rayna had never read Marx or Lenin, but her political evolution in China together with her reverence for Borodin made her eager to learn more about communism in theory and practice.

On the train platform in Moscow on September 7, 1927, they were greeted by a horde of cameramen, all jostling to record Madame Sun's historic arrival. The Russians' special treatment of Madame Sun brought a welcome advantage to Rayna, who was viewed as her companion: both women were given similar deluxe lodgings in the rococo "Sugar Palace," a former sugar baron's mansion remade into a hotel and residence. Rayna got a palatial room and bath. Enjoying lolling in the luxurious bathtub, she chuckled at the irony: "The leaders of the masses of China come to confer with the leaders of proletarian Russia and are housed in a way that rivals Buckingham Palace."[3]

Her mood changed within a few days. Some "blunt talking" by Eugene Chen revealed that there was no paying work ahead, despite his promising remarks en route. And her stay in the Sugar Palace would end October 1. Vague hints were given about a possible international job for Bill with Tass, the Soviet press agency, but meanwhile, the Nationalist News Agency in Shanghai was to be "liquidated," eliminating Bill's job without compensating him for his expenditures on the service. The two of them were "heading for a debacle," Rayna wrote despondently to him. They had debts, no income, and no visible opportunities—and their locations were so far apart that it was frustratingly difficult to communicate about what to do. Telegrams would be impractical and expensive, while letters took at least three weeks to arrive. When Rayna questioned her Chinese and Russian contacts further, she got only "evasions, uncertainties and gestures," she told Bill. "We are high and dry."[4]

Both Rayna and Bill blamed Eugene Chen for misleading them. They did not know that behind their hard fate was a larger reason dooming the Hankou group: Moscow's support was gone. The progress of Chiang Kai-shek's anticommunist armies in China showed that Soviet policy (beginning with Comintern aid to the Guomindang in 1923) had failed. Joseph Stalin, General Secretary of the Communist Party, intended to abandon China for the time being. Stalin was consolidating power for himself, eliminating his rival Leon Trotsky, who opposed his China policy and much else, and turning aside from seeding revolution elsewhere to build socialism in his own country.[5]

Jimmy Sheean reached Moscow just after Rayna swallowed the bleak news from Chen. After nine monotonous days' journey on the Trans-Siberian Railway from Harbin, he was thrilled to find Rayna right away, easily. When she went to meet him, he was "pipped to the gills with vodka, embarrassingly enthusiastic" about seeing her, and spouting "all about his devotion," she told Bill. Sheean insisted on taking her to the opera and fell asleep there almost immediately. She was glad to escape. Yet she welcomed his distracting presence during the next several days, because he countered her depression. She "shelved all thinking" as Sheean whirled her around the city in hired *drozhki* (horse-drawn open carriages) to sample Moscow's theater and concerts, a ballet about China's revolutionary struggle, a military exercise in a city park. They dragged a reluctant Madame Sun to see herself in the newsreel of her arrival in Moscow. "Jimmie is really the most dis-organizing person I have ever known—barring Raph," she told Bill. She nonetheless found his spirits "positively contagious." Both Sheean's fun-loving spontaneity and his infuriating irresponsibility reminded her often of Raph. Sheean was a "blithe companion" who wanted to have a good time, not someone to whom she would unburden herself, because she did not think he was really interested.[6]

Sheean did not see Rayna's anxiety. During these September days with her, he marveled at her clarity—the clarity of a woman who had determined to devote her life to the Chinese revolutionary movement, even in the midst of its fragmentation, even if it meant working clandestinely. As far as he could see, she had figured out how to align her life against the world's "monstrous" social inequities. She had resolved issues that were "the most serious any human has to face" while he still waffled with indecision. Her commitment so inspired him that he changed his plans, in order to remain in Moscow through the winter to be near her. He needed funds to support himself there, so he headed back to London to seek a commission from the North American Newspaper Alliance. Saying he would return in a month, he dashed on to the Leningrad express on September 22 as the train was pulling out, with Rayna and the porter running along the station platform literally throwing his belongings to him.[7]

In fact, Rayna was far from certain about her future. Her former colleagues remained evasive. She resented how Chen and several Russian agents treated her "pretty much as a thing—and a thing that had served its purpose," she wrote to Bill. "It has been a complete shelving of us—nothing could be clearer than that. . . . I feel terribly dumped." In an understandable reversal of her feeling of marital claustrophobia, she missed Bill painfully. Beyond judging the Kremlin spires "magnificent beyond words," she barely explored Moscow because she could not share it with him.[8]

She held out one hope: Borodin, whose overland route from Hankou had not yet brought him to Moscow, might have the magic to create an adequate job for her. When Borodin arrived on October 7, her hope collapsed. All he could offer was a scrap: he could probably employ her to assist him in writing a report on the past two years in China. His presence improved Rayna's social life, because he invited her to outings and the theater along with other friends, but he kept delaying about employing her. Borodin himself was being shunted aside because of Stalin's priorities. He survived, but never regained a significant state position.[9]

At best, Rayna's mood mixed "doggedness and despair." Besides the dim employment horizon, she met excruciating frustration trying to find a place to live. Housing was very scarce and scandalously expensive, because Moscow was bursting with a huge inflow of government and factory workers, already doubling and tripling up in existing residences. Searching for a rental, Rayna saw only "foul holes" without private baths, at stunningly high prices. The bathrooms provided were "simply unspeakable," she reported to Bill, "and used by a few dozen people." For two weeks she benefited gratefully from Jimmy Sheean's help: his acquaintance with a Bolshevik emissary in Beijing led to the man's wife inviting Rayna to share her Moscow room. But the wife also had a baby and a maid, and the crowding made it insupportable for very long. Rayna continued to temporize, staying here and there uncomfortably in one generous acquaintance's overcrowded room and then in another. She never was alone, and never unpacked.[10]

If she could only find employment and housing, Rayna felt inclined to stay in Moscow for six months, to study the Russian language and the Soviet system and prepare herself for further work in China. It did not make sense for Bill to join her, no matter how much they wanted to be together, since no job awaited him and housing was so scarce. Bill decided to move to Manila, in the US territory of the Philippines, where he was likely to find a job on an

English-language newspaper. Manila was relatively close to China, to which they both hoped to return eventually. Once he moved there in mid-October, Rayna felt like joining him "in the contented stupor of the tropics," but she knew that she would become restless if she did. Work for the Chinese revolution was "the only activity" that had ever compelled her fully; she did not want to let it go, even though she was troubled by the intrigue she sensed going on among the Chinese and Russians around her, she told Bill. She "terribly, terribly" missed being free to "talk simply, naturally, honestly." She fantasized about escaping to Zurich, where Helen Freeland had gone to be analyzed by C. G. Jung. Freeland offered to pay Rayna's fare for a Christmas visit, and she longed to go.[11]

Something else was wrong, too. At times during September, Rayna was overcome by a "strange dullness" and her mind was foggy. One day at the Hotel Metropole, where she had established a tiny office, she had to stop and sit down, because she completely forgot where she was going, even forgot where she was. The following day she felt "distracted and in a stupor by turns." She tried to minimize these occasions, but worse symptoms appeared toward the end of October. Her head pounded with an unbearable headache for five days in a row, in a way similar to an episode she recalled from her first days in Hankou. She was "almost blind with pain"; the "incessant pound, pound, pound" sent her searching for a doctor. Medication he prescribed addressed the most hellish pain, but the killing headaches left her utterly "sapped" and her mind confused. These headaches made her ready to "kick over the traces" if a workable arrangement for staying in Moscow did not arrive soon.[12]

When the day for the tenth anniversary celebration of the Bolshevik Revolution arrived on Monday, November 7, Rayna had been experiencing "maddening lapses of memory" for two weeks. She watched the stupendous demonstration of military power in Red Square under a "wretched cloud of headache and foggy mind" and felt "more stunned than impressed," she wrote to Bill. Under a dominating portrait of Lenin, with cannons booming and military music ringing, twenty-five thousand Red Army troops paraded through. Hordes of horse artillery, airmen, parachutists, cavalry on high-stepping horses followed. Then Red Square became a surging sea of the peoples of the Soviet Republics—the Circassians, the Mongolians, the cloaked and fur-capped Cossacks. Mounted on black horses and riding at full gallop with their swords flashing, the Cossacks drew wild cheers from the huge crowd watching. Next came thousands of union workers in leather shirts, armed with rifles—women workers, too, with red kerchiefs and guns on their shoulders—and floods of peasant representatives. Above the grandstands, in a high box atop Lenin's Tomb, stood the fur-clad Soviet leadership, gazing down and saluting, with Stalin directly in the middle. For anyone in the know, including many of the foreign journalists there, Stalin's nearly complete effort to muzzle the oppositionists loyal to Trotsky shadowed the revelry. Public counterdemonstrations and Trotsky himself were jeered and suppressed.[13]

Jimmy Sheean stood next to Rayna surveying it all. He had arrived in Moscow at the last minute. He thought the massive spectacle looked "big, heavy and dead," in contrast to the spontaneous street demonstrations he had seen in China. The thousands of peasants and workers crossing Red Square seemed to him "like sheep," cheering obediently on cue and lacking "that movement and life which constitutes mass feeling." He had relished talking and arguing with Bolsheviks at the Soviet embassy in Beijing, following up on his perception of a contradiction between communist principles and Soviet enactment of them during his Persian travels. Moscow was not dissolving that perception. Attracted as he was to Soviet anti-imperialism, he wondered whether any communist regime could deliver on its big promises.[14]

As he watched together with Rayna for several hours, she told him that she was having one of her awful headaches. It was the first he learned of her suffering.

DOROTHY THOMPSON STOOD watching the tenth anniversary spectacle at the same time. "The communist party understands the sense of the old Roman slogan: Bread and circus for the people," she jotted in her notes. She had arrived by train on November 1 for her anticipated stay in Russia. The Soviet train conductors in high boots and belted blouses charmed her, addressing her smilingly as comrade, though the blizzard she met in Moscow disconcerted her, and the "rather straggly and shabby" cityscape disappointed her at first. The cobbled streets looked very dirty, and the *drozhki* were rusted, the seat coverings worn and ripped, the drivers garbed in "evil smelling" sheepskins.[15]

A sunny day following the snow then transformed the city into something "fantastically beautiful" and "magical": "The muddy streets, the huge, treeless squares, become ribbons of silver and plains of glistening white. Red Square, with the dark Kremlin wall along one side, the clock in the tall tower striking melodiously, the terrific and fantastic church of St. Basil catching [sunshine] on its enameled and twisted and gilded minarets, the long white façade of the Government stores, with their arcades of small shops across the square, the ever present red decorations . . . become against snow festive, almost Christmas-like." She took in breathtaking glimpses of exotic domes and spires, while also noticing that miserable tenements slunk behind freshly painted government offices. The mix of large department stores, crowded government cooperatives, and bazaar-like outdoor booths intrigued her, the latter selling everything from statues of Lenin to plucked chickens and women's cotton underwear.[16]

Thompson wrote lovingly and often to Sinclair Lewis, ruing his absence, saying how much she missed him, sending him kisses. To describe Moscow in familiar terms, she called the city's mood "as puritan & pure as Sauk Center," Lewis's hometown in Minnesota. The sense of mingled "discomfort and enthusiasm" reminded her of the suffrage campaign: "There's an unquenchable social settlement house smell about it," she said. Eager to observe and learn, she did not complain about the bitter cold or the long delay in arrival of her trunks; she borrowed a sweater from the Associated Press correspondent, gloves from a *New York Times* man, and galoshes from Anna Louise Strong, who had come to Moscow from Hankou.[17]

Everything she saw gripped her. After her second full day exploring, she reported to Lewis, "with a few reservations I'm extremely impressed with what I see. There is [sic] volumes to write to correct the American attitude." Her relative open-mindedness diverged from most Americans' readiness to believe that the Soviet system was soul-crushing and deeply antithetical to American values. The United States had joined Allied military efforts to try to prevent the Bolsheviks from consolidating their revolutionary success and would not extend diplomatic recognition to the Soviet regime until 1933. Thompson was among the minority of American intellectuals, journalists, workers, and left-wing liberals who were curious about Soviet society as an "experiment" and eager to see if it would work.

She had come with few fixed opinions, unlike pro-Soviet American visitors, including Anna Louise Strong, the Socialist economics writer Scott Nearing, and Harry Dana, Frances Fineman's onetime Columbia professor friend who was "rabid with enthusiasm" for the Soviet project. Thompson had known them all before re-meeting them in Moscow. She saw them as American types of "self-appointed apologists who, acting as unofficial plenipotentiaries, make a living from Russia."[18]

Thompson crammed in as many kinds of experiences as she could. On a typical day she first waited in the foreign office, hoping to arrange an interview with the Soviet foreign minister, Georgy Chicherin, then visited the Pedagogical Seminar for advice about education and a list of schools to visit, next viewed an exhibition of the art of the Russian nationalities, and after that went to see an ancient monastery where twelve "eternally burning" lamps lighted the tombs. After sharing a long lunch at four o'clock with Junius Wood, the *Chicago Daily News*'s Moscow correspondent (a colleague

Dorothy Thompson in Moscow, 1927.
Source: Dorothy Thompson Papers, Special Collections Research Center, Syracuse University Libraries.

of John Gunther), she attended a performance of Sergei Prokofiev's opera *The Love for the Three Oranges*, and then stopped in to observe an international congress of the Friends of the Soviet Union. Midnight found her in an artists' club in Moscow's bohemian district with a journalist from the Associated Press. While she attended performances, conducted interviews with officials, visited schools and stores and factories and other sites of daily life, she also went out of her way to speak with varied people, from housemaids and *drozhki* drivers to artists and intellectuals. "The more I see the more confused I seem to become," she worried to Lewis.[19]

WHEN DOROTHY THOMPSON and Rayna met is uncertain. Perhaps it was on November 4, when Thompson met Borodin, or a few days later, once Sheean arrived.[20] On Friday, November 11, the two women were talking in Thompson's hotel room, when Rayna fainted. She recovered within an hour or so, made light of the episode, and was able to go with Sheean to an international congress meeting that evening. But the following day, Rayna collapsed again, in a meeting of the Chinese labor delegation. A faithful young Chinese colleague, Zhang Ke, dashed to the Hotel Metropole to tell Anna Louise Strong this alarming news, just before Sheean arrived at the hotel intending to pick Rayna up to go to the ballet. Strong and Sheean headed to the labor delegation's meeting room, not far away. They found Rayna lying on a couch, unconscious. Sheean lifted her gently and carried her a block and a half to the Metropole, to Strong's room. He left her under Strong's care (and went to the ballet).

Rayna was delirious all night—and vomiting, because the local doctor who had been called in gave her ether, to which she was allergic.[21] Sheean dreaded what he might find when he came in to see her the next morning, Sunday, November 13, but Rayna was perfectly sentient, if weak. She asked him to telegraph Helen Freeland in Zurich and ask her to come to Moscow, and to telegraph Samson Raphaelson also. She did not want to telegraph Bill right away, to keep him from worrying. Sheean began searching frantically for a more qualified doctor. Through Walter Duranty, the *New York Times* correspondent in Moscow, Sheean located a well-trained German doctor who spoke English. Dr. Link examined Rayna thoroughly and treated her allergic reaction first; he wanted her to recover enough to be tested by specialists.

Rayna felt so much better by Monday that she asked Sheean to telegraph Freeland and Raphaelson again and say there was no need to come. She stayed in bed in a room next to Anna Louise Strong's; a kind Russian couple named Veprentzov, friends from Hankou whom she called Sonia and Vep, helped attend to her. She seemed much improved during the week, as acquaintances came in to see her, including Sheean, who spent a few hours every afternoon. He thought she was in high spirits all week, gaily reminiscing and joking about some laughable parts of their Hankou experiences. But her headaches recurred. At the end of the week, on Saturday, November 19, Sheean was with her when she had one of her worst headaches ever. By evening, her mind wandered. She melded past, present, and future as if they were all one, speaking of her parents, her Berkeley friends, Raph, and China. In a clear moment she told Sheean to leave so she could sleep.

Sunday morning, November 20, Rayna felt much better; when Sheean came in at midday, they spoke; then she went to sleep. He stayed for several hours, reading to calm his anxiety, and at six that evening Sonia and Vep (who was a medical doctor) came in to spell him. Rayna was breathing very heavily and strangely in her sleep, they all thought. They called Dr. Link; he said it was what he expected, and they should not worry, since "nothing could be done." Sheean, unsure whether to be reassured or alarmed, went away to get some dinner. A couple of hours later the Russian couple called him: Rayna had awakened and asked for him, wanting him to send a cable for her. Though he came quickly, she was asleep again, breathing in an unnatural manner. They again telephoned Dr. Link, who said ominously, "The process I have foreseen is taking its course." He ordered them to get a certified nurse from the Kremlin hospital, which they did. Sonia and Vep stayed in Rayna's room all night. When she woke up for a short time and recognized them, Vep asked her how she felt. She replied, "I'm cold, Vep. I'm dying."[22]

Those were her final words. By early morning, November 21, she was dead. "Little Rayna Prohme—you will remember Vincent Sheean's speaking of her; she was his friend, and a gay red-headed girl who had balled her life up inextricably, but was a charming thing—little Rayna Prohme died this morning, across the street in the Hotel Metropole. Just like that," Dorothy Thompson wrote to Sinclair Lewis. "It is dreadful, Hal, to die alone in a beastly hotel room, in Moscow." Rayna's sudden end made Thompson long to be in Lewis's arms. "I liked her very much in the fortnight I knew her. And now all of a sudden she's dead. . . . And I've wanted all day to run home to you, because it scared me, and I don't feel quite safe anywhere except with you, darling, darling," she told him.[23]

Dr. Link had suspected what proved to be true: Rayna had a brain inflammation caused by an abscess or by encephalitis. An autopsy confirmed that an encephalitic inflammation had been growing in her cerebellum for many months, causing her stupors and headaches since Hankou. It would have been inoperable even if discovered earlier. At the end, her heart stopped beating when the inflammation attacked the brain stem.[24]

Bill Prohme was shattered when he learned by telegram of Rayna's death. The last letter he had received from her was dated October 30; he knew nothing of her final weeks' travail. He raged against "the cruelty of life . . . the obscene nastiness of chance" that had kept him apart from her, thinking that he could have eased her suffering if they had been together. "Everything seems utterly blank for me, nothing matters," he wrote to Lewis Gannett. "I know now how one individual makes a world."[25]

The cremation of Rayna's body took place on Thursday, November 24, Thanksgiving day for Americans. In the open casket, forty tea roses bought on behalf of Bill Prohme surrounded Rayna's face. The coffin was Soviet-style red, and so was the horse-drawn wagon that carried it. Flowers heaped around the casket—chrysanthemums on the top from her father, large wreaths of mums and asters from Borodin and Madame Sun at the sides, brimming baskets of yellow mums from Samson Raphaelson, and red and white ones from Sheean and Strong. More flowers from Eugene Chen and Chinese students were strung along the silk-covered sides. A military band played a revolutionary funeral march as a hundred people trekked two hours across Moscow in bitter weather, accompanying the casket to the modern white marble crematorium. Madame Sun walked the whole way despite frail health, as did Borodin's wife, Eugene Chen and family, the Chinese and the American Labor Delegations, the American correspondents, and many Russians, though not Boro-din himself (who had been told by higher authorities not to attend). Dorothy Thompson walked all the "weary icey miles" following Ray-na's "absurd little coffin, a bright red coffin, in a bright red hearse," she told Lewis.

For several people present, the occasion recalled John Reed's Moscow funeral seven years earlier. Anna Louise Strong offered a eulogy elevating Rayna to the stature of Reed, both being courageous Americans who gave their lives to revolution. Then "the bier, draped in the Red flag and covered with golden flowers, asters, chrysanthe-mums, all the flowers of Rayna's own colours, a heap of gold and red and brown, was placed on the platform. There were speeches in Chinese, Russian and English. . . . Then a signal was given, a switch was turned, and the golden mass of Rayna, her hair and her bright flowers and the Red flag, sank slowly before us into the furnace." Thus Sheean described the end.[26]

He was devastated. "I went all to pieces, off the head more or less," he admitted in a letter to Helen Freeland. In his eyes, Rayna embod-ied devotion to revolutionary service—"like a flame, like a star" that "animated and aroused all those who came near her." He believed that she had become selfless in her dedication to the Chinese masses. She had chosen China for her self. "No personal experience of social injustice, no consideration of personal advantage, drove her into a revolutionary career," he wrote worshipfully; "she was impelled into it by conviction, and she gave it all she had, demanding nothing, holding back nothing." Rayna's outlook burned in his memory in the form of her question, "What do we want to die for? If you are willing to die in the effort to maintain what exists, and what is obvi-ously wrong, that is one thing; but you may choose instead to die in the effort to create a slightly better world."[27]

When Sheean wrote to Milly Bennett to describe Rayna's final days, he tried to explain his feelings: "I think there was nobody on earth even remotely like her. Don't misunderstand; there was never any 'love' business about it; Rayna would simply have howled with laughter at me if I had begun anything like that. But I adored her, I can tell you, as I have never adored anybody in my life." Sheean seemed unaware how far Rayna's certainty had faltered once colleagues cast her aside. Chinese nationalism was the raft she found to cling to, in a sea of decisions about her own life. But in Moscow she was no longer absolutely sure.[28]

Bill Prohme had a clearer sense of how she was torn. "She was ambivalent, really, in her ultimate desires," Bill recognized in a sad letter he typed right away to Dr. Ames. Bill knew how important Ames was to Rayna and wanted to inform him about her recent life and her death. He wrote that Rayna "seemed to thrive on the knowledge she was a part of something big and vital" in China. "She was a real part of it," trusted by the Hankou leaders, Bill emphasized. But he also knew that "she had begun to doubt that the excitement of participation in this struggle was sufficient compensation for concomitant losses."[29]

Sheean fled from Moscow as quickly as possible. Dorothy Thompson's generous sympathy for him at that time created a bond between the two that strengthened through the years. She loaned him the keys to her apartment in Berlin, where he was going from Moscow, and wrote to Lewis, "Hal, dearest, be awfully kind to Sheean; this business of Rayna dying has made him awfully miserable. I've told him . . . he can go and live in my flat. He's a dear boy, and unhappy."[30] Sheean did not take up her generous offer. Instead, he cabled Harold Nicolson as he crossed the Russian border, saying when his train would arrive in Berlin.

Nicolson, who had left Tehran and taken up a new diplomatic post as *charge d'affaires* in Berlin, was delighted to welcome Sheean. But after his arrival and their dinner together, Sheean disappeared from Nicolson's residence. When he was not in his room the next morning, Nicolson worried all day. Not until late afternoon did Sheean phone, saying he was safe. "God knows what he has been up to—he sounded pretty shamed-faced," Nicolson thought. He was forgiving, telling Sackville-West, "I can't help rather liking these

wild irresponsible people even if they <u>do</u> make the hair turn grey."
If Sheean was seeking to ease his despair in a wild spree, Berlin was
the place for it. The city abounded with hustlers, rent-boys, and gay
gathering spots, and though sodomy was a crime, the city's police
let gay social life alone. Sheean stayed on for several more days and
celebrated his twenty-eighth birthday on December 5 with Nicolson.
His paradoxical character appealed to Nicolson, who saw in Sheean
a remarkable mixture "of childishness & romanticism, of softness &
a love of adventure, of idealism & good sense, of deep convictions &
superficial sentimentality."[31]

Distracting himself with action, Sheean set himself a new antifascist adventure. He hoped to expose the little-known method of
exile used by "that swine Mussolini," who was imprisoning his political opponents on the bare volcanic island of Lipari. One prisoner
there was Alfredo Morea, the courageous republican editor who had
pulled a malarial Sheean through Spanish bombardment as they left
the Rif. Sheean's crazy scheme to hail a boat to Lipari and somehow
breach the prison walls proved utterly impossible to fulfill, but the
North American News Alliance took his four articles about Mussolini's obliteration of political dissenters. Still suffering from his
Moscow experience, Sheean returned to Paris and took a minimally
occupying job at the *Paris Times*, a small English-language weekly,
to earn his keep.[32]

DOROTHY THOMPSON REMAINED in Moscow. "I am working awfully hard, eating, thinking, breathing Russia," she told Sinclair
Lewis, "and more confused, more questioning, more doubtful of the
verity of any impression I've gained." Though she continued to as-
sure him, "I love you, with my whole heart, in every way a woman
can love a man or one human soul another," the challenge of getting her story right would keep her there longer than both of them
preferred. She explained, "I find myself caring very much that this
work should be good! and I'm desperately afraid it won't be." Her

findings kept contradicting each other. "Every day I change my mind about everything I'd made it up about the day before," she admitted ruefully.[33]

One day she saw clips from the as-yet-unfinished film by Sergei Eisenstein, *October*, which dramatized the Bolshevik Revolution. She could not have known that Stalin had previewed the film a few days earlier and had ordered Eisenstein to eliminate the scenes that showed Trotsky. But she fully recognized Stalin's aim to crush Trotsky and his partisans when she went to the funeral of Adolf Joffe, who had just committed suicide, two days after the Communist Party expelled Trotsky and put him under house arrest. Joffe had represented the Comintern in negotiating assistance to the Guomindang in 1923, and then had been Soviet representative to Austria, living in Vienna, where Thompson got to know him. Trotsky was "let out" to give Joffe's eulogy, Thompson told Lewis. (It would be his last public speech in Russia.) The scene on that gray and blustery day became "altogether unforgettable" for Thompson, as she watched Trotsky address the crowd in the snowy cemetery, where Joffe's red coffin rested between black flags, with soldiers standing at its head and foot.[34]

Thompson was working at a dizzying pace and scarcely sleeping, yet she found time to write to Lewis every day to say how much she loved and longed for him. They were keeping their relationship a secret from the world as far as possible because Lewis's divorce was still pending. After an evening of subterfuge with two American friends who kept asking questions about Lewis, she burst out in a letter to him, "I do want to mount the Kremlin wall or anything else high & public (the front balcony of the great Komintern building wouldn't be bad, would it?) and tell the world I love and adore you!" But she also wrote firmly, "I love to work." In a Thanksgiving letter, she told him, "I'm thankful for you, for work, and for feeling so well. I don't want anything else in the world."[35]

After Thanksgiving Thompson began counting the days of their separation, thinking she might shorten her stay. Lewis begged her to do so. She seesawed back and forth between her heartfelt desire to be with him and the compelling fascination and difficulty of her assignment. Lewis then solved their problem by deciding to join her in Russia; traveling was second nature to him. He left Berlin for Moscow on November 29. During the next ten days, he frustrated the news media eager to know the celebrated novelist's views of the Soviet Union by speaking of nothing but Dorothy Thompson. Thompson decided to cut her trip a bit short. She had amassed so many notes and thoughts already that staying longer, she decided, would only make it harder to figure out what to say.[36]

The two of them were back in Berlin by the second week of December, both busy with writing. Lewis was completing his novel *Dodsworth* while Thompson finished her Russia articles. She had not expected to find a utopia in Russia. Rather, she was interested in what kind of spirit drove Russians forward under their new form of government and whether the Soviet regime was producing a new sort of person. She put much of her energy into circulating among young people and observing schools, assuming that what she heard and saw there pointed to the future. In contrast to the sense of weariness, even futility, she often found among European intellectuals—who felt that the scepter of the future had passed to the United States— she found that young people in Moscow had amazing confidence in themselves and their country's potential; even if their current conditions were poor, they were sure that the future was bright.

Thompson thought her series of newspaper articles deserved to be a book—and so did Henry Holt & Co., publishers who signed on her project. She had more room to be interpretive in the book, where she likened the optimistic "pioneer" spirit she found in Russia to that spirit in the United States before the Civil War. She reserved her sharpest criticism for relations between the sexes. As she saw it, the suddenly changed conditions of women's civic equality and economic freedom in the Soviet Union, along with very easy divorce, the elimination of church power over marriage, and the decriminalization of abortion, had left women feeling insecure; she thought that more friction between the sexes and a certain sterility in relationships, rather than erotic freedom, had resulted. Her book was one of at least a half dozen credible American and British books of Soviet impressions sparked by the tenth anniversary.[37]

Being apart from Lewis in Russia, and yearning for him so strongly, convinced Thompson that marrying him was the right step. She adored him when he was sober. Sadly, he could never resist drinking for long. A scalding reminder of this interrupted Thompson's happiness two months after they returned to Berlin from Moscow. Out drinking with Harold Nicolson, Lewis missed Thompson's dinner party; then he chattered until midnight "with the incoherence and repetition of the tipsy being very wise," she told her diary. They went to a costume ball next, as planned, but he balked freakishly when the doorman asked for a small fee because he was not in costume. They left. In the taxi going home, Lewis shouted at Thompson "in the foulest language; 'your whoring, half-insane, bastards of friends'—and all the Anglo-Saxon monosyllables," she recounted. She was terrified.

Later, after standing outside in the rain, he was remorseful, but the scene hung in her mind. "I still feel poisoned by the sound of the hatred in his voice," she wrote a full day afterward. "And this time I was part of his hatred. He hated me too. . . . What lies in his soul, when the inhibition is lifted? What contempt, what rage with himself?" She felt not resentment but a great weariness, and a desire to be alone, and calm. She loved him. She saw his personal agony—"this darkness in him which comes up like a tidal wave, drowning his spirit, when drink breaks down the dikes"—as something she could not resent. Yet she wondered if she would be better off without him, concentrating on her work.[38]

Nonetheless, against her own misgivings and friends' warnings, she went ahead with the marriage. She believed Lewis was her soulmate. "It is as my friend that I think of you clearest, love you best," she addressed him. "My comrade." In March 1928, she gave up her newspaper position. She and Lewis were going to live in the United States.

Though she agreed with the plan, it worried her. Life in Europe had led her to think of the United States as "a sterile country." She regarded American civilization as "fundamentally hostile to women," declaring in her diary that the "rights" women had gained were "a shameless (if unconscious) price paid for robbing us of our whole life." Though her own career suggested the opposite, at heart she believed that women and men were essentially different creatures, meant to complement and not to imitate one another. In odd parallel to her critique of Soviet Russia, she thought that the priority set on material gain in the United States and the assumption that ambitious women's aspirations would mimic men's had led to a lack of harmony between the sexes and a failure of deep communication.[39]

Their wedding took place in London on May 14, 1928, amid a distinguished group of invited guests. Since the press followed every move of Sinclair Lewis, the marriage made news on both sides of the Atlantic. Thompson first entered the flash photos of American celebrity not as an accomplished foreign correspondent but as Mrs. Sinclair Lewis. The couple then began a two-month honeymoon hiking in the English countryside. No camping out for them: they lived in a recreational van they outfitted with ice box, sink, commode, table, and bed and drove it from place to place hitched to an automobile. Fulfilling a promise he made, Lewis did not drink at all, but in their close quarters he was often moody. She noted ominously in her diary on August 2, just after the trip ended, "Bad temper is the most destructive of human faults. It supplants trust with fear; it poisons love; it breeds aversion or indifference; it sterilizes emotion. Unless he stops taking me on or casting me off as the mood suits him I shall eventually cease to love H [Hal, her nickname for Lewis]."[40]

They soon embarked on the ocean liner *Hamburg* for their native land, arriving in New York on August 27, 1928. On the pier, the press were waiting for them. The *New York Herald Tribune* asked Thompson if she would join the Lucy Stone League, referring to the band of American women who, as feminists, insisted on keeping their birth names after marrying. Thompson said no, she would be

"Mrs. Sinclair Lewis" in her social life. She added provocatively that the league did not go far enough, because the name game, if real, should insist on children taking the mother's name.[41]

Within a month the couple owned 295 acres in Barnard, Vermont, a property called Twin Farms. Sinclair Lewis was such a restless soul that at forty-three he had never lived in one place for more than six months since graduating from Yale College.[42] But his courtship of Thompson from the start had included a fantasy of the bucolic place where they would live together close to the earth, amid animals and natural abundance. She embraced this dream and Twin Farms fulfilled it perfectly. It included two houses; for the moment they lived in the smaller one and began renovation on the antique larger house, where they planned to live during the warm months from late May to September. During cold weather they would live in or near New York, and for the first winter, they rented a flat in Greenwich Village. Thompson found friends among writers and journalists there.

Lewis, who could not stay put for long, wanted to spend their first Christmas in Hot Springs, Virginia. Thompson found it utterly boring there. Seven months after her wedding, she rued the loss of her correspondent role and missed the lively cosmopolitan community she had inhabited in Europe. "Damn it all," she wrote on Christmas Eve to H. R. Knickerbocker, who had succeeded her in Berlin, "I'm not yet quite adjusted to not having a regular job. I miss you all like the devil." She worried that her achievements as a foreign correspondent would be forgotten. "I begin to live in memory as [only] the smart gal who picked you," she flattered him, while fearing it was true.[43]

Her moods swung up and down during that first winter. "My heart is heavy & rebellious," she told her diary in February 1929. They were in Florida, because Lewis insisted. She recorded bitterly his "sneers" about her European interests and her friends: "'you with your important little lectures. . . . You with your brilliant people. . . . You want to talk about foreign politics which I am too ignorant to understand.' When he talks so my heart freezes up. And then, in a minute he is very sweet again. Oh my God. I really don't know whether I love or hate him—but tonight I was bored with him. I say to myself 'you are totally unimportant & you are married to a man of genius—if you give up your life to making him happy it is worth it.' But it isn't! it isn't! I can really do nothing for him. He is like a vampire—he absorbs all my vitality, all my energy, all my beauty—I get incredibly dull."

She was doing some translations of German writings into English and planning a book, but living with a mercurial husband whose behavior streaked up and down with his drinking was taking a terrible toll. "Can't he see that no human being can do creative work in the atmosphere which he creates about him!" she lamented. "I can't live & work in a world where I cannot plan from one day to the next. . . . And my very mind degenerates." She told herself direly, "It's either give up my work or give up Hal." Yet she cherished their genuine closeness when he was sober, and when she thought of leaving him, economic anxiety assailed her. Her life as Lewis's wife was very comfortable; his books had made him wealthy and they could spend lavishly. She was not sure how she would support herself in the United States, where she felt as yet "ill-adjusted" and had no niche in American journalism. She thought it would "be very difficult to get another European correspondency."[44]

When the warm weather brought the couple to Twin Farms for their first full summer there, both of them were happier. Lewis found it a very good place to write, and Thompson loved the wooded hills and green uplands, the comfortable house, the nearby lake, the cows and chickens and the landscaped garden, of which she was proud. She took pleasure in maintaining a beautiful, well-run home, sustained by numerous household helpers and gardeners. She and Lewis frequently had friends from Europe or New York come to stay.

Still, she missed her job. Welcoming an opportunity to earn her own money and take a break from her husband, she agreed to do a lecture tour through the Midwest in the fall of 1929, to speak about

Germany and Soviet Russia. The public lecture was still a popular form of public education and entertainment. At thirty-six, Thompson was in the first trimester of a pregnancy—very happy to be so— and when she and Lewis were apart, it was easier for her to remember how much they loved each other.[45]

Thompson envisioned the lecture tour as a way to reacquaint herself with her native land. As trains jostled her to St. Louis and back to New York and out to Atlanta and back again, the journey instead reinvigorated prejudices she already had. The audiences she spoke to deepened her impression that material gain and standardization had hijacked American civilization, a view that her husband shared. Berlin and Vienna felt far away as she saw one dishearteningly formulaic Main Street streetscape after another and spent her nights in Pullman cars or tasteless hotels. Lonely, she wrote lovingly to her husband, who outdid himself in amusingly adoring letters. Lewis was restless again after she returned, and the couple went to the Monterey peninsula in California. Thompson thought it sensationally beautiful, "rejuvenating for the body and degenerating for the mind." They then went back to New York, where she gave birth to baby Michael Lewis on June 20, 1930.[46]

Moscow HAD MARKED a turning point. Being alone there, and missing Sinclair Lewis, made Thompson sure she should marry him—a decision that relocated her and radically changed her emotional circumstances and her career. Now she was no longer a foreign correspondent, and she lived in the United States. But her background experiences gave her plenty of material to use in speaking to the curious public in the United States, as she did, for example, at a luncheon in New York hosted by the Foreign Policy Association in January 1929. There she was called upon to speak on "Russia Today" to an illustrious audience, along with economist Paul Douglas, who had been a technical adviser to the American Trade Union Delegation.[47]

International journalism had put Thompson in that position; she was far from wanting to abandon it. But she would have to reinvent her journalist self to stay in the field.

Moscow brought a crushing finale for Rayna Raphaelson, ending her life at thirty-three and closing the curtain on four life-defining years. "One of those flaming personalities who leave a blaze of light behind them," Lewis Gannett wrote in a tribute in *The Nation*. "She groped, as most young Americans do in this erratic age. . . . She drifted to China . . . and there she suddenly ceased drifting. She became a part of the rising tide of Chinese Nationalism." In the *New York Times* notice of her death, Moscow correspondent Walter Duranty waxed sentimental: "She might have lived easily at home," he wrote, "but she preferred to live dangerously in China," giving "her whole being to the Chinese revolution."[48]

The finale of Rayna's life in Moscow reframed Jimmy Sheean's outlook. His memory of her became his polestar, an ideal of political courage against which he would measure himself. She had "inflexibly resolved," he wrote, "never to lie down under the monstrous system of the world."[49] Her death wrested away his closeness to a revolutionary model. Sheean felt this as a tragic burden, which he would lift by writing her story himself.

CHAPTER 7

SHADOWS OVER EUROPE

JOHN GUNTHER ARRIVED in Moscow in June 1928, six months after Dorothy Thompson and Jimmy Sheean left. He was there in his role as "swing man" for the *Chicago Daily News*, replacing the vacationing bureau chief, Junius Wood, whose company Thompson had enjoyed. While many foreign correspondents moved from one newspaper to another, or left the field after a few years as Thompson and Sheean did, Gunther remained with the *News* for a long time. His grit, speed, and flexibility made him very effective at the job. The Chicago paper's excellent reputation in foreign news continued and gave him national exposure through syndication.[1]

As a correspondent, Gunther implicitly embraced the professional ethics of objectivity that Sheean had found confining. He took it for granted that reporters' scruples maintained the integrity of the press, and that quality reporting should be objective, meaning clearly distinguishing between "fact" and "opinion." In the 1930s, nonetheless, thoughtful reporters like Gunther who adhered to the modern standard came to see it was something of a chimera, a goal never to be perfectly reached. Real-world political situations had many angles; "facts" could be construed in more than one way. The best-intentioned reporter might find it a hard road to establish facts objectively viewed and uncolored by subjective judgment.[2] Seasoned reporters working in Europe felt this paradox keenly as they witnessed one political shift after another. The complex and ominous developments they saw demanded interpretation. And not only Fascist Italy's and Soviet Russia's disdain for freedom of the press but also the increasing number of European governments that used censorship and propaganda to control information mounted challenges to the best of the American correspondents.

GUNTHER'S MOSCOW PLACEMENT came with unfortunately bad timing. He was missing the European visit of his mother and sister, a trip he had arranged and paid for; and Frances, at home in Paris, was pregnant. The baby was due in October, and Gunther worried that the *News* would keep him in Moscow past the birth. Eager to be a father, he sent loving wishes to Frances and the baby-to-be virtually every day, assuring her, "I adore you. I worship what you are and what you are going to be." He was proud of his recent raise to $6,600 a year (nearly $100,000 in today's dollars) and wrote to Frances, "Now on to $10,000!"[3]

In Moscow, the demands of his job filtered his experiences of the Soviet system. To produce news reports, he had to navigate one irritating hurdle after another: surveillance on the telephone, gaps in public information, delays for exaggeratedly detailed bureaucratic niceties, and finally, censorship of his outgoing articles. To calm himself, he tried to focus on the historic break made by the Bolsheviks: "I am witnessing what is certainly the most profound social and political experiment since the French Revolution, and one as likely (I do think) to survive and proselytize," he wrote to Frances. "I think that my emotions here are just what they would be had I lived in Paris in 1793. That was Progress. With a big P. So is this. Anyone would be a fool to deny it. And I arrive home definitely uplifted."[4]

Nonetheless, Gunther found it difficult (as Thompson had) to stomach the Soviet Union's most avid American champions, such as Frances Gunther's old friend Harry Dana. Gunther ran into Dana sitting two seats away at Moscow's opera house, with a "dreadful" boyfriend, and at first was happy to talk with him (after insisting that Dana drop the boyfriend "in the nearest gutter"). But he admitted to Frances his adverse reactions to Dana's enthusiasm. "I stiffen against him, and invariably say things I don't really believe, exaggerating my conservative tendencies to offset his radicalism. Result: he thinks I'm a dreadful Tory, an anti-Bol[shevik], and so on; whereas, the way I'm feeling now, I'm quite on the other side."[5]

Gunther's reactions in Moscow stopped up his usual productivity. After three weeks he had not been able to compose even one mail story, which was rare for him. "The more I hear about Russia the less I know," he lamented; both from reading and from talking to people, he became "more uncertain day by day," just as Thompson had. Most of the other American journalists Gunther found in Moscow favored what the Soviets were trying to do, including Walter Duranty, the *New York Times* Moscow correspondent, and Louis Fischer, a *Nation* writer who usually lived in Moscow with his Russian wife. Gunther berated himself, "I wish I would get over my predisposition to <u>balance</u>. It makes me so damned fair."[6] Reporters were supposed to be objective and fair. That he felt abashed about "seeing both sides" reflected the high degree of political attachment among his friends and peers.

After a few more weeks he did begin to write long features, publishing a series that Frances, often his severest critic, loved. "All the pieces had that peculiar charm of familiarness & intimacy with a place & people which is one of the chief powers of your style," she praised him. She went on to suggest ways to sharpen his comparison of Mussolini's and Lenin's ideas. He always welcomed her advice. "Frances is certainly the most intelligent woman I have ever met," he reflected later. "It took me 3 years to realize this." She was filling in for John to some extent at the Paris office of the *News* while he was gone and proved herself quite competent there. At home, she made no pretense of domestic skills and prepared for the baby's arrival by hiring a cook and a baby nurse.[7]

In Moscow Gunther was often lonely. With plenty of time to think, he ruminated long and hard about his future, going through a "severe intensification" of his "recurrent crisis . . . the old business of my driving in tandem—trying to do two things, write & work for a newspaper—and as a result doing neither of them really well." He thought it was time to choose. But he didn't choose. He kept switching back and forth. In July, after a long spate of reasoning, he decided on journalism, because his skill with facts was greater than his imagination; journalism also promised a straighter path to influence. But by early September—after fantasizing that it would be easy to return to Chicago, get into financial journalism and then into finance, and make a pile of money—he chose fiction writing. That year, 1928, was the height of the boom in the United States, with many young men getting suddenly rich in the stock market and a celebrity culture blooming. Gunther's fantasies were unsurprising—and they passed quickly. He decided to stick with the *News* as a "meal ticket" but also continue to write; he had a new novel in progress and ideas for several more. "The thing which does interest me more than anything is human nature," he acknowledged. He counted that inclination on the fiction side of the ledger, but it would color his nonfiction writing as much.[8]

By the time Frances gave birth on September 25, a week early, Gunther had made it back to Paris. They were thrilled with their little girl, naming her Judy. Tragically, she died suddenly in her crib just four months later. The baby's death came on top of another grief for John—his mother's death. The Gunthers had gone hurriedly to Chicago with the baby after learning at Christmastime that John's mother was mortally ill. They arrived ten days too late to see Lizette Gunther alive. Little more than a week later, Judy died from what doctors afterward labeled an unsuspected thymus abnormality. The shock and loss were especially hard on Frances. She felt she was being punished for her several abortions, and a self-lacerating guilt trailed her for the rest of her life. Fortunately, Frances became pregnant again almost immediately, and the Gunthers' marriage survived their grief. John buried his distress, never talked about it, and went back to work.[9]

GUNTHER TRAVELED LITTLE in 1929, until August, when he was sent to Palestine, which was under British administration as a consequence of the great powers' postwar division of the former Ottoman lands. Though it was in an Arab region, Palestine had for several decades been the destination of Zionist settlers from Britain, Europe, and Russia, who aimed to make it a Jewish homeland. In Jerusalem that August, bloody conflict between Arabs and Jews erupted at the Western Wall, a sacrosanct site for both. Each side blamed the other's unwarranted provocation.

Arriving a week after the initial rioting, Gunther tried to sort out what had happened. "I have never had such a tough story to cover," he wrote to Frances once he had been in Jerusalem a few days. "There is no real paper, no official bulletin, no sources, no anything. To cover this story properly means going to the governorate, the deputy commissioner, British headquarters, Zionist Exec[utive], Arab executive, and police twice in a day, and then distilling fact out of the filthiest mess of rumor, slander, lies, prejudice I have ever run into. The way feeling does run here! . . . [and] the resident news people are the closest, stingiest most cub-reportishly jealous crowd I've ever worked with, and a whole batch of high-power shoulder-slapping British war correspondents are worse."[10]

Fortunately for Gunther, Jimmy Sheean was already there. He had been in Jerusalem for more than two months—a "godsend" for Gunther in terms of understanding what was going on. The two men stayed up all night talking, trying to beat the stifling heat by staying outdoors on the roof of the Austrian hospice where Sheean was living. Sheean had been at loose ends in Paris when he decided to go to Palestine to live in one of the communal agricultural settlements that Zionists had planted, to write about it. He floated a proposal to the editor of *The New Palestine* (journal of the Zionist Organization of

America) and quickly got a commission and an advance. Beyond his typical desire to get away, Sheean made the move partly in homage to his recent heroes, Borodin and Rayna, both of them Jews. Ever since his shameful freshman episode fleeing the fraternity, Sheean had become aware of Jews and professed himself an admirer of Jewish traditions, Jewish contributions to international culture, and the "subtle and intense qualities of the Jewish mind."[11]

Sheean's arrival in Jerusalem in June 1929 disrupted his equanimity—and his plans. Palestine struck him forcefully as an Arab country, in which "the Zionist Jews (that is, the modern Jews) were as foreign to it as I was myself." The stark conflict between Arab preexisting settlement and Zionist claims, which had been given life by Britain's Balfour Declaration of 1917, jumped out at him. That war-drawn document promised British approval and support of "the establishment in Palestine of a national home for the Jewish people," but it also promised that "nothing shall be done which may prejudice the civil and religious rights of existing non-Jewish communities in Palestine."

The incompatibility of these two desiderata gripped Sheean. He found the Zionist enterprise dangerously misplaced in an Arab land, and he sympathized with Arab resentment of the Jewish settlers. The postwar British mandate over the area seemed to him a relic of imperialism. Conversations with George Antonius, a high official in the British administration and an urbane, secular Lebanese man, a Greek Orthodox Christian raised in Egypt, had clarified his views. (The Bloomsbury writer E. M. Forster, a friend of Raymond Mortimer, had given Sheean a letter of introduction to Antonius.)[12]

In early July, Sheean canceled his contract with *The New Palestine* and returned the advance, though he had no other financial backing. As he watched petty conflicts over the use of the Western Wall rising during the summer, he contacted the North American Newspaper Alliance (NANA) and was authorized as its special correspondent. The mounting tensions between Arabs and Zionists burst into horrific violence in the last ten days of August. Mayhem spread from the Western Wall to areas farther away, leaving scores of Jews and Arabs dead and hundreds injured. When an attack by Arabs killed a dozen American students at a rabbinic school, outrage filled American newspapers' front pages. Zionists in New York mobilized large rallies, protesting British laxity in allowing the outbreak. (Britain eventually sent battleships to the coast and imposed a state of emergency in Palestine to stop the violence.) Since very few American newspapers had their own reporters in Palestine, they got their information from the US-based Jewish Telegraphic Agency and emphasized Arab violence only.[13]

Sheean's interpretation differed. As an eyewitness to the violence, he was sure that an extremist faction, the Revisionist Zionists led by Vladimir Zabotinsky, had purposely instigated the major conflicts. Although his distress at seeing the deadly results of the Arab massacre of rabbinical students sent him to bed for three days, he interpreted the Arab action as a response to intentional provocations by the Revisionists. In his reporting, Sheean called these extremists "Zionist fascisti," likening them to the thuggish vigilantes who supported Mussolini. "Fiery Zionist Fascisti 'Spoiling for a Fight' Blamed for Massacre" headlined a dispatch by Sheean in the *Toronto Daily Star*, for example. Since he cabled his dispatches, Sheean did not write the headlines, but he used the word *fascisti* in his text and NANA newspapers typically put it in the headline. After Sheean's article appeared in the *New York World*, which had a large Jewish readership, three thousand letters of protest bombarded the editor.[14]

Sticking to his convictions, Sheean testified under oath to Britain's official inquiry following the crisis. He was pleasantly surprised that the British Commission's authoritative Palestine Report vindicated his view. He nonetheless worried about being accused of anti-Semitism when he returned to the United States to embark on a lecture tour. Though no anti-Semite, he thought the Arabs in Palestine had the right to the land. Small numbers of American Zionists

James Vincent Sheean sightseeing in Egypt, 1930.
Source: Private collection, Ellen Sheean and Jane Morton, London.

did hound him as a result. He made it clear that he did not blame Zionism as the root of the conflict, but rather Britain's impossible wartime promise to both sides.[15]

Gunther, while admiring Sheean for being so principled as to return his advance and sacrifice his entrée with American Zionists, remained neutral. "With the Jews I am aggressively independent. With the Arabs ditto," Gunther wrote home. "So the Jews think I am pro-Arab, and the Arabs think I am pro-Jew." While he shared Sheean's assessment that Zionists had instigated the crisis, he did not say so in print. Instead, he sidestepped the issue of who initiated or incited the escalating conflicts (a matter still debated today) in an article on the tangled situation in *Harper's New Monthly Magazine*. With a terrific knack for rendering complex situations deftly, he explained the dilemma with sufficient nuance to make the players and their stakes comprehensible. After sketching the wartime Balfour Declaration, Jewish in-migration to Palestine since 1917, the contiguity of the holy sites for Islam and Judaism, Arab resentment of Jewish settlement, and Zionist disdain of Arabs, he located the cause of the strife in Britain's self-imposed commitment to facilitate a national home for Jews in Palestine *without* prejudicing the rights of Arab peoples there. These were incompatible promises. The British garrison called upon to quell the hostilities would have to stay, Gunther concluded, because the contesting claims by Zionist and Arab inhabitants were not going away.[16]

Gunther's and Sheean's different reactions in Palestine expressed succinctly the contrasting political and reportorial styles of the two men. Both were very effective journalists, but in different ways. Gunther managed to stay level-headedly neutral and to produce clear informational background in conflicted political circumstances, while Sheean got engaged and excited one way or the other and wrote passionately what he thought, regardless of enraging some readers. They appreciated each other's skills and insights.

Though they had been two ships passing in the dark at the University of Chicago ten years earlier, a lasting friendship sprang out of their experiences together in Jerusalem. Still, their personal revelations went only so far. Gunther, who spoke often about the child he and Frances were expecting, uttered not a word about Judy's death. Sheean revealed nothing about his sexual life. In fact he was worried about detection of his "private vices" in Jerusalem if the post office was opening his mail, as he suspected. He warned Raymond Mortimer to be very discreet in writing and to tell Eddy Sackville-West the same. Despite being "sex-starved," he told Mortimer, he had "ignored any opportunities which may have offered *du coté des Arabes*. . . . So it is to be a coward."[17]

GUNTHER'S LIFE GAINED a more stable rhythm in 1930 when the *Chicago Daily News*, recognizing his abilities, made him chief of its foreign desk in Vienna. He was responsible for covering Austria, Hungary, Czechoslovakia, Romania, Yugoslavia, Bulgaria, and Albania. Marcel Fodor, the knowledgeable and generous *Manchester Guardian* correspondent, helped Gunther, as he had helped Thompson, to dig in quickly. The Vienna desk was a promotion and a weighty responsibility, but as compared to his earlier role as roving correspondent its demands were more predictable. That allowed Gunther to write more articles for American magazines. With an acute sense of the European questions likely to interest the American public, he began to place pieces fairly regularly in *Harper's* (owned by the publisher of his novel) and *The Nation*. Frances often suggested topics and offered him cues that produced some of his best analyses. She had given birth on November 4, 1929, to a boy they named John Jr., and in Vienna, the relatively low cost of living meant they could rent a spacious flat and have a housekeeper/cook and a nanny for the baby.[18]

The political fortunes of the areas Gunther covered had shifted radically to the right since Thompson had reported from there in 1925. A menacing trend toward authoritarianism was obvious in much of Europe in the 1920s. In eight European nations, including Austria's neighbors Yugoslavia, Bulgaria, and Poland, representative parliaments were pushed aside by 1930 as authoritarian leaders took over, whipping up nationalism and cultivating popular support by doing so. "Liberalism is on the point of closing the doors of its deserted temple," Benito Mussolini, who had led the way with his Fascist state in Italy, waxed eloquent on the coming triumph of programs like his: "The present century is the century of authority, a century of the Right, the Fascist century." Austria's parliament still operated in 1930, but it was under attack by Austrian fascists and would not last for long.[19]

The political values that most Americans took for granted in their own constitutional government were fast losing ground in Europe. Financial panic and rising unemployment arrested far more American attention when the stock market crash in October 1929 ended

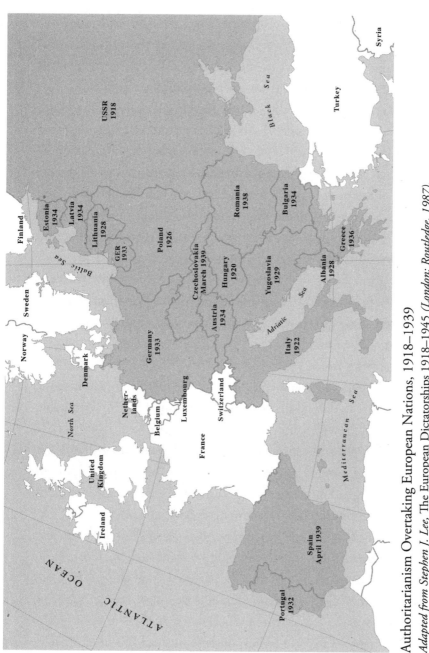

Authoritarianism Overtaking European Nations, 1918–1939

Adapted from Stephen J. Lee, The European Dictatorships 1918–1945 (London: Routledge, 1987).

The date on each country is the year when its representative form of government succumbed to takeover by an internal authoritarian or fascist leader, except for Czechoslovakia, occupied by Germany in March 1939, and Spain, where the Republicans in the Spanish Civil War surrendered to Franco's Nationalist forces in April 1939.

the financial boom. As the economic downturn spread through the world economy, however, it further darkened the political landscape; authoritarian leaders in Europe gained power and adherents by claiming to have solutions for people's economic woes.[20]

Gunther and several other European correspondents for major newspapers repeatedly alerted Americans to the alarming political trend in Europe. Yet their own abilities to report the situation fully and accurately became questionable under authoritarian rule, where freedom of the press was not a value and was handily compromised or quashed. Governments in the countries Gunther covered in Central and Eastern Europe broadcast propaganda as information, and censored what could be learned, read, or written about political affairs. Longtime foreign correspondent George Seldes, who had been expelled from Mussolini's Italy and from Soviet Russia for trying to reveal what these governments wanted to hide, argued in his 1929 book *You Can't Print That* that governments all over Europe prevented the truth from getting out.[21]

Gunther believed he could still do the job well. Countering Seldes, he rose to defend his craft in *Harper's* in 1930, in "Funneling the European News." Without slighting the problems of press control, propaganda, and censorship by reigning governments (and also acknowledging possible biases in reporters or newspaper editors or owners), he argued nonetheless that clever and expert correspondents could and did produce trustworthy news from abroad.

He outlined the pitfalls foreign correspondents encountered and the techniques that he and others used to rise above them. Correspondents in places where the press only parroted what the government wanted to say, Gunther explained, could no longer rely on scouring local newspapers as a major step. Such newspapers were poor guides to the real news. Effective correspondents instead found alternative sources, such as trustworthy local informants; they listened to government spokesmen through a filter of practiced shrewdness; they shared tips with other foreign journalists and used collective wisdom to assess whether political rumors were true or false. To get around censorship in sending their dispatches, they looked for modes of expression and techniques of transmission that were more likely to escape the censors.[22]

The good correspondent should know "personally someone who can tell him quickly and authoritatively what he wants," Gunther wrote, stressing the prime importance of reliable contacts in getting beyond rumors and propaganda. Information-gathering became a "process of reciprocal barter between friends . . . who give news to him and to whom in return he passes on what he knows."[23] That was his own modus operandi. In Vienna, Gunther socialized with local journalists and political figures as well as with American and foreign journalists based there or passing through. A genial glad-hander who viewed all his social life as a crucial way to nourish contacts who might have leads, he thrived in the Vienna coffeehouse culture, knowing how to find his correspondent pals at a chosen regular hour in a chosen coffeehouse, as well as where to find the largest array of newspapers. Gunther's growing love for Vienna became a bond between him and Dorothy Thompson, for it was her favorite city, too.

THOMPSON FOUND HER way back to Europe in 1930, the same year that the Gunthers relocated in Vienna. The stupendous news that Sinclair Lewis had won the Nobel Prize in Literature came to the couple at the end of a summer spent at Twin Farms, where Thompson had enjoyed doting on new baby Mickey (as they called Michael). Of course they made plans to go to the prize ceremony in Stockholm. They had no compunctions about leaving Mickey at home when they departed in the fall. Even when his parents were nearby, he was raised mostly by a nursemaid. At Twin Farms he stayed with his nurse in the smaller house because Lewis could not stand the presence of children when he was writing.[24]

Thompson welcomed the transatlantic journey, and not only for her husband's glory. She had missed Europe—missed the cosmopolitan scenes, and the other foreign correspondents, and being one among them—and she thought ahead about what she might make of being there. In advance of leaving, she shrewdly made an arrangement with the *Saturday Evening Post* to publish any articles she might write. The *Post* was the best-selling general magazine in America, flagship of the Curtis Publishing Company, which also owned the *Philadelphia Public Ledger*, Thompson's former employer. Readers of the *Post* found short stories, jokes, and poems, and long substantive articles on domestic or international political issues, as well as occasional features about celebrities or upper-class sporting life. The magazine's subscribers increased from two million in 1930 to three million in 1938 despite the Depression. Its circulation dwarfed that of *The New Republic*, *The Nation*, *Harper's*, *Scribner's*, and the *Atlantic Monthly*, each having around ten thousand subscribers. As a result, the *Post* had the highest advertising revenue of all magazines and paid its contributors extremely well.[25]

The couple's week in Stockholm in November 1930 was crammed with full-dress Nobel Prize events, about which Thompson wrote for the *Post*. They continued on to Berlin, celebrating the holidays with friends, including John and Frances Gunther, who came from Vienna to Berlin to be with them. Lewis then departed for London while Thompson stayed in Berlin.

She was stunned by what was taking place in Germany. In September 1930, the Nazi Party had won 107 seats in the Reichstag (the federal parliament), up from its previous 12. The party's propaganda successfully exploited the harsh economic downturn: unemployment had jumped even higher in Germany than in the United States at the start of the Great Depression.

Thompson got a powerful first impression by squeezing in among an overflow crowd in the Berlin *Sportpalast* to hear a speech delivered by Joseph Goebbels, Hitler's right-hand man. Military music and uniformed shock troops hopped up the crowd in a hall fluttering with swastika-emblazoned flags. Banners proclaimed "Adolf Hitler Leads Us into a Better Future." Thompson watched fifteen thousand people thrust out their right arms in the Nazi salute and shout

"Heil!" at the entry of Goebbels—who looked "wizened, club-footed and frenetic" to her. He declaimed for two hours on the single theme of Germany's financial and spiritual ruin at the hands of the victors of the world war.[26]

As if a match were lit, Thompson was on fire. Her consternation blazed across the pages of the *Saturday Evening Post*. For herself as much as for her readers she was scrambling to analyze how the modern, admirably civilized, industrially advanced social democratic Weimar Republic could have made way for the popular rise of the Nazi Party. In lengthy articles she examined Germany's disastrous economic conditions—inflation, unemployment, and state indebtedness—and reasoned that young German men's restiveness and lack of economic opportunity primed them for violence. She saw private military forces rising on both right and left. She also wrote about the noxious upswing in national chauvinism and the fragility of parliamentary institutions in several European countries besides Germany.[27]

Thompson returned to Germany in the fall of 1931 for a second visit after spring and summer with her husband and son at Twin Farms. She saw hundreds of thousands of people massing in "monster demonstrations" and felt that revolutionary change was under way. The growing appeal of Adolf Hitler, whose brownshirted storm troops were killing Communists in street battles, defied Thompson's understanding of leadership, of rationality, and of German character. She secured an interview with Hitler—quite a journalistic coup, because he previously had refused interviews with foreigners. Her article about him was published in March 1932 under the screaming title "I Saw Hitler!" with large photographs of Hitler splashed over two pages. It was quickly rushed into print as a very short book, too.[28]

Thompson portrayed Hitler as "the very prototype of the 'Little Man,'" with whom hundreds of thousands of other Little Men—peasants and petty bourgeois who felt the brunt of Germany's economic collapse—could identify. He set himself up "to be loved with fanaticism and emotional abandon," gripping his followers in a "camp meeting atmosphere," she wrote, appealing to "invisible realities, to the emotions, to faith rather than to reason." As an agitator, he was a "genius . . . the most golden-tongued of demagogues"— though what he said, "read next day in cold news print, is usually plain nonsense."

She recognized how central to Hitler's method was his scapegoating of Jews, a point barely noted yet in the American press. Without his insistence that "the Jew" was the root of all problems, she wrote, "the whole thing, both the economic program and the racial, collapses." Having read Hitler's master work *Mein Kampf* thoroughly, she pointed to his contradictory claims that Jews were "worthless democrats and blood-thirsty plutocrats . . . unimaginative rationalists and mystic international conspirators; ritual murderers and bloodless intellectuals, . . . they are dangerous assimilationists and a foreign element in the body politic." Logic did not matter, Thompson concluded. Hitler did not care about gaining intellectuals' approval for his reasoning. Nor did he care about truth. He "does not shrink from lying," she wrote, "nor from advocating the use of the lie" to his purpose.[29]

Thompson invoked American parallels, knowing that the United States, too, harbored illiberal popular impulses like those fostering the Nazi Party, and leaders happy to pump them up. To convey to American readers the phenomenon of Hitler's appeal, she asked them to imagine someone who combined the speaking talents of silver-tongued statesman William Jennings Bryan and crowd-pleasing evangelist Aimée Semple MacPherson, with the publicity skills of Edward Bernays (father of modern advertising) and Ivy Lee, a giant in public relations. This imagined American orator would "unite all the farmers, with all the white-collar unemployed, all the people with salaries under $3000 a year who have lost their savings in bank collapses and the stock market . . . [with] the louder evangelical preachers, the American Legion, the Daughters of the American Revolution, the Ku Klux Klan, the Woman's Christian Temperance

Union . . . and Henry Ford—imagine that, and you will have some idea of what the Hitler movement in Germany means," she wrote.[30]

Though Thompson presented Hitler's modus operandi tellingly, her article soon became an embarrassment. She claimed that this "Little Man" was of such "startling insignificance" that he would never succeed in becoming Germany's dictator. Less than a year later, Hitler assumed power. Thompson was not the only American journalist who underestimated Hitler at that time—just the one to make a bold and mistaken prediction. H. R. Knickerbocker, for example, Thompson's successor in Berlin, thought Hitler was a far weaker person than Mussolini, and in a private letter described him as "a homo-sexual, effeminate corporal with a hyper-sensitive political olfactory nerve," likely to "wilt like a lettuce leaf in hot water" when opposed.[31]

Shaken by events in Germany, Thompson returned in the spring of 1932 to her husband and baby, now living in a new apartment in New York on East 90th Street. She returned to a fraying marriage. Blowups between her and Lewis seemed fatal to their relationship that spring—but once the family moved to Twin Farms in May, the calmer environment there smoothed things over. Lewis was writing a novel with an independent woman at the center, drawing noticeably on Thompson's life and character. The story resonated with admiration of earnestly do-good, small-town-bred values like Thompson's, though its protagonist, Ann Vickers, found her calling as a prison reformer rather than a journalist and her rocky love experiences also differed. Lewis dedicated the book to Thompson, crediting her help for enabling him to write the fictional character. Fifty thousand copies of *Ann Vickers* sold in its first month, and the huge sales (eventually 133,849 copies) bolstered his confidence that he had not lost his touch.[32]

On Thompson's strong initiative (since she planned to go whether or not Lewis did), their family of three went together to live in Vienna for the winter of 1932–1933. Besides renting a flat in town, Thompson took a comfortable villa in the Semmering, an Alpine recreation spot two hours' ride out of town, for the holidays. She planned a holiday house party and beckoned many friends to come stay for a week or more—Marcel Fodor and his wife, H. R. Knickerbocker and his, the Gunthers with their little boy, Johnny Jr., Thompson's sister Peggy and her little daughter, Lillian and Edgar Mowrer, and quite a few others. A cosmopolitan crowd in their thirties and forties, they arrived anticipating rich meals, parlor games, tobogganing, scintillating conversation, and plenty of alcohol long into the night.[33]

One of the guests was Christa Winsloe, a Hungarian writer and artist schooled in Germany. Thompson had known her in the 1920s as a sculptor and society hostess married to an acquaintance of Josef Bard, the Baron Ladislas Hatvany, who also came to the house party although the couple had since divorced. Five years older than Thompson, Winsloe was sophisticated and languorously beautiful, wearing her dark hair in a fashionable mannish style. She had recently become celebrated for her book and stage play about a schoolgirl's out-of-bounds crush on her teacher in a harshly authoritarian all-girls' school. Both story and play, based on Winsloe's own schooling, expressed a politics of antiauthoritarianism by bringing such a forbidden private relationship into public expression. Winsloe's play ended with the girl committing suicide. A female director then turned the narrative into a favorably reviewed film called *Madchen in Uniform* (1931)—somewhat of a *succes de scandale* because of its all-woman cast and theme—and together with the cast transformed the ending so as to affirm love between women. Reviewers of the film minimized suggestions of lesbianism, however, usually interpreting the girl's feelings as an adolescent crush and emphasizing her rejection of the school's authoritarian rule.[34]

Re-meeting Winsloe, Thompson reeled from the erotic charge she felt. "So it has happened to me again, after all these years," she wrote in her diary immediately afterward, jolted by her response. It was not the first time she had been deeply attracted to a woman. She remembered her reverential attachment to a genteelly impressive older woman who favored her during suffragist days—a relationship of maternal longing more than anything else. She also thought back defensively to a Berlin episode when a woman had come on to her and she had responded out of "curiosity," later regretting it: "In the end I hated (and feared) her," deciding that the physical act of "sapphic love" was "a perversion of a love for a man," Thompson protested to her diary. It was "weak" and "ridiculous."

"I'm not that, I'm a heterosexual," she affirmed, writing those words in German. Was she imagining addressing Winsloe? Perhaps she was unaware that the word *heterosexual*, coined in German, now had an English equivalent.[35] Feeling astonished by the "extraordinarily intense erotic feeling" that Winsloe's casual kisses and touches provoked, Thompson told her diary, "I have got to go on writing about this in an attempt to objectify it." How to understand "the sudden indescribable charm in that too-soft face, and the heavy-lidded eyes. . . . Only to be near her; to touch her when I went by"?[36]

It was no wonder Thompson troubled to define her own reactions. Lesbianism inhabited a shifting terrain. Berlin in the 1920s had offered extraordinary space for queer self-presentation and same-sex love, but by the end of the decade, conservative and Nazi rhetoric had made homosexuality a symbol of repulsive degeneration. Similarly, in the United States, the sexualization of social life among bohemians and artists in the 1920s gave some room for bisexuality to be seen in those circles as an illustration of sexual freedom. Lesbian lives could be maintained privately and discreetly in many locations, so long as women partners looked conventionally feminine or were married to men. That kind of latitude contracted during the Depression, as economic hard times made people more conservative on gender roles, while the movies made "sex appeal" a leading part of personality, and heterosexual desire came to be seen as central to defining who men and women were. The up-and-coming young social scientist Margaret Mead, who had passionate sexual relationships with women and with men in the 1920s, watched the tide turn with trepidation. By 1935, she warned other women of achievement that "a person without full sex membership is worse off than a man

without a country." "Full sex membership" implied heterosexual desire as well as conventionally feminine or masculine looks.[37]

Thompson wrestled with her feeling that she was in love. Winsloe's
presence evoked a "strange, soft feeling . . . of being at home, and at
rest . . . a pervading warm tenderness" that stirred her to the core.
"What in God's name does one call this sensibility if it be not love?"
she asked herself in her diary. "This extraordinary heightening of all
one's impressions, this intensification of sensitiveness; this complete
identification of feeling?" She did not know whether Winsloe reciprocated her feelings. She insisted to herself that all she wanted
was "a warm friendship and the opportunity to go on loving her no
more articulately than heretofore." Yet merely speaking the name
"Christa" held magic: "Like holding an amulet in your hand, that
was what saying her name is like. I love this woman. There it stands,
and makes the word love applied to any other woman in the world
ridiculous."[38]

The house party ended when the new year began, and the two
women said farewell. Thompson felt happy to be alone with her husband again, appreciating him and their little son and feeling unusually
affectionate. Her awakened sensuality spilled into a night of unex-
pected and unprotected marital loving. She found it all satisfying—
though she told her diary that "all the time I thought of Christa."
Could these attachments of hers run on parallel tracks? She became
pregnant and imagined contentedly that her marriage had reached a
new plateau. But it was very brief. She miscarried within a month.
In February, Lewis began drinking again and became violent.[39] Her
resort from overwrought emotions was to go back to work, which
meant going back to Germany.

Thompson was in Berlin when the Reichstag, the parliament
building, exploded in flames at the end of February 1933. John
Gunther was there, too, for the *Chicago Daily News*. Even though
Germany was not his territory, he had come on January 30, when the
German president Paul von Hindenburg appointed Hitler as chan-
cellor, forming a coalition government between the conservatives

and the Nazis—but in effect giving political control to Hitler. The jubilation among Nazis and their supporters the night of January 30 was terrific. A huge parade organized by Goebbels marched through Berlin from seven to after midnight. Twenty thousand or more uniformed SS guards, brownshirts, and civilians carried lighted torches and chanted songs as they filled the streets, spurring an uproar of cheering from crowds of onlookers. "Everyone could have fallen into everyone else's arms in the name of Hitler," one woman said. Gunther described Hitler to Frances as "very flabby and feminine, talks with his arms wound round his bosom, husky throaty voice, great sex appeal." He found Goebbels more impressive: "a dapper little man with carefully polished black hair, who drew noises out of the audience—cheers or moans or boos—with the methodical regularity of an engineer playing with organ pipes. . . . Very Billy Sunday-Aimée Macpherson."[40]

Gunther subsequently wrote a penetrating article on the politics of the Reichstag fire, called "Arson de Luxe," published in *Harper's*. It was published anonymously, for worry that Nazi authorities would ban him from Germany if his name appeared. Though a lone crazed perpetrator was found to have set the fire, the Nazi Party immediately circulated accusations that Communists were plotting to take over the government. The party meant to derail votes for Communist delegates in the upcoming March elections. This worked. With Nazi storm troopers terrorizing the opposition, civil rights suspended by emergency decree, and the conservative coalition government in control of press and radio, the Nazi Party gained 44 percent of the March vote. Hitler then jailed most of the Communists who were elected, giving the Nazi Party a majority in a legislature of diminished numbers.[41]

Hitler's party achieved power this way in March 1933 and dispatched his storm troopers over the following year to attack, arrest, and jail—or murder—as many Social Democrats and Communists as possible. Franklin Delano Roosevelt was inaugurated as president of the United States that same month, in an environment of deepening economic crisis: American industrial production had sunk to half of what it was in 1929, and nearly a quarter of the American labor force was unemployed.

Thompson watched the Nazi triumph with unbelieving eyes. The ubiquity of Nazi propaganda, the prohibition and punishment of independent opinion, the terrorizing force of street violence, and the threatening omnipresence of the secret police (the Gestapo) altogether sickened her. She rued her initial miscalculation about Hitler's capacities, seeing that he could speak "utter nonsense" and "still overcome a whole world." Nazi election propaganda "appealed to the basest instincts—hatred, envy, greed, vanity and cheap heroics," she wrote to Lewis. She saw Nazi storm troopers march in formation and bark "with a horrible monotony" the words "Judah Verrecke [Perish the Jews]." They beat up Socialists, Communists, and pacifists as well as Jews with "sadistic and pathological hatred," she said. Italian Fascism seemed to her a mere "kindergarten" compared to the German variety.[42]

Thompson had just read Aldous Huxley's dystopian novel *Brave New World* (1932). As she observed the Nazis implementing their policy of *Gleichschaltung* (roughly translated as "coordination")— which required every government agency, every civil society group, every profession, ultimately every individual, to conform with Nazi dictates—she thought it bore an eerie likeness to the eugenically bred and internally regimented society in Huxley's novel. In Nazi Germany as in *Brave New World*, she wrote, "Nobody will long for any other kind of life, because nobody will get reports of any other kind of life." If anything went wrong, the one out-group, the Jews, always regarded as an alien presence and "a disturbing, decomposing element," was sure "to bear the brunt of the blame."[43]

As she left Berlin in the spring of 1933 Thompson did not return to Lewis, but joined Christa Winsloe in a house Winsloe had rented in Portofino, on the Italian Riviera. How far in advance that reunion had been planned is unclear, but Winsloe had room for Thompson, her little son, and a German child-nurse to stay. Letters flew back and forth between Thompson and Lewis, often loving in tenor, but their relationship remained wobbly. "I thought: I must save myself," she wrote to him from Portofino. "I must, really, now save myself." She felt he was "remote and cold" and remembered how much Josef Bard had hurt her. "I really tried hard not to love you," she told him. "Only," she concluded, "I do love you. I love you too terribly. . . . We've got to go on together, forever, and be kind to each other." For six weeks, nonetheless, she and Winsloe luxuriated in the spring sun of Portofino, contentedly sharing an intense and sweet intimacy while each of them wrote for many hours a day. Thompson did not see the relationship as affecting her sexual identity: this love was "as incarnal as the air," she wrote in a sonnet. To brush off a seeming caution from Lewis, she wrote to him, "have no fears, I ain't thataway. But I am somewhat otherwise and I miss my husband, damn it, frightfully."[44] Did the lady protest too much?

Both women later recalled those six weeks as an idyllic time in their relationship, although the Nazi juggernaut did not halt for them. The articles Thompson wrote in Portofino for the *Saturday Evening Post* pulsed with her alarmed perception that Hitler was preparing for war, disregarding that the Versailles settlement had prohibited German rearmament. She simmered with fury, dumbfounded that Hitler could bamboozle the German people with arguments that hashed the facts. His "only genius," she wrote, was "his power of mass suggestion. . . . He has hypnotized his followers with a vast myth." Picturing Germany as utterly bankrupt, in need of Nazi redemption, Hitler entranced German audiences by blaming all their woes on the Social Democrats who led Weimar, if not on the Allies' rapacious postwar settlement. His claims were propaganda that could "be exploded by a few statistics," Thompson sputtered. By August 1933, she had published eight *Saturday Evening Post* articles on political and economic developments in Germany, each one immensely informed, lengthy and substantive, and five more of similar heft covering related topics, such as the consequences of the breakup of the Austro-Hungarian Empire. The thirteen composed a stunning compendium of information and analysis.[45]

When Thompson returned to the United States in May 1933, she brought Christa Winsloe with her. "I persuaded her," Thompson told her husband, "because for the moment there is absolutely no opportunity for her in Germany, or for anyone of her attitude of mind." As a cosmopolitan antifascist, Winsloe could no longer live comfortably in Berlin. But it was equally true that Thompson did not want to part from Winsloe. Thompson had carried on flirtations and perhaps sexual affairs with men during her marriage to Lewis, while telling herself that she was "happily married too." In that respect she was in step with male foreign correspondents, who were notoriously hard drinkers and unfaithful spouses who justified their lapses by their mobile and stressful lives. Sex had never been a major factor in her relationship with Lewis and was less important as time went on, possibly urging her into outside sexual relationships. "The idea of the exclusiveness of love" was no talisman to her. She told her diary complacently, in connection with an affair with a man somewhat later, that sexual possessiveness was a mistake; "dilemmas" over multiple attachments need not exist for those who were free and courageous, "because each is a specific and separate relation."[46]

The Thompson-Lewis marriage became a ménage a trois, an uneasy and tentative triangle with Winsloe. It worked better when one of the three was away, which happened frequently, because Lewis's restlessness sent him from place to place, Thompson embarked on a lecture tour for six weeks, and Winsloe pursued her ambitions in other corners of the United States, having a brief affair with a man along the way. Winsloe moved to southern France early in 1934 and continued living there except when she was traipsing after the opera singer Ezio Pinza. (Pinza's attractiveness to women was legendary, and Winsloe had fallen madly for him upon hearing him perform.) Both women acknowledged the next year that their intense relationship was over, though a special tie between them endured.[47]

Thompson returned to Germany in 1934. The baneful power of propaganda impressed—and depressed—her again and again. Hitler had done something unique, as she saw it: "Other dictators have murdered democracy. Hitler persuaded it to commit suicide," she wrote. He had done so by the force of his false words and by clamping down on independent opinion in the German press—quite a feat, because German daily newspapers had previously outnumbered those in France, England, and Italy combined. The Reich also banned and criminalized importation and possession of 254 foreign newspapers and periodicals. The success of false propaganda in leading people to assent to authoritarian leadership infuriated Thompson. "All dictatorships," she declared in a speech, "although they rest their power in the last analysis on force, prefer to wield it by consent, and the propaganda power is the means of securing that consent."[48]

Not only Thompson but all American journalists abroad watched with consternation the increasing hold of authoritarian states over public information. By 1935, three-quarters of the inhabitants of Europe and Russia—over three hundred million people—saw their world through the filters of state censorship and propaganda. The problem spread so rapidly that John Gunther updated his picture of reporting from Europe in a second *Harper's* article. He still claimed that foreign journalists in much of Central Europe could send real news, though less so in Germany, "a graveyard of newspapers." Correspondents found "tipsters"—in other words, spies listened cannily to the government press bureau, and cultivated certain social acquaintances inside and outside government, while trying to protect these sources, who were endangering themselves by providing concealed information.

Although sifting truth from propaganda became much harder, the problem of censorship of dispatches was miraculously reduced in the mid-1930s by improvements in long-distance telephone. The telephone created a "veritable revolution" in sending European and Soviet news across borders. Telephoning was immediate, cheaper than previous methods, and impossible to censor directly (unlike cables and mail). Gunther telephoned his stories to the *News* office in Paris, and from there they went by cable or wireless (radio) to the United States. Correspondents in Berlin, Madrid, Rome, Warsaw did the same.[49]

Beyond print, authoritarian states mobilized the preeminent new technology of mass communication, the radio. "No channel of publicity," Thompson observed, was "more exploited for propaganda purposes, both internally in separate countries, and internationally." Unlike in the United States, where radio programs came from many sources and were supported by commercial sponsors, many European countries created just one state-supported radio network. Thompson called the radio a "new revolutionary instrument" because of its central role in an attempted putsch by Austrian Nazis in Vienna in July 1934. Austria's radio network was state-controlled, and the plot—which failed, though the perpetrators assassinated the Austrian chancellor, Engelbert Dollfuss—centered on a broadcast falsely declaring a change in government. An authoritarian state could make a radio message "practically inescapable," Thompson emphasized.[50]

Thompson crossed from Austria into Germany by car in August 1934. As she traveled through the German countryside, she noticed swastika flags bristling from every house; she had been told that watchmen were snooping on every block. She was horrified to see a huge banner saying "Born to Die for Germany!" dominating the hillside of a Hitler Youth encampment of six thousand adolescent boys. More than ever, she felt sure the Nazis were preparing for war. Six weeks earlier, on the "Night of Long Knives," Hitler had engineered the massacre of nearly a hundred of his supposed enemies in his own party and the arrest of a thousand more. He thus cleared the way toward claiming full power when Paul von Hindenburg, the aged conservative who nominally shared government power with him, died early in August.[51]

To confirm his supreme authority, Hitler then called for a plebiscite. Even though there was no chance that the vote would go against him—and he would have retained power regardless—his

Reich put on an immense propaganda campaign. The day of Hitler's culminating speech was declared a national holiday so that everyone could hear the national broadcast of his words. Everyone owning radios was instructed to turn them on and to invite neighbors without radios to join in listening. In every restaurant, theater, public square, and gathering place in every city, loudspeakers were installed to boom Hitler's words everywhere, making it virtually impossible to avoid hearing him. Thompson witnessed this stunning example of Nazi thought control.[52]

Thompson checked into the Hotel Adlon a few days later. Within a day, a messenger appeared at her door to hand-deliver an order from the state, advising her to leave Germany immediately to "avoid formal deportation." She was being expelled. This made front-page news in the United States. The Reich singled her out for her belittling comments in "I Saw Hitler!" and her reporting of Jewish persecution, relying on a recent (and retroactive) law that reserved the government's right to deport anyone whose activities were deemed detrimental to Germany or disrespected its leaders.[53]

She was the first American journalist to be ejected by Hitler's Reich. A few correspondents had already departed—reluctantly—after being warned that their safety could not be assured. They included Thompson's former housemate Edgar Mowrer, whose hard-hitting reporting from Germany for the *Chicago Daily News* won him the Pulitzer Prize in 1933, and Frederick Kuh of the United Press. As Thompson boarded her train for Paris, the remaining foreign correspondents gave her an armful of American Beauty roses and rousing cheers—dreading that there was worse to come. Unless correspondents were willing to conform to state dictates or appear to do so, their continuance was precarious and the pursuit of accurate information meant dramatic daily risks.[54]

THOMPSON'S EXPULSION FROM Germany opened American eyes to the hazards faced by foreign correspondents who tangled with authoritarian governments. Her celebrity at home increased as a result, and she responded to many requests to speak and write about Germany by warning insistently of the dangers of fascism. She had become so sensitive to the slipperiness of the slope toward fascism that she saw its potential in any expansion of central government power—including in President Roosevelt's New Deal. Among the friends with whom she shared her thinking was John Gunther. He came to the United States in the fall of 1934 to explore new job possibilities. Gunther was thinking of ending his years as a foreign correspondent. "Europe I love, & in Europe I have had much pleasure & happiness, but I despair of all the greed & fear & wrangles & wars," he wrote to Frances while en route for his visit. "I feel very green & explorative . . . very American & very eager to see just what kind of a continent & country it was that gave us birth."[55]

CHAPTER 8

TWO BIG BOOKS

"THE CAREERS OF most crack U.S. foreign correspondents can be divided into two phases," declared *Time*, the leading weekly news magazine, in 1936. "In the first they report. In the second they reflect." This pronouncement gestured toward Jimmy Sheean's *Personal History* (1935), a book so phenomenally successful that it inspired a "cloudburst" of imitations by other foreign correspondents. A brilliant turn in Sheean's uneven road, his book recounted his youthful search for self-definition as he confronted flashpoints in world politics. His quest was to ascertain "some relationship between this one life and the millions of others into which it was cast" as he came face-to-face with fascism, communism, imperialism, anticolonial war, and attempted revolution.[1]

Like Sheean, Thompson and Gunther too moved beyond newspaper reporting by the mid-1930s. In doing so they broadened and deepened their influence. Americans who had stayed home wanted to hear from these former foreign correspondents, whose immersion in foreign politics had grounded their perspectives and gained them critical knowledge. Their opinions as global informants matched Americans' rising need to grasp menacing political events occurring around the globe.

SHEEAN DID NOT achieve his huge success with *Personal History* quickly or easily. Immediately after returning from Palestine, he undertook a midwestern lecture tour, giving his controversial assessment of the 1929 violence and attracting audiences of fifteen hundred people, many of them Jewish. These exhausting tours never proved as lucrative as he hoped, and he usually regretted having taken them. Suffering financially as the Great Depression sank in, Sheean was perpetually needy, usually indebted and borrowing from friends. He put his energies into writing fiction in the early 1930s, thinking that was the route to riches, and made New York City (center of American publishing) his home base, even though he disliked it for bringing out his worst habits. Visits to Raymond Mortimer in Gordon Square leavened his existence and kept up his Bloomsbury connections.[2]

Memories of Rayna still haunted Sheean. To recover from the crash of all she had meant to him, he translated the story of his relationship with her into a novel. Sheean titled it *Gog and Magog* against his publisher's strong objections, insisting on using these obscure biblical words indicating strange, dangerously threatening forces, to refer to the vying systems of America and Soviet Russia— though readers would be hard put to understand that. The novel portrayed John, an American in his twenties living in Paris, who traveled to Moscow to follow a lover and bumped into Sheila Rudd, an American redhead burning with idealistic, self-abnegating fervor for communism. Spellbound by Sheila's "spiritual energy," John felt "content to argue in perfect seriousness with this sliver of fire." The two bantered, and argued, until Sheila eventually succumbed to illness and tragic death. Sheila's rigid political views in the novel caricatured Rayna's actual views, making John's opposition easy, though he nonetheless felt her death as a crushing blow.[3]

Sheean knew the novel was not his best work but had felt driven to write it. "Ever since that terrible time in Moscow I have known that this book would have to be written or I should never get over it," he explained apologetically to Raymond Mortimer, knowing his friend was a discerning critic. "All I wanted to do was to get something off my chest. In that sense, it was simply a physical necessity." *Gog and Magog* (1930) sold no better than a novel Sheean had written earlier with similar high hopes, called *Anatomy of Virtue* (1927). Sheean then tried short stories and was elated to place one in the *Saturday Evening Post* for a whopping $600. (In that Depression year, $1,800 was considered an adequate annual household income.) The *Post* sustained Sheean during the early 1930s, publishing nine of his pleasing and clever, if trivial, stories. He published a third novel, *The Tide* (1933), a deceptively lightweight tale set among newspaper reporters. The character of his fictional heroine, a savvy, perceptive, sympathetic reporter, saluted Dorothy Thompson, while the plot gave room for Sheean's political views of British imperialism, Zionism, and political injustice in Palestine.[4]

Writing novels neither exorcised the ghosts of Sheean's past nor gained him a best seller. He was at a low point when Harold Nicolson, visiting New York in 1933, suggested that he write about his experiences during the 1920s. "I had always intended to do such a book sometime, but until he said this it hadn't occurred to me to do it at once," Sheean told Mortimer.[5] He chose the title *Personal History* quite deliberately. He did not mean the overall history of a person but "an account of one person's relationship to the history of the time (1918–1929)," in other words, "the effort of a rather average person in rather un-average circumstances . . . to arrive at a view of the world and of his own place in it." He had in mind as a model *The Education of Henry Adams*. Adams, making his education his subject, discussed only life events that instructed him; likewise, Sheean intended to dwell only on "the relationship between a person and the history in which he lives." Sheean refused to call the book an autobiography and was vexed by others' calling it one. "It leaves out nine-tenths of my autobiography. . . . It leaves out all of a singularly complicated and horrendous 'love-life' for example," he protested to Jamie (Hamish) Hamilton, the publisher of the British edition. "I grow weary of repeating to all and sundry that this is a book on one given theme," he sighed, "not an autobiography or a collection of memoirs."[6]

Personal History took the form of a *bildungsroman* and made its major theme Sheean's growth in placing himself in the world responsibly—finding "a relation of one to many, a place in the chain of cause and effect." He structured the book with "just as definite a form as any novel," he affirmed. He narrated his younger self as a sympathetic if sometimes foolish character, admitting his weaknesses and inviting readers to identify with him, as various enterprises sharpened his outlook. The narrative began with Sheean a freshman in college in 1917, making his cowardly exit from the Jewish fraternity he had naively pledged. Aware of the shabby episode's relevance in the 1930s, he summarized bitterly, "Hitler himself could not have invented a more savage and degrading system of anti-Semitism than that worked out by those little monsters, the undergraduates."[7] Next came New York's fund of metropolitan sophistication and newspaper experience for him. Then he arrived in France, saw Fascism in bud in Italy, developed critical perspectives on intra-European conflicts, entered the dangers and learned the lessons of the Rif, and ventured next to Tehran.

The book's narrative arc rose to its height in a very long chapter called "Revolution," on Hankou and Moscow in 1927, where Sheean's struggle to situate his life responsibly amid the world's chaos and injustices culminated. Rayna's character held center stage. Sheean heightened the contrast between himself and Rayna by depicting himself after his adventure in the Rif as a complacent soul, living a solipsistic life of spectatorship with at most a theoretical interest in Bolshevism. He sketched how dismissible he probably appeared in Hankou to Bill Prohme, whose "violent revolutionary enthusiasm," Sheean imagined, "resented my bourgeois lethargy, my innumerable changes of white silk clothes, my Scotch whisky and Egyptian cigarettes." Rayna, in contrast, embodied unselfish commitment to the cause of justice, uncannily embodied in "the kind of girl I had known all my life."[8]

In his appealing portrait, Rayna retained her sense of fun, while she dedicated herself to the Chinese revolutionary movement at great personal sacrifice. An admirable and affecting character—down-to-earth, sympathetic, prone to teasing rather than censuring him—she was miles more persuasive than his fictional Sheila Rudd. Sheean responded with adoration. In Moscow in September 1927, he wrote, he felt her blazing conviction as a "solar phenomenon": his "world revolved about her."

Sheean's depiction of Rayna bloomed so expressively on the page that it was easy to read *Personal History* as a tragic love story, ending in a "spiral plunge to catastrophe"—although he stated plainly that theirs was never a sexual relationship, that "boudoir 'love' had no part" in it. Many readers assumed nonetheless that he was in love with her (as had several acquaintances in Moscow). That impression was reinforced by his dedication of the book to her, quoting lines from Shakespeare's sonnet 109: "Never believe, though in my nature reigned / All frailties that besiege all kinds of blood, / That it could so preposterously be stained, / To leave for nothing all thy sum of good." He was not in love in a conventional way, but saw her as a shining incarnation of his own highest aspirations, and treasured that model.[9]

Sheean's journey to secure writing commissions so he could stay in Moscow for the winter then complicated the story. Back in London, spouting revolutionary enchantment, he reconnected with Harold Nicolson and associated skeptical friends; they confronted his Moscow enthusiasm with reasonable arguments for gradual rather than revolutionary change and assured him that social legislation under bourgeois governments would eventually correct injustices. Sheean found himself responding willy-nilly to their contentions, and just as much, to the pleasurable offerings of London life. A comfortable month there poised him on a teeter-totter—terribly torn between his attraction to Rayna's righteous commitment and the alternative of finding his worth in the world through a bourgeois life of writing.[10]

James Vincent Sheean, studio photograph, 1935.
Source: Photograph collection at the Tamiment Library, New York University, by permission of the Communist Party USA.

In his dramatic retelling, Sheean returned to Moscow for the tenth anniversary celebration no longer Rayna's acolyte but her savior. He intended to halt the very idealistic dedication that he found so beautiful in her, to bring her back to "the half world in which I wanted to keep on living . . . where men did not die for their beliefs." Yet he was still vulnerable to Rayna's enthralling fervor. He vividly rendered his imbalance between two incommensurable and mutually exclusive alternatives, each having a compelling rationale, in terms shadowing Henry Adams's suspension in his *Education* between two mysterious and opposing sources of energy—the Virgin, emblem of mystical faith, and the Dynamo, emblem of modern technology.

Rayna became in effect Sheean's mirror and opposite, his virtual twin, who had chosen the "live option"—Sheean used William James's term—of revolutionary struggle, the choice he himself was unable to make. Rayna's position dramatized one side of an argument in his own mind, and one that also would have drawn in many readers, because *Personal History* was published at the start of the Communist Party's "popular front" and the height of its recruiting success in the United States. As Sheean staged the conflict in *Personal History*, he argued "tooth and nail" with Rayna day and night for a week—a week he did not know would be her last—to undo her plans to join the Communist Party and to "enter the Lenin Institute to be trained as a revolutionary instrument." (He must have invented the latter point for stronger effect because she would have to be hand-picked by the American Communist Party to enter the new international training institute named for Lenin, and she had no connection to the party.) His tussle with her led to a final contrivance of his, intended to dazzle and ensnare her—a dressed-up "bourgeois evening" of dining and dancing at the Grand Hotel. (This scene also was likely invented.) Rather than succumbing to this lure, she dragged him afterward to a meeting of the international Congress of Friends of the Soviet Union, which moved her emotions more. Sheean narrated Rayna's journey toward death affectingly and suspensefully, picturing himself next to her almost every moment.[11]

Rayna's single-mindedness in Sheean's narrative did not match the devastating feelings of disillusionment that she expressed to Bill Prohme in her letters in the fall of 1927 or the ambivalent longings she expressed to Helen Freeland. Possibly she told Sheean she wanted to join the Communist Party. In an obituary he wrote just after she died, he said that "one can scarcely doubt" that she would have done so had she lived, but this may have been simply his presumption. Its sole confirmation came from Dorothy Thompson, in a letter she wrote to Sinclair Lewis about Rayna's death, mentioning that "Only a week ago we were all talking on her for wanting to join the communist party."[12]

Although Sheean made a fraught and tenuous peace with bourgeois society himself, his revolutionary entanglements in Hankou and Moscow left a permanent stamp. The tragedy of her death stayed with him and did not extinguish the ideal she represented in his eyes. On the final page of *Personal History* he wrote, "Even if I took no part in the direct struggle by which others attempted to hasten the processes that were here seen to be inevitable in human history, I had to recognize its urgency and find my place with relation to it."[13] For years, Rayna continued to speak inside his head as a ghostly alter ego. Borodin, whose intellectual seriousness and reasoned Marxist outlook also came through impressively in *Personal History*, had lent Sheean the "long view" that prevented despair at the failure of a single revolutionary effort. The "long view" embedded a conviction that historical processes would eventually bring the oppressed classes to triumph.

PERSONAL HISTORY WAS published in New York on February 1, 1935. Frances Gunther, no pushover as a critic, wrote to John that she was "really impressed": "400 pages of extremely difficult exposition all built around and held together by a very fine sound intellectual theme—and still appealing enough 'to go like wildfire.'" "I would cut off a leg to write as good a book as this," John Gunther thought to himself about it.[14]

The book did indeed go like wildfire. Reviewers were enthralled, seeing in *Personal History* not only Sheean's own picaresque whirlwind around the globe but also the mercurial potential and wrenching choices set before his generation. "If one wants an overview of the past fifteen years in world history, a sense of all important shifts in the political atmosphere of our epoch, *Personal History* is worth a hundred more articulated and factual volumes," promised a review in *Current History*.

The enthusiastic reception of *Personal History* retrieves the importance of that fraction of Americans to which Sheean belonged, whose youth in the 1920s included venturing into the world and trying out varying political positions. In the left-leaning *New Republic*, a perspicacious review by Malcolm Cowley—whose then little-read *Exile's Return* (1934) would eventually supersede Sheean's as a rendition of their generation abroad—praised the book highly and named its core theme: "like millions of people drifting through post-war society," Sheean wanted "to find a reason for living." Latter-day Bloomsburian David Garnett saw Sheean as "an exceptionally charming example of an attractive class: the American boys who came to maturity after the war." Sheean's argument with Rayna, Garnett wrote, was "a debate which hundreds, perhaps thousands, of the honest young are engaged in arguing for themselves to-day and Mr. Sheean's experience, though it was extraordinarily harrowing and dramatic, was typical of his whole generation."[15]

Sheean began hearing from his readers right away. By early March, ten or twelve letters a day were arriving. At the end of April he was getting "floods and floods" of letters. The book's uptake was "phenomenal in America . . . in the intensity of the response," he told Mortimer. "The language is so extravagant. I am compared to Hamlet, to Candide, to Carlyle, to Pierre Loti, to Henry Adams, to Tolstoy and to Rousseau. . . . I am offered vast sums to lecture, to talk on the radio, to go to Hollywood." Sheean was astonished by the popular reaction. "I never expected this book to be the epidemic it has turned out to be," he told Mortimer. "I seem to have invented (without meaning to do so) a kind of dialect for all the hysterical yearners in America; they write me whole vast letters couched in this dialect taken from my book—things about 'world-ideas' and 'the world-mind' and 'segment of the world-experience' and, above all, again and again, 'the long view.' That simple phrase has apparently made my fortune."[16] Though he sounded cynical, he was truly moved—as well as elated at making money.

One reader's reaction distressed him deeply. Bill Prohme, close to death from a recurrence of tuberculosis, wrote to Sheean from a sanitarium in Honolulu, protesting the book's "shoddy, cheap, exhibitionist and vulgar picture of Rayna." Sheean responded, though he had little hope of altering Bill's judgment. He respected Bill's love for Rayna and felt that Bill was accusing him of having "hideously desecrated something perfect," as he told Helen Freeland. He confessed to Freeland (who wrote him a kind letter) that "things he rakes up . . . give me nervous prostration for days."[17]

Personal History brought Sheean transatlantic fame. It occupied best-seller lists for many weeks, won a National Book Award (in the inaugural year of the prize) and several other awards, and eventually would sell more than two million copies. His photograph shared the company of entertainment stars such as Charles Boyer, Ezio Pinza, and Fred Astaire on a page titled "Heartbeats" in *Vogue*.[18] Walter Wanger, a politically minded Hollywood producer, snapped up the movie rights to *Personal History* for $10,000. Wanger cast the film with noted stars but met delays in moving toward production. Controversy linked to the left-wing sympathies in the story halted Wanger's production again and again. None of Sheean's original characters or plot remained when the film reached the screen as *Foreign Correspondent* in 1940.[19]

Fellow journalists were among those most impressed with Sheean's book. "No book published in our time had a greater direct response from the working press," one affirmed. Within a year, the Moscow correspondent Walter Duranty published his recollections under the title *I Write as I Please*, and Negley Farson, based in London for the *Chicago Daily News*, wrote his *The Way of a Transgressor*. "Since the publication of Jimmy Sheean's 'Personal History,'" John Gunther noted wryly in 1936, reviewing yet another memoir, "the foreign correspondent packs a notebook in his kit . . . and thinks more of future royalties than contemporary datelines." A review of still another correspondent's tale made sure to say that "Vincent Sheean set the standard." When *Personal History* was republished in a Modern Library edition five years after initial publication, the *New York Times* reviewer called it "something of a landmark . . . certainly the most influential of the books in which foreign correspondents began to relate their own lives to the dynamics of international events," a book "still alive, while most of its followers are in limbo."[20]

Journalists later in the twentieth century continued to take Sheean's book as a model. Eric Severeid expressed pleasure in the mid-1970s that his own memoir was thought "a fair match" with Sheean's *Personal History*, "because I loved Jimmy and his book which I read during my honeymoon in a north woods' shack. . . . That book must have unconsciously affected my own attempt." Harrison Salisbury, a World War II correspondent who then reported on Soviet Russia for the *New York Times* and in 1970 founded its op-ed page, formed romantic images of Anna Louise Strong and Borodin from *Personal History*, which he "had gulped down (like tens of thousands of Americans) when it appeared." The book made an appearance in literature, too. After praising the book highly in *The Nation*, calling it "a first-class literary work" in a review, Mary McCarthy used it as a cultural touchstone in her first novel, *The Company She Keeps* (1942). As the novel's hard-boiled protagonist assessed a stranger in a railroad car who wanted to pick her up, she gave him ambivalent approval for praising Vincent Sheean for *Personal History*: "judged by eternal standards, Sheean might not be much, but in the cultural atmosphere of the Pullman car Sheean was a titan."[21]

AT THE FIRST crest of *Personal History*'s success in March 1935, Sheean acquired a "girlfriend," in his own word. He fixed his eye on Diana Forbes-Robertson—called Dinah—daughter of a famous acting family and sister-in-law of Sheean's British publisher Jamie (Hamish) Hamilton, who introduced them late in 1934. In March 1935, the two spent some time together when she traveled with friends to Naples, where Sheean was living because it was the setting for the novel he was writing. They then made a plan to meet in August (suitably chaperoned) at the Salzburg music festival. In late July, Sheean told Raymond Mortimer that he intended to marry Dinah. "There's no doubt that I'm approaching a sort of Crisis in my existence," he told his friend as August began. Mortimer may have been the only person he told. In several letters of the same weeks to John Gunther, Sheean made no mention of a girlfriend or plans to marry.[22]

Meeting in Salzburg for the festival, the couple suddenly went before the American consul and were married on August 24, 1935. Diana Forbes-Robertson was twenty, enthralled with Sheean's worldly wisdom and playfully executed erudition. He was thirty-five, in the flush of new success. She was lovely, and her personality was called "electric," but what else about her convinced Sheean he should marry her remains mysterious. Her extended family may have intrigued him. Her American mother, Gertrude Elliott, was a former actress, and her English father, Johnston Forbes-Robertson, was a renowned and beloved Shakespearean actor. Her mother's sister Maxine Elliott was a glamorous and enterprising American former actress who gallivanted in her youth and captivated aristocratic celebrities who were still her friends in the 1930s, when she was in her seventies. More than once, luminaries such as Winston Churchill and even the Prince of Wales were guests at "Aunt Maxine's" house in Cannes on the French Riviera when Sheean and his wife were also visiting. Sheean developed a personal acquaintance with Churchill that way, starting in 1935 when he was out of power. Churchill read *Personal History* and pronounced it "very subversive."[23]

Sheean seemed heartily delighted with his bride, telling Gunther and other friends about his marriage: "Gal by the name of Dinah, nicest ever I saw, and why didn't anybody ever tell me marriage was the Perfect State? Seems to me I've wasted a lot of time. Maybe it was because I never knew Dinah before." The couple at first lived in Naples. Sheean had conceived a romantic historical tale set in the republic of Naples in 1799, when Jacobin revolutionaries briefly rose against their Habsburg overlords and would-be British captors, only to be brutally defeated and buried. Sheean meant the novel to illuminate "certain revolutionary impulses which are eternal in human nature," as he told Jamie Hamilton, who would publish the novel in

James Vincent Sheean and Diana Forbes-Robertson, 1935 or 1937.
Source: Private collection, Jane Morton, London.

Britain. Failures such as the one in Naples, including the tragic fate of Sheean's heroine Luisa Sanfelice, were only temporary halts in "the raising of further and further classes of people to the surface of life." This was the essence of Borodin's "long view," which inspired Sheean's novel (and may have saved the Hankou group from despair): such "ill-prepared, ill-directed, impractical outbreaks . . . do prepare the spirit of man for the next . . . expression of the revolutionary idea," Sheean affirmed.[24]

Sheean finished writing the novel quickly. Dinah was pregnant and about to give birth when the couple moved to Ireland, land of Sheean's forefathers, in April 1936. He had an "Irish book" in mind, but the move provoked "a maddening effect" in Sheean, he later admitted, tangled with guilt that seems to have arisen from thinking of his Irish grandparents as poor peasants there, while he arrived as a man of privilege. His reaction to fatherhood was equivocal. Their daughter Linda was born in Dublin on May 29, 1936, and Sheean reeled into their rented house dead drunk after an event honoring him, hosted by an authors' society. The family was to move to a different rented house a week later and Sheean complained to Jamie Hamilton that he was "becoming a complete squaw-man under the weight of all these domestic details and difficulties. I'm trying hard now to throw them all off . . . as I haven't written one word in two months." Within two weeks he went off to London to attend a Wagner opera, leaving Dinah and the newborn and nurse in Dublin.[25]

His novel, titled *Sanfelice*, was published in mid-June. Lewis Gannett, who had become a regular book reviewer for the daily *New York Herald Tribune*, saw that Sheean's "glamorous and romantic novel . . . continues the debate upon the value of revolution which he conducted . . . in *Personal History*." Few other reviewers were quite so perceptive, though many quoted a concluding reassurance to the tragic heroine: "The Revolution, Luisa, is eternal; it is the lifting of more and more people to the surface of life. . . . We have failed. . . . But . . . the Revolution has not failed." Reviewers' comparisons to *Personal History* always put *Sanfelice* in the shade, and the novel did not sell very well.[26]

An onslaught of mixed reviews sent Sheean into a tailspin. He had outsize expectations for the novel, even having imagined that it would win the Pulitzer Prize. Because the English reviews more often praised him, he exaggerated the negativity of the American reviews, expostulating to an old friend on July 1: "In America the general tone seems to be 'What's this? This Sheean bastard, whom we don't like anyhow, thinks he can write a novel? We'll learn the son of a bitch!'" A snide review in the *Chicago Daily News* infuriated him unreasonably. The reviewer called *Sanfelice* a superb tale and appreciated it being presented as fiction, while strongly implying that *Personal History* was also fiction and should have been presented as such. Sheean saw "an astonishing venom" in this "libelous goddamn thing."[27]

Two weeks later, in the middle of July 1936, Sheean had a complete bodily and mental breakdown. He was alternately comatose or delirious for about six weeks. His doctors unhelpfully labeled it a "syndrome collapse." His condition was so dire that on August 17 he was flown from Dublin by helicopter to a sanitarium in Switzerland and subsequently transferred to a Geneva clinic. He regained consciousness on August 24, but remained in the clinic until late September, when his doctors declared him fully recovered. Meanwhile, *Personal History*'s continuing success caused many lucrative offers to roll in, leading him to joke by mid-September, "Moral: go loony and get rich."[28]

Shortly after he recovered, Sheean attributed his collapse to "nerves and alcohol." His many doctors and psychiatrists had found no more certain cause. His disappointment with the reception of *Sanfelice* may well have been a trigger, but it was only one of the recent major changes in his life: phenomenal acclaim for *Personal History*, marriage and fatherhood after years of other sexual adventures, residence in his forebears' native land, then a stunning blow to his hopes for *Sanfelice*, which was his fictional reengagement with the revolutionary lesson he learned in China. Before his collapse, Sheean may also have received the news that Bill Prohme had committed suicide on the anniversary of Rayna's death the previous November, taking to the grave his scorn for Sheean's portrait of her in *Personal History*.[29]

Whatever the reasons for Sheean's breakdown, it secured his wife's sole attention. She went with him when he was flown to the sanitarium, leaving the baby with a nurse. The family did not reunite until late September. He gave Dinah immense credit for his recovery into full consciousness. Five doctors had given him up for dead, and only Dinah refused to believe that, Sheean told Raymond Mortimer, saving him "just by her constant presence, the pull of it, which I could actually feel, physically I mean, as a sort of tugging sensation, during the week I spent between here and there, coming out of it." Sheean called the experience "an agony without limit or definition in time—it might have been a hundred years' nightmare." It took him several weeks afterward to suppress memories of the pain of "hang[ing] on to Dinah desperately as the only reality." Sheean ridiculed the reasoning of the Freudian analyst at the clinic who suggested that jealousy of his new daughter had caused his breakdown.[30]

Toward the end of 1936, Sheean and his wife made a visit to Raymond Mortimer that suggested his recovery was less than perfect. Sheean seemed well, talking as expected when the couple arrived, Mortimer reported to Eddy Sackville-West. Then Dinah left the room, "& suddenly," Mortimer recounted, "I perceived that I was listening to a madman. It was, as you may suppose, an appalling shock, & my head is still unsteady. Persecution-mania . . . & referring in all the papers in the past that he was queer!" It is doubtful that Sheean had revealed his sexual history to his wife, and presumably Mortimer did not tell Dinah everything he heard. Sheean was raving that the Jacobin character in his novel *Sanfelice* was being seen as representing King Edward VIII, and that by naming the character Ferri, Sheean was suggesting that Edward VIII—the new king of Great Britain who resigned the throne that December in order to marry Wallis Simpson—"was a Fairy." This was "fantastic beyond belief," Mortimer wrote to Sackville-West. "I got an instant's telephone-talk with Diana, who was very reassuring. She said it was getting better & slighter every day, & that she was not alarmed about it; but it was indescribably agitating & horrible. Poor girl, what a nightmare she has been through!" Mortimer wrote sympathetically.[31]

Frances and John Gunther had been appalled to learn in the summer of 1936 that Sheean was hanging between life and death. Jamie Hamilton, sure that Sheean was about to die, had asked Gunther to write an advance obituary, and Gunther obliged. He called Sheean a legend, marveled at his proficiency in speaking numerous languages "with the utmost fluency, clarity, humor and grace," and praised his friend's brilliant erudition, principled conduct, and inimitable personality. Gunther rated Sheean's intellectual prowess far higher than his own.[32] He had no need to envy his friend's success with *Personal History*, though, because he had published his own knockout best seller that very year. The two men's books could hardly have been more different.

GUNTHER'S WINDING PATH to writing his big book began in the fall of 1934, during his three-month visit to the United States, where he was prospecting for new employment. He was thinking about quitting the *Chicago Daily News* and moving home. When he disembarked in the unfamiliar cityscape of New York, he felt exhilarated but also unmoored. He was alone, and wrote to Frances in Vienna, "I miss you dreadfully, intellectually as well as sexually, my brain trust"—teasingly calling her by the moniker for FDR's circle of highly educated advisers—"Please come and do my thinking for me!" As usual, he kept a vivid running log of his activities to send to her. She was very busy, for she had become Vienna correspondent for the *London News-Chronicle* that year, getting her articles on the front page in July, when Austrian Fascists attempting a coup assassinated the chancellor, Engelbert Dollfuss. She was also filing stories for the *Chicago Daily News* while John was away. He was genuinely "pleased and proud" to see his wife's published stories when he went to Chicago.[33]

Two years earlier they had gone through an extremely bad patch in their often unstable marriage. Frances threatened suicide and seemed set on divorce. She may have had another abortion. John felt afterward that the spring and summer of 1932 were "the worst six months of my life." Yet they emerged from that crisis by the middle of 1934. Both of them were analyzed in Vienna by Dr. William Stekel, a straying psychoanalytic disciple of Freud who practiced his own approach. After six months of seeing Dr. Stekel, John felt miraculously cured of bouts of impotence and of previous asthmatic reactions to cats and dogs, and the Gunther marriage seemed on an even keel.[34]

In New York, Gunther conferred with Carl Brandt, still his literary agent, and met with contacts Brandt set up, including editors at *Vanity Fair*, *The Nation*, and *Fortune*, and Clifton Fadiman, editor in chief at publisher Simon & Schuster. Simon & Schuster was "Gunther-minded" and wanted a book from him, he discovered. The gregarious Gunther spent many of his New York hours in conversations over drinks and meals in restaurants, bars, and at dinner parties. He soon proceeded to Chicago, where the *Chicago Daily News* put him to work writing a series on the cleanup of organized crime since the end of Prohibition the previous year. Paul Mowrer, the accomplished foreign correspondent who had been Thompson's adviser and Gunther's boss in the 1920s, now headed the editorial page of the *News*. Gunther was unhappy to see that Mowrer's editorials fell in line with the conservatism of the paper's new Republican owner, who opposed the New Deal.[35]

The *News* was not alone in opposing Roosevelt. Sixty percent of editorial opinion—reflecting the views of newspaper owners and publishers, not the views of reporters—opposed FDR in 1932, though he swept the election, gaining close to 58 percent of the popular vote and nearly 90 percent of the electoral college. In initiating "fireside chats" via radio, President Roosevelt used the airwaves to skirt newspaper publishers' antipathy, projecting his cultivated voice and personal charisma directly to the American people. Gunther heard him on the radio in late October and decided that "his voice is just as good as they say; . . . one of the most thrilling I have ever heard." FDR also cultivated the Washington press corps, counting on reporters' professional principles to mitigate the conservative bias of their bosses' political views. He was the first president to hold regular press conferences—twice a week—and the first to allow correspondents to question him without having submitted written questions beforehand, though he did not permit them to quote what he said there.[36]

In Chicago, Gunther was sought after for his perspectives on the world. Invited by the Chicago Council on Foreign Relations to lecture on political developments in Austria, he wowed the crowd of four hundred listeners. His discussion of "Seven Questions about Hitler" for the "swellest" ladies' club in town was likewise "jammed." Lunches, dinners, and drinks with people who wanted his company stocked his calendar. "For every date I accept I turn down 5 or 6," he told Frances. "You have no idea how people are after me."[37] Still, he missed Frances "integrally"—thinking of her not "twenty or forty or a hundred times a day" but "always, a perpetual stream in my subconscious." When a Chicago friend who had never met Frances asked John to describe her, he said, after a moment's thought, "Well, I've known her since 1925 and been married to her since 1927, and in nine years I never heard her say a banal thing."[38]

Gunther wanted to educate himself about the United States as much as his American acquaintances wanted to hear about Europe. He took a side trip to Detroit to interview Henry Ford, making sure to see Ford's nostalgia-laden "Dearborn Village" under construction. He soon wrote several long articles on Ford. He accompanied a ward politician rewarding Chicago precinct captains following a Democratic landslide on election night 1934. Every precinct captain was paid off, and politicians crowded in among gangsters and hoodlums to an all-night drinking party.[39]

From Mowrer and others, Gunther heard varying opinions on the new National Recovery Administration (NRA), the controversial New Deal agency that brought industry and labor together to set wage and price codes to stabilize the Depression economy. "People object to the NRA," he told Frances, "because (a) they are Republicans (b) they fear the bill of rights is being sabotaged (c) they think Roosevelt is a communist, (d) they think he is a Fascist (e) they disapprove of Mrs. Roosevelt talking on the radio." He found worry on the left that fascism could emerge from the NRA. The structure of NRA industrial codes bore a strong similarity to Mussolini's corporatism, and the administration unleashed a blanketing blast of "Blue Eagle" propaganda for it. The agency's critics were relieved when a unanimous Supreme Court declared the NRA legislation unconstitutional the following year.[40]

Gunther then returned to New York to meet with fellow correspondents, novelists, politicos, and additional magazine editors to gather their ideas and opinions. He discussed government economic planning with economist Stuart Chase and with an enthusiast for the Tennessee Valley Authority (a New Deal rural electrification project).

He spent hours with his friend Hamilton Fish Armstrong, editor of *Foreign Affairs*, "violently and fruitlessly" discussing whether war was on the way in Europe. Politically minded intellectuals knew Gunther's name because of his occasional essays in *Harper's, The Nation, The New Republic*, and *Foreign Affairs*. Though these publications circulated to relatively small numbers, they had the readers Gunther wanted to impress. His friend, the former correspondent Raymond Swing, now an editor of *The Nation*, told Gunther that President Roosevelt read it "cover-to-cover every week." Invited to one dinner party after another, Gunther met New York thinkers and writers of his generation, including Philip Wylie, James Thurber, Tess Slesinger, John O'Hara, Henry Steele Commager, Suzanne La Follette, Louis Adamic, Donald and Ann Friede, Albert Boni, Edward Bernays, Thomas Wolfe, Max Perkins, Walter Lippmann, and Harry Scherman, cofounder of the Book of the Month Club.[41]

He next headed for Washington, DC, where seeing the White House and Capitol moved him. He stopped into the hearings of the Senate's Nye Committee, which was investigating the influence of bankers and munitions-makers on American entry into the world war. Gunther had just published in *Harper's* a revealing account and implicit indictment of the brisk international trade in armaments in Europe, a subject Frances had suggested he take up. He had the numbers to prove that manufacturing firms in Great Britain, Germany, France, Japan, Czechoslovakia, and the United States were making hundreds of millions of dollars in profits by selling war-making materials to whatever nation would buy, regardless of having signed neutrality pacts or participating in disarmament conferences. His essay implied European readiness for war. Awareness of the potential for another European war haunted foreign correspondents' minds far more than the minds of Americans at home.[42]

In Washington, Jerry Frank, Gunther's old friend from Chicago, now counsel for the New Deal Agricultural Adjustment Act, gave him an earful of gossip about the major players in FDR's administration. Gunther was promised a personal introduction to President

Roosevelt after his Friday press conference. The president's talent in conducting the press conference charmed Gunther, who reported to Frances that FDR delivered every response with "the simplicity, elocution, and suspense-quality of a great actor." His response to a question he did not wish to answer was "a long clever pause," and he satisfied another questioner by merely "twinkling" amusedly. To another question he responded with "Laughter. Tilt of the head. Eyes snap like window panes with sun on them." Roosevelt put the reporters in a marvelous mood while revealing almost nothing new. Gunther met the president face-to-face for three minutes after the press conference, and also gained fifteen minutes to pepper Rexford Tugwell, Department of Agriculture undersecretary and central member of Roosevelt's "brains trust," with questions.[43]

Gunther's three-month trip gave him "an acute attack of Americanitis." Upon returning to Vienna, however, he received a big surprise that shelved those thoughts. The *Chicago Daily News* was making him chief of the foreign desk in London. It was a big promotion. "The London job is the grandest there is in journalism," Jimmy Sheean congratulated him. "The London correspondent of an important American paper is a Personage," he teased his friend lightly; "his self-respect occasionally blooms out a little too much, and becomes frog-chested, but anyhow it's a wonderful thing." Frances embraced the move to London along with John, although he gained status from it while she lost her professional position. Leaving Vienna meant she would have to give up her job as correspondent there for the *London News-Chronicle*. Her editor regretfully accepted her resignation, saying, "If every foreign correspondent were of your calibre [*sic*], my life would be a bed of roses."[44]

There was one wrinkle. Gunther had just committed himself to writing a book. His agent had been urging him for some time to write an overview of European politics; publishers were looking for one and he was well positioned to write it. He had consistently refused because he wanted to write fiction in any spare time he had. Then, during his stay in New York, an agent for Brandt broke through his resistance. She asked Gunther to name the advance he would need to write such a book comfortably. Still reluctant, he named a figure he thought was so outlandishly high that no publisher would bite— $5,000 (roughly $90,000 in today's buying power). To his shock, she got it for him. Cass Canfield at Harper & Brothers, his friend since signing Gunther's first novel in London, combined his own offer with buy-in from a British publisher and a plan that three chapters would appear in *Harper's Magazine*. Gunther was hurriedly packing for his return to Vienna and nursing a terrible hangover when Canfield forced him to sign the contract. "Canfield has got me to write a Europe book for him," Gunther told Ham Armstrong in February 1935, adding, "The idea terrifies me."[45]

His new position made writing the book much harder. He had counted on being in Vienna, where demands on him were comparatively light and he knew everyone he needed to know. Vienna was also close to the European locations where he needed to do research, and London was not. Most important, his new placement meant learning a new political landscape and establishing vital new contacts, and he was expected to cable a news story of 250 to 600 words every day at a minimum. The London foreign desk kept him busy six days a week, eight to ten hours a day.

He finished the book with astonishing rapidity nonetheless. He managed it by drawing on his previous knowledge and extensive notes, repurposing earlier articles of his, conducting research in European capitals during his three weeks of vacation, and borrowing crucial expertise from comradely correspondent friends, who sent him detailed memos about places and people they knew well. He credited several of them as essential informants, especially H. R. Knickerbocker, "who knew more about Hitler, Stalin and Mussolini than any other man in Europe," and "valiantly, brilliantly" brought Gunther up to speed during three long afternoons in London.[46]

"Finished the damned monstrous thing last night!" he wrote in his diary on December 3, 1935. "It runs about 190,000 words and I have done the actual writing in five months. I woke F[rances] up when I tottered in at five in the morning and we celebrated." Gunther had a bound copy in his hands a month later. His publishers had begun to set galleys while he was writing. Once he completed the book, the British publisher hired three different lawyers to scrutinize the text for anything that could be regarded as libelous in Britain. For most of December, when the lawyers urged cuts (and they did), Gunther had to cut and paste and adjust his prose at a furious pace. Nonetheless, the book was published in the United States and Britain on January 13, 1936.[47]

Gunther chose the title *Inside Europe* at the last moment, in November 1935, as he was wearily riding the train to London from Cardiff, Wales, where he had been reporting on the upcoming British elections. He imagined his usage to be unique. The idea of a privileged vantage point "inside" organizations or personal circles was hardly unknown, but it was applied mainly in scandal sheets or Hollywood fan magazines. The press mercifully did not publish personal gossip about government officials, though an anonymous book called *Washington Merry-Go-Round* burst on the nation's capital in 1931, skewering officials from President Hoover on down for their habits, deals, and infighting. Gunther was well aware of the phenomenal sales of that book and its immediate sequel. (The two authors, both reporters, lost their newspaper jobs once they were identified.)[48]

Inside Europe was far more ambitious. Nothing compared to its panorama of contemporary European governance and politics. Germany, Austria, France, Spain, Italy, England, Poland, Czechoslovakia, Yugoslavia, the Balkans, Turkey, and Soviet Russia all were there. Gunther made a good faith effort to be fair to all regimes while maintaining a liberal perspective. His loathing for fascism and dictatorship was obvious, especially regarding Hitler, but he discussed worthy accomplishments in Mussolini's Italy and Stalin's Russia. He assessed right-wing threats to the elected republican government in Spain soberly and viewed the new French Popular Front government as one of few encouraging signs in Europe.

Lively to read and terrifically informative, *Inside Europe* considered economic, religious, cultural, and military dimensions of each country as well as politics, but individual portraits of powerful players predominated. Gunther purposely centered "leading personalities" and draped everything else around them. He sought material for "human rather than purely political portraits" of men in power, pursuing a standard set of queries about each leader's central beliefs, daily routines, moral and intellectual qualities, and attitudes to religion, sex, money, fame, power, and ambition. It was not an approach he chose arbitrarily or merely for effect; he sincerely believed that "the accidents of personality play a great role in history." He felt that events during his lifetime bore this out. Without Lenin being the man he was, would there have been a Bolshevik Revolution? Without Hitler's leadership, would Germany loom over Europe as it did? Fascinated with discerning the relation between major political leaders' individual peculiarities and political outcomes, he never doubted that there was a strong relation. Gunther had acknowledged that "the thing which does interest me more than anything is human nature" when mulling his future career in 1928.[49] It was still so.

In an era when the outsize personalities of Mussolini, Stalin, Hitler, and Roosevelt dominated international news, the primacy of personal leadership seemed to Gunther absolutely explanatory in regard to dictatorships, and no less reasonable to consider in constitutional governments. By animating leaders' personalities in discussion of their political tendencies, his book equipped readers with easily graspable knowledge. Gunther's talent for unspooling a narrative through individual protagonists and antagonists matched the wants of middlebrow readers. He invented lusty conversational idioms to describe powerful leaders and their sidekicks, noting their peculiarities in looks and quirks in behavior as well as their beliefs and policies. By cuing emotional responses, his prose encouraged readers to feel that they grasped the vast political landscape he surveyed. This was the approach that publishers considered a winning formula, and that the recently founded Book of the Month Club prized: arresting the reader's interest through individual characters, whom readers could admire or hate, identify with or find alien. Gunther was supremely good at it.[50]

His approach was akin to what the nineteenth-century German sociological thinker Max Weber called methodological individualism, a mode of analysis positing that intentional individual acts always underlay social phenomena. Weber saw this as a method for interpreting why things happen as they do, because intentions can be traced.[51] Gunther made individuals foremost, but as a modern man in Freud's Vienna, inevitably influenced by Freud's theory of the unconscious and recently psychoanalyzed by Dr. Stekel, he sought hidden motivations as well as more obvious intentions. His psychoanalytic understanding was shallow, matching that of most Americans who bandied about Freudian terms.

In his vivid portrayals of Hitler, Mussolini, and Stalin, Gunther embraced a theory of Stekel's about the psychopathology of dictators, which began with a pattern of bitter, impoverished childhood and an exceptionally strong mother-child relationship, and resulted in an outsize assertion of power over others, serving as anodyne for remembered humiliations. Furthermore, the popular veneration of these dictators stemmed from a postwar generation's need for a father substitute after rejecting their own fathers. Earlier, Gunther had visited Hitler's childhood hometown in Austria to interview relatives and friends who knew him as a child and published an article in *Vanity Fair* contending that Hitler was "a prisoner of infantile fixation." Stressing that claim in *Inside Europe*, he warned dramatically that "it cannot be denied: unresolved personal conflicts in the lives of various European politicians may contribute to the collapse of our civilization."[52]

Gunther's winning style was a key to his book's success. His authoritative voice laid on adjectives and similes, comparisons and analogies, arresting the reader's interest while encouraging the feeling of being very well informed. The republican constitution of Spain, Gunther wrote, for example, "exuded the pure cool aroma of Jean

Jacques Rousseau and Thomas Jefferson." Hitler as chancellor of Germany, quite the opposite, was "about as popular internationally as smallpox." "Mussolini is built like a steel spring. Stalin is a rock of sleepy granite by comparison and Hitler a blob of ectoplasm." Kemal Ataturk, the revolutionary Nationalist leader of Turkey, "the dictator-type carried to its ultimate extreme . . . strides the Turkish landscape like a colossus." Next to Ataturk, "Hitler is a milksop, Mussolini a perfumed dandy." Gunther included jokes: on Austria's tiny size compared to the past Austro-Hungarian Empire, he offered the story of two Tyroleans: "'Let's take a walk,' one said, 'around Austria.' 'No,' replied the other, 'I don't want to get back before lunch.'" He cited funny names: Hitler's bodyguards were named Schraub and Shreck, which in English meant "Screw" and "Fright." Even the chapter titles were stimulating: "Who Killed the German Republic?"; "The Trick by Fire and the Purge by Blood"; "Danube Blues"; "The February Tragedy"; "Duranty's Inferno"—this last, a newspaperman's tease alluding to Walter Duranty in Moscow.[53]

Almost all reviews of *Inside Europe* credited Gunther's broad expertise, praised the book's comprehensive coverage, and found it "vivid and extremely readable from beginning to end." British reviewers were, if anything, more positive than the American. An early rave in the London *Daily Telegraph* by Harold Nicolson—who was by then a Labour Party member of Parliament—delighted Gunther immeasurably and boosted British sales. Nicolson called *Inside Europe* "one of the most educative, as well as one of the most exciting books which I have read for years." Warning that it was "so entertaining that it may seem frivolous," "so comprehensive that it may seem superficial," "so personal that it may seem dramatic," "so exciting that it may seem sensational," Nicolson defended the book as a "serious contribution to contemporary knowledge." He did admit that Gunther's "sense of the picturesque phrase" occasionally led him astray. Nicolson also took the opportunity to praise the United States for giving more scope than Britain did to the valuable type of "perambulatory foreign correspondent" exemplified in Gunther,

John Gunther, studio photograph, 1936.
Source: National Portrait Gallery, London, photograph by Howard Coster.

Thompson, Sheean, H. R. Knickerbocker, the Mowrer brothers, and Walter Duranty. *The Spectator* took exception, contending that journalists were incompetent at writing books, and calling Gunther's "inside" story "even more silly and trivial than the outside one."[54]

Most American reviewers found Gunther's personality sketches "breath-taking" and "highly instructive," but his premise that "the accidents of personality play a great role in history" came in for some sharp criticism, as did his psychoanalytic claims. Gunther's friend Raymond Gram Swing warmly praised the book in *The Nation* but could not swallow Gunther's assertion that "Hitler has an Oedipus complex as big as a house." Lewis Gannett called the psychoanalytic analysis "Nonsense!" but nevertheless loved Gunther's detailed portraits and called *Inside Europe* "the liveliest, best-informed picture of Europe's chaotic politics that has come my way in years."[55]

Jimmy Sheean was another such critic. He endorsed the book for the publisher, calling it "An invaluable addition to our knowledge of the present monstrous age in European politics," but told his friend frankly, "I don't like the central theme, of course (as you would know without my telling you) and I do regard it as absolute nonsense that Kemal [Ataturk] swept the Greeks into the sea because some Greeks had ill-treated his mother, or that Mussolini's political career is due to a 'father-bipolarity' or whatever the hell the Viennese psychiatrist said. There are much sounder reasons than these for the things that happen." Malcolm Cowley's assessment in *The New Republic* verged on scorn. He undermined Gunther's thesis by arguing that collectively experienced social phenomena, rather than individual psyches, propelled history on its path.[56]

Regardless of objections, Gunther's book kept selling and selling. Cass Canfield had set the print run for the American edition at five thousand copies, enough to make a satisfactory profit for Harper & Brothers; the British printing was smaller. When good reviews made sales boom, Harper quickly rolled the presses. Fourteen more US printings were out by August, and the book had been translated into French, Dutch, Czechoslovak, Swedish, Danish, Finnish, and German—though the Gestapo banned *Inside Europe* and suppressed its circulation in Germany.[57]

Seven months after initial publication, Gunther was already preparing a revised edition. Hitler had cavalierly violated an earlier international agreement by marching his troops into the demilitarized Rhineland, and Mussolini invaded and occupied Abyssinia (Ethiopia). To keep the book up-to-date, Gunther made a thousand textual changes, adding fifteen thousand words. He accomplished all that in one week in August while still occupied in London. Matching the momentous rapid-fire events of the mid-1930s—including the abdication of Edward VIII in Britain, the start of civil war in Spain, the Moscow show trials—Gunther repeatedly revised *Inside Europe*, and

Harper sold the book anew, a marketing innovation in the publishing industry. In December 1936, Hamish Hamilton reported that *Inside Europe* was the best-selling nonfiction book by any American published in England in the previous decade.[58]

Although *Inside Europe* shimmered with assurance, Gunther felt cowed by the rapier wits of the British intelligentsia with whom he hobnobbed in London. His social circles included not only correspondents and publishers but also current politicians, former prime ministers, literary stars such as Aldous Huxley, H. G. Wells and Wells's captivating current lover, the cosmopolitan Russian baroness Moura Budberg, the Prince of Wales shortly before he became King Edward VIII, and Wallis Simpson, the American divorcée for whom Edward gave up the throne. Aneurin Bevan, a Labor member of Parliament for Wales, became Gunther's pal, while his favorite conversationalist was the radical journalist Claud Cockburn, who was publishing his own heterodox paper called *The Week* in mimeo form but would soon leave to join a Communist brigade in Spain. Margot Asquith, Countess of Oxford, the unconventional seventy-two-year-old widow of former prime minister H. H. Asquith, also became an adored friend of Gunther. The Gunthers played the brand-new game "Monopoly" with Margot Asquith's son and daughter-in-law, and Frances won—by applying "strictly Marxist strategy," she claimed.[59]

Circulating among intellectual power players in London, Gunther berated himself for his ignorance, as he had done in Vienna five years earlier: "I must <u>know</u>. Politics. Government. Finance. Economics. Psychology. Medicine. and biographies of all great men of affairs." Was it more important for India to be socialist or nationalist? Could the League of Nations hold back an imminent war? These were questions that came up in gatherings Gunther attended, on which he thought he should have firm and intelligent opinions. Lunching with a crowd of London political correspondents made him "want to crawl away for six weeks or six years and read all the books in the world, from Plato down. These people, all about my own age, <u>know</u> so much more than I do; they have a stronger point of view; they can back up any assertion with historical or literary allusions; they know Spinoza and Rousseau and Marx and Thomas Jefferson and John Milton and Lucretius and *Mein Kampf* by heart; they are, in a word, educated in a way that I am not." He tasked himself with almost comic earnestness for his inability to think solidly for a whole hour. "I try to pose questions to myself, 'What do you think of bourgeois morality?' 'What are your leading political ideas?' 'What is your definition of a great man?' and so on, but after a few moments I give up, grab any book to hand, and lose myself in it."[60]

With sales of *Inside Europe* quickly promising to make Gunther rich, London did not hold the Gunthers for very long. He quit his newspaper job, no longer worried about finding another job if he left the *News*. The Gunther family moved to New York in October 1936. As *Inside Europe* became the go-to book for Americans wanting to understand the recent past, the present, and the possible future of Europe, invitations poured in for Gunther to speak and to write articles for wide-circulation magazines. His earnings jumped from $9,812 in 1935 to nearly $47,000 in 1937, equivalent to more than $800,000 in buying power today.[61]

GUNTHER'S SUCCESS SHOWED that American audiences welcomed forceful interpretation of the fast-changing European political landscape. Authoritarian governments' deployment of propaganda and censorship in Europe had meant that he and his peers had been forced to sift and mend shards of news. Necessity made them interpret the news they reported, even while journalistic ethics required opinion to be set off from "fact." Raymond Gram Swing vigorously defended their approach in speaking to the American Society of Newspaper Editors in 1935: "If European news is to be comprehensible at all it has to be explained. If it is explained it has to be explained subjectively," Swing maintained. "There is no getting around it, the man in Europe who is of most value to his newspaper is the man who expresses opinions in his writings."[62] Sheean's *Personal History* had contributed uniquely to American foreign correspondents' winning that point. "Sheean established, as had nobody before him, that what counts is what a reporter thinks," one of his peers praised him; "No book published in our time . . . gave the public better insight into a newspaperman's mind."[63]

As grim news from Europe mounted, Americans wanted explanations that would help them grasp what was going on. Both Sheean and Gunther answered that call in their books, in lectures, and on the radio as well as in print. Most Americans in the 1930s wanted to distance themselves and their nation from intra-European conflicts, as popular surveys, huge memberships in pacifist organizations, and congressional passage of Neutrality Acts indicated. But the very prevalence of assertive antiwar sentiment in the United States showed, ironically, that Americans could not realistically divorce themselves from the rest of the world.[64] As the decade went on, Gunther, Sheean, and, even more prominently, Dorothy Thompson, pressed on the American public the futility of imagining American separation from the fate of Europe.

CHAPTER 9

ANTIFASCISM LOUD
AND CLEAR

B ECAUSE DOROTHY THOMPSON's political intelligence had been
schooled in Europe, she could not rid her mind of wariness
about the spread of fascism. Having seen representative parliaments
and the rule of law give way to authoritarianism in one European
nation after another, she worried whether any nation was immune.
The pattern of Germany's descent into Nazi rule made her especially
leery of concentrated executive power and state control of the economy. When President Roosevelt mobilized Congress to pass extraordinary new economic measures to deal with the Great Depression,
alarm bells rang in her head. She gave John Gunther an earful of her
concerns when she met him in Chicago in October 1934, telling
him her fear that FDR's party would become "dictatorial—Fascist."
The National Recovery Administration especially perturbed her. The
NRA's codification of wages and prices in industry seemed to her
ominously parallel to emergency decrees issued in the Weimar Republic in 1929–1930 and subsequently used by the Nazi Party to
great advantage.[1]

Thompson's political acumen put her on constant alert in the
1930s. She remained critical of what she saw as FDR's overreach and
sharply aware that the Depression evoked in the United States the
kind of economic resentments that had driven ordinary Germans to

look to Hitler as a savior. In 1934, more than one-fifth of the American workforce was unemployed; industries stood still, and drought was turning the southern plains into the Dust Bowl. Homegrown varieties of fascism and communism surged in the United States as well as elsewhere around the globe. While Thompson stayed on alert for warning signs in her own country, it was the alarming progress of fascism in Europe that really claimed her attention. Jimmy Sheean joined her in that. The two of them were among the most insistent voices urging American awareness of the threats implied in fascist militarism and aggression. On that topic, Thompson's effectiveness and celebrity—some would say notoriety—were unequalled.

THOMPSON SAW NO reason to assume that Americans were immune to fascism. She kept her eye on demagogic leaders of right-wing movements in the United States and on President Roosevelt's moves. In fearing that the NRA could slide toward fascism, she was not alone, for other reasonable Americans on both the left and right likened Mussolini's corporatism to the way the NRA operated or saw similarities between Roosevelt's policies to counter the Depression and Hitler's policies of limiting production and manipulating wages and prices.

Sinclair Lewis echoed Thompson's concerns in his satiric novel *It Can't Happen Here*, in which a folksy, popular, yet dictatorial fascist-like politician was elected president of the United States after bamboozling his audiences and the press with propaganda. Lewis dashed off the novel in six frenzied weeks in the summer of 1935. He modeled the antic power of his fictional character on controversial presidential aspirant Huey "Kingfish" Long, a rabble-rousing Louisiana senator (and previous governor) whom Thompson had interviewed in Washington earlier that year. An assassin's bullet put Long out of the way in September. Lewis's novel caused a political sensation when it was published a few weeks later, and it sold 320,000 copies.[2]

Since the Nazi regime had made Germany inaccessible to her, Thompson turned to the United States and began examining New Deal programs devised to relieve unemployment. Her view that Germany's use of public works employment had done more harm than good, making men's resentments fester rather than assuaging them, influenced her inquiry from the start. First going to Washington to interview central administrators, including Harry Hopkins and Rexford Tugwell, she then traveled around the country to speak to workers at Works Progress Administration and Federal Emergency Relief sites. She spoke also with social workers who dealt with recipients of direct aid, and with homeless men residing in transient camps set up for them.

Her three long articles in the *Saturday Evening Post* in 1935 made clear her doubts about the wisdom and efficacy of bureaucratically structured government aid. Life on relief seemed to her an alternative reality of social workers' visits and small checks—a benevolent "serfdom" backed up by government bureaucracy. The men housed in transient camps were treated like children: they led "infantile" lives "without personal responsibility" and would "make excellent shock troops for a radical-Fascist movement," she concluded. Public works projects had the advantage of supplying actual jobs, but she called the projects unnecessarily costly, because of the bureaucratic accounting required. Government power over the economy reeked of fascism to her. "If the state aggrandizes the economic power, for whatever purpose," she believed from what she had seen happen to the Weimar Republic, "then it is driven toward dictatorship by the sheer necessity of fulfilling what always must be its two prime functions: maintaining order and avoiding bankruptcy." Apart from her genuine alarm about germinating conditions for fascist mobilization, Thompson's criticism of New Deal programs resembled what wealthy Republican opponents said of the New Deal.[3]

Thompson's amalgam of New Deal criticism and Europe-bred antifascism puzzled John Gunther. As much as he admired and agreed with her on European matters, he found her objections to the New Deal hard to swallow. His ambivalence influenced the canny and affectionate profile he wrote of her at that time, at the request of the *New York Herald Tribune Magazine*, in which he summarized her affect as "impersonal, disinterested, sometimes brutal, often inconsiderate, generous, excessively single-track in her devotion to compelling enthusiasms, reasonably ambitious and unfalteringly cheerful."[4]

Thompson's views drew the attention of Helen Rogers Reid, wife of Ogden Reid, the owner and publisher of the *New York Herald Tribune*. The Reids were stalwart Republicans, as was the *Herald Tribune* (like most leading newspapers), but they were not among the isolationist hard-liners in the Republican Party. Helen Reid had masterminded the paper's rising prominence since the mid-1920s, and in 1931 she began an important new trend by hiring Walter Lippmann to write a political column. She lured him with an outsize salary, a secretary, a travel budget, and full scope to express himself three times a week. At the time, political columns barely existed—the sole political opinion was typically on the editorial page, the owner's province. Syndicated columns of the 1920s dwelled on personalities, humor, gossip, or homely wisdom and very rarely on political questions. Op-eds did not exist, with one exception: the page in the *New York World*, a Democratic paper, where Lippmann wrote until the paper folded in 1931. Reid's risky hire of Lippmann, whose political views were not easy to place on a standard political spectrum, paid off in readership. Other papers then jumped to hire their own political columnists.[5]

Political columnists became a new phenomenon in the 1930s, but not one of them was a woman until Reid approached Thompson about writing a column in the *Herald Tribune*. Having already put an extraordinary number of women into responsible positions, Reid now offered Thompson a marvelous opportunity, and Thompson gladly grabbed it. She asked for perks like Lippmann's and a firm guarantee of freedom to speak her mind, and Helen and Ogden Reid more or less promised what she wanted. Neither they nor Thompson envisioned significant friction occurring between them.[6]

Thompson named her column On the Record. It began on March 17, 1936, appearing on an ordinary newspaper page (as Lippmann's did) rather than on an opinion page. Producing a thousand to fifteen hundred snappy and meaningful words every Tuesday, Thursday, and Saturday would be no easy ride, Thompson understood, and Lippmann said as much in a welcoming note. Helen Reid had imagined a "woman's voice"; Thompson wrote about whatever was on her mind. She took on national and foreign politics, breaking news, court decisions, cultural innovations, social habits, historical change, intellectual trends. Six weeks into the job, she loved it, she told her friend Alexander Woollcott, a well-known New York drama critic, radio voice, and master of the bon mot. "I hope you are right about it getting to be easier," she replied to Woollcott's praise. "I'm like the gal who is put to teaching French to the High School kids. She means well, but she doesn't know French and keeps just one jump ahead of the class." To John Gunther she confided, "You have no idea how hard it is to write about American politics. This country is in a mess politically. I don't know half time whether I'm on my head or my feet." But she added delightedly, "I have the world's best job."[7]

She made the column provocative, critical of many of FDR's policies at home and vividly antifascist on the European situation. Pathos, condemnation, fierce analogy—all of these contributed to making her political feelings clear. Seventy daily newspapers signed on for syndication rights immediately. Soon that number doubled. Within two years, her column reached between seven and eight million newspaper subscribers. Of seven leading columnists profiled in *The Nation* in 1938, only Walter Lippmann's potential audience of eight million exceeded Thompson's, and not by much.[8]

Packing lots of information into short space, and writing in down-to-earth language, Thompson moved easily from fire-breathing indignation to folksiness from one day to the next. For humor she invented the Grouse—a petulant and satirical character (often assumed by readers to represent Sinclair Lewis) with whom she held spirited dialogues. She did her writing in the mornings at home, at Twin Farms in the warm months and in New York during the winters. A generous hostess at both homes, she had a habit of directing social conversation to spark ideas for her columns. As a result she became known—not always kindly—for pumping knowledgeable people for tips. She trusted a coterie of well-informed male friends to give her insights and corrections on foreign affairs and employed three women as secretaries and research assistants.[9]

Fascism continually pressed on Thompson's mind not only as a monstrous reality in Europe but also as an American possibility. "It Can Happen Here," she titled her column on May 28, 1936, playing on the title of her husband's novel to decry a thuggish vigilante group of white Protestant men who had murdered a relief worker in Detroit. Wherever she saw anti-Semitism she came down on it. She insisted that persecution of Jews ought to concern every American because it was antithetical to principles of democracy. In July she devoted two successive columns to "the lunatic fringe," after the Reverend Gerald L. K. Smith, an effective speaker who attracted Huey Long's supporters, defiantly adopted that phrase in self-description. Her outrage targeted several groups of extremist nationalists in whose rhetoric she saw the early Nazi movement mirrored. They included followers of the anti-Semitic "radio priest" Father Coughlin and of William Lemke, presidential candidate of the miniscule Union Party, who excoriated liberals, socialists, communists, immigrants, and people of color.[10]

"No people ever recognize their dictator in advance," Thompson warned. "When our dictator turns up, you can depend on it that he will be one of the boys . . . and he will stand for everything traditionally American." In her echo of Lewis's novel, she was alluding to what she saw as President Roosevelt's overreach. She admired the president's talents, but his 1937 "court-packing" proposal incensed her. FDR became so frustrated by the Supreme Court striking down New Deal policies that he proposed increasing the number of justices—whom he would have the power to appoint. FDR's proposal never became a reality, but his attempt underlined Thompson's grim belief that the state "is by its nature a predatory instrument." After the president called the Supreme Court a headache, Thompson opened her column with the Grouse "crankily" opining, "'There is one certain cure for a headache. . . . It is cheap, instantaneous and guaranteed. That remedy is decapitation.'" The ridiculousness of such a "cure" led to Thompson playing the Grouse's interlocutor and explaining the unconstitutionality of FDR's scheme. An observation by the Grouse—"'I see . . . that we are going to keep out of war'"— likewise animated her critique of the Neutrality Act of 1937. Certain that Nazi Germany was preparing for war, she repeatedly hammered the point that neutrality legislation was mistaken in theory and practice, a brake on the exercise of American foreign policy.[11]

As if her column were not enough, the radio networks also wanted Thompson. Three national networks (NBC, CBS, and the Mutual Broadcasting Service, MBS) operated in 1936, and Americans owned 33 million radios—eleven times as many as a dozen years before. Surveys indicated an average of three listeners for every radio, which suggested that 80 percent of the population could tune in at once. Thompson accepted a weekly spot on NBC, hosting a short late-evening program on personalities in the news. Her horror at fascist use of radio as a tool in Europe made her appreciate the airwaves' impact; cold newsprint could not match the immediacy of a radio voice. She found it thrilling to address potential millions at once, especially in contrast to exhausting lecture tours. Broadcast, her voice was at once feminine, forceful, authoritative, and elegant, her pronunciation precise, with an accent hinting at upper-class Britain more than upstate New York. She could be heard on radio programs beyond her own, too, when called upon to address particular issues or events.[12]

With programs such as Thompson's, radio moved into political commentary. When radio programs began in the 1920s they were locally broadcast and consisted of sports, music, and entertainment, not news, because the newspaper industry monopolized news broadcasting. Newspaper owners defended their monopoly ever more aggressively when the Depression sank their income from advertising, just as radio programs' popularity zoomed ahead and networks became national. The newspaper–radio battle over control of the news reached a compromise in 1934, allowing stations to broadcast five-minute news briefs twice a day, without commercial sponsorship; newspapers in turn agreed to publish radio program schedules. Radio networks continued to press into news reporting, and over time, the line between news and commentary blurred: NBC hired Thompson to attend both Republican and Democratic presidential nominating conventions in 1936, for example. Still, Americans relied principally on newspapers for news, and especially for foreign news, until the end of the 1930s.[13]

Millions of Americans already listened to Thompson on the radio and read her pithy column three days a week when the *Ladies' Home Journal* came knocking, asking her to write a column that would spark women's interest in politics. The *Journal*'s circulation outran that of every other women's magazine and even that of the *Saturday Evening Post*. Thompson happily agreed to write a column every month for $1,000 each, equivalent to more than $17,000 today. She received six honorary university degrees in 1937; invitations to speak at forums, clubs, dinners, and commencements poured in by the hundreds. Americans debated her views over breakfast tables and at dinner parties, in office breaks and on the street. Whether revering or deploring her, they recognized her as the "First Lady of American Journalism."[14]

Sinclair Lewis could not endure it. When the German situation dominated conversation at home, as it often did during social occasions, Lewis became furious. "Many is the time I have heard him say 'No more *situations* or I will go to bed,'" Jimmy Sheean recalled. "Generally he pronounced it *sityashuns* in order to make it seem more contemptible." Although Lewis had a sudden best seller in *It Can't*

Happen Here, and more than one reviewer judged it his best since *Dodsworth* (1929), he knew that his 1930s novels lacked the brilliance of his earlier fiction. His sense of creative decline contrasted starkly with Thompson's ascent. He "had a horror of being known as 'Mr. Dorothy Thompson,'" Sheean thought, watching the marriage fade into "a hopeless simulacrum." Moments of solidarity between the couple became the exceptions rather than the rule.[15]

In the spring of 1937, Lewis announced that he was leaving. He had become crazy about the theater—writing plays, acting in summer stock, and falling in love with a very young actress, Marcella Powers. Thompson did not see casual infidelity as fatal, but felt stricken by

"He's giving Dorothy Thompson a piece of his mind."

Dorothy Thompson cartoon by James Thurber, in the *New Yorker* May 16, 1936.
Source: Cartoons Collection, New York.

the withdrawal of his love. When Lewis blamed her work for ruining their marriage, she protested unhappily that she loved him intensely, uniquely, and that, quite the contrary to what he thought, her work had saved their marriage. Lewis's "overcharged" presence was "too intense to be born[e]" at times, she explained: "I couldn't live with you, every minute, wholly, . . . [in] so charged and electric an atmosphere. And work has always been my way out." Only "constant baths in the cool air of work" enabled her to return to him whole. (Lewis's "appalling restlessness" had been caricatured by Bernard de Voto as "a kind of electrical disturbance. He wasn't actually spinning like a top or hanging by his toes from the ceiling but you had a dizzy impression that he must be.") Thompson insisted to her husband, "I am grateful to work. Next to you, I love it best of anything."[16]

Very reluctant to see the marriage end, she continued to harbor the belief that she and Lewis would reunite—but they never lived together again. The implosion of their marriage was a source of great pain to her, exaggerated by her previous experience with Bard. Thompson could tell herself rationally that both of her marriages had failed through her husbands' faults as much as (if not more than) her own. Still, the marriages *had* failed. That meant, to her, that *she* had failed. That was a common view of the day and her own heart's view, despite her reasoned justifications of her behavior.

Thompson's distress affected what she wrote in her *Ladies' Home Journal* column, the one public place where she wrote about gender roles, though only occasionally even there. Although as a professional journalist Thompson always downplayed the pertinence of sex to individual capacity or achievement, she identified deeply as a woman and believed women and men had essentially different needs and roles to play in sexual and family relationships. Her first column, in May 1937, championed the lifegiving, civilizing nature of women, echoing gender expectations familiar to *Journal* readers. Addressing "the Girl Graduate" in June, she undermined her self-defense to Lewis by assuring the graduate of high school or college that if she married and spent her life at home, using her husband's earnings wisely and raising her children "to be good people," she should not "feel inferior to women 'with careers.'" It was "harder and rarer," Thompson wrote, "to be a good wife than a good newspaperwoman." Her sense of having failed in two marriages bore on her mind. In a later column she slammed her generation's "illusion" that a happy marriage could accompany a demanding career and sexual freedom. "Making a successful marriage is, by and large, a full-time job for most women," she concluded. She added, "If I had a daughter I would tell her that she had to choose."[17]

Yet through the 1930s she energetically opposed the damaging (and misplaced) Depression-provoked outcry against married women stealing men's jobs and insisted eloquently on wives' need and right to have paid employment of their own. American efforts to eliminate married women's public and private employment fed her suspicions about creeping fascism. In a keynote speech called "The Changing Status of Women," given before thousands of women at a *Herald Tribune* forum in 1934, she deplored retrogressive Nazi dictates for women and urged wariness about American intents "to put women back into the home in order to create extra jobs for men." The impulse "runs counter both to the best interests of women and the best interests of society," she declared firmly. "The traditional activities of women cannot again in the modern world be centered in the home, to any great extent." With the Nazi example in mind, she continued, "a society in which women are reduced to a diminished role will, I am convinced, become in the end a sterile and a dead society tending toward militarism."

She urged her audience to have "in their own minds" the convictions that shaped her attitude: "Work is <u>not</u> merely a job: work is <u>not</u> merely a means of earning money or supplementing a man's income. Work is an essential of life itself as necessary as bread and love; it is the means by which the individual establishes a relation between himself and a larger society than the family unit; it is his—and her— chief medium for growth and development. The chance to choose one's work, and to pursue it, is the chance to become a more effective human being." Her words expressed her own self-justification.[18] She did not stop holding that view, despite her *Journal* columns appearing to deny it. In 1938 in On the Record, for example, she defended wives' employment against a conservative columnist's attack.[19] Her underlying conviction that women deserved to have both love and work persisted, although the demise of her second marriage robbed her of joy in it.

Dorothy Thompson and Sinclair Lewis at Twin Farms, 1938.
Source: Aldon Blackington Photographs, Special Collections and University Archives, University of Massachusetts.
When photographer Aldon Blackington did a series of portraits of New England characters, he sought out Lewis and Thompson at their Vermont home.

THE YEAR 1938 was an alarmingly bad one in Thompson's eyes. Spring began with Hitler's triumph of political chicanery and force in his long-intended "Anschluss," the annexation of Austria to Germany, a direct assault on the prohibition in the Versailles treaty.

Thompson's beloved Vienna was being Nazified. She called the March 12 takeover "the most cataclysmic event of modern history," and wrote in On the Record that it foretold one of two outcomes: either "Germany will dominate the Continent of Europe, or millions of lives will be spent in another war." She pounded out her message that fascism was an "international revolutionary movement" no less than communism, and more dangerous. Italy had joined Germany and Japan in November 1937 in a pact pledging to fight communism wherever it appeared, including inside other countries, and Thompson referred to this "Fascist International" alliance as the "Fascintern," in parallel to the Comintern (the Communist International).[20]

Few Americans could remain unaware of Thompson's furious efforts to budge them from the "supreme illusion" that fascism was not their worry. She repeatedly accented the terrible danger of "ostrichism"—Americans burying their heads in the sand. In her conviction that the "Fascintern" threatened the United States as well as Britain and Europe, she was far ahead of the nation as a whole. Her estimation of the threat was shared by most American reporters in Europe, certainly by Gunther, Sheean, William Shirer, Edgar Mowrer, and H. R. Knickerbocker—and though they wrote influential news articles, essays, and books, none of them had a thrice-weekly column in the Herald Tribune or any comparable mouthpiece. Of all the journalists who aroused Americans to the evils of Nazism in the 1930s, she was the most insistent and best known.[21]

Thompson's continuing condemnation of Nazi measures defining and defaming Jews as an inferior "race" was also exceptional. Many of Thompson's friends in Germany were Jewish and had fled, becoming refugees living in the United States. Her sympathies with them underlay her emphasis, but she also saw a larger issue in Nazi crimes against Jews: these crimes exemplified the social injustices produced when authoritarian governments obliterated liberal legal procedures. Besides speaking and writing eloquently about Nazi persecution, she sponsored Jewish individuals trying to emigrate to the United States, sent money generously to friends in Europe, and supported organizations helping needy exiles. Polls at that time showed that 30 to 40 percent of the American populace embraced a strong anti-Semitism, in sharp contrast to Thompson's sympathies. Prejudice against Jews was widespread. Prestigious universities strictly limited admission of Jews, for example, and prestigious professions rarely advanced them; restrictive covenants in high-end neighborhoods prevented Jews from acquiring property there, and clubs of the well-off refused Jewish members. At least half of Americans believed that Jews had too much influence in the nation's economic life.[22]

Thompson called herself a conservative, but her insistent antifascism complicated any attempt to categorize her. Though her views of the New Deal placed her with conservative critics of FDR's policies, those critics typically saw fascism as more benign than communism and leaned toward isolationism in foreign affairs, the very opposite of her position. Though no fan of communism, Thompson saw fascism as a much greater current menace.

Her stance on the Spanish Civil War indicated how her antifascism aligned her with the left. In 1936, General Francisco Franco led a military revolt that aimed to topple the recently elected left-leaning Spanish government. Much of the Spanish army went with Franco; the Spanish fascist party called the Falange supported him, and so did the Catholic Church. Thompson immediately looked askance at Franco's so-called Nationalists as perpetrators of a "flagrant military rebellion" against a legitimate government, even before it became clear that Nazi Germany and Fascist Italy supported Franco's forces.

Thompson recognized early that the war in Spain was a contest in international power politics, not simply an internal conflict. By 1938 the world knew that Mussolini and Hitler were boosting Franco's insurgents with armaments, munitions, Italian troops, and all-important bombing planes. The Soviet Union, as an enemy of fascism, responded by sending arms, planes, and advisers to the Republican loyalists who were fighting to retain the elected government, but Soviet support was relatively small. Meanwhile, the democracies—

Britain, France, and the United States—did nothing, presenting a "spectacle of indecision and hypocrisy" in Thompson's critical view.

When the United States embargoed any arms shipments to Spain (as prescribed by the 1937 Neutrality Act), Thompson protested that the American position amounted to aiding fascists. She argued repeatedly in favor of lifting the embargo, not hesitating to place herself on the side of communists when they were battling fascist tyranny. Her views on Spain allied her with the international left, while in the United States she joined with right-wing conservatives in regard to the New Deal. Thompson admitted no contradiction there. Both her antifascism and her New Deal critique stemmed from her commitment to upholding liberal democracy as she defined it.[23]

JIMMY SHEEAN AGREED with Thompson's assessment that they were seeing a fateful struggle between liberal democracy and fascism in Spain. As antifascists the two were united, but he did not share her critique of the New Deal. Since recovering from his 1936 breakdown, Sheean had been living with his wife Dinah and their daughter Linda either in an elegant neighborhood outside Paris or else on the coastal cliffs of England above the English Channel—both places loaned by generous members of Dinah's extended family. In seeming withdrawal from politics, he wrote a historical novel centering on a confrontation between the French and English armies in 1745, published as *A Day of Battle* (1938).[24]

The civil war tearing Spain apart galvanized Sheean's antifascist energies. Like Thompson and other antifascists, Sheean saw the Spanish Civil War as a proxy war, heavy with meaning because of German and Italian support for Franco's side and the Soviet Union's aid to the Republican loyalists. Individual democratic, socialist, anarchist, and communist sympathizers from many countries outside Spain, including three thousand or more from the United States, saw it that way, and volunteered their bodies to the Republicans, forming International Brigades to fight Franco's Nationalist forces.

Sheean desperately wanted to get press credentials to report from the front. His frequent source for commissions, the North American News Alliance (NANA), had already given the job of reporting Spain to Ernest Hemingway. In Paris, Sheean happened to see Hemingway departing for Spain and was peeved by his offhand remark, "You stay here and be comfortable, kid: I'll go to Spain for you." Sheean knew he "did not want anybody to go to Spain for me, least of all Ernest." In February 1938, Sheean and his wife traveled to the United States—they had been invited to dine at FDR's White House, along with twenty others—and he looked up Dorothy Thompson in New York right away. When he told Thompson about his eagerness to get to Spain, she quickly arranged for him to talk with Helen Reid, who needed little persuading to offer Sheean press credentials from the *New York Herald Tribune*.[25]

The Sheeans recrossed the Atlantic a month later, bound for Spain. In April 1938 they arrived in Barcelona, capital of the province of Catalonia, where the Republicans were holding out against what seemed like looming defeat. Franco's forces had conquered at least two-thirds of the country. Dinah Sheean was drawn in by accompanying Jimmy there, and when they returned to England, she raised funds to send food and milk to children on the Republican side. Although she was only twenty-three, inexperienced, and diffident about speaking and writing for a political cause, she proved adept at her work with relief and refugee organizations.[26]

Sheean drove with a few other correspondents to the front, three hours away from Barcelona, and found volunteers of the International Brigades in retreat from an onslaught by tanks, troops, and hundreds of German and Italian planes. Silver bodies of Italian aircraft soared overhead, while the unequipped Republicans were using tourist road maps to plot their retreat. Together the correspondents and the exhausted soldiers dodged ongoing air raids. Sheean had not been under fire since the Rif, where forces led by the same General Franco had decimated the Riffians at Alhucemas Bay. Revering the bravery he saw in the International Brigades, Sheean felt that their presence "suffused the total effort with a moral value more precious than their lives, the sense of a world not altogether lost." Among them he sensed "a common conscience in which whatever hope there is for any possible future must rise again."[27]

Sheean's articles, communicated to New York by telephone or radio, emphasized persistent Republican energy even though assaults in April had severed Catalonia from the rest of Republican-held Spain. Much of their population was starving, but the Republicans mobilized to prevent total Nationalist victory. Despite this seeming devastation in April, Sheean's headlines in May told an upbeat story as he moved from Barcelona to Valencia to Madrid: "Loyalist Spirit Is High Despite Daily Bombings"; "Enemy at Its Gates, Madrid Fights on, Gay as Ever"; "Loyalist Spain Viewed as Getting Its Second Wind with Morale Up." Because the *Herald Tribune* syndicated its foreign news, Sheean's articles could be read far beyond New York City.[28]

As Franco's Nationalists advanced in Spain, Sheean raged at "the tragic hypocrisy of 'nonintervention'" by Britain and France. British leadership seemed to him comatose, blinkered in indifference to the aggressive appetite of fascism, making no move to help Spain nor to prevent Mussolini's recent takeover of Ethiopia. Only the valorous commitment of the Spanish Republicans offered him hope: peasants and workers undergoing extreme privation were nonetheless staking their lives on preventing Franco's victory—and doing so with inspiring élan. He saw in their unvanquished spirits the only counter to Western powers' timorousness and "the limitless claims of Fascist imperialism." "Spain alone raised its clenched fist against the bombs."[29]

The Sheeans left Spain in June, headed for Vienna. The Anschluss had taken place when they were en route from New York to Spain, and they found a favorite city hideously transformed. Vienna was a "nightmare," Dinah wrote to a friend in horror. Terror reigned, as the Nazis imposed on the Austrians the "coordination" that had made Dorothy Thompson shudder in Berlin five years earlier. Vienna was "a depressed and harassed shadow of itself" after three and a half months under Nazi rule, Sheean mourned. After investigating, he estimated that fifty thousand people, including aristocrats, liberal Catholics, intellectuals, and other potential dissidents, had been thrown in jail as supposed enemies. Jews were being systematically expropriated and had no rights whatsoever; twenty thousand of them had been imprisoned, and all the rest were under constant threat of arrest. The *New York Times* cited Sheean's findings editorially, labeling the Nazi cruelty in Vienna a "cold pogrom."[30]

The Sheeans went on in September 1938 to Czechoslovakia's Sudetenland, the mainly German-speaking region that Hitler was intent on acquiring. Hitler had stirred up ethnic Germans there to make impossible demands on the Czech government, holding out the threat of invasion by Germany if the demands were not met. If Czechoslovakia were invaded, prior treaty obligations would bring France and the Soviet Union into the fray. Britain's prime minister Neville Chamberlain, determined to avoid war and knowing that Britain would also be drawn in by France, began negotiating with Hitler. Drawn-out negotiations culminated in Britain and France handing Hitler the Sudetenland. The Czech government had no alternative but to succumb. The agreement signed on September 30 in Munich by Germany, Britain, France, and Italy achieved "peace in our time," Chamberlain infamously declared.

Britain's and France's abdication of responsibility disgusted Sheean. Czechoslovakia sacrificed its national independence "as a ransom for the spineless West," in his words. Again, as in Spain, the Western democracies failed to shore up the antifascist side, and the repetition made both failures more appalling. Dorothy Thompson was equally sickened by British and French leaders' willingness "to throw the last democratic republic east of the Rhine into the jaws of the Nazis." She saw the Munich agreement as a death knell for the continent and titled her column about it "Obituary for Europe."[31]

The Munich crisis became a turning point for Americans' awareness of the imminence of war in Europe, and also for reliance on radio for up-to-the-minute news. During Chamberlain's negotiations with Hitler, newsman H. V. Kaltenborn of CBS stayed in the radio studio in New York day and night, receiving reports from abroad by telephone or wireless, translating them himself, and narrating the situation blow-by-blow, making eighty-five broadcasts in eighteen days. No newspaper "extra" could be hawked on the sidewalk as quickly as a voice could speak on the air. Kaltenborn's feat made radio a news phenomenon and his own name a household word. Radio was "a new dimension . . . added to politics and diplomacy," commented critic James Rorty on these broadcasts. "For the first time, history has been made in the hearing of its pawns."[32]

After sending gloomy dispatches from Czechoslovakia's Sudetenland, Sheean returned to Barcelona, aiming to revive his own spirits with a second exposure to the antifascist resistance there. He traveled to a spot near the front one early November day along with Ernest Hemingway, Herbert Matthews of the *New York Times*, and photographer Robert Capa, through a landscape of destroyed villages and shell-marked houses. Dodging barrages of fascist shelling to see the Republican forces in retreat, the foursome narrowly avoided catastrophe themselves. The scene was even worse when Sheean returned to Catalonia two months later, in January 1939. He rushed there when he heard that Barcelona was about to fall. From Figueres, a small town near the French border, he saw the miserable demoralization of the Republican population subjected to merciless bombing. Floods of bewildered and starving refugees streamed toward the Propaganda Office where he and other correspondents took refuge, sleeping at night on the tile floor. Thousands came that way, clutching their small bundles of possessions, hoping to cross the border to France and meanwhile waiting, starving, shivering, and sleeping in the gutters. For the article he owed to the North American News Association, Sheean wrote something close to a funeral dirge. Never before had he mentioned defeat. Now he knew that fascist triumph lay ahead.[33]

In all his newspaper writing in 1938, Sheean spoke interpretively, as an eyewitness. He made that plain to readers. Newspapers publishing his syndicated articles highlighted Sheean's reputation as intrepid journalist and author of *Personal History*. His interpretive angle, based on his firsthand observation and shrewd political reasoning, had become his calling card. "'Objective' reporting" of the events of 1938 was "hardly possible for us who live awash in the tidal wave they set up," he wrote afterward. He wrote the truth as he saw it.[34]

Expanding on his newspaper accounts, Sheean recounted his 1938 experiences in a book he called *Not Peace But a Sword* (1939). Again, as in *Personal History*, he was the central character facing world-historical events, but the book's bitter mood differed entirely from the exploratory dynamic of the earlier work. The contrast measured the distance between the venturesome 1920s and the harrowing 1930s as Sheean lived them. The book's urgent theme was the failure of the Western democracies to face up to fascism. Its eloquence compelled reviewers, and it sold well—a hundred thousand copies its first year—though nowhere near as well as *Personal History*.[35]

Sheean's reputation sparked many invitations to write and to speak, but he was not always in shape to respond. After his 1936 breakdown, he had recurrent episodes of seemingly manic behavior and bouts of disabling drunkenness, especially in New York. Dinah Sheean devoted herself to him during these difficult periods. On their return from Spain to New York in February 1939, he had a bad spell—barely sleeping, exhibiting terrific nervous energy and excitement even without drinking heavily. Dinah described his behavior to correspondent Louis Fischer, who knew Sheean from Moscow and became close to Dinah in Spain, where Fischer too was enmeshed in the antifascist cause. "It's something to do with coming here [to New York]," Dinah explained worriedly, "with . . . the effect that he has on people here—they are very silly about him, lionize him terrifically and fuss over him, and that terrific self-consciousness of his starts getting fretted." Jimmy was "galloping around" at home, repeating a patter she knew from previous episodes—"that he has made a public fool of himself, that everyone on earth knows about it,

James Vincent Sheean in the living room of his bor-
rowed home in England, 1939.
*Source: Photograph collection at the Tamiment Library, New
York University, by permission of the Communist Party USA.*

that it is a shame and humiliation for me, that it is something that he can't help." She went on, "'It,' he has tried to describe to me . . . as some abnormality in himself which everyone recognizes and which has many sides, one of them very obscene. . . . He . . . goes into a sort of trance and shakes he [*sic*] head, and repeats how horrible this all is, and he keeps asking me how I can stand it and he asks himself what is it. . . . He is in agony all the time. . . . He clings onto me as if he were drowning, and it is very hard to be strong and helpful and not to break down too and just howl."[36]

Sheean's outbursts mystified Dinah, although to a contemporary ear they sound like hysterical confessionals about his sexual attraction to men. Very anxious because Jimmy was scheduled to speak on be-half of refugee Spanish Republicans, Dinah (then pregnant with their second child) felt "terrifyingly uncertain" whether he would collapse while speaking. His recovery a few weeks later reassured her, making him "as good a lecturer as any I have ever heard," Dinah told Fischer. She urged Jimmy often to see a psychoanalyst, wanting him to "find out what these things are that trouble him." He resisted huffily.[37]

THE REFUGEES THAT Sheean saw fleeing Spain represented part of a growing international problem that Dorothy Thompson took to heart. Not only were refugees running away from fascism in Spain and Jewish refugees from Nazism in Germany and Austria; displaced political liberals, socialists, monarchists, and aristocrats were exiled elsewhere. Four million people around the globe were already state-less, Thompson pointed out, and their numbers were swelling—where would they go? During the worldwide depression, many countries excluded in-migrants who would become job seekers. Palestine was no longer an open-ended possibility for Jews because Britain in 1936 severely limited Jewish immigration there, responding to Arab resent-ment of a recent Jewish influx.

Thompson saw catastrophe ahead if democratic countries did not act. As she looked around the world, democracy was losing the race it was running against fascism. Refugees were part of the picture, she contended, for "a defeatist attitude toward the refugee problem becomes a defeatist attitude toward democracy itself." Pressing this point in *Foreign Affairs*, she declared that the refugee problem had to "be regarded as a problem of international politics" rather than a matter for "international charity" (as had been typical in the past). She proposed an international agency that would incorporate Jewish agencies' current efforts but would gain the stature, administration, and funding of an effective international body. Her writing goaded President Roosevelt toward American participation in an interna-tional conference on refugees in Evian-les-Bains, France, and she influenced the League of Nations to extend the life of a committee on refugees that would have otherwise expired.[38]

As dire events unspooled in Europe, Thompson was often asked to comment on the radio. Her antifascist fervency produced electrifying effect in the Grynszpan case. A desperate seventeen-year-old Polish-German Jew named Herschel Grynszpan, desolated by the brutal arrest and expulsion of his parents and thousands of others from Poland, was living alone and illegally in Paris, feeling hopeless about his own future. On November 7, 1938, carrying a gun, he walked into the German embassy and shot the first German official he saw. He did not attempt to run away, and French police took him into custody. Goebbels's propaganda ministry immediately directed the German press to describe the shooting as an attack on the Third Reich by "world Jewry." This directive intentionally provoked ferocious storm trooper attacks on Jews, and arson attempts on Jewish synagogues and community buildings in several locales. On November 9, when Grynszpan's victim, Ernst vom Roth, died, Hitler and Goebbels took the opportunity to orchestrate a coordinated nationwide attack on Jews that marked a new stage in Nazi terror. Shock troops unleashed wanton pogroms and looting so destructive that the episode was later called the "Night of Broken Glass," or *Kristallnacht*. Nazi violence killed at least a hundred people that night; thirty thousand Jewish men were swept off to concentration camps in one week. World press reaction was aghast.[39]

Though Thompson knew Grynszpan was guilty, the "unheard-of things" taking place in Germany enraged her more than ever. Grynszpan's plight obsessed her: was he not justified by "a higher justice, that says that this deed has been expiated with four hundred million dollars and half a million existences, with beatings, and burnings, and deaths, and suicides?" she wrote (referring to Jewish losses). France was about to sign a nonaggression pact with Germany, and Thompson focused on whether Grynszpan could get anything close to a fair trial in Paris. "Who is on trial?" she asked her radio audience when she spoke on the General Electric radio hour. "I say we are all on trial. I say the Christian world is on trial. I say the men of Munich are on trial, who signed a pact without one word of protection for helpless minorities." Thompson called the situation a crisis for the human race, for human decency and principles of civilization—"not a Jewish crisis" alone. She demanded that her audience examine themselves. She accused the Western democracies, and Christians, for their own inaction in allowing Germany's perpetration of horrific violence against Jews.[40]

Her forceful eloquence as she spoke of Grynszpan's youth, his character, and his desperation drew an immediate response. Three thousand telegrams arrived (from forty-six of the forty-eight states), along with innumerable letters offering help, and several hundred dollars. Interpreting the response as showing Americans' unified commitment to civil liberties, she then got a number of correspondent friends (including John Gunther, Hamilton Fish Armstrong, and Raymond Gram Swing) together to form a Journalists Defense Fund to raise money for the best possible lawyers for Grynszpan. Thompson publicly insisted that only non-Jews should donate, lest the Nazis take it as a provocation for more retribution against Jews in Germany. Nearly $40,000 came in, more than was needed to pay the top-notch lawyer already hired to defend the boy. (Thompson sent the remaining money to refugee organizations.) Grynszpan's fate was overborne by larger forces before very long. When France fell to the Nazis in June 1940, he was sent to prison under German supervision.[41]

Reams of anti-Semitic hate mail landed at Thompson's door because of her efforts for Grynszpan. Her stance of "ruthless indignation," as one writer characterized it, inevitably elicited critical comment, not only about her as a bluntly opinionated political columnist but also about her as a woman. *Time* magazine called Thompson a "Passionate Pundit" who was "never at a loss for an answer, almost invariably incensed about something," and whose "column has pleased a national appetite for being scolded." Behind such commentary flickered unspoken female stereotypes—the censorious

Dorothy Thompson at NBC Radio microphone, late 1930s.
Source: Dorothy Thompson Papers, Special Collections Research Center, Syracuse University Libraries.
Studio conditions appear to be spare and cold.

schoolmarm, the nagging mother, the harpy. As her impact on public opinion gathered momentum, Thompson became all the more newsworthy herself. The urgency of her columns and radio addresses attracted many additional invitations to speak and write, and she took them. Thousands of people attended her lectures. She was constantly in the public eye. She was both rewarded and reviled for her strong stands, receiving awards for her valiant efforts on behalf of refugees.[42]

In a 1938 series on eight major political columnists, *The Nation's* literary editor Margaret Marshall wrote an astute sketch of Thompson, calling her "the most interesting and dramatic personality" of the eight, and summing up what made her compellingly readable and influential and also a magnet for ire. Every one of Thompson's anti-fascist columns "reads like a tour de force," Marshall wrote, admiring her "positive, disinterested and passionate conviction" regarding the persecution of Jews and other victims of fascism. Not surprisingly, Marshall, who was on the left, thought Thompson's writing on foreign affairs "much superior" to her sniping at the New Deal. But Thompson was likely to sink into "hysteria" even in antifascist mode, Marshall wrote. "Outrage is her favorite mood." Marshall appreciated Thompson's antifascist sincerity but could not stomach her always taking a "high moral tone," acting as a "self-appointed anti-fascist Joan of Arc" in a voice always righteously hectoring, always "dealing in ultimate truths." These "alarmist tendencies of her emotional nature" were especially dangerous when Thompson applied fascist analogies to the United States—erroneously and perniciously, in Marshall's view, in a way attractive to reactionaries.[43]

Thompson's behavior made sensational news again when the German-American Bund held a mass "Pro-America" rally on February 20, 1939, in New York's Madison Square Garden. The Bund was a small Nazi clone group, but the rally was huge, with twenty thousand in attendance and Nazi flags and insignia strewn about. Passing by Madison Square Garden on her way to give a speech elsewhere, Thompson went in and seated herself in the press gallery. She yelled "Bunk!" and laughed out loud at the malignant stupidity of the Bund's officious parading and their pronouncements from *Mein Kampf.* The Bund's storm troopers quickly hustled her out of the hall, and she had a police escort outside, generating lots of publicity. A woman's laugh as the ultimate affront to male self-importance hit a public nerve, as much as her unadorned ridicule of fascism did.[44]

That June, *Time* magazine put Thompson on its cover, with a story balancing uneasily between respect and smart-alecky derision. In the wake of the Grynszpan episode, the profile claimed that Thompson could "do more for a cause than almost any private citizen in the U.S." The story credited her column with being "sensationally informative," as a result of her "sound reportorial instinct" and "astonishing capacity to read and absorb"; it called her career in journalism "one of the most phenomenally successful." *Time* then took Thompson down a few notches by deeming her a "clubwoman's woman" who was "read, believed and quoted by millions of women who used to get their political opinions from their husbands, who got them from Walter Lippmann." The implication that Thompson was read only by women was demonstrably false, but the emphasis on her sex was typical.

Time's article summed up Thompson as a "plump, pretty woman of 45, bursting with health, energy and sex appeal" who "was not afraid to pour into her column whatever emotion she felt." That was accurate. (Men remarked on her sexual appeal well into her forties, often surprised to find a woman so capable in male-dominated domains also very attractive.) A severer critic charged that Thompson's emotionalism, together with her ability to "write rings around any other newspaper columnist," made her impact on readers very dangerous. A *New Yorker* profile archly damned her with faint praise as "half mother and half firebrand," with the "double talent for brooding in print over the welfare of mankind and at the same time inflaming it to further disasters."[45] All Thompson could really be blamed for was sticking to her principles and honestly expressing them with very great effectiveness.

She and Sheean became ever closer friends at this time—both of their political barometers screaming the same level of antifascist alarm, both distressed that the generality of Americans did not understand how fearsome was the threat. Neither of them was surprised that the Munich accord—which they both despised—failed to prevent Hitler from invading Czechoslovakia in March 1939 and occupying the whole country. That June, the Sheeans rented the smaller house on the Thompson-Lewis property of Twin Farms and stayed there for the summer, a practice that would continue for numerous years. Almost every evening Jimmy and Dorothy were in company, usually with additional friends similarly concerned, carrying on the kind of table-pounding discussion that Sinclair Lewis hated. It made

Dinah Sheean feel "like two cents," as well. Dorothy Thompson was twenty years older than Dinah, and so were many of her friends. She made no effort to pull Dinah inside the circle of debate, and Jimmy could be even harsher.[46]

Sheean and Thompson did not agree on everything, and that made their mutually respectful arguments all the more intense. Thompson explicitly rejected what she called "the totalitarian state" whether it occurred on the left or the right, under communism or fascism. Sheean was comfortable allying with Communists during the mid-1930s Popular Front, when the international Communist Party welcomed Socialists and other non-Communists into unified antifascist effort, and the numbers of so-called fellow travelers swelled. In New York, Sheean joined the left-wing League of American Writers, a group initiated by Communist writers in 1935 and then augmented with non-Communists, almost every one a fervent partisan of the Spanish Republicans. The League saw Sheean's name as an advantage. He signed the 1937 call to the League's second Congress of Writers, tried to help the group raise money, and spoke at the third Congress in June 1939, where he stressed that writers could not stand apart from social forces and should find solidarity with workers "in the mines, on the railroads, in the cotton fields . . . American workers, industrial and agricultural, white and black."[47]

Even as Stalin's one-man rule disillusioned many Communist sympathizers, Sheean joined several hundred others in August 1939 in an open letter titled "To All Active Supporters of Democracy and Peace," defending Soviet practices against charges of equivalency to fascism. But later that same month, when the Soviet Union signed a nonaggression pact with Germany, Sheean was through. In *The New Republic* he published a crushing disavowal of his long-standing "act of faith" in believing the best of Communist intents.

It was his first-ever public criticism of the Soviet Union. Previously, Sheean explained, he had swallowed his doubts about Stalin's policies and focused on "the magnitude of the historic effort" made by the Soviet Union, including its antifascism and its anti-imperialist foreign policy. He could do that no longer. Stalin had become a "personal dictator of an enslaved and terrorized state," Sheean wrote: Stalin's purges had eliminated independent thinkers from Soviet leadership, and his policies of forced industrialization and collectivization caused "monstrous sacrifices" for millions of peasants. In a second article Sheean called the Nazi-Soviet nonaggression pact the last straw. When harsh pushback from some readers rolled in, he underlined how "difficult it was" for him "to surrender an obstinate hope and enumerate some very repellent facts."[48]

THE WAR THAT Sheean and Thompson thought inevitable became a reality on September 1, 1939, when Hitler invaded Poland. Britain and France then declared war on Germany. In public opinion polls that autumn, Americans overwhelmingly favored the Allies, but thought their own country's greatest problem was staying out of the war. Only 2.3 percent of those surveyed wanted to enter the war at once and send the US Army to help Britain, France, and Poland (though an additional 1 percent would enter with the Navy and Air Force only). Almost the entire American population preferred not even to send military supplies. Seventy percent thought US entry into the first world war had been a mistake.[49]

Thompson immediately recommended lifting the American arms embargo to belligerents. That step would give the United States flexibility going forward, without requiring any other immediate action, she contended. Arguing against diehard isolationists in the Senate, she soon advocated repealing the whole Neutrality Act, to "untie the President's hands" and allow the United States to use its great power. Sheean, not so constantly in public view as Thompson, was bolder, saying that the United States should enter the war at once. On a lecture tour through the Midwest in the winter of 1939–1940, he was disheartened to find his audiences generally feeling that the war in Europe had little to do with them.[50]

To Sheean and Thompson, the war felt very close indeed. Both of them went to Europe in the spring of 1940, the period called "the phony war" because Hitler's aims beyond seizing Czechoslovakia and Poland seemed unclear. The war seemed to be suspended—but not for long. In April, German troops invaded Denmark and Norway. Thompson and Sheean, both in Paris, had talked into the predawn hours of May 10, when word arrived that more than a hundred German army divisions, thousands of bombers, and airborne troops were attacking the Netherlands and Belgium. German mobile armored units soon swept into France, where French forces mobilized but proved no match for the Nazi assault. Italy joined the war as Germany's ally on June 10, 1940, and four days later German troops marched into Paris. France capitulated on June 22. Photographs of Hitler in front of the Eiffel Tower circulated the globe. The fall of France had taken only six weeks. Britain, where Winston Churchill had just succeeded Neville Chamberlain as prime minister, was now the sole restraint on German gains.[51]

These circumstances were so unanticipated in Washington, DC, that panic ensued, forcing a sudden major reorientation in American policy—toward rearmament, first of all. Military preparedness had slid so far amid neutrality sentiment and the Depression that the United States stood twentieth in world rankings of military powers; the American navy was concentrated only in the Pacific, because of expectations of relying on the British navy in the Atlantic. After FDR gave several major speeches on the need for appropriations, Congress speedily pushed through $8 billion for military buildup (or $144 billion in current dollars). In September 1940, President Roosevelt responded to Prime Minister Churchill's desperate plea for assistance by masterminding a unique State Department agreement: fifty American destroyers went to Britain in exchange for American leases on a number of critically positioned British bases. As strictly a trade, the plan cleverly avoided the Neutrality Act's prohibitions.[52]

With war resuming on the continent, the Sheeans left Paris and returned to their house on the cliffs above the English Channel. That area of the coast was expected to be the first target of German bombing. Sheean stopped in several coastal towns to interview British residents, reporting to the North American News Alliance on families' calm firmness as they evacuated their children. He anticipated that "America will be fighting for its life very soon." Heavy bombing along the Channel coast began in August—hundreds of German planes at one time, combatted by the Royal Air Force. The attack spurred Dinah to gather war letters of her compatriots and publish a collection of them, giving the proceeds to the British-American Ambulance Corps.[53]

This was the first war to be broadcast into American living rooms. Wireless capability for overseas broadcast in 1938 was still halting, often fading out or failing, but improvements by 1940 made eyewitness programs from Europe into a new norm. Edward R. Murrow of CBS was broadcasting nightly from London, drawing huge numbers of listeners as he narrated ordinary Britons' daily experiences of the war.

Sheean happened to be with Murrow on the evening of September 7. The two men walked together to the tidal area of the Thames River, when air raid sirens suddenly shrieked, antiaircraft fire rent the air, and a booming hail of bombs began. Murrow and Sheean jumped for cover into a nearby haystack as bursts of flame exploded in the night sky again and again, turning the moon red. Billows of smoke filled the air and spiky shreds of shrapnel flew all around. Sheean's dispatch, published in numerous newspapers, wrote of unforgettable "fires, flares and flashes," "apocalyptic" in their scale. "The world was upside down," Murrow told American listeners in his next broadcast, adding, "Vincent Sheean lay on one side of me and cursed in five languages."[54] It was the start of "the Blitz," the merciless German bombing of London that went on night after night, and sometimes by day, too, from September 1940 to May 1941.

DOROTHY THOMPSON, VINDICATED in her Cassandra-like warnings that Germany intended war, was facing a political quandary at home.

That year, 1940, was an election year, and President Roosevelt was running for an unprecedented third term. As a writer for the *Herald Tribune*, Thompson was expected to support the Republican Party's candidate, but most Republican leaders were anti-interventionist and FDR came far closer to her own foreign policy views. She was more than relieved in August when the Republican Party convention nominated a surprising dark horse, political novice Wendell Willkie, a successful businessman who was an internationalist. Helen and Ogden Reid were keen for Willkie, too.

As weeks ticked by, Thompson continued to ruminate over her choice for president. She admired Willkie but also deeply valued President Roosevelt's efforts to move the United States toward commitment to the Allies. FDR not only called for rearmament and put through the destroyers-for-bases deal but also fostered congressional passage in 1940 of the Selective Service Act, initiating the military draft, despite its probable unpopularity in an election year. Thompson had a private interview with FDR in the White House on October 1 (a meeting plotted by her friend Morris Ernst, the preeminent civil liberties lawyer in New York and a Roosevelt partisan). She then stunned her readers—and the Reids—by endorsing FDR for president in her column on October 9. She explained in telling detail that Roosevelt's experience equipped him far better than Willkie to lead the nation in such perilous times, though she hastened to affirm Willkie's equal devotion to democracy and the national good.[55]

Thompson's sudden abandonment of the Willkie cause infuriated the Reids. Republican subscribers inundated the *Herald Tribune* with letters, many of which the Reids published. Only a few applauded the paper for allowing such a renegade her freedom of speech. Most took quite the other side, appalled that the paper published her column, denouncing Thompson and saying she spoke nonsense. Ogden Reid told Thompson that letters were running 19 to 1 against her. She stood her ground, of course. In a second column, she reasoned further that the Axis powers wanted the president to be defeated because they feared FDR's leadership more than that of any Republican challenger. (German shortwave broadcasts had revealed that to be true.) The *Herald Tribune* refused to publish that column, though it appeared in papers elsewhere on October 14, through syndication. The *Herald Tribune* did print the column four days later, prefaced by Thompson's expression of pain at finding herself at odds with the Reids and many readers. The *Herald Tribune*'s editorial that day argued flatly against Thompson's position but credited her "habitual fairmindedness and rightmindedness" in avoiding any implication that Willkie was an appeaser of fascism.[56]

FDR made the most of Thompson's support. She spoke on his behalf during the weeks remaining in the campaign and contributed material for him to use in speeches. A foreign policy speech he gave on November 2 followed Thompson's draft almost word for word, and his principal speechwriter rated it his best. Once FDR won his third term and the question of what the United States should do ignited ever more intense debate, Thompson continued to send the president memos and drafts of material, whether solicited or not. She allied herself with his aim to move popular opinion toward material support for the Allies.[57]

By supporting Roosevelt, Thompson had broken an unspoken pact with her employers at the *Herald Tribune*. She was not surprised that the Reids did not renew her contract in the spring of 1941. The *New York Post* stepped into the place of the *Herald Tribune*, becoming her flagship, and a separate new syndication contract sent On the Record to more numerous newspapers than ever, so she did not suffer materially. Nonetheless, she felt the loss of the *Herald Tribune* audience as a blow, because she hoped to move weighty Republican readers toward her antifascist point of view. The *New York Post*'s subscribers were typically working-class and middle-class Democrats, many of them Jewish and already strongly antifascist.[58]

Opinions about Thompson polarized as she continued to stress American responsibilities to the Allies. She railed against the America First Committee, an anti-intervention group founded in the fall of 1940. Charles Lindbergh, still wildly admired for his 1927 solo flight across the Atlantic, was the group's featured speaker, and his speeches often were broadcast nationally. Lindbergh made it clear that he sympathized with the Nazi vision for world organization and expected Germany to win the war. Sure that Lindbergh was a fascist at heart, Thompson condemned his views in numerous columns. Lindbergh had to be judged "in light of the only two possible choices for America, fascism or resistance," she wrote. She bore down equally hard, though less often, on Father Coughlin, the anti-Semitic radio priest who supported a militaristic "Christian Front."[59]

Thompson's enemies called her a warmonger. When Congress was discussing the Lend-Lease bill that would allow American armaments to go to Britain, women picketers from a "Mothers' Crusade" tried to hang an effigy of Thompson on the gates of the White House, though the police prevented it. In Los Angeles, when she was about to speak, several hundred picketers blocked traffic near the auditorium where six thousand people were crowding in to hear her. Her cheering squad rivaled the force of her opponents, though, especially in New York. Three thousand supporters filled the Waldorf-Astoria's huge ballroom on May 6, 1941, for a grand fête honoring her. New York governor Herbert Lehman lauded Thompson's "outstanding services to the cause of democracy and freedom," saying that "no voice has been more potent, no mind more searching, no heart more courageous" than hers, in "the struggle between democracy and dictatorship." Thompson was seated beside Wendell Willkie, who added his praise. (He had accepted his defeat graciously.) President Roosevelt sent "hearty greetings and all good wishes," saluting Thompson's "clear and consistent defense of democracy." Winston Churchill sent terse eloquence across the sea: "She has shown what one valiant woman can do with the power of the pen. Freedom and humanity are grateful debtors." In her own speech, Thompson urged the huge audience to "demand unitedly that America be put at once on a total war footing."[60]

Both she and Sheean traveled to areas at war in 1941. Thompson made a month-long summer trip to England, hosted by the adoring editor of the London *Sunday Chronicle*, who had been reprinting many of her columns. Her radio speeches had been broadcast in England during the Blitz, and her celebrity was such that she was welcomed as a heroine. The press followed her every move. She broadcast almost every day she was there, met with British leaders and with heads of governments-in-exile in London, visited munitions factories and bomb shelters, addressed the House of Commons, had tea in Buckingham Palace with Queen Consort Elizabeth, and spent a weekend with Prime Minister Churchill.[61]

Sheean looked toward Asia, where Japanese attacks had battered China since 1937. He crossed the Pacific and over five weeks stopped in Auckland, Singapore, the Dutch East Indies, Bangkok, Hong Kong, Chungking, and the Philippines, reporting on what he saw there for the *Herald Tribune*. He toured American bases in Guam and Wake Island last and returned to New York on December 1, 1941. Beginning a lecture tour, he estimated that the United States would be attacked by Japan within the next ten days.[62]

On December 7, 1941, the Japanese attacked American and British targets—Pearl Harbor in Hawaii, Guam, Wake Island, the Philippines, Hong Kong, and Malaya. Dorothy Thompson wept when the United States declared war on Japan the following day. Despite urging the nation to assume "a total war footing" six months earlier, she did not welcome war as anything but an absolute necessity. Her quest to make her country confront fascism directly had succeeded, but it was not a victory she could celebrate. She had no taste for military glory and was well aware of war's potential to create undesired results. A war intended solely to destroy Germany or Japan was not worthwhile, she declared to her *Ladies' Home Journal* readers. The war effort would be "futile unless we fight it for a new world of co-operation."

Her public campaign to rouse Americans' awareness was over. A private ending followed three weeks later in the Woodstock, Vermont, courthouse when Thompson received the decree of her divorce from Sinclair Lewis. Memories of the "years of intense pleasure & blackest pain" of their marriage flashed through her mind. Now she felt neither pain nor pleasure. "To have felt too much," she mused, "is to end in feeling nothing."[63] Barely an ashy residue of her charged relationship to Sinclair Lewis remained, but her passionate journalism would kindle again to alight on new objects.

CHAPTER 10

WAR OUTSIDE AND
WAR INSIDE

In blacked-out London, the ferocious *ack-ack-ack* coming from antiaircraft guns in Hyde Park sounded like all hell let loose. Residents in the Dorchester Hotel across the street stood the noise, to feel safe. The elegant hotel's reinforced concrete and steel construction justified its bomb-proof reputation, which attracted visiting dignitaries, cabinet ministers, "airmen off duty and tarts on duty" (as society photographer Cecil Beaton noted after his stay), and wealthy Londoners who preferred the hotel to their own homes. The hotel's basement bomb shelter awaited when air raid sirens screamed, but even the dining room was rated sufficiently secure.

John Gunther was living there in the fall of 1941, his bed warmed by fellow American Lee Miller, a sexual nomad and talented photographer working for British *Vogue*.[1] Their trysts in wartime London reflected how much Gunther's life had changed since *Inside Europe* made him a celebrity and its riches freed him from the *Chicago Daily News*. Like Dorothy Thompson and Jimmy Sheean, Gunther too parlayed his previous work in foreign correspondence into new genres in the late 1930s. He made the most of his accumulated expertise to become a trusted source for whatever in the world Americans wanted to know.

As HUNDREDS OF thousands of people made *Inside Europe* their ready reference, Gunther realized he had found a winning formula in book writing. He intended to stick with it. In his diary he echoed *Time*'s earlier comment, deciding that "The only political journalism worth doing, it seems to me, is reflection after the event."[2] Before leaving his *News* post in London, he concentrated on updating *Inside Europe* to keep pace with fast-changing events. But once the family relocated in New York City in October 1936, Gunther began planning his next project.

He had no small plans. He had decided that his second book should cover all of Asia, though he sensed (appropriately!) that this book would be better titled "Outside Asia" than "Inside," because he had nothing like the familiarity with Europe that had undergirded his first venture. To compensate for his ignorance of the politics, culture, and history of a continent far larger than Europe, he made elaborate plans for his route—consulting foreign offices, ambassadors, State Department officers, other journalists, businessmen, and travel bureaus beforehand, and assembling material to take with him. He intended to put his feet down in every country he would cover and do all the research and interviewing himself, writing his notes by hand, usually immediately after he conducted an interview rather than during it. Thus he pinned the methods he knew from a dozen years as a correspondent to the project of a long and varied book. Lots of background reading would supplement what he learned on site.[3]

Together with Frances, John began the Asia trip on October 31, 1937, barely a year after moving to New York. Eight-year-old Johnny was enrolled in a progressive school in New York and stayed in his nanny's care during his parents' eight months away. They packed "lightly," Frances joked—taking with them seventeen pieces of luggage, plus a huge canvas bag holding about a hundred books and a leather bag holding John's morgue of relevant newspaper clippings. Traveling to fourteen countries, they eventually logged thirty thousand miles. John was writing along the way, sending numerous articles to the North American News Alliance (NANA) on such topics as Chinese morale under Japanese attack, and composing longer feature articles for magazines. He felt he needed to keep earning solid fees en route because he paid for the trip himself. Later he toted up his direct costs at more than $15,000, equivalent to about a quarter million today.[4]

Frances at first felt reluctant about accompanying John. She thought, resentfully, that he would probably "use" her, "the way he did in the Europe book, & then even completely forget he has used me," she wrote in her diary. John's phenomenal success with *Inside Europe* had ignited a slow burn in her. One month after the book came out (when they were still in London), he was "submerged overwhelmed deluged with invitations," and she admitted to her diary that she felt "wildly frantically blankly envious." *Inside Europe* depended—very significantly, in her view—on her suggestions and analyses; prestigious magazines such as *Collier's* ignored her nonetheless and solicited John's contributions. John dedicated *Inside Europe* to "my wife in love and friendship" and credited Frances by name for several pithy comments. That meant little to her when he "proceeded to forget the hundreds of other lines he appropriated from me without quotation. . . . He has literally—even honestly—forgotten! he tells me things I told him!"[5]

Since leaving Vienna she had been depressed on and off. Though she had welcomed moving to London, it meant dropping her newspaper job to focus on her own writing, in which she often met frustration. Her aggrieved mood may also have related to vague memories of adolescent sexual abuse, stirred up in her analysis with Dr. Stekel, and still plaguing her once the family moved to New York. Her various projects, big and small, proved difficult to complete. Like many other ambitious and talented women of her generation, she had been astonishingly blithe at first, assuming she had the freedom to pursue her self-set goals, only to find that wifehood and motherhood freighted her with unanticipated constraints, sometimes self-imposed. Whether because of an unwarranted sense of inadequacy or exaggerated perfectionism, she could not deliver on the ambitious ideas she conceived. She published one story in the 1930s, but her drafts of plays and additional stories and extensive research for a book on imperialism came to naught. She recognized her own incapacity, saying to John, "I am a Penelope writer. I spend all afternoon unknitting what I wrote in the morning."[6]

John readily agreed that his authorship was indebted to her. When he was traveling alone in September 1936, pursuing research for a revision of *Inside Europe*, he wrote that he was helpless without her. "Never again will I try to do a job of work without you around to harry, provoke, help, stimulate, guide & corral me," he affirmed fondly. "Everything I do is jointly yours & I know & appreciate it." He thought she had "much more talent" than he did himself, encouraging her, "I think your insight, political & human, and gift of phrase amount to genius." He had cheered on her newspaper writing in Vienna and had high hopes for her independent writing. "I shall be so proud & happy when you finish a real job," he told her. He recognized her particular weakness, which was exactly the opposite of his own strength—"you haven't got staying power, endurance, which I happen to have." He hoped to help her gain those abilities in New York and imagined their "glorious" new life: "We will work all morning, play all afternoon (you must learn tennis), read all evening, & screw all night."[7]

Frances chastised herself for resenting her husband's fame, thinking it was "ridiculous being jealous of one's own husband." She condemned herself for being "mean, picayune, petty, low" in having such feelings. Nonetheless she had them. "Maybe I ought to be glad just to be used," she considered, "but I want to assert myself too as such—at least to get my due for what is my worth—that's only fair. . . . I don't want a 'to my wife in love and friendship & owing to her patient collaboration,' etc.—I want a by-line." When she decided she would go to Asia with John, she determined that she would take her own notes and write about the trip herself, too, in a journal format.[8]

Hers was the same dilemma faced by numerous capable wives of writer-husbands in the mid-twentieth century, who served as crucial but silent collaborators in their husbands' work—as muses, researchers, intellectual catalysts, amanuenses—while never gaining public recognition. Frances Gunther rebelled against that inequity, believing she deserved better. In Shanghai she made common cause with the wife of Edgar Snow, another traveling American journalist whose recent book on the Chinese Communists, *Red Star over China*, both Gunthers admired greatly. Helen Foster Snow thought Frances had a comparatively good deal, saying to her, "Your husband quotes you, he gives you credit—Mine never does—he uses all my lines, & I never get any credit."[9]

The Gunthers began their round-the-world journey on an Italian ship, the SS *Conte de Savoia*. Not long into the transatlantic passage, the captain and two other officers brought out their marked-up copies of *Inside Europe* for John's autograph, much to the Gunthers' surprise, because the book was banned in Italy. Apparently, Italian prohibitions did not mean very much! Their first stop was Egypt, not because John was writing about it but because Frances had never been there and it was a good place to land. Frances occupied herself in Cairo taking intelligent notes and buying a Koran, thinking she might write a book on comparative religion. She saw the sights, recording amusingly though acidly, "Riding a camel is like a cross between masturbating and being seasick." They were entertained more than once by a cosmopolitan Egyptian businessman named Aziz Elouis Bey and therefore met Lee Miller, who was then Elouis's wife. The marriage was a surprising turn for Miller, who at eighteen had been a Condé Nast model in New York, then Man Ray's photography apprentice, muse, and lover in Paris, next a photographer with her own studio in New York. She was not yet thirty.[10]

John had set a frantically busy schedule. Both he and Frances trotted day after day through dizzying sequences of excursions, lunches, dinners, evening parties, receptions in every country they visited, with some very lengthy journeys to go from one country to the next. They stopped for only a few days in many countries, but spent nearly two months in India and twelve days each in Palestine and the Philippines. John's assumptions about American readers' interests figured in his arrangements. Because Japan's military had been conquering territory in China since 1937, the Gunthers spent the whole second half of their trip in China, Japan, and Manchukuo (the regime Japan had set up in Manchuria). The book John would write emphasized East Asia, assessing whether China could survive and resist Japanese takeover and trying to answer the question of "how fascist is Japan?"[11]

Their stay in Palestine proved consequential for Frances Gunther, because her Jewish identity, rarely important to her before, surfaced there. She was breathless at Jerusalem's beauty, recording, "There's something about the place—the elevation, the brilliant sunshine, the extraordinary delicate blush pink of the stones, dazzling in the sunshine, the hills changing color every moment in the translucent atmosphere . . . there's something about the place that invites you, excites you to rapture." She and John met with Zionist leaders Chaim Weizmann and David Ben-Gurion—who would become the first president and prime minister of the state of Israel a decade later—and traveled all around.

In her journal Frances expressed violently personal Zionist views. At that time, Britain was considering partitioning Palestine, because Arab discontent over the extent of Jewish settlement had burst into armed rebellion. She knew that if she were Arab, she would say, "To hell with the Jews! . . . am I the Jew's keeper?—I should say not! Let the English give them Wales! Let the Americans give them Florida!" But she opposed partition and was a Jew, so she said, "To hell with Arabs!—throw 'em out! they have 4 other Arab states to go to— make 'em go—drive 'em out with bayonets, mustard gas! here we are and here we stay!" The exit of Palestinian Arabs to Iraq, Saudi Arabia, Transjordan, and Syria looked to her perfectly feasible.

Though her intellect acknowledged arguments on both sides, she justified to her own satisfaction the "right" of Jews to live in Palestine because of their ancient history there and because (she assumed) Jews had nowhere else to go. Only modern Jews concerned her: she envisioned extirpating the orthodox even more brutally than the Arabs: "First I'd string up all the Jews at the Wailing Wall—my god, wailing! how sickening, humiliating—after 5000 years of history, & wailing! . . . Chloroform 'em—fumigate 'em—shame 'em—put 'em into decent clothes—make 'em build roads—and if they resist, cremate 'em, curls & all. Then take the children and bring them up as decent human beings." Frances expressed these extreme views only in private, but they no doubt influenced her husband, who slanted his treatment of Palestine in *Inside Asia* toward the Zionist side enough to arouse criticism. "Zionism is an emotional and practical necessity to countless Jews," he concluded, and "should become the best single solution to the refugee problem." He echoed his wife: "The Arabs might conceivably go into Transjordan or Iraq, where there is plenty of room."[12]

Frances also adopted the cause of immediate freedom for India, when the Gunthers traveled there at the turn of the year. "The essential point seems to me," she wrote in her diary, "if the British treat the Indians badly, they will want to be free; & if the British treat the Indians well, they will also want to be free. The desire to be free (of the British) is over & above 'treatment.'" She had long been a fierce critic of British imperialism, but her passionate embrace of Indian nationalism in 1938 was rooted in something more personal. While in India she fell in love with Jawaharlal Nehru, Gandhi's heir apparent—an urbane, British-educated, cosmopolitan man, infinitely committed to Indian freedom and attractive to many women. He reciprocated with gracious friendship. Her feelings about Nehru as her *beau ideal* drew her away from John.[13]

Nehru, Weizmann, and Ben-Gurion were only three of the many leaders the Gunthers met. John had entrée to diverse notables everywhere—industry heads, generals, party activists, Dutch, French, and British imperial officials, princes and princesses, youth organizers, and reform leaders such as the Indian jurist B. R. Ambedkar (a prime mover for rights for the so-called Untouchables). The Gunthers met Gandhi, Philippine president Manuel Quezon, and Prime Minister Fumimari Konoe of Japan. They had a rare audience with Generalissimo Chiang Kai-shek—who was leading the temporarily united military forces of the Nationalists and Chinese Communists against the Japanese—and with Madame Chiang. "Is this the face that launched a thousand airships?" Frances jotted in her diary about Madame Chiang. John used the line in *Inside Asia* (crediting her); he also quoted her quip "There is Methodism in his madness," about Chiang, who was a Christian. The Gunthers also met and spoke with the usually inaccessible Zhou Enlai, a central Communist political officer and negotiator, reaching him through the intercession of Agnes Smedley, an American radical writer who had been in China for a decade and had embedded herself with the Chinese Communist army at war.[14]

Frances took critical and envious private notes on her husband's technique for getting his informants to speak freely. He warmed them up by asking obvious questions and praising the answers as highly valuable, to the end that "in the mellow atmosphere, his informant melts, & gets really confidential, & tells him things he wouldn't tell another soul." John never contradicted his informant even if aware that he was lying or wrong; he never argued, but listened "with rapt attention" and asked his usual questions "as tho[ugh] he had just thought of them that minute, inspired by their presence."[15] With such extraordinary access wherever he sought it, and methods to draw out his informants, Gunther brought home tremendous material to work up into a book.

THE GUNTHERS RETURNED to New York in the fall of 1938. Taking a modern apartment on Central Park West at 90th Street, they filled its shelves with relics acquired during their travels and with several

thousand of John's books. A few thousand more books went in a separate office space Gunther had rented, where he hired a secretary to
deal with his mail and small tasks. *Inside Europe* was still selling close
to a thousand copies a week and had been translated into fourteen
languages. To overcome sales resistance as Gunther's revised editions
were published, Harper & Brothers offered "trade-ins," a complete
novelty based on the carmakers' model: buyers of the new edition got
fifty cents credit if they turned in an earlier version. During his first
five weeks back in New York, Gunther refused thirty invitations to
speak, so many people wanted to hear from him—though he was glad
to address the Council on Foreign Relations, now an august body of
diplomatic types and scholars well funded by foundation grants.[16]

His social engagements were often political engagements in that
anxious November of 1938, as he quickly integrated himself into
networks of acquaintances—journalists, publishers, editors, and
the like—who were looking worriedly at Europe just as he was, not
the least bit comforted by the recent Munich agreement. When he
had dinner with editors of *The Nation* magazine and poet Archibald
MacLeish, they argued over how democracy could be saved, whether
China could withstand the Japanese advances, whether liberals
should encourage the United States to rearm, and how to keep fascism out of Latin America. Gunther thought MacLeish (who wrote
for Henry Luce's business magazine *Fortune* during the 1930s and
situated himself politically on the antifascist left) very "solid." After
dinner the two men stayed up talking together till 3:00 a.m., joined
by H. R. Knickerbocker and his wife, Agnes. Gunther and "Knick"—
his correspondent pal from Europe whom he credited with enabling
him to finish *Inside Europe* so quickly—continued talking until six
in the morning.[17]

A few days later Gunther had dinner with "Ham" Armstrong
(who edited *Foreign Affairs*, the journal of the Council on Foreign
Relations), Dorothy Thompson, Raymond Gram Swing, and a few
others, to discuss drafting a manifesto on the dangers facing democracy and how the United States ought to respond. Once they drafted

such a document, they imagined gathering thousands of signatures and gaining national impact. Thompson, concerned about fascist nations' ability to mobilize their young people through ideological pronouncements, especially stressed the need for the United States to assert a "positive philosophy" of democracy and the rule of law.[18]

The news from Germany about the devastating pogrom against Jews called *Kristallnacht* was making Gunther feel grim. He did not hear Thompson's radio speech about Grynszpan, the young Jew who shot the Nazi official in Paris; he confessed himself "unable to face listening to the radio regularly" (though he left unclear whether this was because current news upset him too much or because he shied from the medium). He promised Thompson to help her effort in any way he could, when she asked. With one of the picturesque metaphors that seemed to spring to his mind effortlessly, Gunther marveled that Thompson had "become a sort of combination of the Goddess Minerva and the engines of the Normandie" (a new superfast French ocean liner) while remaining "delightfully feminine." When he attended a huge luncheon event to benefit the radio program called *Town Meeting of the Air*, the host mentioned Thompson's campaign to save Grynszpan and "a perceptible ripple, a gush of breath and excitement, stirred through the entire crowd" of seventeen hundred people. Gunther wondered how many other names would provoke that reaction.[19]

During another typical day or two in November, Gunther paid $25 (more than $400 today) to attend a luncheon benefit for republican Spain, where he heard addresses by witty poet Dorothy Parker and by Bennett Cerf, president of Random House Books. Gunther sat with publisher Max Schuster and discussed Schuster's idea of publishing a translation of the whole of *Mein Kampf*, since only parts of it had been published in English. That evening he dined with the couple who owned the *Reader's Digest*, then on its rise to become the most profitable middle-class magazine of the century. The DeWitt Wallaces were eager to publish selected chapters of Gunther's book on Asia, and he accepted their offer gratefully, beginning what he later called his "long, fruitful association" with the *Reader's Digest*, a financial boon.

The next day Gunther promised foreign correspondent Jay Allen that he would contribute a three-hundred-word sketch of Manuel Azana, the prime minister of republican Spain, one of the ten Spanish Loyalist heroes whose portrait busts by sculptor Jo Davidson were being exhibited in a New York benefit. Gunther wrote 268 words for the exhibition catalog in thirty-five minutes and felt pleased with his efficiency. (His sketch was the shortest of the ten in the catalog, while Jimmy Sheean's on Dolores Ibarruri, "La Pasionara," was the longest.) He also wrote a draft of the manifesto about democracy that the dinner group had discussed. Later in the month, following Jay Allen's successful face-off against a Catholic priest on Spanish issues at the Foreign Policy Association, Gunther brought Allen and a crowd of foreign correspondent pals and their wives home with him, where they stayed up till three o'clock talking. He gave a lunch the next day for Allen, inviting Ham Armstrong and political scientist Harold Laski, among others, and they chewed on the shockingly pro-German and anti-British statements made by Joseph Kennedy, recently appointed US ambassador in London.[20]

At the same time, with the superhuman dispatch that Gunther made his norm, he was racing through the writing of *Inside Asia*. In five months he completed the 575-page book, which followed the model of *Inside Europe* in its lavish array of snappy individual profiles. "Very nearly each country is dominated by a man," Gunther justified his continued emphasis on personalities. It followed that having a grasp of these individuals and their circles was essential to understanding the country's politics. He had an informal list of basic items he wanted to find out about each important person: his "sources of power," his "leading ideas," the turning points and motivations of his career, his current ambitions, his health, education, basic philosophy of life, and his attitudes toward "women, religion, friends, money, war, race."[21] By interviewing leaders' friends and associates, Gunther acquired anecdotes quirky or frivolous enough to give readers a sense of special access to knowledge.

The Asian portraits rarely dazzled quite as brightly as those in *Inside Europe*, but Gunther injected startling or amusing metaphors and parallels. Gandhi was "an incredible combination of Jesus Christ, Tammany Hall, and your father" and "a sort of etherealized Houdini," in that he escaped British imprisonment when he entered a fast. Nehru was "an Indian who became a westerner; an aristocrat who became a socialist; an individualist who became a great mass leader"—a rational, modern agnostic in a country of "colossal medievalism" and "religious fanaticism." (Gunther loved to impart information in the form of paradoxes.) One could learn from Gunther that Chiang Kai-shek had a bullet-proof limousine with windows almost an inch thick and that the things he liked best were "poetry, mountains, and his wife"; or that the Chinese puppet emperor installed by the Japanese in Manchukuo was six feet tall, weighed only 102 pounds, and was kept "locked up like a case of mumps."[22]

Gunther excelled in summarizing political background and deftly sketching the economic, industrial, and agricultural features relevant to each country's political culture. Unlike Sheean, who made himself the main character as well as the narrator, Gunther prided himself on keeping his own experiences, no matter how picturesque, off the table. As he concluded *Inside Asia*, he did not try to sum up the massive continent as a whole because the countries he visited were so diverse. Nor did he think it made any sense to postulate an "Asian mind," though he saw certain realities shared in common everywhere, including desperate poverty and "religious bondage and repression." Resolutely secular himself, Gunther did not look for any more complex meaning harbored in religious belief. As he assessed the likelihood of change occurring, he put his finger on the shaping force of Western powers' predatory imperialism and the ways it had generated local and regional pushback in the form of nationalism. He could foresee that the days of European imperialism in Asia were numbered.[23]

Harper produced Gunther's book super-rapidly, publishing it on June 8, 1939. "*Inside Asia* Guntherizes practically everything east of Suez," the *New York Times* reviewer immediately informed readers, implying that to "guntherize" was to explain an improbably huge area cogently. The book was "authoritative, useful and entertaining," almost all reviewers chorused, saying that Gunther brought Asia alive and provided a guide to contemporary events. "The Most Competent One-Man Reportorial Job Ever Undertaken," announced the subhead of an enthusiastic review in the *New York Herald Tribune*, to Gunther's satisfaction. The reviewer saw little prejudice in Gunther's account, crediting him with being "open-minded, fair-minded and tolerant," despite the book's array of opinionated generalizations (about ethnic groups) that would be unacceptable today. If reviews were not quite as ecstatic as for *Inside Europe*, they were good enough for *Inside Asia* to glide onto best-seller lists right away. An eminent jury, on which Dorothy Thompson served, unanimously named it one of the ten "most important" nonfiction books of 1939—as *Inside Europe* had been in 1936, making Gunther the only two-time winner of that award.[24]

Gunther's celebrity got a new shine not only from *Inside Asia* but also from speaking on the radio. Radio networks regularly drew on well-known print journalists to comment on the mounting political pressures of 1938 and 1939, and Gunther's ability to charm and inform in print made him a prime candidate to do so on the air. He did not seek radio work but accepted when the NBC networks (or programs such as *Town Hall of the Air*) came after him. His fame and his store of knowledge also made him an early panelist on *Information Please!*, a radio game show that zoomed to popularity as soon as it started in 1938. Hosted by Gunther's friend Clifton (Kip) Fadiman, the show enticed listeners to compete with panelists on fast-paced questions about piecemeal information, usually abounding in puns and clever wordplay.[25]

Radio proved a good source of income, but compared to writing, the medium meant little to him. "Nothing is real to me unless it is a book," he told his diary. "I can never remember a word of my broadcasts." He did more of them nonetheless. He said yes when NBC, moved by the seeming imminence of war, asked him to do a dozen live updates from Europe. He was going to Europe to research his next revision of *Inside Europe* in the summer of 1939 anyway, and the North American Newspaper Alliance had commissioned him to write newspaper articles while there. Broadcasting across the Atlantic had just been made feasible by improvements in wireless communication, but it was not perfect. On his first broadcast, he felt "terribly let down" that static spoiled Frances's ability to hear him. "It was to you, for you, I was talking," he wrote her. His chatty and fond letters described indulgent purchases in Paris and Geneva and suggested they should buy a house with the riches reaped by sales of *Inside Asia.*[26]

With uncanny timing, Gunther was in Moscow in August 1939, when the nonaggression pact between Germany and the Soviet Union was announced. He quickly left for London, arriving there just as Germany invaded Poland; he was standing in Parliament's press gallery when Britain declared war on Germany on September 3. His newspaper articles about the fast-changing situation appeared frequently in American newspapers between August 19 and September 22. It was not yet a "world" war, he told readers, since only Britain, supported by France and Poland, declared war on Germany. The rest of Europe was still neutral and Japan was at war only with China.[27]

On September 11 he received news that Frances was deathly ill with peritonitis from a ruptured appendix, and he booked passage home right away. Fortunately, a second cable arrived three days after the first, before his ship sailed, reporting that she was out of danger. His passage home in September was fateful nonetheless. On shipboard, Gunther conceived a relentless sexual passion for Agnes Knickerbocker, H. R. Knickerbocker's young wife. Agnes was traveling with their small children, escaping European danger while Knick stayed abroad. A redheaded Texan who won the Pulitzer Prize in 1931 for foreign correspondence from Germany and Russia, Knick

John Gunther and Frances Fineman Gunther, 1937.
*Source: Frances Fineman Gunther Papers, Schlesinger Library,
Radcliffe Institute for Advanced Study, Harvard University.*

was extremely possessive about his sexy wife, though he thought nothing of straying sexually himself. He had freely related his many sexual adventures to Gunther, including his conquest of Agnes within twenty-four hours of meeting her when she was sixteen. Knick's typical badinage infused a letter welcoming Gunther to stay in his "five room villa" in Berlin, which noted that a "maid can also be furnished in type desired, please name age, weight, height and character of mammary glands preferred."[28]

The shipboard affair tumbled Gunther into years of painful, secret, devastating attachment to the wife of his colleague and friend. It was not the brief infidelity taken for granted among foreign correspondents but a nearly obsessive and self-destructive passion on his part. How could he have so betrayed Knick? And so meanly injured Frances? All that can be said is that his behavior was not unique in his social stratum. Walter Lippmann, for example, began a love affair early in 1937 with the wife of his best friend, Hamilton Fish Armstrong. Both the Lippmann and the Armstrong marriages shattered when a misdirected letter revealed the affair to Armstrong after eight months. Two divorces followed. Lippmann then happily married Armstrong's former wife. Armstrong eventually remarried, too, but never again spoke to Lippmann.[29]

Gunther saw Agnes Knickerbocker seldom because she and her children lived in Texas. Both distance and secrecy made their affair depend on telephone calls and letters. Living a lie, Gunther saw Knick and Agnes together socially when they came to New York now and then, and he conferred with Knick as he would have formerly, to maintain the facade that nothing had changed.

John's new love transformed his relationship to Frances. The fondness he had expressed in letters before he encountered Agnes on the ocean passage disappeared. He did not tell Frances right away that he was in love with someone else. They went on living together, and John made sure to spend time with Johnny, relishing his relationship with his son, while his interactions with Frances stiffened. He carried on much of his social life without her. Frances was already ambivalent about their relationship. In a critical mood during their Asian trip, for instance, she had commented in her diary that their "'happy marriage'" was "a false front, put up by us, decently and courageously I think, because he, or at least I believe in the discipline of formalized public appearance." She depended on their marriage more than John did, nonetheless, for status, security, and support.[30]

GUNTHER'S PUBLIC REASONS for uneasiness that fall of 1939 added to his private trepidation about the secret affair with Agnes Knickerbocker. His liberal friends were confounded and gloomy, uncertain how to read what was going on in Europe. The Nazi-Soviet nonaggression pact puzzled everyone; Germany's aggressive moves stalled strangely after the invasion of Poland; and then Soviet Russia burst into war against Finland at the end of November. Gunther was on the air for NBC often, speaking about Europe, Russia, and India and China, too, now that he was seen as an Asian expert. He became so used to fan mail that he no longer read it but simply had his secretary say if letters were pro or con. While he was offering commentary all the time, he criticized himself (as he had in Europe) for taking a purely reportorial stance, retreating into "being just an eye and an ear" and lacking deep convictions. "I am far too deeply addicted to compromise," he chided himself. He was nonetheless pleased when Kip Fadiman told him that Janet Flanner (the esteemed columnist on France for the *New Yorker* under her nom de plume Genêt) liked his writing a lot "because it shows <u>balance</u>. I don't go off the deep end like Dorothy and Sheean."[31]

He wrote for hours during the day—revising *Inside Europe* again, preparing radio scripts—yet often talked and drank long past midnight at friends' homes or in swanky nightclubs like 21. His social circles expanded to include British friends from London, social gadfly Elsa Maxwell, and publisher Henry B. Luce and his accomplished wife, Clare Boothe Luce, whose 1936 play *The Women* became a movie that year. Gunther was trying to write a play himself. He took a winter break in Miami in January 1940, arriving a few weeks before a planned secret meeting with Agnes. Tortured with desire for her, he went to prostitutes (usually two per night). Back in New York in the spring of 1940, he alternated between depression and wild craving for Agnes. When Frances went to the Caribbean in April, John easily found women to have sex with—either willing dates or prostitutes at "Polly's," a famous upscale brothel in New York. Soon he was also romancing the Hollywood screen actress Miriam Hopkins, who lived both in Hollywood and in New York.[32]

The news from Europe changed radically in the spring of 1940 when Germany invaded Denmark and Norway, then moved into

Belgium and Holland, and began advancing in France. Though crazily tormented with thoughts of Agnes, John broadcast news commentary often in April and every day in May, when the Nazis marched through France. He was a ready voice of expertise about Europe, while his mental life seesawed between pathos and sordidness. "The source of my dissatisfaction & unhappiness is the failure of my marriage," he declared in his diary in June 1940, after another tryst with Agnes, who distressed him by saying that she could not leave her husband. "This explains my lack of will & purpose, confusion about the war, lack of faith, lack of feeling & conviction, my continued misdirection & ineptness."[33]

Gunther refocused his roiling mind by traveling widely in Latin America—alone. Archibald MacLeish (whom FDR had appointed Librarian of Congress) had suggested Latin America for Gunther's next book, perhaps because FDR and the State Department were very concerned about Nazi penetration there. Gunther embraced the idea. He began by going to Washington, where Undersecretary of State Sumner Welles gave him numerous letters of introduction to Latin American leaders. Welles also instructed every US embassy and consul to look out for Gunther's arrival. Over the next five months, until February 1941, Gunther traveled to all twenty Latin American nations (missing the presidential campaign of 1940 that proved so consequential for Dorothy Thompson). He covered almost twenty thousand miles and consulted more than four hundred individuals, including seventeen of the twenty heads of state.[34]

When Gunther returned to the United States, he had another secret rendezvous with Agnes and then began painfully yet effectively cranking out *Inside Latin America*. On Mother's Day in 1941, John told Frances that he was in love with someone else, without naming who it was. A month later he presented her with a financial plan for their separation, devised with the help of lawyer Morris Ernst. She refused it. They argued loudly at dinner, in front of Johnny, scaring the boy. John nonetheless exited to his office to finish the chapter he was writing on the president of Mexico, even while feeling "utterly possessed, mad, crazy" with thoughts of Agnes—"really, out of my mind."

Gunther proved astonishingly able to write chapter after chapter while wracked by shifting emotions. He sought release in frequent sprees at Polly's, which were made easier once Frances and Johnny left to spend the summer of 1941 in Los Angeles with Frances's brother Bernard Fineman, a film producer. John had also found himself a "regular girl"—a lovely New York socialite and budding novelist half his age, nicknamed Bubbles for her lighthearted disposition. They met at a party in June 1941. She was intelligent, beautiful, and thoughtful, and became his steady girlfriend—though he continued to patronize Polly's and go out with Miriam Hopkins when he could. He appreciated Bubbles more and more; only thoughts of Agnes kept him from proposing marriage to her.[35]

He was writing hard over the summer of 1941, though he gave parties that lasted till near dawn when foreign correspondent buddies such as Walter Duranty or Jay Allen visited New York. Knick and Agnes came to town, requiring the deceitful necessity to invite them to his parties and see them together socially—and to get together with Knick alone as he would have, before. How could Gunther face this man? He did, just as he kept to a killing deadline. *Inside Latin America* had been promised as a Book of the Month Club selection for November. He had to finish it by September 3, and on August 18 he still had six countries to cover. He began writing one country per day—four thousand to five thousand words each—with record hours of work, and a record night of boisterous sex at Polly's when he sent ten chapters to the printer. By his fortieth birthday on August 30, he was almost finished.[36]

The night before his deadline he was beset by "savage, lonely, unbelievable thoughts" of Agnes. "Unendurable," he called them—but he finished the manuscript in time, and delivered it before noon on September 3, since every minute counted. Next he was on the air for an NBC "European roundup," a regular gig for which he was confident enough not to prepare. After that, he got very drunk. He had been turning in his chapters to be typeset as he finished them, and he began going over proofs two days later, completing his checking and fixing them. By September 10 his work was done. The next day he sat for eminent studio photographer George Platt Lynes for a publicity photo. ("Fairy," Gunther noted in his diary.)[37]

As before, Harper worked a miracle in publishing speed and on October 29, 1941, released a first printing of 215,000 copies of *Inside Latin America*. Gunther's vivid impressions of twenty leaders and nations—educated impressions, though lightly gathered—had great appeal. He spliced these together with political commentary about both the poverty and the rich resources of every nation and the relative visibility of fascist imprints—or, on the other hand, friendliness to the United States. He said little about race and nothing about racism. Recognizing that most of the Latin American peoples were racially mixed, in parallel to the United States, he saw this mainly as a potential "problem." As much as *Inside Latin America* described another continent, it was a USA-focused book, seemingly built on the assumption that all penetration and influence by the United States would be beneficial. Gunther regarded "Yankee imperialism" (naming it as such) as a thing of the past, and presented the new American imperialism of siting military bases in the Caribbean as highly reasonable in the context of Nazi threats to the Western Hemisphere.[38]

Some American reviewers embraced the book as "a rapid and reliable once-over survey," others somewhat more circumspectly as a "superb piece of reporting, but with the defects that are inevitable in the whirlwind approach to the problem of a continent." Reviewers were becoming shrewder in assessing what "to guntherize" meant. *Inside Latin America* stayed at number one or two on the *Publishers Weekly* best-seller list for twenty-eight weeks even though spokesmen in several Latin American countries said Gunther was dreadfully misguided. Fourteen Latin American scholars in the United States got together to condemn the book in a signed statement. "Far from constituting a reliable introduction" to the continent, the scholars declared, Gunther's book was a "danger" to the enterprise of educating readers in the United States. They thought it bad for "the cause of inter-American understanding," without specifying exactly why. Such criticism bothered Gunther little, so long as the book continued selling well.[39]

Before the book's release, Gunther was on his transatlantic way to broadcast from London at war. He got in touch with Lee Miller as soon as he arrived at the Dorchester Hotel, knowing she was already staying there, and she came up to his room at 1:15 a.m. She had left Elouis in favor of a new partner, English surrealist painter Roland Penrose, but that hardly kept her away from John, or from *Life* magazine photographer David Scherman, with whom she had a relationship during the war. In the torrent of destruction caused by the Blitz and in the blacked-out years, illicit sexual liaisons flamed up in London. Amid the ghoulish horror of war, people seized erotic freedom as a counter, making love to defy death.[40]

NBC had again commissioned Gunther to give a series of on-the-spot live broadcasts from London. He did so for two months—until a phone call from Lee Miller told him the news of Pearl Harbor. He booked passage from London to New York as soon as he could get out, which was December 12, 1941. In a ship darkened and camouflaged to evade German U-boats, he crossed on what would be the last regularly scheduled American transatlantic passage. He knew that everything familiar was about to change.[41]

WAR NOW SPANNED the world. The United States declared war on Germany and Italy as well as Japan by December 11. Britain and its allies the Netherlands, New Zealand, and Australia declared war on Japan. China declared war on Japan, Germany, and Italy. The Soviet Union did not declare war on Japan, but Germany had launched a surprise attack on Russia six months earlier, breaking the Nazi-Soviet pact and bringing the Soviet Union into alliance with Britain against Germany and Italy.

Soviet troops in sub-sub-zero temperatures were heroically keeping the German army from reaching Moscow when Gunther returned to New York at the end of 1941. He left a miserable Christmas dinner with Frances and Johnny early and went to Ham Armstrong's cocktail party, reconnecting with Thompson and Sheean there. Supper with friends at Bennett Cerf's followed. Gunther was reassessing how to be most useful now that the United States was at war. At lunch the next day, his publisher Cass Canfield urged him to take up *Inside USA*, a project he had been mulling for some time. (Canfield also conveyed the happy news that *Inside Latin America* was sending him royalties of $13,000, the equivalent of more than $200,000 today.) Gunther consulted other friends. Archibald MacLeish, now working in war information, advised doing the American book. Gunther began to feel that *Inside USA* would be his magnum opus. He told his diary, "it is my <u>destiny</u> to write it."[42] Yet he hung back from starting.

About his marriage he was more decisive. He and Frances separated in February 1942, though their son Johnny wept at the news. Frances established her separate residence in Madison, Connecticut, where Johnny lived with her until going to boarding school, and John made his on Park Avenue near 61st Street in Manhattan. Dorothy Thompson lived in easy walking distance, in an east 48th Street townhouse she had recently turned into a combined home and office. Meanwhile, Gunther's emotions were on a roller coaster between his fondness for his girlfriend Bubbles and his quixotic passion for Agnes, with whom he had four rendezvous between March and May of 1942. He had a rival in a Hollywood producer who proposed marriage to Bubbles in June; the competition made John value her more and think about marrying her. He continued to visit Polly's, though admitting "bad conscience" more than once, worrying, "Am I degenerating into a drunken lecher?" But he answered himself, "no I'm lonely, & I want love, that's all."[43]

Frances resisted divorce, in part because as "Mrs. John Gunther" she had more weight in her advocacy for Zionism and for Indian freedom. She became vocal in both these causes during the war years.

Her emotions and behavior toward John zigzagged crazily, but she pursued political advocacy steadily. She helped representatives of the Irgun, a militant Zionist paramilitary group, to raise money in the United States, and poured an ardent commitment to the Indian cause into public speaking and writing as never before. Nehru, imprisoned by the British for most of the war, responded to her letters, feeding her persistent fantasies about him and also nerving her to write three essays urging Indian freedom, published in *Common Sense*, a small liberal-to-socialist magazine. Encouraged by praise for the articles, she turned them and her related speeches into a short book, *Revolution in India*. These were unique accomplishments for her. Wanting to improve her knowledge and credentials to seek a worthwhile job, she began taking courses in international relations at Yale University in New Haven, not far from Madison.[44]

Still unsure what he should do, John worked on a revision of *Inside Asia* and resumed being man about town. His social life drew on a cosmopolitan mix of people in newspapers, theater, books, magazines, radio, and Hollywood. Parties at restaurants or homes, lunches and dinners at expensive restaurants, "café society" at the Stork, 21, and the Colony—these were his haunts. He was "everybody's best friend. The one good friend all . . . had," a correspondent affirmed. Gossip columnists took note of his whereabouts (and of the woman on his arm, to his annoyance). Whenever foreign correspondent friends, including Louis Fischer, William Shirer, Quentin Reynolds, Jay Allen, came through New York City, he treated them and traded political views and personal gossip. These men did not forget each other. Gunther kept up with the women, too, not only Thompson but also Martha Gellhorn, Virginia Cowles, and Anne O'Hare McCormick. He saw Clare Boothe Luce more often, discussing his play with her, but she was shifting gears, preparing to run for Congress from Connecticut. Gunther celebrated with her when she won in 1942.[45]

Washington's needs, New York's intelligentsia, and Hollywood's bright lights intersected during the war, as the new availability of

commercial plane travel facilitated the creation of a bicoastal creative community of Americans, supplemented by European refugees. Though Gunther was not dazzled by Hollywood's appeal,
he responded positively when Darryl Zanuck, executive head of
Twentieth-Century Fox, got in touch with him in April 1942, seeking his help on a documentary on the US Signal Corps. Gunther was
flying back and forth to Washington often that month, taking over
foreign news analysis on Raymond Gram Swing's radio show while
Swing was vacationing. He said yes to Zanuck and also to film director
Frank Capra, then employed by the Office of War Information, who
wanted Gunther to work on the propaganda series Why We Fight,
which would be shown to millions of new American soldiers to pump
up their understanding of the abominations of German, Italian, and
Japanese fascism. Gunther lived and worked in Hollywood for four
weeks in the summer of 1942. He reconnected with Elsa Maxwell,
who seemed to know everyone, and in his spare time he socialized
with stars such as Jack Benny, Ginger Rogers, Marlene Dietrich, and
Dietrich's lover the French actor Jean Gabin. Bubbles was in town
with her other suitor, causing Gunther some tense moments.[46]

When Gunther returned home in the fall, it was taken for granted
that he was a wise head on all matters international. He often went
to Washington to get inside information on US war strategies and
Allied hopes. On one of those visits at the end of September 1942,
he saw Jimmy Sheean, who was wearing a captain's uniform. Sheean
had joined the Army Air Forces (AAF) at forty-one, Gunther noted
in his diary, "because he was having one of his old nervous break-
downs. He said he stayed up all night drinking and playing music, couldn't work, felt that he had been a warmonger for 20 years,
and couldn't stand the youngsters going out to get killed for him
and Dinah." Sheean chose the air force because it had impressed
him mightily when he toured Guam and Wake Island just before
Japan attacked. He was commissioned as a captain on May 28, 1942,
telling Ham Armstrong, "I think it will be the making of me (or

breaking, maybe)," adding that he believed in the AAF "more than in anything else we have."

Sheean sounded frustrated with his assignment when he spoke with Gunther that September, saying (in Gunther's account) that "a child of 10 could do all the work he is supposed to do. He stands with a pointer and explains Asia to General Arnold every morning." (Henry H. "Hap" Arnold, a three-star general, was the commanding general of the Army Air Forces and directed activities for the air war against Germany and Japan.) Later that evening, Gunther saw Sheean again, so "blind drunk" that "he could hardly stand," in Gunther's observation—a repeat of behavior Gunther had seen too often in New York. Sheean was soon sent to North Africa, where he worked with generals and other higher-ups, often serving as a French translator. He was promoted to the rank of lieutenant colonel after a year. Though virtually nothing is known of his intelligence work, it seems rarely to have been onerous or dangerous.[47]

When Gunther was in Washington he was usually seeking grist for his broadcast mill. This meant speaking with members of FDR's administration such as journalist Elmer Davis, head of the Office of War Information, and with foreign representatives such as China's minister of foreign affairs T. V. Soong and Soviet ambassador Maxim Litvinov. He was on the air frequently. When Operation Torch, the Allies' landing in North Africa, succeeded early in November, he spoke at length on the radio several nights in a row. Attending a dinner for Wendell Willkie, who was seen as a credible presidential candidate for 1944 although FDR's electoral votes had crushed his in 1940, Gunther picked up several tips from army officers and the assistant secretary of war and then listened to Willkie speak for two hours about the war and the foreseeable postwar world. Gunther was secretly pleased (though also embarrassed) that Willkie, while speaking, turned toward him frequently with remarks such as "John, you are really an expert on these things and you know that what I am saying is right" or "as John knows better than I do."[48]

"Isn't it about time another one of John Gunther's 'Insides' came out?"

John Gunther cartoon by Helen Hokinson, in the *New Yorker*, 1944.
Source: Condé Nast, New York.

Feeling remiss for remaining uninvolved in reporting the war, and anticipating an Allied invasion somewhere in Europe early in the summer of 1943, Gunther contacted both the North American Newspaper Alliance and NBC Radio. Both gave him press credentials to report the war from North Africa, and his stature and luck got him the plum assignment to cover General Dwight D. Eisenhower, Supreme Commander of the Allied Expeditionary Force. Eisenhower was about to lead the surprise Allied invasion of Sicily. Because

Gunther traveled with Eisenhower, he became the first American reporter to see the successful invasion up close and to write about it. He broadcast along the way numerous times, wrote dozens of news articles distributed through subscribers to NANA, and returned to New York after eleven weeks. The war was nowhere near won, and he was still waffling on what to do next.[49]

NEITHER JOHN GUNTHER'S nor Vincent Sheean's wartime mode could or would be Dorothy Thompson's. Her mixed feelings about Germany, the "problem child of Europe" (in her words), made her distrust what the war might bring.[50] Yet she wanted to serve her country when it was fighting fascism. Fortunately, William Paley, the head of the Columbia Broadcasting System (CBS), soon came to her with a proposal she took up eagerly. Paley's idea, to beam propaganda into Germany to encourage popular resistance to Hitler, fit Thompson's worldview and capabilities perfectly. She saw real potential for Germans to rise up against the Third Reich, and with zeal she began composing scripts addressed to an imagined friend in Berlin named "Hans."

Thompson's speeches circulated in Germany (in German) via CBS shortwave radio between March and September 1942. Her words unveiled the heinous evils of Hitler's regime, and stressed that Nazi victory over the Allies was impossible. Thompson was speaking from the heart. She believed that a significant break could occur within Germany, with Allied incentives and encouragement. How far her words made a difference is impossible to gauge, but Joseph Goebbels found the broadcasts distressing enough to decry Thompson as "the scum of America" and to wonder in his diary how it happened that a "dumb broad" could so defame the Führer.

She published the scripts in English later that year under the title *Listen, Hans!* In a preface, she appraised the internally warring tendencies she saw in the German psyche—between extreme order and intemperate boundlessness, rationalism and sentimentalism, idealism and nihilism. These paradoxes, as she saw them, explained Germans' susceptibility to Hitler but also supported the likelihood of recovering Germany to Western civilization. Reviewers praised the book generously, especially the enlightening preface.[51]

Thompson loathed everything about the Nazis, but she did not believe that Germans had a uniquely evil or militaristic streak. Germany had a divided soul, as her introduction to *Hans* explained. She weighed in early and loudly in the popular and policy discussion (which began almost as soon as the war did) on treatment of Germany after Allied victory. Opposing any intention to grind Germany into dust, she insisted that such a postwar plan took the wrong approach entirely: in the short run, Allied plans to weaken Germany fatally, if announced, would lead Hitler's armies to fight harder to prevent Allied victory; and in the long run, a revived and recivilized Germany would be needed to halt Soviet power in Europe.

A war plan to annihilate rather than reconstruct the enemy made no sense to her in any case. She had said that to her *Ladies' Home Journal* readers at the outset. The Allies' announcement in January 1943 of the goal of "unconditional surrender" by the Axis exasperated her. She objected that Allied policy was misguided: publicizing such an inflexible punitive goal was bound to be counterproductive, for it precluded a negotiated peace and quashed the possibility for oppositionists to Hitler to emerge and negotiate with the Allies. As much as she wanted to extirpate fascism, she felt the goal of "unconditional surrender" tainted the war effort.[52]

Thompson's seeming generosity to Germany perplexed many readers of her column on both left and right, and angered others. Many saw it as a reversal of her earlier vehemence about the Nazi threat. Her righteous certainty became a target for satire. Thompson combined "the appearance of Brunnehilde with the gusto of General Patton and the holy fire of a crusading apostle," jeered a sketch of her as "God's Angry Woman," noting accurately enough that Thompson's current views had thrown her admirers a "curve ball." A slashing portrait of "Dorothy Thompson, Cosmic Force" insolently disparaged her as a "lady mental welterweight" with "limitless faith in herself, her intuitions, her judgments and her place as wet nurse to destiny." Mocking her with allusions to her sex, the male author praised Thompson's outstanding ability to "rearrange the post-war map of the world between 10:30 A.M. and 12:30 P.M. with as little effort as another woman whipping up a sponge cake." His critique wallowed in a sexism not yet named in 1944 and all the more effective in ridiculing Thompson.[53]

Despite the opposition her views attracted, Thompson argued repeatedly that Germany must be "salvaged," not crushed, and brought back into European fellowship after the war—both to sustain peace and to limit the Soviet Union's presence in Europe. In a public fracas in 1944, she was accused of being pro-German for refusing to sign a manifesto of the Writers' War Board because it denounced a German "will-to-aggression" in perpetuity. Thompson's refusal to condemn Nazi atrocities as uniquely German, while she also objected to the Allied policy of unconditional surrender, began to isolate her. Sorrow deepened her desolation about the direction that the war had taken when Lieutenant Wells Lewis (Sinclair Lewis's son from his first marriage) was killed by a German sniper late in 1944. She loved and treasured Wells as her own son and was inconsolable about losing him, especially because she could not affirm that he had not died in vain.[54]

To her own amazement, however, Thompson found renewed marital happiness during the war. Very soon after her divorce from Lewis, she fell in love passionately, sensuously, mind-alteringly, the way she had fallen for Bard. A Czech painter named Maxim Kopf, born in Vienna and raised and educated in Prague, arrived uninvited at Twin Farms to paint Thompson's portrait. (Another refugee very grateful to Thompson had sent him.) Kopf had been jailed for months in Paris as a suspected spy and then transferred to a concentration camp, but luckily benefited from a singular political arrangement that enabled several hundred Czech refugees to leave the camp for the United States. A burly, lusty man over six feet tall, muscular from being overworked in the concentration camp, Kopf was moderately talented and wholly dedicated to his art, exuberant about life despite his own hard and knockabout path. Both he and Thompson were nearing fifty. The sexual attraction between them was immediate.

She was astonished and overjoyed. "My personal life was a total failure—my life as a woman," Thompson described her state of mind when they first met. Kopf provided the remedy: "To Maxim I was always a woman first and last." Worldly and self-confident—able to speak seven languages badly, it was said—Kopf did not mind that Thompson and her circle were intense analysts of international issues and he was not. Their surprising match was solid. One problem got in the way: he was married. He had married Lotte Stein, a German Jew, partly so that she could enter the United States on his passport, but Stein did not think the marriage was now dispensable. Thompson leaned hard on her; rumors flew that she forked over large sums before Stein gave in.

In June 1943, Thompson and Kopf were married in the Universalist Church near Twin Farms in a buoyant ceremony among friends. She joked to Alexander Woollcott about having "a low strain of masochism" in being "tempted to attempt the impossible" again by marrying. A little embarrassed to be marrying again at her age, she was ecstatically happy with Maxim Kopf, "the man I ought to have married in the first place," she told Jimmy Sheean.[55]

Sheean's own marriage was not faring well. Dinah Sheean's attachment to him flagged during his years away in the air force. He sensed that she saw his departure as "a relief" after he spent three weeks' leave with her and their children in 1944. "Long separations in the war and the difficulty in getting unwound from it on return" had made "a mess of many people's lives," he reflected. It was true that the war disrupted many couples' relationships, but he was deflecting warning signs about his own marriage by generalizing the matter.[56]

The shell that was the Gunthers' marriage ended with divorce that spring of 1944, the very month that John's tormenting entanglement with Agnes Knickerbocker exploded—because Knick discovered it. Gunther was ready to be free of his hobbling passion and did not mourn its ending. He had already recognized his own folly, admitting to himself that "the amount of time, energy, ingenuity, imagination, etc., I put into this love affair could run a government for 5 years." Frances Gunther was stunned to learn that unremarkable Agnes Knickerbocker was the woman John had left her for. The Knickerbockers' marriage survived, but not the friendship between the two men. Knick indicted John: "I consider you a person without honor."[57] With an agonizing chapter of his life closed, Gunther looked ahead. It was time to act on his long-simmering intent to write *Inside USA*. He could see America's postwar global dominance coming.

CHAPTER 11

THE AGE
OF ADJUSTMENT

ALLIED VICTORY IN Europe in May 1945 did not relieve
Thompson's heavy heart. Week after week her columns analyzed, criticized, and condemned the conduct of the "total" war
and the "phantom peace." Thompson despaired over the Potsdam
agreement signed that summer by President Harry Truman, Joseph
Stalin, and British prime minister Clement Atlee, and not only because it would demilitarize Germany and set up four zones of occupation. The agreement ratified Soviet advances into Eastern Europe;
it also allowed Eastern European countries bordering Germany to
expel ethnic Germans, thus making homeless refugees of twelve to
fourteen million people whose only crime was being German. Her
moral indignation had no bounds. Her friendship with many German refugee intellectuals and artists, to whom she offered generous
help and fellowship, influenced her views. Jimmy Sheean, living at
Twin Farms in the summer, felt "rather submerged here in guttural
Mittel Europa voices and condemnation of the Allies," he told John
Gunther. "Fully half of all talk is in German." He thought it was bad
for Thompson's perspective.[1]

Thompson traveled to Germany that summer and saw the hideous
extermination camp of Dachau. The camp had been liberated three
months before, so she did not witness putrefying corpses stacked like

cordwood or walking skeletons barely recognizable as human beings, but she had read the reports. Cheek by jowl with the gas chambers, she saw the sedate homes of SS administrators—Schubert's *Lieder* still on their pianos, volumes of Goethe on their shelves. This stupefying juxtaposition spoke to her of the malevolent potential of modern civilization to warp the human soul. She had to infer that modernity had certainly not left barbarism behind; it had succeeded in systematizing barbarism scientifically. This, rather than a unique monstrousness of Germans, or Nazis, was the terrifying "Lesson of Dachau" for her: "When civilized man, with his science, his technique, his organization, his power, loses his mind, he becomes the most terrible monster the world has ever seen," she wrote in the *Ladies' Home Journal*.[2] What took place in Germany could happen in America, she implied.

In her condemnation of Nazi outrages all along, she had demanded that her listeners not separate themselves from the horrors taking place. When she exhorted listeners about Herschel Grynszpan's case, "Who is on trial? I say we are all on trial," she was accusing everyone in Western nations for tolerating Nazi methods. After the Red Army liberated the Majdanek death camp, near Lublin in the summer of 1944, her column on the atrocities uncovered there hammered the same theme. "These crimes were committed by human beings. They can no more be separated from the human race than their victims," she wrote. "Every individual bears a responsibility for the whole of mankind. Human civilization is based on the recognition of that responsibility. The moment any one denies this responsibility he makes himself an accomplice of humanity's crimes. The moral crisis of our times has arisen from the denial of this responsibility."[3]

Her definitions of morality and responsibility grated against critics for whom the villainy of the German perpetrators was foremost. Thompson's wartime insistence on salvaging rather than destroying Germany had alienated many people. After Allied victory, an increasing chorus rebuked or abandoned her, claiming she had more sympathy for the Nazis than for their millions of victims. She soon compounded the insult (in their eyes) by becoming a critic of Zionist efforts to establish a Jewish state in Palestine.

Before and during the war, American Zionists had prized Thompson for denouncing anti-Semitism and advocating unrestricted Jewish migration to Palestine. To these supporters' shock, her opinions shifted after she traveled to Palestine in 1945. As she learned more about the conflicts between Zionists and resident Arab Palestinians, Thompson became sympathetic to the Arab position. Taking an increasingly pacifist position, she was also appalled by the violence of Zionist paramilitary groups avidly contesting British dominion at that time. When the Irgun blew up the British administrative headquarters at the King David Hotel in Jerusalem, killing ninety-one people inside, Thompson was aghast.[4]

She supported Arab claims in 1946 and 1947, gaining enemies who vilified her as an anti-Semite—even as pro-Nazi. She was neither. She believed that it was "all right to change your opinion . . . if it's the second opinion that is right," and she defended her views about Palestine to her editor at the *New York Post* as being based on facts. A barrage of protest mail landed at the *Post*'s door nonetheless. In March 1947, without explanation to Thompson, the *Post* stopped printing her column. Because her syndication contract was independent of the *Post*, she continued writing On the Record, and it appeared three times a week as always, elsewhere, but not in New York.[5]

The *Post*'s action certainly distressed Thompson, but postwar international relations burdened her mind more. She had little hope for the new United Nations, thinking that its plan to rely on cooperation among great nation-states was unrealistic, because each country would defend and pursue only its own interests. To keep the peace, she thought only binding international law, with the compulsion of an international armed force behind it, would be effective. But in the *Ladies' Home Journal* she called for world disarmament and looked to women to bring it about. "If No One Else—We the Mothers," her column declared.[6]

In Thompson's melancholy assessment, the world was in the midst of a moral crisis. Words had lost their meaning; basic values such as truth, and the rule of law, were being cast to the winds. Only a spiritual resurgence could save humanity, she asserted more than once: "The whole of our civilization is sick for a living ethos. Its experiments and adjustments fail for the lack of an integrating faith." The "secular religions" of communism and fascism had left people wanting because they did not address the soul, she believed, and modernity's materialism and technology provided insufficient moral nourishment. "It is the concept of the infinite and the eternal and of something beyond and more important than personal happiness which gives sense and dignity to human life and cohesion to society," she maintained.[7] She was not alone in seeing evidence of moral debasement in the gas chambers, the atom bomb's destructiveness, and both sides' purposeful obliteration of civilians.

LIKE THOMPSON, JIMMY Sheean saw no real peace when the war ended. He was living in New York when the American atomic bomb decimated Hiroshima, and he wrote in his diary, "Unimaginable. . . . The whole thing passes belief." John Hersey's later account of the atomic devastation, told through the eyes of six survivors, terrified Sheean, whose long awareness of the geopolitical context of US-Soviet antagonism made the atomic era all the more frightening. "There has been no time in human history when the power of life and death has been so dangerously concentrated in two immense states," he brooded anxiously. Two giants now straddled the globe. Only "an irresistible will for peace on both sides" would "prevent a world-wide antithesis" between the two.

Deploring the postwar American move to replace the Nazi enemy with the Soviet one, he hated to see the American press manufacture "crisis" by stressing Soviet aggressions. Winston Churchill's heralded speech of March 1946 in St. Louis, declaring that "an iron curtain has descended across the Continent," made Sheean fume. The "iron curtain" metaphor for suppressions of freedom in the Soviet sphere of influence in Eastern Europe stuck, though Sheean regarded it as counterproductive bluster. He could see rationality in the Soviet aim to surround itself with compatible states in Eastern Europe.[8]

Government persecution of suspected American Communists deepened Sheean's downbeat mood. He helped raise money to defend friends on the executive board of the Joint Anti-fascist Refugee Committee, a relief group founded during the Spanish Civil War, who were called to testify before the House Un-American Activities Committee (HUAC). All of them were charged with contempt of Congress for refusing to reveal their records and would serve jail time. He joined protests against HUAC's prosecution of Hollywood writers, actors, and directors for supposed Communist ties.

Dorothy Thompson did not share Sheean's views of Soviet Russia. She decried regimes where she saw "party programs dominating the whole of life" and "adherence to or rejection of them determining whether men and their families survive or perish." She also made it plain that she regarded the Communist Party in the United States as a criminal conspiracy, not a party in the parliamentary sense. She thought Communist Party membership should be made a crime—but, ever a civil libertarian, she agreed with Sheean that the abusive hunt for "Reds" in America was highly unfair so long as belonging to the party was legal. Because civil liberties and the freedom to dissent were such central values to her, she criticized the persecutory tactics of HUAC and Senator Joseph McCarthy more than once. Even though communism was anathema to her, she also repeatedly objected to an American foreign policy that would police the world to keep communism at bay.[9]

Though they argued, the two were closer than ever. Sheean habitually rented the smaller house on Thompson's beloved Vermont property, Twin Farms, from May to October. He could concentrate there far better than in New York, and Thompson was nearby, ready to talk. She had Maxim by her side, too, leavening her outlook with private pleasures. Sheean was not so fortunate. Dinah divorced him in January 1946. "I still can hardly believe it," he admitted to himself a week after the decree. He had taken Dinah's commitment to him for granted and never imagined how dreary life would be without her. When the federal government began hounding him to pay long-neglected income taxes, financial worries assailed him as well, because he was unable to pay what he owed. The United States made up for the extraordinary military expenses of the war partly by enlarging the tax pool, making nearly two-thirds of Americans subject to federal income tax in 1945, compared to 7 percent in 1940. Very high rates were set for upper brackets.[10]

Sheean's gloom about the world—and himself—shadowed his latest book, *This House Against This House*. The book's opening and concluding scenarios expressed his pessimism about the likelihood of a lasting peace, while the middle offered views of the war during his service in North Africa, Italy, India, and China. More reviewers warmed to these war episodes than to his sober ruminations. Several put Sheean's method of "personal journalism" on the examination table. The sharpest critic concluded drily, "One wonders if this type of intimate, first-person journalism hasn't about outlived its usefulness as a serious contribution to world thought." This did not bode well for Sheean's ability to earn a living.[11]

In the fall of 1946, ready for an exit from New York, Sheean undertook a reporting task unique for him. He went to Lawrenceburg, Tennessee, where twenty-five African Americans were on trial for attempted murder, after shots fired in a melee in their neighborhood wounded four white policemen. Walter White, head of the National Association for the Advancement of Colored People (the principal civil rights organization in the United States), asked him to go to Lawrenceburg and write about the trial, and Sheean roused himself to oblige: "I know the case and my sympathies are already deeply engaged." He had not taken any stand on racism before, but he had been exposed to explicit antiracism in the American Communist Party during the 1930s, through the League of American Writers.[12]

He found the trial in Lawrenceburg a greater scandal than he had imagined. The prosecution was free to spew vicious words and threaten violence, while the NAACP defense lawyers were "muzzled to a degree one had never believed possible in the United States," Sheean wrote. His articles, relating the prosecutor's outrageous courtroom bullying, made local white authorities so furious that the local commissioner of public safety called Sheean a "Communistic bastard" and a "lying son of a bitch." The next astounding development was the verdict: the all-white, all-male jury acquitted twenty-three of the twenty-five men accused, since no evidence tied them to the shots fired. Two were convicted on lesser charges than murder. The outrageous travesty of legal procedure in the courtroom troubled the jurymen—who were ordinary white farmers and workers—as much as himself, Sheean concluded. The acquittal so heartened him that he affirmed the "splendor" of American values, "in spite of many contradictions."[13]

If the outcome of the trial was cheering, Sheean found the state of the world and his own life quite the opposite. He regarded any acceleration of US-Soviet tension warily. When President Truman sent massive support to Greece and Turkey early in 1947 to prevent the spread of communism toward the Mediterranean, Sheean saw it as an ominous "move of the greatest significance." It upset him. Yet he sensed in the public a dismaying "atmosphere of fatalism and apathy" on international issues. Dorothy Thompson agreed. When the *New York Post* dropped On the Record, the editor's sole explanation was that the column was "dull." Though Thompson suspected a cabal working against her, she felt constrained from arguing that "the editors do not find my column dull. . . . Maybe they do," she explained her position to John Gunther. "What is or is not 'boring' varies with the public mood. . . . I think all serious commentators have suffered, with the public and sponsors, since the war; the interest in public affairs and especially international affairs has certainly lapsed since the war."[14] While Thompson seemed resigned to the public becoming disaffected with what she had to say, Sheean looked in a new direction to heal his malaise.

JOHN GUNTHER, IN contrast to his two friends, had his finger on the pulse of the reading public. Turning from foreign continents to his own, he spent almost three years researching and writing *Inside USA*, investing more time and care in it than in any of his previous books. Familiarity bred not contempt but something like realism. Covering fifteen Asian or twenty Latin American countries in less than a year had not fazed him, but getting a grasp of all forty-eight states seemed to him daunting. He consulted more people than ever before on his initial outline and made very careful plans, sending a set of three questions ahead of time to all forty-eight governors. (He received replies from all but one.) Then he began thirteen months of travel, crisscrossing the nation, going to every state, aiming to discover "who runs things" and what was distinctive about each one. He conducted so many interviews that he sent nine hundred thank-you notes once he finished.[15]

Inside USA was published in May 1947. Its 979 pages sold for the whopping price of $5 at a time when most books cost no more than $3. Its print run of half a million was the largest ever in the publishing history of the United States. The Book of the Month Club chose the book to be its first choice selection for June and committed to buy nearly 400,000 copies. Harper & Brothers printed another 125,000, expecting general demand to be large—as it certainly was. "Three days after it was published, it accounted for ninety per cent of the day's book business done at Macy's," reported Richard Rovere in a glowing *New Yorker* profile of Gunther. "Nothing like that had ever happened before."[16]

Inside USA was Gunther's "most spectacular performance" yet, a reviewer wrote in awe. One could hardly *not* admire this behemoth of a book, bursting with the variety and vitality, the contradictions and disparities, distances and convergences that Gunther found in his native land. Gunther told his readers that he wrote for a "man from Mars, or the moon" who knew nothing about the United States.[17] His findings were geographical and political, economic and anecdotal, statistical and gossipy, critical and jokey, partly travel guide but altogether a political assessment of how and whether democracy was working in dozens of locales. (He left out the national structure and federal government, planning to write a second book on them.) Individual personalities did not dominate *Inside USA* as much as they did Gunther's earlier books, although he sketched scores of state and city leaders, supplying plenty of evidence of inventiveness, community solidarity, and public-spirited leadership. Though the book arrayed the heterogeneity of places, attitudes, and politics Gunther found, he concluded that the phrase *e pluribus unum* fit the expansive country very well. Public questions being debated in diverse locations converged.

Again and again, Gunther recurred to "a dominant and supremely difficult American problem, that of the Negro," as he moved from state to state. The exquisitely detailed rules of Jim Crow that he first saw in Atlanta—a modern city, not a backwater—appalled him. He was reminded of the caste system in India. Having absorbed important lessons from Gunnar Myrdal's recent study, *An American Dilemma* (1944), he devoted a chapter to lynching, segregation, the white primary, and the poll tax in the South, and also pointed out insidious discrimination against African Americans (notably in housing and education) from California to Missouri and Michigan. Nonetheless he described "the Negro" as the overall "problem"—not white racism. The unevenness of the nation's bounty was clear in Gunther's evidence that pockets of poor Americans persisted, hungry and ill-housed, amid overwhelming American productive might. The sheer bravura and colorful plethora of the nation came through nonetheless as cause for delighted wonder.

The mood pervading *Inside USA* was ebullient, in acute contrast to the tragedy shadowing its author. In April 1946, Johnny Gunther—a smart and unpretentious sixteen-year-old with musical talent, a gift for science, and a clever way with words—was diagnosed with a malignant brain tumor. It was a mortal illness. The Gunthers searched for specialists, trying every medical avenue, from orthodox to experimental, to beat it. More than thirty specialists were brought into the case eventually. Johnny himself remained hopeful, enduring two major surgeries and facing his ongoing debility with extraordinary courage and cheerfulness. The tumor seemed miraculously (and inexplicably) to have been put on the run in the early months of 1947, but that was temporary. Soon the malignancy regrew faster.

For months, while frantically searching for alternative treatments and supporting his son as best he could, the pained father was writing *Inside USA* at his usual furious pace. He had found a new ballast for his personal life in Jane Perry Vandercook. He had met her briefly several years before, and they became reacquainted and close during the year of Johnny's illness. Ending his years of romantic and sexual fits and starts, Gunther found a new soulmate in a vital and beautiful woman sixteen years his junior. Frances Gunther, heartbroken too about her son's condition, confronted it courageously, devoting herself to Johnny and bending her creativity to make his life as worthwhile and enjoyable as possible. She and John were equally loving parents, and their indelible angst over Johnny brought them together in the shared aim to save him.[18]

It was a lost cause. Johnny became ever more precious to his parents as he showed forbearance through long hospitalizations and peculiar diet regimes, through near blindness in one eye and a drooping arm and leg. Toward the end (though not knowing that it was), he determined that he would graduate with his class at Deerfield Academy, despite having lost a year and a half of school. He studied with a private tutor, passed all his exams, and then insisted on limping heroically down the aisle at the graduation ceremony. A tall, wavering figure with his head swathed in bandages, he received his high school diploma with the others. A few weeks later his life ended, on June 30, 1947.[19]

If the booming success of *Inside USA* offered distraction for John, Frances Gunther had nothing comparable. Johnny's illness interrupted all that she had been trying to build for her single life since 1941. Though she held herself together well during the year and a half of crisis, it wholly depleted her. To say she was devastated would understate it. The death of Johnny, the golden child who had redeemed her guilt about her abortions and the loss of baby Judy, brought her momentum to a halt.

With a hole in his heart for his lost son, John Gunther visited Jimmy Sheean at Twin Farms one month later. It was a good week for both—"about as good a week as I have ever had," Gunther thought. Sheean felt that Gunther had helped him "immeasurably," too, simply "by his sanity." Sheean had lost six weeks of the summer in a mental whirlwind, brought on by his struggle to understand how the "good war" to defeat fascism had brought in its train the cataclysmic power of atomic fission and a darkly threatening bipolar standoff.[20]

Gunther did not dwell on his loss during the visit, though the question why Johnny had to die—and whether he bore some responsibility—haunted his mind. Evenings were spent at Dorothy Thompson's house, drinking, talking, arguing. When the friends talked about the possible meanings of Johnny's death, it was only one of infinite topics, including, was Christianity dead? did free will or determinism rule? how did poetry differ from prose? were people always so corrupt as in the present? should a samurai-type elite rule? "I am blank with admiration, at a) Jimmy's erudition; b) D's vitality," Gunther told his diary. "I would be worn out for a week, after one such slugging talkfest that she puts on nightly." He noted that "Jimmy wants Dinah to come back. He is lost without her. Never knew till now that only she gave his life meaning." But Gunther thought his old friend nonetheless seemed "remarkably fine," not drinking much, "wonderful with the kids"—Sheean's daughters were there for the summer—"helps clear the table, reads & studies seriously. . . . I have never known him to be better, or liked him so well."

Gunther noted down a remarkable (not to say maniacal) conversational riff that took place one evening, when Sheean called himself "'the greatest American legend,'" and went on to say "that generals & ambassadors quailed before his name, that nobody has made a greater contribution to intellectual life of USA, (*Personal History* was greatest seller Modern Library ever had, till it brought out *War & Peace*), that his 'genius' is absolutely indispensable, that he is probably the greatest living American master of English prose, and that his work is bound to live because of its fermenting influence on a whole generation & more, & that D[orothy] T[hompson] will be president because he 'wills' it. . . . Clare [Boothe Luce] is to nominate her, & the speech that D. will make will sweep her in." Sheean was "in deadly earnest, his eyes flashing a positive sulphuric blue fire," Gunther wrote in astonishment. "A <u>woman</u> as president, who believes in peace, who lost one son in a war, and who had another of military age. I listened goggle-eyed." Thompson demurred, saying she was not qualified, though she did not dispute him on the principle. Sheean's insistence on a woman president who would symbolize peaceful intentions was spurred by his fearful vision of an atomic battle between the United States and USSR that would put "life itself" in question. His mental anguish led him to seek farther.[21]

SHEEAN WAS READING widely, trying to comprehend a postwar situation he saw as disastrous. He found promise in the Bhagavad Gita, one of the most sacred Sanskrit texts of Hinduism, and in the writings of Mohandas Gandhi, the spiritual leader of the movement for Indian independence and initiator of the practice of nonviolent civil disobedience. He was paying close attention to the fateful events in India that summer of 1947 by listening to BBC broadcasts. Britain gave up its colonial rule in August. Partition of its former colony into two independent states, India (mostly Hindu) and Pakistan (mostly Muslim), followed, setting off the migration of millions from one geographical area to another. Partition sparked ruinous civil chaos and sectarian violence. In September, to call a halt to the murderous conflicts, Gandhi began fasting in nonviolent protest.[22]

Sheean became anxious to get an assignment that would take him to India. He felt an urgency about it, he told Thompson, because he had a premonition that within six months Gandhi would be assassinated—by a Hindu. Though most Indians revered Gandhi as a saint, his acceptance of the partition and his insistence on nonviolence in the midst of civil strife had made him controversial. Sheean trusted his unusual premonition because of previous extrasensory insights of his that were rationally inexplicable unless he was "psychic," as he casually used the label. In April 1945, for example, when he was on his way to San Francisco for the meeting that would plan the United Nations, Walt Whitman's lines about Abraham Lincoln's death—"my captain lies, fallen cold and dead"—kept going through his mind. The next day he learned that FDR had died. Then again, in October 1946, while driving in a car with a friend discussing something unrelated, he heard a click in his head, and the sentence "There goes Goering's dream" passed through his mind. The next day he was astonished to read that Goering had committed suicide at almost exactly the same time.[23]

The editor of *Holiday* magazine agreed to pay for the trip to India, and Sheean added assignments from the *Herald Tribune*. He began traveling in November, stopping in London, Paris, Vienna (still occupied by Allied forces), Prague, and Rome. Everywhere he went, he socialized with familiar journalists and local diplomatic personnel. He continued to Cairo, where the Arab League was meeting, for long talks with national and anticolonial leaders he knew from his earlier efforts. He had access to them because his reputation as a world-spanning journalist held, despite lackluster reception of his recent books.[24]

He arrived in Karachi, Pakistan, at the very end of December 1947 and stayed for two weeks. Pakistan and India had been at war over the disputed Kashmir region since October. While Sheean was in Karachi, communal violence arrived there—a deadly riot of resident

Muslims against arriving Sikhs, resulting in hundreds of deaths and injuries despite the quick response of police and army. Sheean wrote about the outbreak, but his purpose there was to understand the conflict between Pakistan and India better. His interview with Muhammad Jinnah, the founding leader of Pakistan, proved frustrating; Jinnah cannily said nothing new. Sheean then spoke with several other high officials and composed a substantial piece for the *Herald Tribune*, detailing Pakistan's side in its conflict with India.[25]

On January 13, 1948, Sheean learned that Gandhi had begun a new fast on behalf of Hindu-Muslim unity, and rushed to Delhi. He immediately sent a note to Jawaharlal Nehru, who had become India's first prime minister. A few days later he had the opportunity of an hour's conversation with Nehru—following the hour Nehru spent with American photographer Margaret Bourke-White, whose acquaintance Sheean made—and came away impressed with the Indian leader's temperament. On January 17, set as a day of prayer, Sheean saw hundreds of people line the Delhi streets in processions, praying for peace between Pakistan and India and calling for Mahatma Gandhi to end his fast. Nehru publicly responded to the impact of Gandhi's fast by promising that India would pay Pakistan a huge sum that Pakistan claimed it was owed.[26]

When Gandhi ended his fast the following day, and resumed holding public prayer meetings as he had done earlier, Sheean wrote in his journal: "Never did there live a man who was not only mythopoeic and mythogenic in the highest degree like this, but was also fully conscious of it and collaborated so with destiny." A bomb was thrown—to no effect, fortunately—at the first public prayer meeting, strengthening Sheean's confidence in his own foresight: "I have believed since last summer that if he is to be killed it must be (for India's sake) by a Hindu and not by a Muslim. This is in the logic of every sacred drama in the entire history of religion," he recorded. He had in mind the pattern in Christianity (and many other religions and founding myths) in which an inspired leader becomes a martyr, to serve the larger good.[27]

Pleased to get a summons from Nehru on January 26, Sheean hoped Nehru was answering his request for help in gaining access to Gandhi. Nehru did help with that, but when they met, Nehru had Sheean's *Herald Tribune* article on Pakistan in hand and spent the next two hours—barely stopping to take a breath—refuting Sheean's presentation of Pakistan's point of view. "There is no doubt whatever that he gave me hell," Sheean thought afterward. Nehru's effort measured his estimation of Sheean's potential impact on world opinion. While not regretting what he had reported on Pakistan, Sheean had the benefit of understanding India's point of view far better.[28]

On January 27, Sheean was able to meet and speak with the Mahatma face-to-face, following Gandhi's public prayer meeting. From prior reading he knew that Gandhi defined action as righteous if it was undertaken selflessly, without desire for its specific gains, or "fruits." Now, he was able to ask Gandhi the question that burned in his mind: How could it occur that righteous action, including "righteous battle," could produce catastrophic results? Gandhi answered that battle could not be righteous; a righteous cause undertaken with violence ceased to be righteous, because means and ends could not be evaluated separately. When Sheean indicated that he was referring to the war against Nazism, Gandhi said "with great dignity and a sort of gentle sadness, almost with pain, that our ends may have been good but our means were bad and this was not the way of truth but the way of evil." Gandhi added that "it is madness to try to erase a whole nation like Germany or change overnight a spirit like that of Japan."

Very moved by the answer Gandhi had given, Sheean returned the following day for another lesson. Gandhi discussed the nature of reality, and Sheean absorbed his teaching that the one living reality was the spirit of God, which pervaded all things, even a stone; all physical existence was a manifestation only. Departing, he let his mind roam over topics for subsequent lessons, feeling gratified and uplifted in imagining Gandhi as his guru (master or teacher). The following day, January 29, he nonetheless stayed away, taking up an opportunity to join a contingent accompanying Nehru on a speaking tour outside

Delhi. (Exhausted afterward, Sheean marveled that Nehru, though speaking for hours, "doesn't seem to get tired at all.")²⁹

Back in Delhi on January 30, Sheean hurried to prepare for Gandhi's prayer meeting at five o'clock in the afternoon. He stood with another journalist near the front of the garden where Gandhi would address the crowd. The Mahatma emerged from his residence as usual with a grandniece supporting him on either side. He was taking his place in front when several shots rang out. Gandhi fell to the ground, bleeding heavily, and died within minutes. Hearing the shots, Sheean was jolted into a semiconscious daze. The assassin—a Hindu extremist—had proved his premonition accurate. As Gandhi was carried away, Sheean was hardly aware of what was going on around him. Biblical lines such as "Father, why hast thou forsaken me?" ran through his head.

Sheean fell into spiritual turmoil for a full week afterward. During that time he "realized the self" in the Hindu sense, he said, meaning that he accepted God. He renounced materialism—meriting Dorothy Thompson's sincere approval—and determined that he would undertake "no great or commanded act except for the truth of the action, not its possible fruits." On February 6, fully conscious in the real world again, he began attending the early-morning chanting of the Bhagavad Gita on the bank of the Jumna River. The ritual chanting continued until February 13, when Gandhi's ashes were to be scattered in the Ganges. Sheean and several million others went to that ceremony; he traveled on the special train bearing a large urn of Gandhi's ashes.³⁰

Sheean then began writing about these experiences. He felt transformed by accepting the reality of an all-pervading metaphysical presence he could call "god." He made nonviolence central to his moral outlook. It was less the uniqueness of Gandhi's principles (which Sheean recognized were ancient) than the way Gandhi enacted and wholly embodied these principles that inspired Sheean's new convictions. After publishing several articles recounting his premonition, his wish for Gandhi's help, his talks with Gandhi, the assassination, and his new beliefs, he expanded the same narrative into a book titled *Lead, Kindly Light* (1949), which was the name of a favorite Christian hymn of Gandhi's. The hymn was often played at Gandhi's public prayers, signaling his religious toleration.[31]

Lead, Kindly Light was well-timed. A great many Americans were looking for spiritual renewal after a war that had ravaged their sensibilities. They were seeking to restore "sense and dignity to human life," in Dorothy Thompson's words. Most people nourished that widespread hunger within the organized religions they knew, lending Christian churches greater institutional and psychological power than before the war. Thompson herself returned ineffably to her Methodist roots and proposed values she expressly called Christian as the surest salve for the postwar moral crisis she perceived. President Truman and other politicians took political advantage of the trend, upholding Americans' religiosity as a "weapon" against "godless" Communism. But not all resorts to spiritual values were opportunistic. Sheean's Gandhian lessons and his mission to create an international will for peace found an eager audience. The moral search and the spiritual resolution he expressed in *Lead, Kindly Light* struck a chord in the postwar American public, vaulting his book to best-seller lists for several months.[32]

SHEEAN'S BOOK SHARED the best-seller lists in 1949 with John Gunther's latest, in a neat convergence. Gunther had written a memoir of his son Johnny's struggle. In turning his emotions into words on the page, he found a mode of healing. His narrative of Johnny's cancer was as compellingly readable as a detective tale, turning and twisting with sudden seeming gains, crushing disappointments, then new possibilities for treatment. Tragedy lurked at every moment, but the book was not lugubrious. Johnny's thoughtful and sunny personality and his gallantry in facing formidable odds emerged from the clever conversations his father quoted. Frances Gunther contributed a moving afterword.

The book as a whole was uplifting, despite its tragic ending. Gunther titled it *Death Be Not Proud*, the opening line of a seventeenth-century sonnet by John Donne. Whether John or Frances Gunther believed in an afterlife for the Christian soul, which was the premise underlying Donne's sonnet, is doubtful. John did not budge from his secularism, unlike Thompson and Sheean—and unlike Frances. After Johnny's death she embraced her identity as a Jew and decided to move to Palestine, where the state of Israel was established in May 1948. She transformed her life, finding some comfort in religious belief and in participating in building Israeli society.[33]

John's marriage in 1948 to Jane Perry Vandercook, who became his companion in writing and life, began a new phase for him also. He quickly rolled out four books in three years after *Death Be Not Proud*, all of them expansions of magazine articles he had been commissioned to write: one on postwar conditions and leaders in Eastern Europe called *Behind the Curtain* (1949), and short studies, partially memoir, of American leaders Roosevelt, MacArthur, and Eisenhower. Somewhat abashed that "guntherize" had become a verb, he then spent three years, with his wife's help, on *Inside Africa* (1955), a book equal in scale to *Inside USA*. He plotted and researched the book with the curiosity and sense of discovery of his earlier books, but it became more and more difficult to keep up the killing pace he had set as a young man. Through failing eyesight and worsening health, Gunther continued to research and write a slew of books, and—still the good friend and bon vivant—to host memorable parties.[34]

Gunther stayed a close friend of Sheean, though many others thought Sheean had gone off the deep end, between his drinking habit and his confidence in his "psychic" gift. Dorothy Thompson was loyal, too, and hoped for Jimmy's sake that he and Dinah would reconcile. Dinah Sheean never stopped thinking about her ex-husband, though she fell for a series of younger men in love affairs that began exhilaratingly, only to crash sooner or later. Though painfully alive to Jimmy's faults, she still appreciated him for his sometime brilliance, his playfulness and erudition, and the glamour of his many worldly exploits. Stinging from a bad affair in the fall of 1949, she saw renewed virtues in Jimmy. He had been writing tender letters to her proposing that they begin a new start in life. She agreed to meet him in December. The result was their remarriage, on December 17, 1949, in London, and a trip to India together in 1950.[35]

Their reconciliation was brief. Within a few years they were snarling at one another with ugly accusations, and they separated again, but did not divorce. One of the things Dinah was seeking was a more fulfilling sexual life than she had with Jimmy, but whether she knew by then that he was attracted to men is not certain. She took up a life of her own, new love relationships (none of which lasted), and a series of jobs. Jimmy, still hounded by the IRS and in a financial hole, tried writing books of many sorts, including his own musical autobiography, two more middling novels, and biographies of Thomas Jefferson, Mahatma Gandhi, Oscar Hammerstein, and Giuseppe Verdi. The most valuable was his unique short memoir of Edna St. Vincent Millay (whom he had known only for a few years before her death in 1950), highlighting her unusual relationship with birds.[36]

Sheean's behavior in the late 1940s and 1950s was erratic. His political judgments of Cold War politics were often lucid and sharp, as he turned his longtime anti-imperialism into a prescient focus on the decolonizing world. Sheean perpetually turned outward, while the Cold War climate nudged most Americans away from internationalism. He knew he was pursuing "subjects which lack interest for the large public," as he wrote to Ham Armstrong, hoping nonetheless that *Foreign Affairs* would publish his pieces on Ceylon and India. (It did.) When a conference of nonaligned Asian and African countries was planned to take place in Bandung, Indonesia, in 1955, Sheean made sure to find a magazine to send him there. He told Thompson after the meeting, "We'll all be dead before the results are in, but I think Bandung was the most momentous gathering since the Congress of Vienna."[37]

He was right about Bandung and its role in the consolidation of a "Third World" concept. But Sheean's concerns with Asia, and with international peace and preventing atomic war, also led him to write hectoring letters to Nehru, to Madame Sun Yat-sen, to Nan Pandit, giving advice and chastising them for missteps. (Nan Pandit was Nehru's sister, head of the Indian delegation to the United Nations from 1946 to 1958, and Indian ambassador to the United States from 1949 to 1951.) Sheean always meant well, but his letters were out of control. His astounding hubris suggested a delusional sense of his own omniscience and his ability to predict the future. During the Korean War (1950–1953), he turned his attention to American politics, ingratiating himself with Adlai Stevenson, governor of his native state of Illinois. He urged Stevenson to run for the presidency in 1952—sure that Stevenson and Eisenhower would face each other for the presidency, long before the likelihood emerged. He was equally certain that Stevenson would win. Stevenson responded generously and kept up the acquaintance. When Eisenhower swept the election, Sheean had "the biggest shock" he could recall and apologized to Stevenson for "the overweening confidence with which I bedevilled you."[38]

All the while, Sheean valued Dorothy Thompson's friendship immensely. Concerned about her health and spirits, he worried in 1950 that she seemed "almost to have lost her interest in public affairs and international relations" because "her views no longer command much attention and it depresses her to go on expounding in a vacuum." She soldiered on, writing On the Record, though it brought her little satisfaction. "Ours is the age of adjustment and togetherness—and to hell with it!" she said of the 1950s. She remained very glum about the world situation, telling an acquaintance, "my picture of the future is too grim for me to wish to commit it to words, for either public or private consumption."[39]

Still, her social life was stimulating, full of friends and convivial parties, and her husband's tender love brought her much happiness.

That idyll imploded in 1958, when Maxim Kopf had a series of heart attacks. He died that July. They had been married fifteen years, and Thompson, numb with grief, was not certain how to go on—though she did go on. She wrote her final column for On the Record the next month, August 1958, and determined to spend her energy on writing her autobiography. But she found no energy for ambitious writing. Her health declined. After she had a heart attack in July 1959, she aged rapidly.

Thompson looked more ill than well in the Christmas season of 1960, when Jimmy and Dinah Sheean went to the airport to see her off to Lisbon to visit her grandchildren, Michael Lewis's two children. Jimmy felt "an irresistible sense of farewell" as Thompson boarded the plane. She who had devoted herself to the fate of Europe succumbed there to a fatal heart attack on January 30, 1961. Her tombstone stated, by her own choice, only her married name and one word of description: "Dorothy Thompson Kopf—Writer."[40]

PUBLISHERS EAGER TO find a biographer for Thompson saw Vincent Sheean and John Gunther as prime candidates for the job. Neither of them really wanted to do it, but the large fee attracted Sheean. He decided to limit his book to the Thompson-Lewis marriage. (Sinclair Lewis had died ten years before Thompson.) When given access to Thompson's papers, Sheean was surprised to see that she had carefully saved many revealing personal materials, and he inferred that she wanted their contents to be known. He decided to let the couple speak for themselves, for the most part, in the book he titled *Dorothy and Red* (1963). He reprinted swaths of Thompson's diaries and letters and fewer of Lewis's, knitting them into a narrative with his own commentary. Under the heading "A Rather Strange Interlude," he included all of Thompson's musings about Christa Winsloe. Some old friends—William Shirer, for instance—were shocked, but few reviewers remarked on it. The episode must have reverberated most for Sheean. Only then did he learn that his beloved friend had more in common with him than he had been aware.

Dorothy's and Red's intimate words, combined with Sheean's aptly expressed memories, created an absorbing and poignant story, and reviewers liked the book. Good sales hoisted it briefly to the best-seller list. One London review began by remarking that twenty-five years earlier "it would have been unnecessary to identify Dorothy and Red," because they were almost as celebrated as Franklin and Eleanor Roosevelt. Yet obscurity for Thompson and critical dismissals of Lewis had already swamped them, the reviewer noted. Thompson's career had dropped into backwaters as quickly as it had ascended in the 1930s, in fact. Young people did not know who she was, Sheean found out while writing the book, and it motivated him further.[41]

The reviewer took it for granted that obscurity would be "the fate of the greatest of journalists." It was true for Jimmy Sheean himself, who outlived Thompson by sixteen years. In the summer of 1968, distraught over turns in American politics, Sheean moved to the small Italian town near Lago Maggiore that he had loved since 1934. He never returned to the United States. Even though *Personal History* was republished in 1969, a simpler narrative of American writers' and artists' hedonistic sojourns in Paris in the 1920s overtook and supplanted it.[42]

Dinah Sheean joined her husband in Italy in 1969, and the two of them found surprising peace with one another in his last years. "Jimmy and I had our honeymoon at the wrong end, in the final years," she said after he died, thinking of writing a memoir about him. By then she could talk about his sexuality. She had asked Raymond Mortimer if he thought Jimmy was bisexual, and received the answer, "'of course, you silly, didn't you know?'" It did not distress her. A few weeks before his death, fading from cancer, Jimmy had said to Dinah, "You are my best friend." She took this as his supreme accolade.[43]

John Gunther should have had a better shot at lasting fame because he continued to write books that sold well. In his last decade he was working on his final continent. "Inside Australia" would have been another full-scale study on his established model, but it was incomplete when he died in 1970. His name and "inside" had been synonymous for more than three decades. Regardless, the book of his that lasted longest was none of those informative tomes but *Death Be Not Proud*, a family story of gallantry and sorrow that spoke to the ages.

CODA

O N May 8, 1945, the day the Allies declared victory in Europe, Jimmy Sheean exulted in relief. He was in San Francisco for the meeting that would plan the new United Nations organization. The happy news set him oddly on edge, "a little unsure" as he looked forward. His past career had moved in lockstep with the progress of fascism. Ever since catching a glimpse of Mussolini's "thugs" in 1922, he reflected, "My comings and goings, my work and thus to a considerable extent my life, had been ruled by it"—to the extent that "my own private decisions were governed by the doings and sayings of these monsters." What was to be next? he asked himself.[1]

The rise to prominence of Thompson and Gunther, too, had taken place in tandem with fascism's advances in Europe. Deeply drawn in by the world-historical events they witnessed, all three became "as seasoned and weatherwise in the developing process of Fascism and war as anybody," in Sheean's words. They had begun in the 1920s without such cares, in an experimental spirit, but the demise of liberal governments challenged by authoritarian leaders had gripped them all, becoming a leitmotif in their writings. As they clocked long, productive, wearying years revealing and interpreting the dangerous political ferments roiling the world, Americans looked to them as public intellectuals and authoritative experts. Their continent-spanning knowledge vaulted them into becoming celebrities, sought after in little towns and big cities across the United States. They had access to world leaders in and out of power: John Gunther interviewed dozens of prime ministers, presidents, and generals at length as well as rising and deposed leaders such as Leon Trotsky and Zhou En-lai; Vincent Sheean became a personal friend of Winston Churchill, of Jawaharlal Nehru, of Adlai Stevenson; Dorothy Thompson met the Queen Consort of England and was consulted by President Franklin Roosevelt. By the end of the 1930s correspondents such as they had "become political powers capable of influencing their nations and helping to determine the outcome of the war," an attentive critic judged, often better than diplomatic personnel in assessing what was going on.[2]

The defeat of fascism made 1945 a turning point for these three, and for other major American journalists abroad between the two world wars. None could pursue the task in the same way. Nor could a younger generation of would-be journalists start out as they once had twenty-five years before. Geopolitical reality had changed because of the war's outcome. When Gunther, Thompson, and Sheean first became foreign correspondents in Europe and Rayna Raphaelson went to China, their own nation was just emerging into world power. American dollars, policies, and know-how had global impact, but their possible extent was yet to be seen. The potential global heft of the Bolshevik regime in Russia was similarly inchoate. Young Americans in the 1920s who wanted to live abroad, like these four, could be relatively open-minded as they watched various parties jockeying for position around the globe. They could be naive explorers discovering the world for themselves as they learned journalism.

In contrast, with fascism decisively defeated in the second world war, the United States and the Soviet Union vied for supreme influence—wartime allies now global foes. Was the twentieth century going to be, as Henry Luce contended in 1941 it should be, "the American Century"—or, rather, the century in which Soviet Communism became preeminent?[3] And would the opposition between the two behemoths mean "Cold War" only, or actual war? For many years, reality teetered between those alternatives, while the atomic annihilation of Hiroshima and Nagasaki made the possibility of future war more frightening than it had ever been.

These tense circumstances conditioned the roles of American journalists abroad after 1945. "The day of the old-style foreign correspondent is over," one experienced hand opined even before the war ended. "More and more correspondents are veering to personal impression and editorial stuff." As compared to the indeterminate, if turbulent, world scene of the 1920s and 1930s, the bipolarity of the new postwar era offered starker choices. The buildup of American national security apparatus, including the global presence and covert designs of the CIA, also had consequences for American journalists abroad, who might become unwitting agents of their government. In 1958, Dorothy Thompson noted that potential for current journalists as she contrasted her own career, saying, "Nobody did our homework for us. There was not a press attache in an American embassy. . . . None of us was an agent of American Policy. . . . None of us was ever arrested as a spy even by totalitarian governments. They knew we weren't. . . . Nowadays with the Counter Intelligence Service being what it is, nobody can be sure."[4]

Leading journalists abroad in the 1950s could not help envying the celebrity and influence of their predecessors. The chief correspondent in London for CBS in 1953, Howard K. Smith, saw none among his associates abroad "whose work can vie in its impact or popularity with that of the men of the Great Age" between the two world wars. He named only men—Sheean, Gunther, Shirer, Duranty, and a couple of others—though Thompson ought to have been on his list. Rather than concluding that his contemporaries had fewer talents, he thought (somewhat defensively) that the politics of the two eras made the difference: in the 1930s, clarity about fascist aggression had sparked journalists to provide sharp analysis and dramatic accounts, unlike the present "dreary story of the development of the cold war," which did not.[5]

Whether or not Smith was justified in taking the onus off talent, he was right to emphasize changing times. Technological advances as well as geopolitical shifts altered the face of foreign reporting. When Sheean, Gunther, and Thompson rose to the top of their game in the 1920s and 1930s, awareness of what was going on in the world depended on print media—if not newspapers, then magazines and books—and getting reliable news from foreign nations required having responsible staff located there. Mass production of cheap print was well established; phenomenal numbers of newspapers flourished and were supported by massive advertising. Because of radio's limits, Americans did not typically tune in for foreign news until the beginning of the second world war. Radio's shock to newspapers beginning in the mid-1930s was akin to social media's current disruptive effect, in that a single broadcast could go directly to the ears of millions at once, with untold power to shift opinion, inspire anguish or reverence, and inculcate belief. The accelerating improvements in telecommunication also led foreign news sources to diversify, rarely depending any longer on a given intrepid reporter on site. After 1945 the advantages of radio, and then television, meant that newspapers would never again command the proportion of advertising income or hold the popular sway they had earlier. Nor would print altogether. The printed word became one among many communicative modes (and the least "audiovisual" of them) in the twentieth century, only to gain speedier, fiercer competitors in the twenty-first.

The global trajectories etched by Thompson, Gunther, Sheean, and Raphaelson, and the reputations they achieved, could not have materialized in the same way at any other time. Rather than that particularity consigning these "greatest of journalists" to obscurity (as the London reviewer of *Dorothy and Red* would have it), it should award them roles as players on the stage of history. Journalism of the past has been far too easily taken for granted, its products treated as ephemera. Print journalists created the public sphere during the interwar years; to neglect their impact warps understanding of history. Today, as tweets and their consequences assault us every day, it is plain that the modes and content of public communication have power of their own; they are part of politics, part of society, and can become motors of change. It was no less true in the unstable decades between the world wars.

Uncanny parallels between the interwar era and ours leap to mind even though the very definition of journalism now is made chaotic by social media's lightning punch. A look around the globe today reveals dangerous political trends akin to those Thompson, Gunther, Sheean, and Raphaelson saw—authoritarian populist leaders destroying democracy from within, legal rule corrupted by partisan intentions, right-wing social movements wreaking violence on ethnic and religious minorities, crowds of refugees finding no nation willing to take them in, and political discourse being led by insults, lies, hyperbole, and purposeful distortions of history.

Americans again are divided, as in the interwar decades, on the question of international responsibilities versus inward-facing nationalism. It was in the 1920s that a contest began between cosmopolitanism and provincialism in American culture, politics, and conduct of foreign affairs. These days the two sides are known as "blue" America versus "red," where they were earlier seen as urban versus rural, coasts versus heartland, or internationalist versus isolationist, but however named, the contention has continued. With their cosmopolitan and sexually daring lives, the four in this book inhabited a leading edge among Americans of their age. Their emergence does not erase the insular tendencies observable in the United States then, for Congress did shrink immigration, the Ku Klux Klan did resurge, religious fundamentalists did pit biblical knowledge against the science of evolution—but it puts the focus on countertendencies pointing to an alternative future.

The insistence of international journalists like Thompson, Gunther, Sheean, and Raphaelson on looking outward countered the limitations of provincialism. They became vitally concerned with what was going on in the whole world rather than only in their own backyards, and tried to judge squarely if and how the United States should interact with the rest of the world. They saw the United States as one people in a larger universe of many peoples, one actor among many, and wanted to see it act responsibly both abroad and at home. These assumptions underlay the way they reckoned with politics abroad and the interpretations they brought home.

The four in this book chose journalism at a time when the integrity of the press was a controversial issue, as it is today. The question whether the press could speak truth to power was squarely on the table. Press agentry was a newly rising profession, and the first world war had generated fears, intensified by fascism's rise, of governments' ease in manipulating the public through propaganda. Then and now, thoughtful people believed freedom of the press essential to the survival of democracy. Then and now, alarming changes threatened to suppress public knowledge and smother criticism of powerholders. "The people cannot govern unless the people know," a critic warned in 1936, summing up, "Deprive the populace of real news—and you disarm it."[6] Awareness that control of public information can dictate political outcomes was a legacy of those years. Today that awareness could not be more crucial.

Acknowledgments

MY PATH TO completing this book has been long and winding, and I have accumulated many debts along the way, all of which I am happy to acknowledge.

First, my thanks for fellowships that have supported my research and writing, at the Center for Advanced Study in the Behavioral Sciences in 2008–2009, at the National Humanities Center for the spring of 2016 when I held the Birkelund Fellowship, and at the Radcliffe Institute for Advanced Study at Harvard University in spring 2017. I am grateful to have been able to rely all along on research support from Harvard University.

I could not have written the book as it is without the kind permission and help of Mrs. Jane Gunther and Nicholas Gunther, for the Gunther material, and of Carol Simons and Joel Raphaelson for the Raphaelson material. I am extremely grateful to all of them. I also would like to thank Tom Grunfeld for helping me reach the Simons and Raphaelson descendants. One of the (few) advantages of having begun this project rather long ago is that in London in 2013 I was able to meet Ellen Sheean, who gave me permission to use Vincent Sheean materials and loaned me several photographs. More recently, I have had the great pleasure of becoming acquainted with Jane Morton, Ellen Sheean's daughter, who has been the soul of graciousness in granting approval of my use of Sheean materials and supplying letters and a photograph of Diana Forbes-Robertson Sheean. Early in my discovery of Frances Fineman Gunther's papers in the Schlesinger Library, Mary von Euler was both kind and generous in responding to my queries and sending me additional material. I am heartily grateful for all these privileges.

Many individuals have helped me with specific queries. Peter Carroll was endlessly and graciously helpful in correcting my errors about the Chinese Nationalist revolution of the 1920s, and Mohamed Dauodi continuously, learnedly, corrected me on everything I got wrong about the Rif; both of them have been invaluable colleagues to me. Any remaining errors are mine only. I am also very much obliged to Margot Canaday for taking some pictures for me in the Princeton archives, and to Charlotte Brooks, Herrick Chapman, David N. Hempton, Mark D. Jordan, Richard Kaye, Christopher Reed, Stephen Vider, Alan Wald, and my colleagues in the History Department at Harvard, Emma Dench, Alison Frank, Mary Lewis, Erez Manela, Terry Martin, and Derek Penslar, for readily helping me with their expertise on particular points.

Co-fellows at the National Humanities Center in spring 2016, especially Vince DiGirolamo, April Masten, Janice Radway, Daniel Walkowitz, and Judith Walkowitz, commented usefully on my intentions for this book, and Vince and April gave me very helpful comments on a particular chapter. Co-fellows at the Center for Advanced Study in 2008–2009, including Steve Barley, Kimberle Crenshaw, Cori Hayden, Woody Powell, Lani Guinier, Abigail Saguy, Shinobu Kitayama, David Lake, Hazel Markus, Kate Stovell, and Winddance Twine, contributed to my thinking with constructive criticism of an earlier version of the project. Friends at various points, often long ago, gave me welcome feedback and/or encouragement that mattered a great deal, including Lizabeth Cohen, Ellen Dubois, Estelle Freedman, Dolores Hayden, Jill Lepore, Katherine Marino, Christine Stansell, Laura Wexler, and Alan Wolfe. More recently, I benefited greatly from Andrea Volpe's extensive advice, Susan Faludi's encouragement and comments, and small but crucial responses from Peter Hulme, Emma Cott, and Joshua Cott. I'm very grateful to all of them—and I hope others who also helped will forgive me for failing to mention them.

I owe the biggest debt to the reading/writing group I shared with Ann Braude, Carla Kaplan, and Susan Reverby over the past five years. When the going is tough, it is camaraderie like theirs that pulls one through, and I am forever grateful for the laughter and solidarity in our meetings and for their generous and constructive criticism as I wrote and rewrote my chapters.

I appreciate having had the assistance of many graduate students (most of whom are now faculty members) and a few undergraduates who photocopied documents for me. They included Jesse Gant, Alexandra Harwin, Emily Remus, Josie Rodberg, Emma Rothberg, Brian Young, and Davor Mondom. Others did more than photocopy, and even though it turned out that the research assistance I received from Francesca Annicchiarico, Tom Arnold-Foster, Lila Corwin, Betty Luther Hillman, Pearle Lum, Katherine Marino, Claire Nee Nelson, and Tsvia Reinstein figured barely or not at all in this book, I wanted to thank them. I am very much obliged to Ann Marie Wilson for her expert recovery and presentation of the information I needed from *Notable American Women*, and to Taryn Perry and Hayden W. Stone for doing the same from the *American National Biography*. Cate Brennan at the National Archives and Records Administration did me important favors in regard to the passport photographs, and I am extremely thankful and obliged to her.

Archival materials are at the heart of this book. I am deeply indebted to archivists and reference librarians at several institutions who were patient and constructive with my numerous requests. As always, Sarah Hutcheon, Ellen Shea, and Diana Carey at the Schlesinger Library answered my every query or request with expertise and alacrity, and I can't thank them enough. Collections at two libraries in particular were crucial to my research over many years: the Special Collections Research Center at Syracuse University, and the Special Collections Research Center at the University of Chicago. Staff in both places always responded quickly and efficiently to my requests, and I am immensely grateful. My thanks also to Kathryn Neal, Associate University Archivist at University Archives, UC Berkeley, for finding information about Rayna Raphaelson's enrollment, and to Cara Setsu Bertram, Reference Specialist at the University Archives, University of Illinois, for finding evidence of Samson Raphaelson's appointment for me. Suzy Taraba, Director of Special Collections & Archives, Olin Library, Wesleyan University, helped me hugely with the Fred Millett papers. Jennifer Hadley also answered my questions about that collection more recently. Constance Brown, Registrar, Barnard College, and Hilary Thorsen, Public Services Archivist, Barnard College Archives, chased down information about Frances Fineman for me. Staff at the Princeton libraries, especially AnnaLee Pauls, were also notably ready and willing to help, numerous times. Fred Burchsted at Harvard jumped to help whenever I contacted him asking about a reference work or database. Brooke Andrade at the National Humanities Center was brilliant in answering obscure requests. To all of these I've mentioned and numerous others at other libraries whom I haven't mentioned, I want to offer hearty thanks and recognition of the work you do, so essential to the writing of history.

In the editorial process, I greatly valued Lara Heimert's and Brandon Proia's intelligent and constructive feedback, Katie Lambright's responsiveness, and Mike Morgenstern's mapmaking skill. Melissa Veronesi was a pleasure to work with in production—a dream of efficiency and cheeriness. I am happy to thank them all.

To my children Joshua Cott and Emma Cott, my never-ending appreciation and love for their consistent interest.

Nancy F. Cott

Permissions

The author gratefully acknowledges permissions from the following:

Jane Morton, London, to use and quote from James Vincent Sheean materials, including photographs and documents from her private collection

Jane Gunther, New York, and Nicholas Gunther, Davis, California, to use and quote from John Gunther materials

McIntosh and Otis, Inc., and the Special Collections Research Center, Syracuse University Libraries, to use and quote from Dorothy Thompson materials

Carol Simons and Joel Raphaelson, to use and publish photographs and documents from their private collections of Rayna Raphaelson, Samson Raphaelson, and William Prohme materials

Mary von Euler, to quote from Frances Fineman Gunther materials in the Schlesinger Library

The National Portrait Gallery, London, to reproduce Howard Coster's photograph of John Gunther

The Communist Party USA, to reproduce two photographs of Vincent Sheean

Cartoons Collection, Inc., to reproduce a James Thurber cartoon

Condé Nast, to reproduce a Helen Hokinson cartoon

The Lilly Library, Indiana University, to quote from the Vita Sackville-West Manuscripts

Abbreviations Used in Notes

INDIVIDUALS

DS	Diana Forbes-Robertson Sheean
DT	Dorothy Thompson
FF and FFG	Frances Fineman, Frances Fineman Gunther
HFA	Hamilton Fish Armstrong
HN	Harold Nicolson
JB	Josef Bard
JG	John Gunther
JVS	Vincent Sheean
LB	Louise Bryant
R	Rayna Simons Raphaelson (Prohme)
RHR	Rebecca Hourwich Reyher
RM	Raymond Mortimer
RW	Rebecca West
RWL	Rose Wilder Lane
SL	Sinclair Lewis
SR	Samson Raphaelson
VSW	Vita Sackville-West

ARCHIVAL COLLECTIONS

DT-SYR	Dorothy Thompson Papers, Special Collections Research Center, Syracuse University Libraries
DTColl	Dorothy Thompson Collection, Special Collections Research Center, Syracuse University Libraries
FFG-SL	Frances Fineman Gunther Papers, Schlesinger Library, Radcliffe Institute for Advanced Study, Harvard University
JG II	John Gunther Papers, Addenda II, Special Collections Research Center, University of Chicago
JVS-SYR	Vincent Sheean Papers, Special Collections Research Center, Syracuse University Libraries
JVS-WHS	Vincent Sheean Papers, Wisconsin Historical Society
LC	Library of Congress

ABBREVIATIONS USED IN NOTES

MHS   Massachusetts Historical Society
RBML   Rare Book and Manuscript Library
RBSC   Rare Books and Special Collections
RHR-SL   Rebecca Hourwich Reyher Papers, Schlesinger Library, Radcliffe Institute for Advanced Study, Harvard University
SCRC   Special Collections Research Center
UC   University of Chicago
WHS   Wisconsin Historical Society

BOOKS

Asia   John Gunther, *Inside Asia* (New York: Harper & Bros., 1939).
IE   John Gunther, *Inside Europe* (New York: Harper & Bros., 1936).
ILA   John Gunther, *Inside Latin America* (New York: Harper & Bros., 1941).
IUSA   John Gunther, *Inside U.S.A.* (New York: Harper & Bros., 1947).
PH   Vincent Sheean, *Personal History* (New York: Doubleday, Doran, 1935).
D&R   Vincent Sheean, *Dorothy and Red* (Boston: Houghton Mifflin, 1963).

PUBLICATIONS

Annals   *Annals of the American Academy of Political and Social Science*
Atl M   *Atlantic Monthly*
Ayer's   *N. W. Ayer and Son's Newspaper Annual and Directory*
CDN   *Chicago Daily News*
Ch T   *Chicago [Daily] Tribune*
DBG   *Daily Boston Globe*
G & M   *Globe and Mail* [Toronto]
LHJ   *Ladies' Home Journal*
NYT   *New York Times*
NYHT   *New York Herald Tribune*
OTR   On the Record
PL   *Philadelphia Public Ledger*
SEP   *Saturday Evening Post*
TNR   *The New Republic*
WP   *Washington Post*

GENERAL

f.   folder
n.d.   no date
ts.   typescript

Notes

INTRODUCTION

1. Quotation, Joseph Freeman. "The Green Hat," Joseph Freeman Papers, Box 155, folder 5, Hoover Institution. Randomly selecting in *American National Biography* the surnames beginning with *A, B, C, D, E, F, L,* and *S,* I assessed biographical sketches of 965 of the 2,267 individuals born in the United States from 1896 to 1908 (thus in their 20s in the 1920s): 23 percent of them lived a year or longer in a foreign site between 1920 and 1940. (The proportion would be larger if residence abroad earlier or later were included.) Similarly checking 256 of all the 286 women of the same age cohort in *Notable American Women* (excluding 30 who were not American-born), I found that 36 percent did the same. Potential overlap of women's names between the two samples was ignored. Examples of young Americans influenced by foreign residence in the period include Donald Friede, *The Mechanical Angel* (New York: Knopf, 1948); Marjorie Worthington, *The Strange World of Willie Seabrook* (New York: Harcourt, Brace, 1966); Cass Canfield, *Up and Down and Around* (New York: Harper & Row, 1971); Bettina Berch, *Radical by Design: The Life and Style of Elizabeth Hawes* (New York: Dutton, 1988); Peter H. Oberlander and Eva Newbrun, *Houser: The Life and Work of Catherine Bauer* (Vancouver: University of British Columbia Press, 1999); Emily Hahn, *No Hurry to Get Home* (Seattle: Seal Press, 2000); Gregg Andrews, *Thyra J. Edwards: Black Activist in the Global Freedom Struggle* (Columbia: University of Missouri Press, 2011). On those in high arts, see especially Wanda Corn, *The Great American Thing: Modern Art and National Identity, 1915–1935* (Berkeley: University of California Press, 1999), 3–190; Carol Oja, *Making Music Modern: New York in the 1920s* (New York: Oxford University Press, 2000); Brent Hayes Edwards, *The Practice of Diaspora: Literature, Translation, and the Rise of Black Internationalism* (Cambridge, MA: Harvard University Press, 2003); Laura Doyle and Laura Winkiel, "Introduction: The Global Horizons of Modernism," in *Geomodernisms: Race, Modernism, Modernity* (Bloomington: Indiana University Press, 2005), 1–16; Douglas Mao and Rebecca L. Walkowitz, "The New Modernist Studies," *PMLA* 123, no. 3 (2008): 737–748. Ernest Hemingway, *A Moveable Feast* (New York: Scribner's, 1964), enshrined a classic portrait of the literary expatriates, well countered by Brooke

Blower, *Becoming Americans in Paris* (New York: Oxford University Press, 2011). Morrell Heald, *Transatlantic Vistas: American Journalists in Europe, 1900–1940* (Kent, OH: Kent State University Press, 1988), was exceptional in placing journalists in the transatlantic migration of the creative younger generation.

2. The extensive literature undermining the notion of US isolationism in the 1920s began with Scott Nearing and Joseph Freeman, *Dollar Diplomacy* (New York: B. W. Huebsch, 1925), and has expanded hugely since, although the idea lives on. Recent very helpful contributions include Daniel Gorman, *The Emergence of International Society in the 1920s* (Cambridge: Cambridge University Press, 2012), and Brooke L. Blower, "From Isolationism to Neutrality: A New Framework for Understanding American Political Culture, 1919–1941," *Diplomatic History* 38, no. 2 (2014): 345–376.

3. See John Maxwell Hamilton, *Journalism's Roving Eye: A History of American Foreign Reporting* (Baton Rouge: Louisiana State University Press, 2009), 124–296; Heald, *Transatlantic Vistas*; Robert William Desmond, *Crisis and Conflict: World News Reporting between Two Wars, 1920–1940* (Iowa City: University of Iowa Press, 1982).

4. Vincent Sheean [JVS], *Personal History* (New York: Doubleday, Doran, 1935), 310, 53.

CHAPTER 1: ORIGINAL ROVER BOY

1. Vincent Sheean [henceforth JVS], "Major and Minor," *Musical Leader* [Chicago], clipping n.d. but before October 1919, enclosed in JVS to Fred Millett, postmarked October 6, 1919, Fred B. Millett Papers, Special Collections and Archives, Wesleyan University. All letters from JVS to Millett are in this collection. See also JVS to Ruth Falkenau, November 7, 1919, f. 1, Box 1, Sheean-Falkenau Correspondence, UC, on his preference for "Vincent"; JVS, *Personal History* (New York: Doubleday Doran, 1935) [*PH*], 42, and George Seldes, *Tell the Truth and Run* (New York: Greenberg, 1953), 167, for the usual but false story of his name; John Gunther [JG], "London on Edge," *Atl M* 159, no. 4 (April 1937): 395–396. Pana's population was 5,500 in 1905, 8,000 in 1919, *N. W. Ayer and Son's Newspaper Annual and Directory* [hereafter *Ayer's*] for 1905, p. 183; 1919, p. 230, http://lcweb2.loc.gov/diglib/vols/loc.gdc.sr.sn91012092/default.html.

2. JVS, *PH*, 14 ("map"); for his height (although it mistakes his hair and eye color), Department of State Passport Application James Vincent Sheean #106979, December 14, 1921, RG 59, entry 534, National Archives and Records Administration [NARA]; JG, "James Vincent Sheean" [ts., c. 1949], on his "candid baby blue" eyes, Box 7, JG II. Carl Edward Johnson, "A Twentieth Century Seeker: A Biography of James Vincent Sheean" (PhD diss. [Mass Communications], University of Wisconsin, 1974), covers his childhood and youth, 3–27, 55n38.

3. JVS, *First and Last Love* (New York: Random House, 1956), 28–29, 48–50.

4. JVS, *Bird of the Wilderness* (New York: Random House, 1941), 257–258 (quotation).

5. JVS, "Reunion: A Story," *Harper's Monthly* 166 (April 1933): 529, characterization of himself arriving at college; JVS to Millett, postmarked October 12, 1919.

6. JVS, *PH*, 9–19, first published as "My Friend the Jew," *Atl M* 154 (November 1934): 400–409; JVS to Millett, postmarked October 12, 1919.

7. Fred Millett to Helen Mills, May 27 [1918], July 5, 1918 (quotations); JVS to Millett, November 29, 1919; George Sherburn to Fred Millett, May 9, 1919, Millett Papers; Fred B. Millett, *Graduate Student II: Two Academic Years, 1916–1918* (Whitman, MA: Washington Street Press, 1957), 16–17; Fred B. Millett, *Chicago Elegies* (Middletown, CT: James D. Young, 1939), 11.

8. Johnson, "Twentieth Century Seeker," 31–52; JVS, *PH*, 19–21, and *First and Last Love*, 37–48. See Wayne Koestenbaum, *The Queen's Throat: Opera, Homosexuality, and the Mystery of Desire* (New York: Poseidon, 1993).

9. George H. Douglas, *The Golden Age of the Newspaper* (Westport, CT: Greenwood, 1999), 158–160 (quotation, 159); Shelley Fisher Fishkin, *From Fact to Fiction: Journalism and Imaginative Writing in America* (Baltimore: Johns Hopkins University Press, 1985); Jean Marie Lutes, *Front Page Girls: Women Journalists in American Culture and Fiction, 1880–1930* (Ithaca, NY: Cornell University Press, 2006), 123–128, 192–193nn10–11; Daniel Leab, *A Union of Individuals: The Formation of the American Newspaper Guild 1933–36* (New York: Columbia University Press, 1970), 4–11, on conditions in newspaper work in the 1920s.

10. *Ayer's* for 1920, part 1, 13. Number of households in 1920 (including approximately 91 million adults over age fifteen) calculated from *Historical Statistics of the United States, 1789–1945* (Washington, DC: Bureau of the Census, 1949), 25–26 (Series B 1–12 and B 31–39) and 29 (series B 171–181). There were 1,286 daily American newspapers in 2016, according to Amy Watson, "Number of Daily Newspapers in the United States from 1970 to 2016," Statista, May 29, 2019, https://www.statista.com/statistics/183408/number-of-us-daily-newspapers-since-1975/. Paid circulation in 2017 was just under 31 million; Amy Watson, "Paid Circulation of Daily Newspapers in the United States from 1985 to 2018 (in thousands)," Statista, July 10, 2019, https://www.statista.com/statistics/183422/paid-circulation-of-us-daily-newspapers-since-1975/. The US population in July 2018 was over 327 million, including at least 250 million adults over the age of eighteen; US Census, "Quick Facts: United States," https://www.census.gov/quickfacts/fact/table/US/PST045217. William S. Gray and Ruth Munroe, *The Reading Habits of Adults: A Preliminary Report* (New York: Macmillan, 1929), 259–260, 262, and passim. The survey queried very large numbers of adults in every state but concentrated on the Northeast and Midwest, including Chicago.

NOTES TO PAGES 12–16

11. John William Tebbel, *The Compact History of the American Newspaper* (New York: Hawthorn Books, 1963), 239, on the *Herald-Examiner*; Michael Schudson, *Discovering the News: A Social History of American Newspapers* (New York: Basic Books, 1978), esp. 79–159; Simon Michael Bessie, *Jazz Journalism: The Story of the Tabloid Newspapers* (New York: Dutton, 1938); JVS to Millett, August 5, 1919.

12. JVS to Millett, December 22, 1919; JVS to Millett, "Monday night," postmarked September 30, 1920; JVS to Millett, May 1, 1920; and JVS to Millett, "Monday night," n.d.; "Barbara Behave," University of Chicago Blackfriars Records, Special Collections Research Center [SCRC], UC, http://news.lib .uchicago.edu/blog/2009/05/19/university-of-chicago-blackfriars-records/.

13. JVS to Millett, May 1, 1920; JVS to RM, March 9 [1930], Collection of RM materials, Box 4, f. 3, Princeton; JVS to Millett, postmarked July 24, 1919; "Monday night," n.d.; JVS to Millett, September 30 and October 2, 1920 (double postmark); Millett, *Chicago Elegies*, 11–12. See Bridget Gillard Read, "Dear Professor Millett: Reading an Archived Life" (master's thesis, Wesleyan University Honors College, 2012); William Wright, *Harvard's Secret Court: The Savage 1920 Purge of Campus Homosexuals* (New York: St. Martin's, 2005); Tony Ray Meyer, "Frat Boys Called Fags: Queer Fraternity and Homosocial Culture in the Harvard Secret Court of 1920" (thesis [History], Harvard University, 2011). Cf. Nicholas Syrett, *The Company He Keeps: A History of White College Fraternities* (Chapel Hill: University of North Carolina Press, 2009), esp. 188–207.

14. JVS to Millett, March 21, 1919 ("screw"), March 24, 1919, and May 1, 1920.

15. JVS to Millett, December 22, 1919, "Monday night"; see JVS to Ruth Falkenau, June 21, July 2, 1920, Box 1, Sheean-Falkenau Correspondence.

16. JVS to Millett postmarked November 29, 1919, but written weeks earlier.

17. JVS to Millett, postmarked December 12, 1920.

18. Susan McDermott Sheean, b. September 3, 1868, d. January 21, 1921. *Illinois, Deaths and Stillbirths Index, 1916–1947*; JVS, *PH*, 23. Stephen Mallarme's poem, "*Brise Marine*" [Sea Breeze], begins "*La chair est triste, hélas! 'Fuir, la-bas fuir'*" (Alas, how sad the flesh! To flee, to flee far away).

19. Malcolm Cowley, *Exile's Return: A Narrative of Ideas* (New York: Norton, 1934) (quotation) 69–72; Christine Stansell, *American Moderns* (New York: Metropolitan Books, 2000); Michael Soto, *The Modernist Nation* (Tuscaloosa: University of Alabama Press, 2004), 98–99; George Hutchinson, *The Harlem Renaissance in Black and White* (Cambridge, MA: Harvard University Press, 1995), 367–369; Ann Douglas, *Terrible Honesty* (New York: Farrar, Straus and Giroux, 1995), 64–67.

20. *Ayer's* for 1922, 695, puts *New York Daily News* circulation at 443,643; the *New York Times* [hereafter *NYT*] claimed 327,216, and the *New York World*, 330,000. See Bessie, *Jazz Journalism*, esp. 75–93, 234; Douglas, *Golden Age*, 225–232; Kevin G. Barnhurst and John Nerone, *The Form of News: A History* (New York: Gilford Press, 2001), 203–252; William R. Hunt, *Body Love: The*

Amazing Career of Bernarr MacFadden (Bowling Green, OH: Bowling Green State University Popular Press, 1989), 135–145.

21. JVS, *PH*, 25–26; Millett, *Graduate Student II*, 9–19 (quotation, 14); JVS to Millett, postmarked March 21, 1919; postmarked March 24, 1919. His operetta "Barbara Behave" included a Bolshevik character, a humorous and stereotyped cardboard villain.

22. Virginia Gardner, *"Friend and Lover": The Life of Louise Bryant* (New York: Horizon Press, 1982), 220–225 (quotation from Reed), 13; JVS to Virginia Gardner, September 8, 1971, Box 7, f. 20, Virginia Gardner Papers, Tamiment Library, New York University.

23. Louise Bryant [LB] to Anne Dennis Bursch, February 13, 1922, quoted in Gardner, *"Friend and Lover,"* 238; Mary V. Dearborn, *Queen of Bohemia: The Life of Louise Bryant* (Boston: Houghton Mifflin, 1996), 169–178.

24. JVS to LB, June 19 [1922], LB Papers, Box 7, f. 97, Sterling Memorial Library, Yale University; Gardner, *"Friend and Lover,"* 256.

25. Robert Wirth and Erez Manela, introduction, *Empires at War: 1911–23* (New York: Oxford University Press, 2014); Odd Arne Westad, *The Cold War: A World History* (New York: Basic Books, 2017), 1–128.

26. JVS passport application sworn on December 14, 1921. Warren I. Susman, "The Pilgrimage to Paris: The Backgrounds of American Expatriation, 1920–1934" (PhD diss., University of Wisconsin, 1958), 192–208; Daniel T. Rodgers, *Atlantic Crossings* (Cambridge, MA: Harvard University Press, 1998), 3–75; Akira Iriye, *Cultural Internationalism and World Order* (Baltimore: Johns Hopkins University Press, 1997), 51–90; Nancy L. Green, *The Other Americans in Paris: Businessmen, Countesses, Wayward Youth, 1880–1941* (Chicago: University of Chicago Press, 2014).

27. Foster Rhea Dulles, *Americans Abroad: Two Centuries of European Travel* (Ann Arbor: University of Michigan Press, 1964), 141–142, 153–158; Eunice Fuller Barnard, "The Swelling Tide of Foreign Travel," *NYT*, May 6, 1928, 77; Brandon Dupont, Alka Gandhi, and Thomas J. Weiss, "The American Invasion of Europe: The Long Term Rise in American Travel, 1820–2000" (National Bureau of Economic Research Working Paper 13977, May 2008), http://www.nber.org/papers/w13977.

28. Ernest Hemingway, *Dateline: Toronto: The Complete Toronto Star Dispatches, 1920–1924*, ed. William White (New York: Scribner's, 1984), 88; Cowley, *Exile's Return,* 79–80; William G. Bailey, compiler, *Americans in Paris, 1900–1930: A Selected, Annotated Bibliography* (Westport, CT: n.p., 1989), supplies the exchange rate figures in appendix.

29. Scott Donaldson, *Archibald MacLeish: An American Life* (Boston: Houghton Mifflin, 1992), 127; Roger Baldwin, "The Capital of the Men without a Country," *Survey* 58 (August 1, 1927): 460–467; Claude McKay, *A Long Way from Home*, ed. Gene Andrew Jarrett (New Brunswick, NJ: Rutgers University Press, 2006), 187, 189 (original work published 1937); William A. Shack, *Harlem in Montmartre: A Paris Jazz Story between the Great Wars* (Berkeley: University of California Press, 2001), 63–71.

30. JG to Helen Hahn, March 30, April 3 [1925], "Original letters to Helen," Box 5, JG II. Bruce Reynolds, *Paris with the Lid Lifted* (New York: George Sully & Co., 1927), exemplifies the sex tourism guide; Alain Corbin, *Women for Hire: Prostitution in France After 1850* (Cambridge, MA: Harvard University Press, 1990), 336–337.

31. William Shirer, *Twentieth-Century Journey*, vol. 1 (New York: Simon & Schuster, 1976), 268–269, 410, 436–438, 463–464, 468.

32. Lutes, *Front Page Girls*, 145–149, 197n91; Brenda Wineapple, *Genêt: A Biography of Janet Flanner* (New York: Ticknor & Fields, 1989). Virgil Thomson to Leland Poole, April 21, 1922, quoted in Anthony Tommasini, *Virgil Thomson: Composer on the Aisle* (New York: Norton, 1997), 100, see also 64–71, 91–100, 122–124; Steven Watson, *Prepare for Saints* (New York: Random House, 1998), 26–29. On Berlin, Christopher Isherwood, *Christopher and His Kind 1929–39* (New York: Farrar, Strauss and Giroux, 1976), 15–35; Robert Beachy, *Gay Berlin: Birthplace of a Modern Identity* (New York: Knopf, 2014), esp. 187–219.

33. Susman, "Pilgrimage to Paris," 205, estimate from his extensive research; Frederick Hoffman, *The Twenties: American Writing in the Postwar Decade* (New York: Viking, 1955), 28–29, concluded similarly from a small sample; Brooke Blower, *Becoming Americans in Paris* (New York: Oxford University Press, 2011), 272n12, on periodicals.

34. John Maxwell Hamilton, *Journalism's Roving Eye: A History of American Foreign Reporting* (Baton Rouge: Louisiana State University Press, 2009), 112, 130–131, 162–163; Eric Hawkins with Robert N. Sturdevant, *Hawkins of the Paris Herald* (New York: Simon & Schuster, 1963), esp. 76–77, 100–101; Whit Burnett and Martha Foley, "Your Home-Town Paper, Paris," *American Mercury*, 1931, 24–31; Irene Corbally Kuhn, "Paris in the Twenties," in *Remembrance of Things Paris*, ed. Ruth Reichl (New York: Modern Library, 2004), 4, 6. The Paris *Herald* swallowed the Chicago *Tribune*'s European edition in 1934, resulting in the *Herald Tribune*.

35. JVS, *PH*, 27–35.

36. JVS, *PH*, 36; Robert William Desmond, *Crisis and Conflict: World News Reporting between Two Wars, 1920–1940* (Iowa City: University of Iowa Press, 1982), 327–334; George Seldes, "Our Journalistic Noblesse," *The Nation*, March 25, 1936, 375–377.

37. Shirer, *Twentieth-Century Journey*, 1:258, 345. Seven US newspapers syndicated their foreign news in the 1920s, according to Desmond, *Crisis and Conflict*, 290: *Chicago Tribune [Ch T]*, *Chicago Daily News [CDN]*, *New York Times [NYT]*, *New York Herald Tribune [NYHT]*, *Christian Science Monitor*, *New York World*, and *Philadelphia Public Ledger [PL]* (joined with *New York Evening Post* in 1924). NB: Though the masthead read "Chicago Daily Tribune" the newspaper was generally known as the *Chicago Tribune* and locally as the *Tribune*.

38. Schudson, *Discovering the News*, 4; Hamilton, *Journalism's Roving Eye*, 225–227; Milly Bennett, *On Her Own: Journalistic Adventures from San Fran-*

cisco to the Chinese Revolution, 1917–1927, ed. A. Tom Grunfeld (Armonk, NY: M. E. Sharpe, 1993), 13–16.

39. Kuhn, "Paris in the Twenties," 4–5; Edward Gibbons, *Floyd Gibbons: Your Headline Hunter* (New York: Exposition Press, 1953), 61–73, 85–94, 132; Hamilton, *Journalism's Roving Eye*, 140–141.

40. JVS, *PH*, 37–38.

41. Sally Marks, *The Illusion of Peace: International Relations in Europe, 1918–1933* (Hampshire, England: Palgrave Macmillan, 2003), 45.

42. See Marks, *Illusion of Peace*, 54–59.

43. JVS, *PH*, 39–41 and articles in *Ch T*, May 6, 1923, 3; June 10, 1923, 3; November 10, 1923, 2; November 13, 1923, 2; November 24, 1923, 2; December 15, 1923, 5, among others.

44. JVS, *PH*, 41, 81. John F. V. Keiger, *Raymond Poincaré* (Cambridge: Cambridge University Press, 1997), 274–311, offers a balanced view.

45. JVS, *PH*, 44–50; JVS, "Turk No Longer Sick Man; Europe Surrenders All," *Ch T*, July 10, 1923, 11; "Allies Censor League Debate on Italian Row," *Ch T*, September 29, 1923, 4; and "Small Nations Angry as League Session Closes: Stirred by Lack of Action in Italo-Greek Row," *Ch T*, September 30, 1923, 4. Cf. Marks, *Illusion of Peace*, 22–24, 67–68.

46. JVS, *PH*, 62–76; "American Reporter Jailed by Spaniards: Accused of Sending Harmful News, State Department Calls for Report," *Washington Post* [*WP*], March 19, 1924, 3; "Frightened Spanish Dictatorship," *Ch T*, March 20, 1924, 8; Henry Wales, "Tribune Writer Can Leave Spain 'In a Few Days': Paris Press Assails Dictator," *Ch T*, March 20, 1924, 11; JVS, "Reporter's Life in Spain Is Bit of Opera Bouffe: Tribune Man Tells How He Was Arrested," *Ch T*, March 31, 1924, 13.

47. JVS, *PH*, 60–61.

48. Jay Allen, "Vincent Sheean," *Atlanta Constitution*, November 26, 1939, F9; JVS, *PH*, 52, 77–82.

CHAPTER 2: BLUE-EYED TORNADO

1. Carl Zuckmayer, *A Part of Myself* (New York: Harcourt, Brace, 1970), 141; loan application quoted in Peter Kurth, *American Cassandra: The Life of Dorothy Thompson* (Boston: Little, Brown, 1990), 48.

2. Dorothy Thompson [DT] to Rose Wilder Lane, [September 19, 1921], in William Holtz, ed., *Dorothy Thompson and Rose Wilder Lane: Forty Years of Friendship* (Columbia: University of Missouri Press, 1991), 21.

3. On her life before 1920, DT, autobiographical ts., 3, Box 114; DT to Mrs. C. B. Wade, March 23, 1951, Box 38, DT-SYR; Kurth, *American Cassandra*, 21–45. Kurth's biography is extremely helpful.

4. DT to Mr. Wright, June 11, 1920, Box 35, DT-SYR.

5. DT, diary of 1920, Box 59, and autobiographical writings, Box 114, DT-SYR; Kurth, *American Cassandra*, 43–47.

6. DT to Ruth Hoopla, February 10, [1921], DT Coll., SYR SCRC [a small collection separate from DT-SYR]; DT, diary of 1920, September 1, [1920]. See Julia L. Mickenberg, "Suffragettes and Soviets: American Feminists and the Specter of Revolutionary Russia," *Journal of American History* 100, no. 4 (2014): 1021–1051.

7. DT autobiographical ts., 6; Department of State Passport Application Dorothy Thompson #157976, RG 59, May 24, 1920, including letter signed by Alexander Sachs (Assistant Executive Secretary, Zionist Organization of America) to Passport Bureau, Customs House, New York City, May 20, 1920.

8. DT to Beatrice Sorchan, June 26, [1920], Box 35, DT-SYR; Kurth, *American Cassandra*, 47–48, on INS.

9. Kurth, *American Cassandra*, 79–80, 91; DT passport application for physical description; DT to Ruth Hoopla, February 10, [1921].

10. Kurth, *American Cassandra*, 51–53; see https://www.independent.ie /irish-news/1916/thinkers-talkers-doers/terence-macswiney-triumph-of-blood -sacrifice-34495537.html.

11. DT, diary of 1920 [late September].

12. DT, diary of 1920; DT to Ruth Hoopla, February 10, [1921]; DT to Beatrice Sorchan, October 22, [1920], Box 35, DT-SYR; see also DT to Beatrice Sorchan, November 13, 1920; on the strikes, Gwynne Williams, *Proletarian Order* (London: Pluto Press, 1975).

13. DT to Beatrice Sorchan, September 26, October 22, 1920; DT, diary of 1920 [October]. See DT, "Guilietti [*sic*], the Sailor Who Has Italy By the Ears," [Louisville, KY] *Courier*, January 23, 1921, SM4. Marion Sanders, *Dorothy Thompson: A Legend in Her Time* (Boston: Houghton Mifflin, 1973), 49–54, and Kurth, *American Cassandra*, 54–56, also recount the episode.

14. DT to Beatrice Sorchan, December 9, [1920], Box 35; DT, diary of 1920, November 27.

15. DT to Beatrice Sorchan, December 9, [1920].

16. See Nancy F. Cott, *The Grounding of Modern Feminism* (New Haven, CT: Yale University Press, 1987), 175–211, 269–284; Mary Lou Roberts, *Civilization without Sexes* (Chicago: University of Chicago Press, 1994).

17. DT to Ruth Hoopla, February 10, [1921]; Susman, "Pilgrimage to Paris," 165–167; Nancy L. Green, *The Other Americans in Paris: Businessmen, Countesses, Wayward Youth, 1880–1941* (Chicago: University of Chicago Press, 2014), 17–18.

18. Kurth, *American Cassandra*, 49–59; Sanders, *Dorothy Thompson*, 41–62. On Mowrer, John Maxwell Hamilton, *Journalism's Roving Eye: A History of American Foreign Reporting* (Baton Rouge: Louisiana State University Press, 2009), 169–175.

19. DT to Beatrice Sorchan, November 18, December 9, [1920]; Stefan Zweig, *The World of Yesterday*, trans. Anthea Bell (Lincoln: University of Nebraska Press, 2009 [original work published 1942]), 313; Thomas K. McCraw, *Prophet of Innovation: Joseph Schumpeter and Creative Destruction* (Cambridge, MA: Harvard University Press, 2007), 104.

20. Robert William Desmond, *Crisis and Conflict: World News Reporting between Two Wars, 1920–1940* (Iowa City: University of Iowa Press, 1982), 353–360; Hamilton, *Journalism's Roving Eye*, 265–267; Kurth, *American Cassandra*, 59–60; DT, "Buying Panic Seizes Viennese: Crowds Start 'Runs' on Shops," *WP*, October 7, 1921, 11.

21. Zuckmayer, *Part of Myself*, 340; Helmut Gruber, *Red Vienna: Experiment in Working-Class Culture 1919–1934* (New York: Oxford University Press, 1991), 13–30, 147; Eve Blau, *The Architecture of Red Vienna, 1919–1934* (Cambridge, MA: MIT Press, 1999); Kurth, *American Cassandra*, 60–67.

22. DT, Conversations with Fodor, 1960, Box 126, DT-SYR; Vienna quotation in Mildred Tideman diary, November 16, 1931, Box 6, JG II.

23. DT, "Coffee in Vienna . . . ," *PL*, Sunday, January 8, 1922, quoted in Sanders, *Dorothy Thompson*, 66.

24. DT to Rose Wilder Lane [RWL], [September 14, 1921], August 13, 1921, in Holtz, *Dorothy Thompson and Rose Wilder Lane*, 23, 15; William Shirer, *Twentieth-Century Journey*, vol. 1 (New York: Simon & Schuster, 1976), 439. DT insisted that her relationship with Fodor was "as sexless as that between two sixty-year old cronies." Lane, daughter of Laura Ingalls Wilder, was then an aspiring novelist, not yet the right-wing libertarian ideologue she later became. See https://fee.org/articles/rose-wilder-lane-isabel-paterson-and-ayn-rand-three-women-who-inspired-the-modern-libertarian-movement/.

25. John Gunther, "Blue-Eyed Tornado," *NYHT Magazine*, January 13, 1935, 6, including quoted exchange with Pedlow; Kurth, *American Cassandra*, 66–71; Sanders, *Dorothy Thompson*, 65–70.

26. Conversations with Fodor, Box 126, DT-SYR. See her second passport application, Department of State Passport Application Dorothy Thompson #43492, RG 59, with additional letter from *PL*, dated April 19, 1922.

27. Kurth, *American Cassandra*, 50–63, 74; headline quoted, *LA Times*, January 1, 1923, 1. See DT, "Amazing Hungary," *Contemporary Review* [London], July 1, 1921, 329–336; DT, "FASCISTI STIR SOUTH EUROPE: Victory Causes Worrying in Official Circles; Jugo-Slavia Responsive to Bulgar Overtures; Tyrolean Sharpshooters to Resist Italians," *LA Times*, November 2, 1922, I, 8; DT, "Tells Fate of Bulgar Leader: Stambulivsky [*sic*] Butchered by Revolutionists," *LA Times*, July 15, 1923, I, 13; DT, "Austrians Put Faith in Krone: Feeling of Nation's Stability Found Growing Steadily," *LA Times*, August 14, 1923, I, 5; DT, "Music and Culture Thrive in Poverty-Stricken Vienna," *WP*, June 25, 1922, 21.

28. Sanders, *Dorothy Thompson*, 72–73; Kurth, *American Cassandra*, 86–91; Peter F. Drucker, *Adventures of a Bystander* (New York: Harper & Row, 1979), 54; Zuckmayer, *Part of Myself*, 141; cf. Shirer, *Twentieth-Century Journey*, 1:450.

29. Margaret Case Harriman, "The It Girl" (Part I), *New Yorker*, April 20, 1940, 24–30; Kurth, *American Cassandra*, 68.

30. Gunther, "Blue-Eyed Tornado," 6, 7, 22; Kurth, *American Cassandra*, 83–87. Historians have stressed newspaperwomen's disadvantages, for example, Patricia Bradley, *Women and the Press: The Struggle for Equality* (Evanston, IL:

Northwestern University Press, 2005); Linda Lumsden, "'You're a Tough Guy, Mary—and a First-Rate Newspaperman': Gender and Women Journalists in the 1920s and 1930s," *Journalism and Mass Communication Quarterly* 72, no. 4 (Winter 1995): 913–921.

31. DT, "On Women Correspondents and Other New Ideas," *The Nation*, January 6, 1926, 11–12; Caroline Moorehead, *Gellhorn: A Twentieth-Century Life* (New York: Henry Holt, 2003), 39–40.

32. Kurth, *American Cassandra*, 76–82; JVS, *Dorothy and Red* (Boston: Houghton Mifflin, 1963) [*D&R*], 13–17; DT, diary [1935–1936], Box 59, DT-SYR.

33. DT to Gertrude Tone, typed excerpt, [early 1922], DTColl; DT to RWL, September 3, [1921], and [September 14, 1921], in Holtz, *Dorothy Thompson and Rose Wilder Lane*, 20, 22–23; Sanders, *Dorothy Thompson*, 77–78, on the apartment. DT to Josef Bard [JB], April 26, [1927], Box 1, DTColl, notes their marriage four years before. All DT–JB correspondence in DTColl is in Box 1.

34. DT to JB, April 1, 1926, December 16, 1926, March 28 [1927], DT-Coll.; Louis Untermeyer, *Bygones* (New York: Harcourt, Brace, 1965), 82–83; JVS, *D&R*, 4; see DT to RWL, June 25, [1928], in Holtz, *Dorothy Thompson and Rose Wilder Lane*, 75: "I am sure I saw in Josef Bard a creative talent to express my own creative instinct and will."

35. Gunther, "Blue-Eyed Tornado," 6, 7, 22; Desmond, *Crisis and Conflict*, 353–356.

36. Lilian T. Mowrer, *Journalist's Wife* (New York: William Morrow, 1937), 215–222 (quotation, 221), 191–193 (quotation, 192).

37. DT, diary, 1935–1936 (recalling that time), Box 59, DT-SYR; DT to RWL, September 3, [1921], in Holtz, *Dorothy Thompson and Rose Wilder Lane*, 18–19. See Nancy F. Cott, "Marriage and Women's Citizenship in the United States, 1830–1934," *American Historical Review* 103, no. 5 (December 1998): 1440–1474.

38. DT to JB, December 1926–early January 1927, quoted in Kurth, *American Cassandra*, 101, and see 94–104; DT to JB, April 3, May 7, [1927], DTColl. Viz. DT to JB, [mid-1927]: "you gradually build up a picture of me, to fit the situation. . . . I, the militant suffragette; I, the careerist." Cf. Eileen Agar, *A Look at My Life* (London: Methuen, 1988), 55–70.

39. DT to RWL, January 10, 1927, Holtz, *Dorothy Thompson and Rose Wilder Lane*, 38–39; DT to JB, March 3, 1927, DTColl; see DT letters to JB, 1926–1927, Box 44, DT-SYR. She consulted psychoanalyst Theodore Reik three times, in her pain.

40. DT to RWL, January 17, [1928] (looking back), Holtz, *Dorothy Thompson and Rose Wilder Lane*, 68; DT to JB, May 7, 1927, n.d. "later in the conference," and n.d. "Sunday night," DTColl.

41. DT to JB, "Later in the conference" [early May 1927, in Geneva], DT to JB, November 17, 1927 (quotation), DT, 5-page sketch, "To-Day's Germany: 'The Forming Face of Germany' to Be Illustrated with Cartoons, Portraits, Jokes," [1927], DTColl.

42. DT, sonnet dated May 25, [1927], "How grand it is, this falling out of love," DTColl, and copied in DT to RWL, January 17, [1928], Holtz, *Dorothy Thompson and Rose Wilder Lane*, 68–69; DT to JB, n.d. [June 1927], July 11, 1927, DTColl.; and see Arthur H. Hirsch, *Sexual Misbehavior of the Upper Cultured* (New York: Vantage Press, 1955).

43. Kurth, *American Cassandra*, 105–108; DT, diary, September 21, 1927, Box 59, DT-SYR; JVS, *D&R*, 22–23.

44. DT to JB, July 11, 1927, DTColl; DT, "The Boy and Man from Sauk Center," *Atlantic* 260 (November 1960): 46.

45. SL, "All Prizes, Like All Titles, Are Dangerous," Letters of Note, September 28, 2012, original letter published May 26, 1926, http://www.lettersofnote .com/2012/09/all-prizes-like-all-titles-are-dangerous.html; John Hersey, "First Job," *Yale Review* 76 (March 1987): 189.

46. JVS, *D&R*, 22–26; Kurth, *American Cassandra*, 104–110; DT to JB, July 26, [1927], DTColl.

47. JVS, *D&R*, 27–29; DT to JB, August 22 [1927], DTColl.

48. DT to RWL, December 25, [1927], in Holtz, *Dorothy Thompson and Rose Wilder Lane*, 63; DT to JB, November 17, [1927], May 7, 1927 ("monstrous"), July 11, 1927 ("never ever"), DTColl.

49. DT to JB, August 22, [1927], DTColl.; Hersey, "First Job," 185; Carl Van Doren quoted in Hersey, "First Job," 189.

50. DT, diary, September 9, 1927, Box 59, DT-SYR; see JVS, *D&R*, 23.

51. DT, diary, September 16, 1927, Box 59, DT-SYR.

52. DT, diary, September 16, September 21, 1927, Box 59, DT-SYR.

53. DT, "Hindenburg Has a Birthday," *The Nation*, October 26, 1927, 447–448.

54. DT to JB, December 13, [1927], DTColl.

CHAPTER 3: LUCKIEST YOUNG UPSTART

1. JG, "Autobiography in Brief," *Story*, May 1938, 93; JG, Green notebook I (handwritten), 113, Box 2, JG II.

2. Quotations in previous paragraphs, JG, "Autobiography in Brief," 89–91; see also Jay Pridmore, *John Gunther: Inside Journalism* [exhibit catalog] (University of Chicago Library, 1990); Department of State Passport Application John Gunther #171869, RG 59, vol. 3782, May 12, 1922, NARA, and actual passport, Box 3, JG II.

3. H. L. Mencken, "The Literary Capital of the U.S.," *The Nation*, April 17, 1920, 92; JG, "Higher Education in America: The University of Chicago," *Smart Set* 67, no. 4 (April 1922): 67–77; Pridmore, *John Gunther*, 10–11; Ken Cuthbertson, *Inside: The Biography of John Gunther* (Chicago: Bonus Books, 1992), 17–23.

4. Ben Hecht, *A Child of the Century* (New York: Simon & Schuster, 1954), 162–163, 250. See Neil Harris, "The Chicago Setting," in *The Old Guard and the Avant-Garde: Modernism in Chicago 1910–1940*, ed. Sue Ann Prince (Chicago:

University of Chicago Press, 1990), 3–22; Bernard I. Duffey, *The Chicago Renaissance in American Letters: A Critical History* (East Lansing: Michigan State College Press, 1954), 141–147; Samuel Putnam, *Paris Was Our Mistress* (New York: Viking, 1947), 35–45.

5. Harry Hansen, *Midwest Portraits* (New York: Harcourt, Brace, 1927), 10.

6. JG, "Autobiography," 92 (quotation); Hecht, *Child*, 249; Cuthbertson, *Inside*, 23, 32–34; JG, "The Return of Joe Vesley," *The Best News Stories of 1923*, ed. Joseph Anthony (Boston: Small, Maynard, 1923), 60–64; JG, "A Visit to Teapot Dome," *The Best News Stories of 1924*, ed. Joseph Anthony and Woodman Morrison (Boston: Small, Maynard, 1924), 163–169. Editor Anthony selected the "best" from about three thousand stories nominated by newspaper editors.

7. Cuthbertson, *Inside*, 30–31.

8. David Paul Nord, *Communities of Journalism* (Urbana: University of Illinois Press, 2001), 125–128; John Maxwell Hamilton, *Journalism's Roving Eye: A History of American Foreign Reporting* (Baton Rouge: Louisiana State University Press, 2009), 162–165.

9. See Mary Lou Roberts, *Civilization without Sexes* (Chicago: University of Chicago Press, 1994), and Carolyn J. Dean, *Sexuality and Modern Western Culture* (New York: Twayne, 1996), 36–43. *The Green Hat* soon became a long-running Broadway hit in New York and eventually the film *A Woman of Affairs*, memorably starring Greta Garbo.

10. JG, Green notebook I, 83, 95.

11. JG to Helen, November 17, [1924], "Original letters to Helen," Box 5, JG II, henceforward "Log to Helen."

12. JG, Log to Helen, [October 1924].

13. Robert W. Desmond, *The Press and World Affairs* (New York: D. Appleton-Century, 1937), 55–75; Robert W. Desmond, *Crisis and Conflict: World News Reporting between Two Wars, 1920–1940* (Iowa City: University of Iowa Press, 1982), 250–253, 290–303.

14. JG to family, November 7, [1924], Box 5; quotations in this and preceding two paragraphs, JG, Log to Helen, November 1, [1924], November 6, [1924], JG II. JG and Lewis probably met at Schlogl's; Mark Schorer, *Sinclair Lewis: An American Life* (New York: McGraw-Hill, 1961), 304–305, shows Lewis in Chicago in 1924.

15. JG, Log to Helen, November 28, [1924] (first quotation) and March 28, 1925 (second quotation).

16. JG to family, December 8, [1924], Box 5; Log to Helen, December 5, December 9, [1924].

17. JG, Log to Helen, November 7, 11, 13, 16, 19, [1924]; Al Silverman, *The Time of Their Lives* (New York: St. Martin's, 2008), 219–222.

18. JG to family, November 28, [1924], Box 5; Log to Helen, November 8, [1924].

19. JG, Log to Helen, November 8, [1924].

20. My account is indebted to Kevin G. Barnhurst and John Nerone, *The Form of News: A History* (New York: Guilford Press, 2001), 203–252.

21. JG, Log to Helen, November 24, November 28, [1924].

22. Desmond, *Press and World Affairs*, 127–137; James E. Abbe, "Men of Cablese," *New Outlook* 162 (December 1933): 27–32.

23. JG, Log to Helen, November 7, December 1, [1924].

24. JG, Log to Helen, December 1, [1924], February 23, [1925]; see Hamilton, *Journalism's Roving Eye*, 194.

25. JG, Log to Helen, December 1, December 12, [1924].

26. JG, Log to Helen, November 8, [1924]; Pridmore, *John Gunther*, 11; Carl Rollyson, *Rebecca West: A Saga of the Century* (London: Hodder & Stoughton, 1995).

27. JG, Log to Helen, December 19, December 21, [1924], January 12, March 11, [1925]; Rollyson, *Rebecca West*, 80.

28. JG, Log to Helen, March 11, 12, 24, [1925], "Christmas week" [1924]; Rollyson, *Rebecca West*, 70–94.

29. JG, Log to Helen, February 14, March 27, [1925].

30. JG, Log to Helen, March 30, 31, April 6–11, [1925].

31. JG, Log to Helen, May 20, [1925]; JG to family, April 15, April 25, 1925, Box 5.

32. JG, Log to Helen, January 10, February 12, May 21, 23–24, May 26–30, [1925]; Frances Fineman job-seeking description [1925], f. 1; Frances Fineman [hereafter FF], untitled ts., n.d. [1925], f. 103, FFG-SL; FF to Harry [Henry Wadsworth Longfellow] Dana, October 18, 1924, H. W. L. Dana Papers, Longfellow House National Historic Site; FF, "The Moscow Theatre," *NYT*, January 11, 1925, X2. NB: Item numbers in the digital inventory of FFG-SL correspond to folder numbers.

33. JG, Log to Helen, May 29, June 5, [1925]. Jimmie Charters, *This Must Be the Place: Memoirs of Montparnasse*, ed. Hugh Ford (New York: Collier Macmillan, 1989), 39–40, on Ford's parties.

34. JG, Log to Helen, June 3, June 7, 1925.

35. Cuthbertson, *Inside*, 68–69.

36. Carol Gruber, "Academic Freedom at Columbia University 1917–1918," *AAUP Bulletin* 58 (September 1972): 297–305, esp. 300–302. FF is named in "Active Work in Socialism," *Barnard Bulletin*, March 27, 1916, 4; "Something New and Big: The University Labor League," *Barnard Bulletin*, April 2, 1916, 6; "The University Labor League," *Barnard Bulletin*, April 11, 1916, 4; and "Socialist Club," *Barnard Bulletin*, May 15, 1916, 4. Frances Fineman student file, Radcliffe College Student Files, 1890–1983 RGXXI, Series I, Box 38, Radcliffe College Archives, SL, includes letters from the Barnard dean to the Radcliffe dean, never using the word *expulsion* and stipulating only that Fineman associated with the wrong friends in the Columbia School of Journalism.

37. FF to [Professor] George Pierce Baker, May 5 and May 26, 1919, Box 10, folder 836a, George Pierce Baker Papers, Houghton Library; FF student file;

fragmentary autobiographical material including personal chronology, f. 1; FF, 2p. untitled ts. n.d. [1924–1925], f. 103, FFG-SL.

38. FF, unbound journal, c. 1923, p. 34, f. 110; stories, f. 103, 122–124; FFG-SL; copy of FF to editor of *New Statesman*, (3p.), on feminism [1924–1925] Box 6, JG II.

39. See Andrea Tone, *Devices and Desires: A History of Contraceptives in America* (New York: Hill and Wang, 2001), and "Making Room for Rubbers: Gender, Technology and Birth Control before the Pill," *History and Technology* 18, no. 1 (2002): 51–76.

40. See FFG, "The Graven Image of False Gods," n.d. [1937?], f. 103 FFG-SL; Leslie J. Reagan, *When Abortion Was a Crime: Women, Medicine, and Law in the United States, 1867–1973* (Berkeley: University of California Press, 1997), and Robert L. Dickinson, "Medical Reflections upon Some Life Histories," in *The Sex Life of the Unmarried Adult*, ed. Ira S. Wile (New York: Vanguard, 1934), 193. Abortion examples occur in Helen Lawrenson, *Stranger at the Party: A Memoir* (New York: Random House, 1975), 26; Caroline Moorehead, *Gellhorn: A Twentieth-Century Life* (New York: Henry Holt & Co., 2003), 42–66; and Elinor Langer, *Josephine Herbst* (Boston: Little, Brown, 1983), 56–72.

41. JG to FF, June 19, December 31, 1925, and additional correspondence 1925–1926, Box 22, JG II.

42. See Rollyson, *Rebecca West*, 85.

43. JG to Rebecca West [RW], c. December 1925, quoted in Rollyson, *Rebecca West*, 85; this letter cannot be found currently in the Gunther collection at the University of Chicago cited by Rollyson.

44. Hamilton, *Journalism's Roving Eye*, 169–175, on Mowrer; JG to FF, December 31, 1925; Cuthbertson, *Inside*, 60–64.

45. JG, *A Fragment of Autobiography* (New York: Harper & Row, 1961), 5; cf. JG, "All Spain is Against Him, but Dictator isn't Worried," *DBG*, January 9, 1930, 19; "City of Contrasts," *DBG*, February 21, 1930, 16; "France and Russia Near Diplomatic Breach," *Atlanta Constitution*, February 5, 1930, 1; "Feminization Features Spring Styles at Paris," *Atlanta Constitution*, February 1, 1930, 1; JG, London diary, orig. (ts.), December 17, 1935, Box 19, JG II.

46. JG, *The Red Pavilion* (London: Martin Secker, 1926); JG, Log to Helen, May 20, [1925]; "In the Huxley Manner," *NYT*, January 30, 1927, 8; RW to JG, [December 1926] in Bonnie Kime Scott, ed., *Selected Letters of Rebecca West* (New Haven, CT: Yale University Press, 2000), 89–90; JG, Green notebook I, ts., 1931, 96, Box 2, JG II; Cuthbertson, *Inside*, 58–59, 64–66, and see 74–75, 85, on Gunther's slighter novels *Eden for One* (1927) and *The Golden Fleece* (1929).

47. FF to JG, May 26, 1926; JG to FF, n.d. [fall 1926] (first page missing), Box 22, JG II.

48. JG to FF, n.d. [fall 1926] (first page missing), and November 2, 1926, Box 22, JG II.

49. Telegrams, November 1926, Box 22; Helen Hahn to JG, February 8, 1927, Box 24, JG II. A cryptic unsigned cablegram from New York, January 29,

1927, presumably from Fineman, to JG in London, suggests they may have agreed to marry and soon divorce. The telegram says, "Arriving February marriage Rome divorce Paris September Wire Conventional proposal family consumption necessary." "Rye letters," Box 6, JG II. I found no corroborating evidence for Cuthbertson's explanation, *Inside*, 67, 71–72, that Frances claimed she was pregnant.

50. JG Russian log, June 20, [1928], Box 2, JG II.

CHAPTER 4: THE FREEST MAN ON ANY NEWSPAPER

1. JVS, *Personal History* (New York: Doubleday, Doran, 1935) [*PH*], 94; Michael Goebel, *Anti-Imperial Metropolis: Interwar Paris and the Seeds of Third World Nationalism* (New York: Cambridge University Press, 2015), 149–150, 151–166. Sheean recounts his Rif ventures in *PH*, 83–161. The French Communist Party strongly opposed French intervention in the Rif. David H. Slavin, "The French Left and the Rif War," *International Journal of Middle East Studies* 26, no. 1 (January 1991): 5–32; David Drake, "The PCF, the Surrealists, Clarte and the Rif War," *French Cultural Studies* 17 (2006): 173–188.

2. James A. Chandler, "Spain and Her Moroccan Protectorate 1898–1927," *Journal of Contemporary History* 10, no. 2 (April 1975): 312; Shannon E. Fleming and Ann K. Fleming, "Primo de Rivera and Spain's Moroccan Problem, 1923–1927," *Journal of Contemporary History* 12, no. 1 (January 1977): 85–99; C. R. Pennell, "Ideology and Practical Politics: A Case Study of the Rif War in Morocco, 1921–1926," *International Journal of Middle East Studies* 14, no. 1 (February 1982): 19–33. Michael Brett and Elizabeth Fentress, *The Berbers* (Oxford, England: Blackwell, 1996), 188–191, link Riffians to Berbers ethnically.

3. JVS, "Spanish Ruler and 60,000 Men in Moors' Trap," *Ch T*, September 10, 1924, 4.

4. JVS, "Spain's Foreign Legion Battles Rebels 2 Days," *Ch T*, December 20, 1924, 16; *PH*, 83–86.

5. George Seldes, *Lords of the Press* (New York: Julian Messner, 1938), 283, 291.

6. JG to Helen Hahn, December 9, 1924, Box 5, JG II; JVS, *PH*, 86–87; John Maxwell Hamilton, *Journalism's Roving Eye: A History of American Foreign Reporting* (Baton Rouge: Louisiana State University Press, 2009), 170–171.

7. JVS, *PH*, 86, 92–93.

8. Edward Gibbons, *Floyd Gibbons: Your Headline Hunter* (New York: Exposition Press, 1953), 160–179 (quotation, 177); Hamilton, *Journalism's Roving Eye*, 232–233.

9. JVS, "The Story of Abd El-Krim," *Asia*, September 1925, 721–742, for preceding four paragraphs.

10. JVS, "Dead of Spain Choke Up Roads in North Africa," *Ch T*, February 10, 1925, 4; "Moorish General Ridicules Spain Efforts in Riff," *Ch T*, February 9, 1925, 6; JVS, "My Meeting with Abd El-Krim," *Asia*, October 1925, 845–857ff.

11. JVS, *PH*, 116; Jay Allen, "Vincent Sheean," *Atlanta Constitution*, November 26, 1939, F9. Hank Wales was probably the "superior." According to Robert William Desmond, *Crisis and Conflict: World News Reporting between Two Wars, 1920–1940* (Iowa City: University of Iowa Press, 1982), 334, Wales succeeded Gibbons as chief of the Paris bureau in 1924.

12. Michael Schudson, *Discovering the News: A Social History of American Newspapers* (New York: Basic Books, 1978), esp. 122–145, 151–157, and Michael Schudson, *The Good Citizen: A History of American Civic Life* (New York: Free Press, 1998),188–232.

13. JVS, *PH*, 117; Malcolm Cowley, *Exile's Return: A Literary Odyssey of the 1920s* (New York: Viking-Penguin, 1951), 223; see John William Tebbel, *A History of Book Publishing in the United States*, vol. III (New York: Bowker, 1978), esp. 45; Claudia Dale Goldin and Lawrence F. Katz, *The Race between Education and Technology* (Cambridge, MA: Belknap Press of Harvard University Press, 2008).

14. JVS, *PH*, 117–119; [editorial comment], *Asia*, August 1925, 710. Robert Cantwell, "Journalism—Magazines," in *America Now*, ed. Harold Stearns (New York: Charles Scribner's Sons, 1938), 351– 355; Theodore Peterson, *Magazines in the Twentieth Century* (Urbana: University of Illinois Press, 1975 [original work published 1964]); John William Tebbel and Mary Ellen Zuckerman, *The Magazine in America, 1741–1990* (New York: Oxford University Press, 1991).

15. David S. Woolman, *Rebels in the Rif* (Stanford, CA: Stanford University Press, 1968), 169–196; Henry Wales, "Riff Offensive Worries Paris," *LA Times*, May 20, 1925, 5; Henry Wales, "French Parliament Votes to Support War in Morocco," *Ch T*, May 30, 1925, 2; and see articles without byline, "Costs of Riff War Worry Painlevé," *NYT*, May 21, 1925, 2; "Painlevé Explains Situation," *NYT*, May 4, 1925, 2; "Spain's Riff Border Hampers French," *NYT*, May 12, 1925, 6; "Uproar in [French] Chamber Ends Riff Debate," *NYT*, May 29, 1925, 2; "Riffians Undaunted after Six Weeks' War," *NYT*, June 2, 1925, 2; "French Plan Drive with Aid of Spain," *NYT*, June 12, 1925, 2; "France and Spain Sign Blockade Plan," *NYT*, July 9, 1925; "Paris Sees Chance of Peace with Riff," *NYT*, July 24, 1925, 5; "Abd El-Krim Demands Independence of Riff," *NYT*, August 11, 1925, 14; "Painlevé Rejects Riff Independence," *NYT*, August 15, 1925, 5; "Petain is Expected to Crush Riffiansans," *NYT*, August 17, 1925, 3.

16. JVS, *PH*, 117–119; Desmond, *Crisis and Conflict*, 251–252.

17. JVS, *PH*, 119–155, for his second trip into and out of the Rif.

18. JVS, *PH*, 130.

19. JVS, "Krim Fearless During Battle," *LA Times*, October 20, 1925 [dateline Ajdir, September 24, 1925, by courier to Tangier], 4. The beach landing at Alhucemas Bay was a model for the D-Day landings. See Woolman, *Rebels*, 67–68, 188–193, and Sebastian Balfour, *Deadly Embrace: Morocco and the Road to the Spanish Civil War* (New York: Oxford University Press, 2002).

20. JVS, "Riff War's End Still Distant," *LA Times*, November 8, 1925, 3; "Spanish Riff Victory Myth," *LA Times*, November 10, 1925, 10; "Abd El-Krim

Reported Ready to Give Spanish Lively Winter," *The [Baltimore] Sun*, November 14, 1925, 2.

21. JVS, *PH*, 142–147.

22. JVS, *PH*, 148–155; see Roi Ottley, "'Personal History' of a Legionnaire," *NY Amsterdam News*, January 18, 1935, 9.

23. "Riff Peace Terms Held by Writer," *LA Times*, November 4, 1925, 4; and see JVS articles in the *LA Times* and Baltimore *Sun*, November 24, 25, 26, and 27, 1925; *PH*, 155–158.

24. Woolman, *Rebels*, 196–214.

25. JVS, *PH*, 160. For similarly blinkered views among American critics of imperialism in Sheean's generation, see David A. Hollinger, *Protestants Abroad* (Princeton, NJ: Princeton University Press, 2017), and Samuel Zipp, "Dilemmas of World-Wide Thinking," *Modern American History* I (2018): 295–319.

26. Shirer, *Twentieth-Century Journey*, 1:234 (on snow); JVS, *An American among the Riffi* (New York: Century Co., 1926); JVS to Rose Mary Fishkin, London, n.d. [1924], Sheean-Falkenau Correspondence, Box 1, f. 4; *PH*, 45; regarding Lacretelle, James Lees-Milne, *Harold Nicolson: A Biography, 1886–1929*, vol. 1 (London: Chatto & Windus, 1980), 53–55.

27. JVS, *PH*, 162–181; JVS, "Balancing the Persian Budget," *Asia*, January 1927, 46–53; Emily Rosenberg, *Financial Missionaries to the World: The Politics and Culture of Dollar Diplomacy, 1900–1930* (Cambridge, MA: Harvard University Press, 1999), 183–186.

28. JVS, *PH*, 162–165.

29. JVS, *PH*, 162–168.

30. JVS, *PH*, 168–172.

31. JVS, *The New Persia* (New York: Century Co., 1927), 201.

32. On Nicolson, *Oxford Dictionary of National Biography*, http://www.oxforddnb.com; Lees-Milne, *Harold Nicolson*, 185–199; Norman Rose, *Harold Nicolson* (London: Jonathan Cape, 2005), 112–122. On his "native Iranian tongue," Harold Nicolson [HN] to Vita Sackville-West [VSW], October 28, 1927, Box 3, Vita Sackville-West Mss., Lilly Library, University of Indiana, Bloomington; all HN–VSW letters cited are in the same location.

33. Rose, *Harold Nicolson*, 75–83; Lees-Milne, *Harold Nicolson*, 139–149.

34. HN to VSW, May 9, 1926, Box 2; Lees-Milne, *Harold Nicolson*, 54–55; RM to HN, August 16, 1955, quoted in Lees-Milne, *Harold Nicolson*, 400n60, and see 234–237; HN to RM, January 1, 1926, Box 3, f. 5, Collection of RM, Princeton; Rose, *Harold Nicolson*, 137–138, 140–141.

35. Rose, *Harold Nicolson*, 137–142 ("open secret," 138), 241; HN to RM, August 24, 1925 (1), Collection of RM, Box 3, f. 5; Lees-Milne, *Harold Nicolson*, 46, 89, 215, 234–237, 366–368; HN to VSW, November 8, 1933, quoted in Rose, *Harold Nicolson*, 139; VSW to HN, Sunday, May 23, [1926], May 31 [1926], Lilly. *Tapette* is French slang, equivalent to "pansy" or "fairy." Cf. Matt Houlbrook, *Queer London* (Chicago: University of Chicago Press, 2006), 195–215.

36. On Raymond Mortimer [hereafter RM], *Oxford Dictionary of National Biography*, http://www.oxforddnb.com. Mortimer became literary editor of the British weekly *The New Statesman* by 1935. Christopher Reed, "A Vogue That Dare Not Speak Its Name," *Fashion Theory* 10, nos. 1–2 (2006): 39–71; Christopher Reed, "Design for (Queer) Living," *GLQ* 12, no. 3 (2006): 377–403.

37. Frances Partridge, *Memories* (London: Victor Gollancz, 1981), 96; Robert Skidelsky, *John Maynard Keynes, I* (London: Macmillan, 1983), 128–129 ("higher sodomy"), 142–145, 242–253 ("friends," 243), and *II* (London: Macmillan, 1992), 10–11; David Gadd, *The Loving Friends: A Portrait of Bloomsbury* (London: Hogarth Press, 1974), esp. 184–185; Raymond Mortimer, *Duncan Grant* (Harmondsworth, England: Penguin Books, 1944), 7; Raymond Williams, "The Bloomsbury Fraction," in *Problems in Materialism and Culture* (London: New Left Books, 1980), 148–169; John Maynard Keynes, "My Early Beliefs," quoted in Skidelsky, *John Maynard Keynes*, I:142–143.

38. Both "homosexual" and "heterosexual" appear by the 1890s in the *Oxford English Dictionary* but only in clinical/specialist usage; "homosexual," meaning drawn to one's own sex, was in use in the 1920s, but not commonly. Nicolson and Sackville-West called men "buggers" and women "sapphists" if inclined toward their own sex. Cf. Matt Houlbrook, *Queer London*, 195–215, and his "'The Man with the Powder Puff' in Interwar London," *The Historical Journal* 50, no. 1 (March 2007): 152.

39. HN to VSW, May 8, 1926, Box 2; RM to Eddy, May 18, 1926, RM Letters to ESW, Princeton; HN to VSW, May 9, May 21, 1926, Box 2.

40. HN to VSW, May 14, 1926; see HN–VSW letters, May 8–June 7, 1926, Box 2; HN, diary, May 1926, Balliol College, Oxford; JVS, *PH*, 174; HN to VSW, June 3, June 7, 1926.

41. HN, diary, July 4, 1926, Bailliol; JVS, "A Russian Medley," *Asia*, June 1927, 488; *PH*, 185.

42. JVS, *PH*, 172; JVS to RM, October 9, [1926]; RM to Eddy Sackville-West, [postmarked February 24, 1928], Box 1, f. 1, RM Letters to ESW. See also JVS to RM, August 19, [1926], October 4, [1926].

43. Rene Crevel, *A Difficult Death*, trans. David Rattray (San Francisco: North Point Press, 1986), 25, 73; JVS to RM, Monday, [November 1, 1926], November 27, [1926], "Thursday—just after taking castor oil" [November or December 1926]; Bruce Reynolds, *Paris with the Lid Lifted* (New York: George Sully, 1927), 199–200. On McCown's promiscuity, see HN to RM, August 25, 1925, Box 3, f. 5, and JVS to RM, "Paris-Sunday" [November–December 1926], Collection of RM.

44. Nancy Cunard, *These Were the Hours* (Carbondale: Southern Illinois University Press, 1969), 87–88; Lois Gordon, *Nancy Cunard* (New York: Columbia University Press, 2007), 107, 115, 117, 141; Lees-Milne, *Harold Nicolson*, 107; Rose, *Harold Nicolson*, 82; JVS to RM, "Good Friday" [April 1930]; see McCown letters in Virgil Thomson Papers, Yale University music library, esp. January 11, 1923.

45. 46 Gordon Square was the circle's *"monument historique"*; Skidelsky, *John Maynard Keynes*, I:243–245, 294, 333. Gadd, *Loving Friends*, 2–3, 50–51; Pamela Todd, *Bloomsbury at Home* (New York: Harry Abrams, 1999); Richard Kaye, "Bloomsbury," in *The Gay & Lesbian Literary Heritage*, ed. Claude J. Summers (New York: Henry Holt, 1995); JVS to Falkenau, October 13, [1927], Sheean-Falkenau Correspondence, Box 1, f. 2, UC. (Whether the meeting with Woolf took place is unclear.) Michael Yoss, *Raymond Mortimer: A Bloomsbury Voice* [pamphlet #20, Bloomsbury Heritage Series] (London: Cecil Woolf, 1998), 5, quotes Clive Bell describing a party at Mortimer's as "a regular bugger gathering with a smattering of English girls." See JVS–Mortimer letters (esp. 1929–1930) and Mortimer–Eddy Sackville-West letters, de-la-Noy Coll., on JVS and Eddy.

46. JVS, *Gog and Magog* (New York: Harcourt, Brace, 1930), 80. Cf. Donald Friede, *Mechanical Angel* (New York: Knopf, 1948), 134, "anything you did was permissible as long as it did not hurt anyone else."

47. JVS, *PH*, 310–311.

48. JVS to RM, "Monday-Vienna" [November 25, 1929]; John Maynard Keynes to Lytton Strachey, April 1906, quoted in Skidelsky, *John Maynard Keynes*, I:192, and see 191–204. Douglas B. Turnbaugh, *Duncan Grant and the Bloomsbury Group* (London: Bloomsbury Books, 1987), 75, mentions Grant's interest in Sheean in 1930–1931.

49. JVS to JG, April 8, [1930], Box 35, JG II; RM to Eddy Sackville-West, June 6, 1927, February 24, 1928, RM Letters to ESW; Frances Partridge, *Love in Bloomsbury: Memories* (Boston: Little, Brown, 1981), 138–139; HN to VSW, November 29, [1927], Box 3.

50. JVS, *PH*, 315–318.

CHAPTER 5: WITH HER WHOLE HEART

Author's note: For Chinese transliteration, I have used current spelling (pinyin) except for the name of Chiang Kai-shek, because it is so much more recognizable to English speakers spelled that way.

1. See Rayna Simons Raphaelson [hereafter R] to Rebecca Hourwich Reyher [hereafter RHR], ts., n.d. [1921–1922], folder 85.6, RHR-SL. All letters from R to RHR are in this location.

2. R to Dr. Ames, April [*sic*] 1923, R to Dr. Ames, n.d. [spring 1923], f. 10, Box 8, Edward Scribner Ames collection, UC SCRC. All letters to Ames are in this location unless otherwise noted. Dorothy Day, *The Long Loneliness: The Autobiography of Dorothy Day* (New York: Harper, 1952), 47 ("aureole"); Milly Bennett, *On Her Own: Journalistic Adventures from San Francisco to the Chinese Revolution 1917–1927*, ed. A. Tom Grunfeld (Armonk, NY: M. E. Sharpe, 1993), 49 (stopping traffic).

3. R to RHR, ts., n.d. [early 1923], RHR-SL. See RHR's biographical sketch at https://hollisarchives.lib.harvard.edu/repositories/8/resources/6010.

4. Robert D. Sampson, "Red Illini: Dorothy Day, Samson Raphaelson, and Rayna Simons at the University of Illinois, 1914–1916," *Journal of Illinois History* 5, no. 3 (2002), is valuable for those years despite errors on Rayna in China; R to [sister] Gracie [Simons], ts., n.d. [1921], Frank Glass Papers, Box 1, f. 9, Hoover Institution [hereafter Glass Papers]; and Samson Raphaelson [SR], "Family Tape" #2, October 15, 1969, RS 26/20/28, University of Illinois Archives.

5. R to EE [*sic*] [Ernestine Evans], September 10, [1926], in RHR-SL 79.1; Day, *Long Loneliness*, 46–48, and 69; R to Gracie, ts., n.d. [1921].

6. *Reporting the Chinese Revolution: The Letters of Rayna Prohme*, by Baruch Hirson and Arthur J. Knodel, ed. and introduction by Gregor Benton (London: Pluto Press, 2007) [hereafter Hirson], 18, on the marriage. Rayna's surname presents problems; Hirson and other historical accounts call her Rayna Prohme in 1926–1927, but she used the surname Raphaelson. I use her first name because she preferred it: see R to Helen Freeland, October 22, [1926], in Hirson, 41–42, "Raphaelson means nothing to me, I dislike Prohme; Simons is unthinkable. I have no feeling of identity with anything but Rayna." *Reporting the Chinese Revolution* is an essential source, reprinting Rayna's letters to Bill Prohme and to Grace Simons in the Frank Glass Papers, Box 1, f. 9, at the Hoover Institution, and Rayna's letters to Helen Freeland. I cite Hirson's printed versions whenever possible. See also Peter Rand, *China Hands* (New York: Simon & Schuster, 1995), 33–63. On Rayna's independent aims, see R to Grace, n.d. [1921], and cf. Nancy F. Cott, *The Grounding of Modern Feminism* (New Haven, CT: Yale University Press, 1987), 143–240.

7. SR to Stuart Sherman, January 21, January 29, 1919, January 20, 1920, March 18, 1920, Stuart Sherman Papers, Box 4, University of Illinois Archives.

8. Bennett, *On Her Own*, 49; Hirson, 22–24; Bill Prohme to SR, May 7, 1920, in collections of Joel Raphaelson and Carol Simons. "Raph" wrote the story "The Day of Atonement," in Mill Valley—see SR to Sherman, April 2, April 14, July 1, 1920, Sherman Papers. First published in *Everybody's Magazine*, January 1922, it was the basis for the film *The Jazz Singer* (1927), starring Al Jolson.

9. Prohme to SR, October 22, December 28, [1920], in Carol Simons's collection; University of California at Berkeley "Catalogue of Officers and Students, 1920–21"; "Transactions of the Board of Trustees, July 26, 1920 to June 13, 1921," *University of Illinois Bulletin* 19, no. 32 (April 3, 1922): 101.

10. R to RHR, ts. on Stadium letterhead, n.d. [1921]; R to RHR, n.d., handwritten; R to RHR, ts., n.d. [1921]; R to RHR ts., n.d. [spring 1923]; R to RHR, n.d. [1922]; R to RHR n.d. [late spring 1923]: "Yours is the only friendship I have ever had which is built on an immediate intuitive liking and love. It was wonderful finding you two years ago in Chicago." RHR to Ames, June 22, [1922].

11. R to RHR, n.d. [late 1921 or early 1922]; R to Ames, n.d. [late spring 1922]; R to Ames, n.d. on NWP letterhead; see Raphaelson to Sherman, July 13, 1922, Sherman Papers.

12. R to RHR, ts., n.d. [spring 1922], RHR-SL; R to Ames, n.d. [1922]; R to RHR, September 12, 1922. Rayna Raphaelson, "The Hedonism of Disillusionment in the Younger Generation," *International Journal of Ethics* 32, no. 4 (July 1922): 379–397, arose from a philosophy seminar paper of hers.

13. R to RHR, beginning "A note from Ena . . . " [late 1922]; R to RHR, n.d. [September 1923], from Beijing. Rayna Raphaelson passport application, April 16, 1923, Department of State Passport Application Series #2496, RG 59, Container 4172, vol. 12, gives proof of her divorce "prior to Sept 22, 1922." Alfred Cahen, *Statistical Analysis of American Divorce* (New York: Columbia University Press, 1932), 21; J. Herbie DiFonzo, *Beneath the Fault Line: The Popular and Legal Culture of Divorce in Twentieth-Century America* (Charlottesville: University Press of Virginia, 1997).

14. R to RHR, n.d., beginning "I haven't heard from you in days"; R to "Dearest Ena," ts., n.d. [January or February 1923], RHR-SL; R to RHR, March 2, 1924; R to Ames, from Beijing, December 11, 1923, noted that on repaying her debts she would "be just penniless . . . the wealthiest state I've been in for over five years."

15. R to "Dearest Ena," ts., n.d. [January or February 1923]; John Dewey and Alice Chipman Dewey, *Letters from China and Japan*, ed. Evelyn Dewey (New York: Dutton, 1920), 200, 247.

16. See American coverage: J. B. Powell, "Red Envoy to Beijing Opposes Chinese Soviet: Dr. Sun and Joffe Reach Accord," *Ch T*, January 27, 1923, 9; "Alliance Predicted of Russia and China," *NYT*, January 28, 1923, 55.

17. For the Guomindang's 1920s history, I rely principally on C. Martin Wilbur, *The Nationalist Revolution in China, 1923–28* (Cambridge: Cambridge University Press, 1983); Stephen Kotkin, *Stalin: Paradoxes of Power, 1878–1923* (New York: Penguin, 2014), 626–627.

18. See Catherine Ladds's excellent overview, "China and Treaty-Port Imperialism," *The Encyclopedia of Empire*, 1st ed., ed. John M. MacKenzie (New York: Wiley, 2016).

19. R to Ames, April [*sic*] 1923; R to Gracie, June 21, [1925], Glass Papers, Box 1, f. 9. On Pacific routes, see US Bureau of Foreign and Domestic Commerce, *Commercial Travelers' Guide to the Far East* (Washington, DC: US Government Printing Office, 1926), 69–70, 136.

20. R to RHR, March 2, 1924 (describing previous spring); R to Ames, April [*sic*] 1923; R to RHR, ts., n.d. [April–May 1923]; R to RHR, ts., n.d. from Beijing [September 1923].

21. Bennett, *On Her Own*, 234, 170–171, 51, 49; see William Prohme draft registration, May 23, 1917, *World War I Selective Service System Draft Registration Cards, 1917–1918* (Washington, DC: NARA). He was born in Kings County, New York, June 19, 1887.

22. R to RHR, March 2, 1924.

23. R to RHR, n.d.; Rayna Raphaelson, "We Meet at Sea," *American Review* 2, no. 3 (May–June 1924): 283–290 (quotation, 283).

24. See Irene Corbally Kuhn, "Shanghai: The Way It Was," *LA Times*, October 19, 1986; R to Dr. Ames, December 11, 1923, RHR-SL.

25. R to Helen Freeland, October 22, [1926], Hirson, 39–40; Bennett, *On Her Own*, 70–71.

26. See David Strand, *Rickshaw Beijing: City People and Politics in the 1920s* (Berkeley: University of California Press, 1993); Bennett, *On Her Own*, 83, 97, 112, 165.

27. R to RHR, n.d. [September 1923]; R to Gracie, ts., n.d. [September–October 1923], Glass Papers; R to RHR, n.d. [September–October 1923].

28. R to her mother, n.d. [December 1923], Carol Simons collection; R to Dr. Ames, December 11, 1923; R to RHR, n.d. [September–October 1923].

29. R to RHR, March 2, 1924.

30. R to RHR, March 2, May 31, [November 1,] [1924]; Bennett, *On Her Own*, 51; on R's limited sexual experience, R to Gracie [Simons], August 7, [1927], Hirson, 85; R to RHR, February 26, [1926].

31. R to RHR, March 2, 1924; Bennett, *On Her Own*, 49–76. Rayna Raphaelson, *The Kamehameha Highway: 80 Miles of Romance* (Honolulu: Percy M. Pond, [1925]); Rayna Raphaelson, "Americans All," *American Review* 4 (March–April 1926): 129–138; R to Gracie, June 4, [1925], Glass Papers. No evidence of legal marriage between Rayna and Bill has surfaced. In China she still preferred to be Raphaelson; see R to "Beanie darling" [Bill], August 25, [1927], Hirson, 95, "I used my old name."

32. R to RHR, eight handwritten and three ts. pages looking back on the abortion, February 26, [1926], plus another page dated March 1; R to SR, July 6, 1925, December 17, [1926], Joel Raphaelson collection; R to Grace, June 4 and June 12, [1925], Glass Papers.

33. Wilbur, *Nationalist Revolution*, 24–25; Hung-ting Ku, "Urban Mass Movement: The May Thirtieth Movement in Shanghai," *Modern Asian Studies* 13, no. 2 (1979): 197–216.

34. R to [Ernestine Evans], n.d. [spring 1926], RHR-SL Box 79, f. 1.

35. R to RHR, February 26, [1926]; R to [Ernestine Evans], n.d. [spring 1926], RHR-SL Box 79, f. 1; cf. Hallett Abend, *My Life in China, 1926–1941* (New York: Harcourt, Brace, 1943), 43–54. Grover Clark acquired the *Beijing Leader* in 1925 and sold it in 1928; Robert Desmond, *Crisis and Conflict: World News Reporting between Two Wars, 1920–1940* (Iowa City: University of Iowa Press, 1982), 194.

36. R to RHR, February 26, [1926]; R to Helen Freeland, October 22, [1926], Hirson, 40–41. Rayna's sister Grace was living with them then; R to Grace, January 6, [1927], Hirson, 53–54.

37. This is a reasonable surmise; precisely how and when Bill and Rayna met Chen remains uncertain. See R to Helen, February 19, 1927, Hirson, 66: "It wasn't much more than a year ago that I wrote a letter to Eugene Chen, who had just gotten out of jail." Yuan-Tsung Chen [later Eugene Chen's daughter-in-law], says in *Return to the Middle Kingdom* (New York: Union Square Press,

2008), 164–165, that Rayna attended Chen's press conference on December 13, 1925, where they met.

38. Wilbur, *Nationalist Revolution*, 24–25.

39. R to RHR, February 26, 1926.

40. Bill Prohme to Lewis Gannett, November 12, 1926, December 27, 1926, f. 958-1, Lewis S. Gannett Papers, Houghton Library. Gannett got to know Bill and Rayna on his travels in China in 1925–1926.

41. R to Ernestine Evans, September 10, [1926], RHR-SL, 79:1.

42. For previous three paragraphs, Wilbur, *Nationalist Revolution*, esp. 27–33, 47–68; Tien-wei Wu, "Chiang Kai-shek's March Twentieth Coup d'Etat of 1926," *Journal of Asian Studies* 27, no. 3 (1968): 585–602.

43. Bennett, *On Her Own*, 49–76.

44. R to Gracie, January 6, [1927], Hirson, 53; R to Helen Freeland, October 29, 1926, Hirson, 42–44.

45. R to Helen Freeland, October 29, 1926, and December [1926], Hirson, 44, 48; Bill Prohme to Lewis Gannett, November 12, 1926, Gannett Papers, f. 958-1.

46. R to Helen Freeland, October 22, December 31, [1926], in Hirson, 40, 49.

47. R to "Dear Brat"[Gracie], February 16 [1927], Hirson, 64; Henry Francis Misselwitz, *The Dragon Stirs* (New York: Harbinger House, 1941), 20–23.

48. R to Helen Freeland, January 31, [1927], and February 19, [1927], Hirson, 56–57, 66–68 (quotation, 67); R to "Dear Brat" [Grace], February 16, [1927], Hirson, 63–64; Wilbur, *Nationalist Revolution*, 76–77.

49. Wilbur, *Nationalist Revolution*, 6–9; see Dan N. Jacobs, *Borodin: Stalin's Man in China* (Cambridge, MA: Harvard University Press, 1981).

50. Wilbur, *Nationalist Revolution*, 77–85, 99–108.

51. R to Helen Freeland, February 19, March 19, [1927], in Hirson, 66–68, 72.

52. R to Helen Freeland, March 19, [1927], Hirson, 72–73; Wilbur, *Nationalist Revolution*, 6–9; see Jacobs, *Borodin*.

53. Wilbur, *Nationalist Revolution*, 88–93. Misselwitz, *Dragon Stirs*, 32–51, reprints the American report of the "outrages."

54. Wilbur, *Nationalist Revolution*, 94–124; Yu Chang-gen, *Zhou En-lai: A Political Life* (Hong Kong: Chinese University Press, 2008), 31–42.

55. Anna Louise Strong, *China's Millions* (New York: Coward-McCann, 1928), 15, 34; "Karl von Wiegand Arrives to Cover China Story for Hearst," *China Weekly Review*, May 7, 1927, 264; "More Newspapermen Arrive in Shanghai," *China Weekly Review*, May 28, 1927, 351; JVS, "Hankow in Throes of Social Change Led by Russians," *The Sun*, May 19, 1927, 11; Misselwitz, *Dragon Stirs*, 65–66, 87–102.

56. JVS to LB, February 25, [1927], March 29, 1927, Louise Bryant Papers, Box 7, f. 28; JVS to RM, April 31 [*sic*], 1927, Collection of RM Materials. See JVS, "China's Rift Spreading," *LA Times*, April 18, 1927, 2, and "Communism is his Foe, Chiang Kai-Shek Says," *The Sun*, May 1, 1927, 9.

57. JVS, *PH*, 213–214, 216, 229. Cf. William Chamberlin, *The Confessions of an Individualist* (New York: Macmillan, 1940), 121–135.

58. Bill Prohme to Lewis Gannett, May 14, 1927; Randall Gould, *China in the Sun* (New York: Doubleday, 1946), 70–71.

59. Bill Prohme to Lewis Gannett, May 14, 1927, Gannett Papers; Strong, *China's Millions*, 34.

60. Bennett, *On Her Own*, 141–164; "Beijing Stirred by Arrests of Two Americans," *China Press*, April 7, 1927, 3; "American Woman Released in China," *The Sun*, April 10, 1927, 2.

61. Bennett, *On Her Own*, 214–215, 234–235; Gould, *China in the Sun*, 69–70, 114–121; Tracy B. Strong and Helene Keyssar, *Right in Her Soul: The Life of Anna Louise Strong* (New York: Random House, 1983), 122–142, esp. 126.

62. JVS, *PH*, 222, 224–226, 240–241 (quotation, 226); Strong, *China's Millions*, 37–41 (quotation, 40); see Bennett, *On Her Own*, 224–226.

63. R to Gracie, August 24, [1927], Hirson, 91–92; JVS, *PH*, 238.

64. R to Helen Freeland, August 6, 1927, Hirson, 81–82.

65. Bill Prohme to Lewis Gannett, July 17, [1927], f. 958–2, Gannett Papers; Bennett, *On Her Own*, 291n1.

66. R, diary of July 31, Hirson, 76–77; R to "Dear Gracie," August 7, [1927], Hirson, 84, paraphrasing the resignation letter; R to Helen Freeland, August 6, 1927, Hirson, 81–82; R to SR, August 8, [1927], Simons collection.

67. On the escape, Hirson, 86–90; R to Gracie, August 7, August 24, [1927], in Hirson, 83, 92.

CHAPTER 6: MOSCOW PASSAGE

1. JVS, *PH*, 259, 246–251 (quotation, 249); JVS to LB, August 24, [1927], Louise Bryant Papers, Box 7, f. 98.

2. R to Beanie [nickname for Bill] darling, "on train," September 6, 1927; *Reporting the Chinese Revolution: The Letters of Rayna Prohme*, by Baruch Hirson and Arthur J. Knodel, ed. and introduction by Gregor Benton (London: Pluto Press, 2007) [hereafter Hirson], 101–102; R to Gracie [Simons], August 24, [1927], Hirson, 92.

3. R to Beanie darling, September 7, 1927, Hirson, 103–105.

4. R to Billium [nickname for Bill], September 16, 1927, Hirson, 108–109; R to Beanie darling, September 21, September 22, 1927, Hirson, 110–113 (quotations, 110, 113).

5. Steven Kotkin, *Stalin: Paradoxes of Power: 1878–1928* (New York: Penguin, 2014), 625–652; Dan N. Jacobs, *Borodin: Stalin's Man in China* (Cambridge, MA: Harvard University Press, 1981), 301–307.

6. R to Billium, September 16, September 21, 1927, Hirson, 109–111 (cf. JVS, *PH*, 261–263, 267–269); R to Beanie, September 22, 1927, Hirson (quotations, 110, 113); see also 141.

7. R to Beanie, September 22, 1927, Hirson, 113; JVS, *PH*, 270–272, 262; JVS to Ruth Falkenau, October 13, [1927], f. 2, Box 1, Sheean-Falkenau Correspondence.

8. R to Beanie, October 18, September 7, October 7, 1927, Hirson, 128, 103, 120–121.

9. See R to [Bill], October 19, October 18, 1927, Hirson, 127–129, and commentary, 160–161; Jacobs, *Borodin*, 248.

10. R to Billium, October 8, 1927, Hirson, 123–126 (quotation, 125); R to Beanie, [c. October 11 or 12, 1927], Hirson, 127; see R to Beanie darling, September 25, 1927; R to Helen darling, September 28, 1927; R to Beanie darling, October 7, 1927, Hirson, 114, 118, 121; and further letters on housing, Hirson, 121–128.

11. R to Billium darling, October 8, 1927, Hirson, 124, 126; R [to Bill], October 19, 1927, Hirson 128–131 (quotations, 130).

12. R to Beanie, September 21, September 22, October 26, October 30, 1927, Hirson, 111, 113, 132; R to Billiam, November 2, 1927. See also JVS to Samson Raphaelson, November 21, 1927, Samson Raphaelson Papers, RBML, Columbia University.

13. R to Bill, undated fragment [early November], R to Beanie, November 9, 1927, 139–142, 139, 140, 142; DT, copy of telegram to *Press Daily Chronicle* (London) in DT, Notes on Russia, Dobkin Family Collection of Feminist History (courtesy of Glenn Horowitz Bookseller); Igor Torbakov, "Celebrating Red October," *Scando-Slavica* 64, no. 1 (2018): 7–30; Nikos Kazantzakis, *Russia: A Chronicle of Three Journeys . . .* (Berkeley, CA: Creative Arts, 1989), 187–197; Kotkin, *Stalin*, 650–651; Walter Duranty, "Red Army Marches in Soviet Capital," *NYT*, November 8, 1927, 3; "Russian Opposition Defies Soviet," *NYT*, November 9, 1927, 34; "Trotsky Show Rivals Moscow Celebration," *NYT*, November 11, 1927, 6.

14. JVS, *PH*, 283–284, 246–251; JVS, "Asia at Moscow," *Asia,* March 1928, 221–226 (quotations, 224).

15. DT, "The 10th anniversary celebration," Notes on Russia; DT to SL, November 1, [1927], Wednesday eve [November 2, 1927], Box 47, f. 1927–1928, DT-SYR. All DT–SL correspondence of 1927 is in this folder.

16. DT, Notes on Russia.

17. DT to SL, Wednesday eve [November 2, 1927]; DT to SL "Thurs." [November 3].

18. DT to SL, Wednesday eve [November 2, 1927]; DT, Notes on Russia; DT to SL, Friday [November 4], November 8 [1927].

19. DT to SL, Friday the 11th [of November 1927].

20. DT to SL, Friday [November 4, 1927].

21. Tracy B. Strong and Helene Keyssar, *Right in Her Soul: The Life of Anna Louise Strong* (New York: Random House, 1983), 139.

22. The best sources on Rayna's illness and death as described in previous paragraphs are JVS to Miss [Helen] Freeland, November 21, 1927, January 3,

1928, Hirson, 143–148; JVS to Samson Raphaelson, November 21, 1927, Raphaelson Papers, Columbia; JVS to Milly Bennett, December 7, 1927, f. 6, Box 5, Milly Bennett Papers, Hoover Institution Archives; and William Prohme, mimeographed ts. "Rayna Simons Prohme: A Report on the last months of her life," 11 (on her last words), RHR Papers, 85.6. Prohme traveled to Moscow to consult Rayna's friends and colleagues there, and then composed and sent this report to friends.

23. DT to SL, Monday [November 21, 1927].

24. JVS to Milly Bennett, December 7, 1927, Bennett Papers.

25. Bill Prohme to Lewis Gannett, November 25 [1927], Gannett Papers, f. 928–2, Houghton; Prohme to Samson Raphaelson, November 22, 1927, Joel Raphaelson collection.

26. DT to SL, Thursday, Thanksgiving, [1927]; Anna Louise Strong, ts. "Rayna Prohme's Funeral," Carol Simons collection; William Prohme, mimeographed ts. "Rayna Simons Prohme: A Report" (with précis of funeral speeches); [Walter Duranty], "Rayna Prohme Dead: Devoted to Chinese," *NYT*, November 22, 1927; JVS, *PH*, 301. Strong and Sheean arranged for flowers requested by Joseph Simons, Samson Raphaelson, and Bill Prohme. An AP account of the funeral, dateline Moscow, November 24, 1927, generated short articles in *LA Times*, November 25, 1927, 17; *WP*, November 25, 1927, 5, and elsewhere.

27. JVS to Miss Freeland, January 3, 1928, Hirson, 147; JVS, "Rayna Prohme," *The Matrix* [Austin, TX], February 1928, 4, 21; see Louis Fischer, *Men and Politics: An Autobiography* (New York: Duell, Sloan and Pearce, 1941), 157–158.

28. JVS to Milly Bennett, December 7, 1927; JVS to Miss [Helen] Freeland, January 3, 1928, Hirson, 147.

29. Bill Prohme to Edward Scribner Ames, November 27, 1927, Ames collection, Box 8, f. 10.

30. JVS, *Dorothy and Red* (Boston: Houghton Mifflin, 1963), 57, 73–77; DT to SL, Thursday, Thanksgiving, [November 24, 1927].

31. HN to VSW November 28, [1927], Box 3, VSW mss., Lilly; HN diary, daily jottings, November 27–December 6, 1927, Bailliol College Archives; HN to VSW, November 29, December 6, 1927, Box 3, VSW mss. Lilly; Robert Beachy, *Gay Berlin* (New York: Knopf, 2014), esp. 187–219; see also JVS to Ruth Falkenau, December 7, 1927, Sheean-Falkenau Correspondence.

32. JVS to Ruth Falkenau, October 13, [1927], Sheean-Falkenau Correspondence; JVS, "Mussolini Exiles Live Lonely Days on Islets," *LA Times*, January 29, 1928, 8; "Italy Grades Her Exiles," *LA Times*, January 30, 1928, 2; "Italy's Exiles Get Daily Dole," *LA Times*, January 31, 6; "Italy's Heroes Fill Jails," *LA Times*, February 1, 1928, 9; *PH*, 306–307, Ron Weber, *News of Paris* (Chicago: Ivan Dee, 2006), 144–147, on the *Paris Times*.

33. DT to SL, November 16, November 17, November 18, 1927.

34. DT to SL, November 18, 1927; Kotkin, *Stalin*, 651–652.

35. DT to SL, November 21, November 25, 1927.

36. Mark Schorer, *Sinclair Lewis: An American Life* (New York: McGraw-Hill, 1961), 494–496.

37. DT, *The New Russia* (New York: Henry Holt, 1928); see Lewis Gannett's review, "Lenin's Land," *NYHT Magazine*, October 14, 1928; and Thompson's remarks in *Russia Today* (New York: Foreign Policy Association, 1929), 3–8, 24–25. Additional books include Ivy Lee, *Present-Day Russia* (New York: Macmillan, 1928); Anne O'Hare McCormick, *The Hammer and the Scythe* (New York: Knopf, 1928); Roger N. Baldwin, *Liberty under the Soviets* (New York: Vanguard, 1928); Theodore Dreiser, *Dreiser Looks at Russia* (New York: Liveright, 1928).

38. DT, diary, February 12, 1928, Box 59, DT-SYR. Peter Kurth, *American Cassandra: The Life of Dorothy Thompson* (Boston: Little, Brown, 1990), 110–114.

39. DT, diary or letter fragment, March 12, [1928], DT diary, September 30, 1927, Box 59, DT-SYR. See DT, "Is America a Paradise for Women? 'NO,'" *Pictorial Review* 30 (June 1929), using evidence from Robert and Helen Lynd's then new study *Middletown* (1927), paired with Sinclair Lewis arguing "YES"; Schorer, *Sinclair Lewis*, 519; Kurth, *American Cassandra*, 139–141. In her article Thompson pointed to "the womanly principle in the universe, the love which cherishes and incubates as contrasted with the outgoing, procreative force, which is masculine."

40. DT, honeymoon diary, August 2, [1928], Box 59. See Marion K. Sanders, *Dorothy Thompson: A Legend in Her Time* (Boston: Houghton Mifflin, 1973), 133–141, on the wedding and honeymoon. (They were legally married in a registry office because Anglican clergy would not marry two divorced people.) See, e.g., "Sinclair Lewis to Wed Writer: Miss Thompson American Newspaper Correspondent," *DBG*, April 24, 1928, 16; "Sinclair Lewis Weds," *Philadelphia Inquirer*, May 15, 1928, 3. Newspapers in Yorkshire, Coventry, Sheffield, Birmingham, Nottingham, and Gloucester as well as London, and in Canada, Ireland, and Scotland, reported the marriage. See www.britishnewspaperarchive .co.uk

41. "Lewis Returns from Europe's Main Streets," *NYHT*, August 28, 1928, 36.

42. "Sinclair Lewis Home with Bride," *NYT*, August 28, 1928, 12; "Novelist Buys an Estate," *NYT*, September 20, 1928, 57; Kurth, *American Cassandra*, 115.

43. DT to Knick, December 24, [1928], H. R. Knickerbocker Papers, RBML, Columbia University.

44. DT, diary, February 13, 1929, Box 59, for quotations in this and the previous paragraph.

45. DT to JB, August 20, [1930], October 10, [1928], DTColl [small collection at Syracuse separate from DT-SYR].

46. DT to JB, August 20, [1930]; Kurth, *American Cassandra*, 146.

47. Pamphlet, *Russia Today* (New York: Foreign Policy Association, 1929).

48. Editorial paragraph (unsigned), *The Nation,* December 7, 1927, 617; [Duranty,] "Rayna Prohme Dead," *NYT,* November 22, 1927, 4. Duranty noted accurately that she was not a member of the Communist Party.

49. JVS, *PH,* 270.

CHAPTER 7: SHADOWS OVER EUROPE

1. John Maxwell Hamilton, *Journalism's Roving Eye: A History of American Foreign Reporting* (Baton Rouge: Louisiana State University Press, 2009), 162–172.

2. Michael Schudson, *Discovering the News* (New York: Basic Books, 1978), esp. 122–145, 151–157; *The Good Citizen: A History of American Civic Life* (New York: Free Press, 1998), 188–232.

3. JG–FFG correspondence, April 1928; JG to FFG, September 9, [1928], Box 22; JG, Russian log [compendium of JG letters and journal for FFG], June 6, [1928], Box 2; JG, note to FFG, July 11, [1928], Box 22, JG II.

4. JG, Russian log, June 20, [1928], Box 2, JG II. On Soviet censorship, Robert W. Desmond, *Crisis and Conflict: World News Reporting between Two Wars, 1920–1940* (Iowa City: University of Iowa Press, 1982), 35–48.

5. JG, Russian log, June 8, June 20, [1928], Box 2, JG II.

6. JG to FFG, June 24, [1928], and Russian log, June 26, [1928], Box 2; Green notebook I, orig. (1931), handwritten, Box 2, JG II.

7. FFG to JG, August 2, 1928, Box 22, JG, Green notebook I, orig. (1931) handwritten, Box 2; FFG to JG, December 1928, Box 22, JG II.

8. JG to FFG, September 9, [1928], from Baku, Box 22; JG, Russian log, July 1, [1928], Box 2, JG II.

9. FFG, Memorabilia, f. 46, 47, FFG-SL.

10. JG to FFG, Jerusalem, Sunday [September] the 8th, [1929], Box 22, JG II.

11. JG to FFG, Sunday [September] the 8th, [1929], Box 22; JVS, *PH,* 333–389, (quotation, 333) on Palestine.

12. JVS, *PH,* 337, 340–341; Susan Silsby Boyle, *The Betrayal of Palestine: The Story of George Antonius* (Boulder, CO: Westview Press, 2001), 146–148.

13. JVS, *PH,* 342–343, 359–360, 363–364; Boyle, *Betrayal of Palestine,* 148. The Western Wall formed part of the ancient Jewish Temple and also the Muslim holy site Haram esh Sherif. See Arieh Bruce Saposnik, "Wailing Walls and Iron Walls," *American Historical Review* 120, no. 5 (December 2015): 1653–1681; Hillel Cohen, *1929: Year Zero of the Arab-Israeli Conflict* (Waltham, MA: Brandeis University Press, 2015); David Klatzker, "British Jerusalem in the News," *Middle East Quarterly* 1, no. 4 (1994); Lawrence Davidson, "Competing Responses to the 1929 Arab Uprising in Palestine," *Middle East Policy* 5, no. 2 (May 1997): 93–112.

14. JVS, "Troops Rush to Quell Warfare in Palestine: Fiery Zionist Fascisti 'Spoiling for a Fight' Blamed for Massacre," *Toronto Daily Star,* August 26, 1929, 1; JVS, "12 Americans Die in Palestine War . . . Zionist Fascisti Blamed,"

BDG, August 26, 1929, 1; JG to FFG, September 8, 1929, Box 22, JG II. See Boyle, *Betrayal of Palestine*, 146–160; Klatzker, "British Jerusalem in the News"; Charles D. Smith, *Palestine and the Arab-Israeli Conflict* (New York: St. Martin's, 1996), 78–80.

15. JVS, "The Palestine Report," *The Commonweal*, April 30, 1930, 737–739; JVS to JG, January 29, April 8, 1930, November 20, [1929], "secret and confidential," n.d. [August 29 or 30, 1929], Box 35, JG II; Boyle, *Betrayal of Palestine*, 146–160.

16. JG to FFG, Sunday, [September] the 8th, September 27, 1929, Box 22; JG, "The Realities of Zionism," *Harper's New Monthly Magazine* 161 (July 1930): 202–212. See JG, "James Vincent Sheean," premature obituary, Box 31, JG II.

17. JG, Green notebook II, Box 2, JG II; JVS to RM, November 17, November 25, and "Monday," [1929].

18. Ken Cuthbertson, *Inside: The Biography of John Gunther* (Chicago: Bonus Books, 1992), 86–87; FFG Memorabilia, f. 46, 47, FFG-SL; JG, handwritten Green notebook II, Box 2; JG to FFG, September 9, [1928], Box 22; FFG to JG, February 14, 1933, Box 23, JG II; JG, "Autobiography in Brief," *Story*, May 1938, 94.

19. Benito Mussolini, *Le Fascisme* (1933), quoted in Mark Mazower, *Dark Continent: Europe's Twentieth Century* (New York: Knopf, 1999), 16; see E. J. Hobsbawm, *The Age of Extremes* (New York: Pantheon, 1994), 109–141.

20. Ira Katznelson, *Fear Itself* (New York: Liveright, 2013), esp. 3–18, 29–83, 103–117; Kiran Klaus Patel, *The New Deal: A Global History* (Princeton, NJ: Princeton University Press, 2016), 45–47; cf. DT, "The Death of Democracies," *Vital Speeches of the Day* 3, no. 12 (April 1, 1937).

21. George Seldes, *You Can't Print That* (New York: Payson and Clarke, 1929).

22. JG, "Funneling the News," *Harper's Monthly Magazine* 160 (April 1930): 635–647.

23. JG, "Funneling the News," 640–641.

24. Marion K. Sanders, *Dorothy Thompson: A Legend in Her Time* (Boston: Houghton Mifflin, 1973), 152–158.

25. Peter Kurth, *American Cassandra: The Life of Dorothy Thompson* (Boston: Little, Brown, 1990), 154. In 1938, the *Post*'s circulation was 3 million and its "pass-along" figure (i.e., the presumed number of individuals who read a given copy) was 12.9 million. John William Tebbel and Mary Ellen Zuckerman, *The Magazine in America, 1741–1990* (New York: Oxford University Press, 1991), 172–181; Robert Cantwell, "Journalism—Magazines," in *America Now*, ed. Harold Stearns (New York: Scribner's, 1938), 345–355.

26. DT, "Poverty de Luxe," *SEP*, May 2, 1931, 6; see Richard J. Evans, *The Coming of the Third Reich* (New York: Penguin, 2004), 255–265.

27. DT, "Poverty de Luxe"; "Something must Happen," *SEP*, May 23, 1932; "The State Dictates," *SEP*, February 6, 1932; "The Gray Squirrel Complex," *SEP*, February 20, 1932; "Will Gangs Rule?" *SEP*, June 23, 1932.

28. DT, "Will Gangs Rule?" 6; DT, "I Saw Hitler," *Hearst's International combined with Cosmopolitan* 92, no. 1 (March 1932): 32–33, 160–164; DT, *I Saw Hitler!* (New York: Farrar and Rinehart, 1932).

29. DT, "Back to Blood & Iron: Germany Goes German again," *SEP*, May 6, 1933, 4; DT, *I Saw Hitler!*, 29–30, 30, 31, 34; see DT, "The Record of Persecution," in *Nazism: An Assault on Civilization*, ed. Pierre Van Paassen (New York: Harrison Smith and Robert Haas, 1934), 1–24.

30. DT, *I Saw Hitler!*, 34–35. Organizational names for which she used acronyms are spelled out here.

31. DT, *I Saw Hitler!*, 13, 14; H. R. Knickerbocker to Percy Winner, June 18, 1932, quoted in Andrew Nagorski, *Hitlerland* (New York: Simon & Schuster, 2012), 75.

32. Kurth, *American Cassandra*, 170–175; Mark Schorer, *Sinclair Lewis: An American Life* (New York: McGraw-Hill, 1961), 573–583, including sales figures; Richard Lingeman, *Sinclair Lewis: Rebel from Main Street* (New York: Random House, 2002), 386–388; Sanders, *Dorothy Thompson*, 172–173.

33. Kurth, *American Cassandra*, 159, 176–177.

34. See valuable treatments in Ruby Rich, "Maedchen in Uniform: From Repressive Tolerance to Erotic Liberation," *JumpCut* 24–25 (March 1981): 44–50, and Sara Gwenllian Jones, "Madchen in Uniform: The Story of a Film," *Perversions* 6 (Winter 1995/1996), 7–46.

35. See "heterosexual" in *Oxford English Dictionary*, first usage in 1927. DT, diary, December 28, [1932], Box 59, DT-SYR, for quotations.

36. See "heterosexual" in *Oxford English Dictionary*, first usage in 1927. DT, diary, December 28, [1932], January 2, [1933], Box 59, DT-SYR, for quotations.

37. Lois W. Banner, *Intertwined Lives: Margaret Mead, Ruth Benedict, and Their Circle* (New York: Knopf, 2003), esp. 269–273, quoting Mead's "Sex and Achievement," *Forum* 94 (1935) on 273; John D'Emilio and Estelle Freedman, *Intimate Matters* (Chicago: University of Chicago Press, 1988, 1997), esp. chapters 10–13, and a contemporary comment, Gilbert Seldes, "Good Old Sex Appeal," *New Republic*, April 21, 1926, 275.

38. DT, diary, December 28, [1932], January 2, [1933].

39. DT, diary, January 2; Kurth, *American Cassandra*, 183, on Lewis smashing up the apartment and hitting her.

40. Evans, *Coming of the Third Reich*, 310–311; JG to FFG, Berlin, [February 1933], Box 23, JG II.

41. [JG], "Arson de Luxe," *Harper's* 167 (October 1933): 641–649; JG to Hamilton Armstrong, January 23, 1934, f. 15, Box 33, Hamilton Fish Armstrong Papers; DT, "Back to Blood & Iron"; Evans, *Coming of the Third Reich*, 328–349.

42. DT, "Room to Breathe In," *SEP*, June 24, 1933, 54ff.; DT to SL, March 13, [1933], Box 48, DT-SYR; DT, "The Problem Child of Europe," *Foreign Affairs* 18, no. 3 (April 1940): 389–390.

43. DT, "Room to Breathe In."

44. DT to SL, March 25, March 30, 1933, Box 48, DT-SYR; Kurth, *American Cassandra*, 185–190; JVS, *Dorothy and Red* (Boston: Houghton, Mifflin, 1963) [*D&R*], 239–246.

45. DT, "Back to Blood & Iron," 70; "What This Country Needs Is—," *SEP*, August 18, 1933. During the mid-1930s, *SEP* published sympathetic accounts of Nazi Germany also, according to Michaela Hoenicke Moore, *Know Your Enemy: The American Debate on Nazism* (Cambridge: Cambridge University Press, 2010), 62–63.

46. DT to SL, March 30, 1933; DT, diary, December 28, [1932], November 7, [1935]; DT, "Holograph, Sinclair Lewis," Box 99, DT-SYR.

47. Kurth, *American Cassandra*, 192–196, 216–218, 342–343; Sanders, *Dorothy Thompson*, 193–194.

48. DT, "What This Country Needs Is—," 9; DT, "Propaganda in the Modern World," October 18, 1935, *Vital Speeches of the Day* 2, no. 3 (November 4, 1935): 67; Evans, *Coming of the Third Reich*, 406–409; Desmond, *Crisis and Conflict*, 419.

49. JG, "Dateline Vienna," *Harper's* 171 (July 1935): 199, 202, and 207; Albin E. Johnson, "300 Million Citizens of Europe Living under Iron Rule of Censorship," *Editor & Publisher* 67, no. 7 (June 30, 1934); Robert W. Desmond, *The Press and World Affairs* (New York: D. Appleton-Century, 1937), 138–169; Desmond, *Crisis and Conflict*, 419–432.

50. DT, "The Great War of Words," *SEP*, December 1, 1934, 8–9, 68–70. See *Annals* 177 (January 1935), "Radio: The Fifth Estate"; and Stephen Kotkin, "Modern Times: The Soviet Union and the Interwar Conjuncture," *Kritika* 2, no. 1 (Winter 2001): n.s. 111–164 on "illiberal modernity."

51. DT, "Goodbye to Germany," *Harper's* 170 (December 1934): 45–47; Richard J. Evans, *The Third Reich in Power* (New York: Penguin, 2005), 31–41.

52. Frederick T. Birchall, "Hamburg to Greet Hitler as Hero at Key Talk of Campaign Today," *NYT*, August 17, 1934, 1; Frederick T. Birchall, "Hitler Declares Hand was Forced by Hostile World," *NYT*, August 18, 1934, 1.

53. Frederick T. Birchall, "Dorothy Thompson Expelled by Reich for 'Slur' on Hitler," *NYT*, August 26, 1934; John Elliott, "Nazis Eject Sinclair Lewis's Wife for 1931 Article Criticizing Hitler," *NYHT*, August 26, 1934, 1.

54. Elliott, "Nazis Eject Sinclair Lewis's Wife," 1; Birchall, "Dorothy Thompson Expelled," 1; Hamilton, *Journalism's Roving Eye*, 262–282; Nagorski, *Hitlerland*, 122–129.

55. JG to FFG, October 3, [1934], Box 23, JG II.

CHAPTER 8: TWO BIG BOOKS

1. "Reflective Reporter," *Time* 27, no. 13 (March 30, 1936); Charles Poore, "Books of the Times," *NYT*, February 3, 1940, 15 ("cloudburst"); JVS, *Personal History* (New York: Doubleday, Doran, 1935), 185; John Maxwell Hamilton, *Journalism's Roving Eye: A History of American Foreign Reporting* (Baton Rouge: Louisiana State University Press, 2009), 204–205, on imitators.

2. JVS to JG, letters of late 1929 and 1930, Box 35, JG II; JVS to RM, Gibraltar, [1934], Collection of Raymond Mortimer Materials, Box 3 Folder 35, RBSC, Princeton (source for all JVS–RM correspondence).

3. JVS, *Gog and Magog* (New York: Harcourt, 1930), 244–245 (quotation); JVS to RM, March 9, [1930]; cf. "America and Russia, Gog and Magog," in JVS, *This House Against This House* (New York: Random House, 1946), 383.

4. JVS to RM, "Monday-Vienna," [November 25, 1929], May 25, [1930]; JVS to JG, May 5, [1930]. On his hopes for *Anatomy of Virtue*, see JVS to RM, October 26, [1926]. His stories appeared in the *SEP* on June 28 and July 26, 1930; February 28 and November 7, 1931; September 3 and November 6, 1932; January 14, February 18, and April 15, 1933. JVS, *The Tide* (New York: Doubleday, Doran, 1933), 165–167.

5. JVS to RM, August 5, [1935]; Norman Rose, *Harold Nicolson* (London: Jonathan Cape, 2005), 176–177.

6. JVS to JG, November 29, [1934], JG II; JVS to Jamie Hamilton, March 7, [1935], April 8, [1935], April 21 (Easter), Box 1, f. 26, May 3, [1935], Box 1, f. 27, Sheean Papers, WHS—the location for all JVS letters to Hamilton.

7. JVS, *PH*, 262, 14. JVS correspondence with Ellery Sedgwick (*Atlantic Monthly* editor), 1934–1935, Sedgwick Papers, MHS, shows that by March 1934, Sheean had outlined the book and arranged to publish several chapters in the *Atl M*: "My Friend the Jew," *Atl M* 154, no. 3 (October 1934): 400–409; "Youth and Revolution," 154, no. 5 (November 1934): 513–520; "Following the Gleam," 154, no. 6 (December 1934): 658–668; "Finale in Moscow," 155, no. 1 (January 1935): 57–69.

8. JVS, *PH*, 230, 216.

9. JVS, *PH*, 261, 263. Witnesses in Moscow, and some later historians, who assumed Sheean had fallen in love with Rayna include Louis Fischer, *Men and Politics* (New York: Duell, Sloan and Pearce, 1941), 156–158; Peter Rand, *China Hands* (New York: Simon & Schuster, 1995), 51–53; Baruch Hirson and Arthur J. Knodel, *Reporting the Chinese Revolution: The Letters of Rayna Prohme*, ed. and introduction by Gregor Benton (London: Pluto Press, 2007) [hereafter Hirson], 61, 166; Peter Kurth, *American Cassandra: The Life of Dorothy Thompson* (Boston: Little, Brown, 1990), 122–124.

10. JVS, *PH*, 272–281.

11. JVS, *PH*, 277 and 285–286. See Gidon Cohen and Kevin Morgan, "Stalin's Sausage Machine: British Students at the International Lenin School, 1926–37," *Twentieth-Century British History* 13, no. 4 (January 2002): 327–355.

12. See chapter 6 and Rayna's letters in Hirson, 119–143. JVS, "Rayna Prohme," *The Matrix* [Austin, TX], February 1928, 21; DT to SL, Monday [November 21, 1927], Box 47, DT-SYR.

13. JVS, *PH*, 398.

14. FFG to JG, [March 1935], Box 23; JG, London diary ts., September 13, 1936, Box 19, JG II. JG made his comment upon reading the book a second time.

15. John Chamberlain, "The World in Books," *Current History* 41 (March 1935): 4; Malcolm Cowley, "Books in Review: The Long View," *TNR*, February 20, 1935, 50–51; David Garnett, "A Hero of Our Time," *New Statesman and Nation*, May 4, 1935, 641 (reviewing the British edition, titled *In Search of History*). Garnett had met Sheean through Raymond Mortimer. See also S. K. Ratcliffe, "An Impassioned Reporter," *The Spectator* 153 (May 3, 1935): 739; R. Duffus, "Mr. Sheean's Post-War Odyssey," *NYT*, February 3, 1935. See Nancy F. Cott, "Revisiting the Transatlantic 1920s: Vincent Sheean vs. Malcolm Cowley," *American Historical Review* 118 (February 2013): 46–75.

16. JVS to Jamie Hamilton, February 25, March 7, [1935]; JVS to RM, April 28, [1935]; JVS to JG, January 31, 1935, Box 35, JG II.

17. JVS to Lewis Gannett, February 25, [1935], f. 1080, and William Prohme to Lewis Gannett, July 12, 1935, f. 958, Gannett Papers, bMS Am 1888, Houghton; JVS to Helen Freeland, September 24, [1935], Hirson, 153–155.

18. *Publishers Weekly* 129 (May 16, 1936): 1949; *Vogue*, April 1, 1936, 74; "Librarians List 20 Books Most Widely Read in '35," *NYHT*, December 31, 1935, 6A; Alice Payne Hackett and James Henry Burke, *80 Years of Best Sellers* (New York: Bowker, 1977), 119 (2 million or more sold as the standard for inclusion); Keith Justice, *Bestseller Index* (Jefferson, NC: McFarland & Company, 1998), 277.

19. Hamilton, *Journalism's Roving Eye*, 205; "Screen News," *NYT*, September 8, 1936, 23; June 29, 1938, 15; April 14, 1939, 28; October 3, 1939, 27; February 2, 1940, 19; "But They'll Keep the Title," *NYT*, January 21, 1940, 119; B. R. Crisler, "Gossip of the Films," *NYT*, August 22, 1937, X7; Margaret Thorp, *America at the Movies* (New Haven, CT: Yale University Press, 1939), 211–213; and Desley Deacon, "'Films as Foreign Offices': Transnationalism at Paramount," in *Connected Worlds*, ed. Ann Curthoys and Marilyn Lake (Canberra: Australian National University Press, 2005), 139–156, explain Wanger's difficulties.

20. Kenneth Stewart, *News Is What We Make It* (Boston: Houghton Mifflin, 1943), 198; JG, "Potential Battlegrounds," *Saturday Review* 15, no. 1 (November 14, 1936); Alexander Werth, "Men and Scoops," *New Statesman and Nation* 11 (January 18, 1936); Charles Poore, "Books of the Times," *NYT*, February 3, 1940, 15.

21. Eric Severeid, *Not So Wild a Dream*, 2nd ed. (New York: Atheneum, 1976), viii; Harrison Salisbury, *A Time of Change* (New York: Harper & Row, 1988), 200–201, and "The Amerasia Papers," *NYT Book Review*, September 19, 1971, 2; Mary McCarthy, "One Man's Road," *The Nation*, March 6, 1935, 282–283; and *The Company She Keeps* (New York: Harcourt, 1970 [original work published 1942]). McCarthy's story appeared first in *Partisan Review* 8, no. 4 (July 1941), and put Negley Farson's *The Way of the Transgressor* in this place—then changed to Sheean for the novel.

22. JVS to Lewis Gannett, February 25, [1935], Gannett Papers, bMS Am 1888, (1080); JVS to RM, July 24, August 3, [1935]; JVS to JG, June 29, July 24, August 2, [1935], Box 35, JG II.

23. Marriage certificate issued by US Department of State shows they were married by a vice-consul of the United States in Vienna city hall, August 24, 1935; see Diana Forbes-Robertson Sheean [DS] to Leland Stowe, June 27, 1949, f. 4, Box 23, Leland Stowe Papers, WHS; on Churchill and Maxine Elliott, JVS, *Between the Thunder and the Sun* (New York: Random House, 1943), 27–66, mention of *PH* on 55.

24. JVS to JG, October 3, [1935], Box 35, JG II; JVS to Irita Van Doren, September 5, [1935], Irita Taylor van Doren Papers, Box 8, LC; JVS to Jamie Hamilton, November 8, [1935], Box 1, f. 27.

25. JVS to RM, October 11, [1936]; JVS to Jamie Hamilton, Saturday [June 6, 1936], folder 28.

26. JVS, *Sanfelice* (Garden City, NY: Doubleday, Doran, 1936); Lewis Gannett, "Books and Things," *NYHT*, June 17, 1936, 19. John Gunther thought it was "very nearly a masterpiece: serene, bold, ambitious, somber, magnificently written." JG, ts. London diary, Friday, April 3, [1936], Box 19, JG II. All subsequent citations to "ts. London diary" are in this location. Other reviews were Ralph Thompson, "Books of the Times," *NYT*, June 17, 1936, 21; L. P. Hartley, "Man's Inhumanity to Man," *Guardian and Observer*, April 26, 1936; "New Books: A Selected List," *London Mercury* 345 (1936): 86.

27. JVS to Jamie Hamilton, November 8, 1935, 27; JVS to Bill Stoneman, July 1, [1936], William Stoneman Papers, Bentley Historical Library, University of Michigan. The review was Sterling North, "Book of the Week," *Chicago Daily News*, June 17, 1936, 25.

28. "Vincent Sheean is Ill," *NYT*, August 17, 1936, 17; JVS to Jamie Hamilton, September 15, September 24, [1936], f. 29; JVS to RM, October 11, [1936]; JVS to Dr. Rhine, April 8, 1952, copy in Box 27, DT-SYR.

29. JVS to RM, October 11, [1936]; see Hirson, 156–159.

30. JVS to RM, October 11, [1936].

31. RM to ESW, Box 1, folder 3, n.d. [December 1936 or early January 1937], in RM Letters to ESW, RBSC, Princeton. JVS to RM, January 12, [1937], noted that he visited Mortimer "a couple of weeks ago."

32. JG, premature obituary of Sheean, Box 31, JG II.

33. JG, October 13, October 22, November 28, [1934], USA log [daily journal written for FFG], Box 2, JG II; JG to Vernon Bartlett, Esq., *London News-Chronicle*, February 1, 1934; FFG to Mr. Smith, *News-Chronicle*, f. 64; FFG clippings, f. 130–132, FFG-SL.

34. JG, [September 1932], Green notebook II (1931–1934) handwritten, and JG, Green notebook II, ts.; JG, USA log, October 6 and 20, Box 2, JG II;

35. JG, USA log, October 4, 5, 15, 1934.

36. JG, USA log, October 24, [1934]. George E. Reedy, "The First Great Communicator," *Review of Politics* 54, no. 1 (1992): 152–155; Leo C. Rosten, "President Roosevelt and the Washington Correspondents," *Public Opinion Quarterly*, January 1937, 36–52; Betty Winfield, *FDR and the News Media* (Urbana: University of Illinois Press, 1990); Stewart, *News Is What We Make It*,

205–206; William Hard, "Radio and Public Opinion," *Annals* 177 (January 1935): 105–113.

37. JG, USA log, October 12, October 24, November 2, 1934.

38. JG, USA log, October 27, October 11, 1934.

39. JG, USA log, November 7, 1934.

40. JG, USA log, Friday, October 19, October 4, 1934; John Garraty, "The New Deal, National Socialism, and the Great Depression," *American Historical Review* 78, no. 4 (1973): 907–944, esp. 913–914; Nelson Lichtenstein, *A Contest of Ideas* (Urbana: University of Illinois Press, 2013), esp. 159–161.

41. JG, USA log, October 4, November 3, November 22, November 28, 1934. JG published at least thirteen articles in *The Nation*, seven in *Harper's*, two in *Foreign Affairs*, two in *TNR*, one in *SEP*, 1930–1935.

42. JG, "Slaughter for Sale," *Harper's* 168 (May 1934): 649–659.

43. JG, USA log, December 7, 1934.

44. JG to William Bullitt, January 26, 1935 ("Americanitis"), William C. Bullitt Papers, Box 34, f. 787, Manuscripts and Archives, Yale University Library; JVS to JG, March 28, [1935], Box 35, JG II; Foreign editor of the *News-Chronicle* to FFG, April 8, 1935, f. 64, FFG-SL.

45. JG, USA log, December 9, [1934]; JG, *A Fragment of Autobiography* (New York: Harper & Row, 1961), 6–8; Cass Canfield, *Up and Down and Around* (New York: Harper's Magazine Press, 1971), 121–123; JG to Hamilton Fish Armstrong [HFA], February 11, 1935, HFA Papers, Box 33, folder 15.

46. JG, *Fragment*, 8–9.

47. JG, ts. London diary, December 3, 1935, December 5, 1935, January 13, 1936.

48. JG, *Fragment*, 12–13. Gunther was unaware of Herbert Bayard Swope's *Inside the German Empire* (1917) or Walter Lippmann's use of an insider/outsider distinction in *The Phantom Public* (1925). In 1927, Frances Gunther suggested that John write a "Behind the Scenes account of modern European politics. . . . Note down all the 'inside' stories you hear & you'll have plenty of material." FFG to JG, Sunday, November 27, 1927, Box 22, JG II. "Basically, it was her idea," JG acknowledged in "Autobiography in Brief," *Story* (1938), 95. See Anon. [Drew Pearson and Robert Allen], *Washington Merry-Go-Round* (New York: Liveright, 1931); *More Merry-Go-Round* (New York: Liveright, 1932); Richard L. Strout, "Washington in 1931," *WP Book World*, July 22, 1984, 225; George Douglas, *The Smart Magazines* (Hamden, CT: Archon Books, 1991), 26–31, 76–93; Neal Gabler, *Winchell: Gossip, Power and the Culture of Celebrity* (New York: Knopf, 1994), 64, 80–94.

49. JG, *Fragment*, 9–11; JG, *Inside Europe*, 13th ed. (New York: Harper & Bros., 1936), xiii; JG, Russian log, July 1, [1928], Box 2, JG II.

50. Janice Radway, *A Feeling for Books* (Chapel Hill: University of North Carolina Press, 1997), esp. 280–283; Joan Rubin, *The Making of Middlebrow Culture* (Chapel Hill: University of North Carolina Press, 1992).

51. Joseph Heath, "Methodological Individualism," *Stanford Encyclopedia of Philosophy*, published February 3, 2005; revised January 21, 2015, http://plato .stanford.edu/archives/spr2015/entries/methodological-individualism/.

52. JG, "Has Hitler a Mother Complex?" *Vanity Fair*, October 1934; *Inside Europe*, 13th ed. (May 1936), xiii; JG, "Stalin," *Harper's* 172 (December 1935): 19–32; "Hitler," *Harper's* 172 (January 1936): 148–159; "Mussolini," *Harper's* 172 (February 1936): 296–308.

53. JG, *Inside Europe*, 179, 86, 161, 183, 270, 379.

54. Alexander Werth, "Men and Scoops," *New Statesman and Nation* 11 (January 18, 1936); Harold Nicolson, "Guide Which Makes Foreign Affairs Exciting," *Daily Telegraph*, January 17, 1936, 9; Goronwy Rees, "The Inside Story," *The Spectator*, January 24, 1936, 139; Eugene Young, "Views behind the Scenes in Europe's Chancelleries," *NYT Book Review*, February 16, 1936, 19.

55. Raymond Gram Swing, "Europe as Portraiture," *The Nation*, March 4, 1936, 285. While praising it, Swing called *Inside Europe* "Not quite satisfactory as history." Lewis Gannett, "Book and Things," *NYHT*, February 8, 1936. Only Gannett mentioned Gunther having and quoting "a wife with an intuitive gift for understanding human beings." Gannett and Frances Fineman were briefly romantically involved; FF to Lewis Gannett, letters May–August 1917, Gannett Papers, bMS Am 1888, (499), Houghton.

56. JVS to JG, January 23, [1936], Box 35, JG II; Malcolm Cowley, "The Personal Element," *TNR* 86 (February 12, 1936); John Chamberlain, "Books of the Times," *NYT*, February 8, 1935, 13, also objected. Reviewers on the left (such as these) were the most negative. Gunther knew he was "assaulted by some of the Marxists for paying too much attention to personality. Of course I paid too much attention to personality. But that was the idea of the book." ts. London diary, March 2, 1936.

57. "Book Notes," *NYT*, August 27, 1936, 19; Richard Rovere, "Inside," *New Yorker*, 31, 36.

58. JG, ts. London diary, August 11, 1936; Charles Poore, "Books of the Times," *NYT*, November 13, 1937, 17; "Book Notes," *NYT*, December 19, 1936, 17; January 30, 1937, 15; Rovere, "Inside." The fourth and fifth editions came out in 1937, a "peace" edition in 1938 and soon a "war" edition.

59. JG, ts. London diary, December 19, 1935, re Cockburn, "There is no one, all in all, I like better in England"; May 20–21, 1936 ("Monopoly").

60. JG, Green notebook II, ms. page dated Vienna, December 1931, Box 2; ts. London diary, February 27, February 19, 1936.

61. JG, ts. London diary, February 28, April 13, 1936; JG, notes on earnings, Box 2, JG II.

62. Raymond Gram Swing, "The Big News in Europe, What It Means, and How to Get It," *Proceedings of 13th Annual Convention of American Society of Newspaper Editors* (National Press Club, Washington, DC, April 18–20, 1935), 91–113 (quotation, 92). The session also featured Dorothy Thompson.

63. Stewart, *News Is What We Make It*, 198.

64. See Brooke L. Blower, "From Isolationism to Neutrality: A New Framework for Understanding American Political Culture, 1919–1941," *Diplomatic History* 38, no. 2 (2014): 345–376.

CHAPTER 9: ANTIFASCISM LOUD AND CLEAR

Author's note: As far as possible I cite Dorothy Thompson's column, On the Record, from the *NYHT*, where it appeared until early 1941, and cite it in a different newspaper only when the best copy in the ProQuest digitized historical newspapers database is elsewhere.

1. JG, USA log, November 18, [1934], Box 2, JG II; DT, "The Death of Democracies: How to Avoid It: By Facing Realities" (speech before the Harvard Club, March 13, 1937), *Vital Speeches of the Day* 3, no. 12 (April 1, 1937).

2. Marion Sanders, *Dorothy Thompson: A Legend in Her Time* (Boston: Houghton Mifflin, 1973), 204; Sinclair Lewis, *It Can't Happen Here* (Garden City, NY: Doubleday, Doran, 1935); Mark Schorer, *Sinclair Lewis: An American Life* (New York: McGraw-Hill, 1961), 607–612.

3. DT, "The Death of Democracies"; DT, "The Wrong Side of the Bed," On the Record [hereafter OTR], *NYHT*, December 3, 1937, 21; DT, "Our Ghostly Commonwealth," *SEP* 208 (July 27, 1935); "Dream Your Own Millions," *SEP* 208 (August 10, 1935); "Vitamins and the Green-plush Rabbit," *SEP* 208 (August 24, 1935).

4. JG, "A Blue-Eyed Tornado," *NYHT Magazine*, January 13, 1935, 6; JG, USA log, November 18, November 25, [1934].

5. Richard Kluger, *The Paper: The Life and Death of the New York Herald Tribune* (New York: Random House, 1986), 171–181, 286–289; Ronald Steel, *Walter Lippmann and the American Century* (New York: Vintage Books, 1981), 269–282; Michael Schudson, *Discovering the News: A Social History of American Newspapers* (New York: Basic Books, 1978), 144–160; Charles Fisher, *The Columnists* (New York: Howell, Soskin, 1944), 10–12; Lynn Gordon, "Why Dorothy Thompson Lost Her Job," *History of Education Quarterly* 34, no. 3 (Fall 1994): 285–290; Janice Radway, *A Feeling for Books* (Chapel Hill: University of North Carolina Press, 1997), 180–181.

6. Peter Kurth, *American Cassandra: The Life of Dorothy Thompson* (Boston: Houghton Mifflin, 1990), 218–219; Gordon, "Why Dorothy Thompson," 295–296. The president's wife, Eleanor Roosevelt, launched her unique column, My Day, on December 30, 1935.

7. DT, "The Corporations Tax Bill," OTR, *NYHT*, March 17, 1936, 21; Kurth, *American Cassandra*, 219; DT to Woollcott, May 6, 1936, Alexander Woollcott Papers, MS Am 1449 (1653), Houghton Library; DT to JG, July 1, August 4, 1936, Box 35, JG II.

8. Margaret Marshall, "Columnists on Parade," *The Nation*, February 26, 1938, 246, cites Thompson's column in 140 papers with 7.5 million subscribers, Lippmann's in 160 papers with 8 million. Columns of Eleanor Roosevelt,

Westbrook Pegler, David Lawrence, Heywood Broun, and Hugh Johnson each had between 3 and 6 million subscribers; *The Nation*, March 5, 1938, 273, 276; March 12, 1938, 300; May 21, 1938, 42.

9. Kurth, *American Cassandra*, 253–265; Sanders, *Dorothy Thompson*, 286–288.

10. DT, "It Can Happen Here," OTR, *NYHT*, May 28, 1936, 23; DT, "The Lunatic Fringe," OTR, *NYHT*, July 21, 1936, 17; July 23, 1936, 17A; see DT, "Unpublished Items in the Dies Report," OTR, *NYHT*, January 24, 1940.

11. DT, "Ruffled Grouse," OTR, *The Sun*, February 17, 1937, 13; DT, "Peace! It's Wonderful!" OTR, *NYHT*, May 3, 1937, 15.

12. David Holbrook Culbert, *News for Everyman* (Westport, CT: Greenwood Press, 1976), 15–17; Kurth, *American Cassandra*, 209–211. William Paley Center, NYC, offers public access to several of DT's broadcasts.

13. Kurth, *American Cassandra*, 224; "The Struggle between Press and Radio," in *The Newspaper and Society*, ed. George L. Bird and Frederic E. Merwin (New York: Prentice Hall, 1947), 538–559; T. K. Carskadon, "The Press-Radio War," *TNR* 86 (March 11, 1936): 132–135. Herman S. Hettinger, "Broadcasting in the U.S.," *Annals* 177 (January 1935): 1–14, found news occupying less than 1.5 percent of key stations' programming over one week (tested in 1934).

14. Kurth, *American Cassandra*, 232; Sanders, *Dorothy Thompson*, 224; John William Tebbel and Mary Ellen Zuckerman, *The Magazine in America, 1741–1990* (New York: Oxford University Press, 1991), 155–156; Don Wharton, "DT," *Scribner's*, May 1937, 9–10 (calling her "First Lady of American Journalism").

15. JVS, *Dorothy & Red* (Boston: Houghton Mifflin, 1963) [hereafter *D&R*], 255, 263; Schorer, *Sinclair Lewis*, 610. *It Can't Happen Here* was reviewed by John Chamberlain, *NYT*, October 21, 1935, 17; Benjamin Stolberg, *NYHT Book Review*, October 20, 1935; Lewis Gannett, *NYHT*, October 21, 1935, 3.

16. DT to SL, April 29, 1937, in JVS, *D&R*, 293–300 (quotations, 296–297). See Kurth, *American Cassandra*, 242–250; Schorer, *Sinclair Lewis*, 627–633, and quoting DeVoto's *We Accept with Pleasure*, 588.

17. DT, "To Live and Create Life," *LHJ* 54, no. 5 (May 1937): 12; cf. her diary, early November 1935, Box 59, DT-SYR; DT, "To the Girl Graduate," *LHJ* 54, no. 6 (June 1937): 12; DT, "If I Had a Daughter," *LHJ* 56, no. 9 (September 1939): 4, 41.

18. DT, "The Changing Status of Women," ts., Box 98, DT-SYR, delivered September 27, 1934. See "Roosevelt Sure Nation Has 'Both Feet on Ground' . . . Dorothy Thompson Condemns Fascism," *NYHT*, September 28, 1934, 1; DT, "The Married Woman's Right to Earn," *Equal Rights*, February 29, 1936, 411–412. Cf. Lois Scharf, *To Work and to Wed: Female Employment, Feminism, and the Great Depression* (Westport, CT: Greenwood Press, 1980).

19. DT, "Women at Work," OTR, *NYHT*, December 21, 1938, 14.

20. DT, introduction to Kurt Schuschnigg, *My Austria* (New York: Knopf, 1938), reprinted in DT, *Let the Record Speak* (Boston: Houghton Mifflin, 1939), 157; DT, "Fascism Marches On," OTR, *DBG*, November 8, 1937, 14; DT,

"Anti-Red Pact Likely to Be Signed in Rome Today: Fascist International," OTR, *The Scotsman*, November 6, 1937, 17; DT, "Wake Up to Live!" OTR, *NYHT*, March 16, 1938, 21; Richard J. Evans, *The Third Reich in Power, 1933–39* (New York: Penguin, 2005), 646–664.

21. Michaela Hoenicke Moore, *Know Your Enemy: The American Debate on Nazism, 1933–45* (Cambridge: Cambridge University Press, 2010), 41–77, esp. 45.

22. Kurth, *American Cassandra*, 298–301; Sanders, *Dorothy Thompson*, 247–248; Moore, *Know Your Enemy*, 72–73, summarizes polls of American attitudes toward Jews.

23. DT, "Lessons of Spain," OTR, *DBG*, April 19, 1937, 14; DT, "The Embargo against Loyalist Spain," OTR, *NYHT*, May 6, 1938; DT, "Intervene with Food," OTR, *DBG*, November 21, 1939, 21 (quotation); DT, "The Unneutrality Bill," OTR, *NYHT*, February 24, 1937, 21; "The Unneutrality Bill II," OTR, *NYHT*, February 26, 1937, 21; "The Unneutrality Bill III," OTR, *NYHT*, March 1, 1937, 15; DT, "The Liberal Spirit" (speech delivered November 18, 1937), *Vital Speeches of the Day* 4, no. 4 (December 1, 1937).

24. JVS, *D&R*, 261–263; JVS, *A Day of Battle* (New York: Literary Guild, 1938).

25. JVS, *D&R*, 285 (quotations), 286–288; "Roosevelts Give Dinner for 22," *WP*, February 25, 1938, X16; "Ocean Travelers" list, *NYT*, February 2, 1938, 16; March 12, 1938, 14.

26. Regarding Dinah Sheean, see "$1,000,000 Campaign for Refugees Planned," *NYT*, March 17, 1939, 11; "Drive Aids Spain's Exiles: Spanish Rescue Ship Campaign Opened by Mrs. Sheean," *NYT*, January 21, 1940, 31; "$3,000 Donated to Help Refugees Reach Mexico," *NYHT*, November 16, 1940, 4.

27. JVS, *Not Peace but a Sword* (New York: Doubleday, Doran, 1939), 269 (quotation), 42–80; "Vincent Sheean Sees Catalonia Rally for Republic's Last Stand," *NYHT*, April 3, 1938, 1; JVS, "Hour of Danger Has Barcelona Keyed to Fight," *NYHT*, April 25, 1938, 2; JVS, "Sheean Says Generals in Spain Guide Battles with Road Maps," *NYHT*, May 4, 1938, 10; Sebastian Balfour, *Deadly Embrace: Morocco and the Road to the Spanish Civil War* (Oxford: Oxford University Press, 2002).

28. JVS, "Loyalists Insist Franco is Halted and Still Believe They Will Win," *NYHT*, May 5, 1938, 1, and "Loyalist Spirit is High . . . ," *NYHT*, May 22, 1938, 8; "Enemy at its Gates . . . ," *NYHT*, May 24, 1938, 1; "Loyalist Spain Viewed as Getting Its Second Wind . . . ," *NYHT*, May 27, 1938, 6; Robert William Desmond, *Crisis and Conflict: World News Reporting between Two Wars, 1920–1940* (Iowa City: University of Iowa Press, 1982), 253.

29. JVS, *Not Peace*, 86, 233.

30. DS to Louis Fischer, July 4, 1938, Box 11, f. 19, Louis Fischer Papers, RBSC, Princeton University Library; JVS, "Good-bye, Vienna," *TNR* 76, no. 1239 (August 31, 1938): 98–99; JVS, "Austrian Jews Forced to 'Give' Wealth to Nazis," *NYHT*, July 7, 1938, 7A; JVS, "50,000 Jailed in Austria in 3½ Months

of Terror Leaving Nazis Supreme," *NYHT*, July 5, 1938, 1; JVS, "Wrath of Nazis in Austria Falls on Aristocrats," *NYHT*, July 6, 1938, 2; [editorial] "Cold Pogrom in Vienna," *NYT*, July 9, 1938, 12.

31. JVS, *Not Peace*, 200–234, 271–325 (quotation, 233); DT, "Obituary for Europe," OTR, *WP*, September 21, 1938, 11; DT, "'Peace'—And Crisis Begins!" OTR, *WP*, October 1, 1938, X9. See Evans, *Third Reich*, 665–679, and Kurth, *Cassandra*, 266–267.

32. Culbert, *News*, 70–83; James Rorty, "Radio Comes Through," *The Nation*, October 13, 1938, 372–374.

33. JVS, "Sudeten Uprising Quickly Crushed," *NYT*, September 24, 1938, 4; "Czechs in Prayer Preparing to Die," *NYT* September 29, 1938, 7; "Vincent Sheean Tells of Trip in Czech-Less Sudeten Area," *DBG*, October 4, 1938, 4; "Hitler's Grand Entry into Karlsbad Like a Super-Movie, Reports Sheean," *DBG*, October 5, 1938, 1; JVS, *Not Peace*, 326–363; JVS, "Spanish War Seen Near Its End," *NYT*, January 28, 1939, 5.

34. JVS, "The Doom and the Glory of Czecho-Slovakia," *NYHT*, May 14, 1939, H3.

35. "Sheean's Book Analyzes Current Europe," *Hartford Courant*, August 20, 1939, SM6; Barnet Nover, "Europe in the Year of Munich," *WP*, July 30, 1939, B10; R. L. Duffus, "A New Book by Vincent Sheean," *NYT*, July 30, 1939, BR1; Wilbur Needham, "Sheean Pens Graphic Report of Europe Today," *LA Times*, July 30, 1939, C6; "22 Books Top 100,000 Sales Mark in Year," *Ch T*, January 3, 1940, 18.

36. DS to Louis Fischer, February 15, February 17, 1939, Fischer Papers. Paul Preston, *We Saw Spain Die* (London: Constable, 2008), 213–262, profiles Fischer well.

37. DS to LF, March 21, 1939, February 15, 1939, April 10, 1939, Fischer Papers.

38. DT, "Refugees," OTR, *NYHT*, April 6, 1938, 21 (first quotation); DT, "Refugees: A World Problem," *Foreign Affairs* 16, no. 3 (April 1938): 375–387 (second quotation, 377); Kurth, *American Cassandra*, 280; DT, "The Nansen Committee Extended," OTR, *NYHT*, May 13, 1939, 19A.

39. Richard J. Evans, *The Coming of the Third Reich* (New York: Penguin, 2004), 580–592.

40. DT, Radio speech, November 14, 1938, in *Let the Record Speak*, 256–260.

41. DT, "To a Jewish Friend," OTR, *WP*, November 14, 1938; DT, "Give a Man a Chance," *WP*, November 16, 1938; JG, diary, November 15, 1938, Box 19; Kurth, *American Cassandra*, 281–284. See Journalists Defense Fund documents in DT correspondence, Box 35, JG II; Gerald Schwab, *The Day the Holocaust Began* (New York: Praeger, 1990); Anthony Read and David Fisher, *Kristallnacht* (New York: P. Bedrick, 1990); Jonathan Kirsch, *The Short, Strange Life of Herschel Grynszpan* (New York: Liveright, 2013).

42. Don Wharton, "DT," *Scribner's*, May 1937, 9–10; "Passionate Pundit," *Time* 32 (August 22, 1938); "Refugee Committee Honors Dorothy Thompson

at Dinner," *WP*, January 25, 1939, 5; "1,100 to Attend Dinner for Dorothy Thompson," *NYHT*, January 22, 1939.

43. Margaret Marshall, "Columnists on Parade," *The Nation*, February 26, 1938.

44. Sanders, *Dorothy Thompson*, 235–236; Kurth, *American Cassandra*, 286–289; DT, "To the Intolerant!" OTR, *NYHT*, February 22, 1939, 21; cf. Helene Cixous, "Laugh of the Medusa," *Signs* 1, no. 4 (Summer 1976): 875–893.

45. "Cartwheel Girl," *Time* 33 (June 12, 1939): 24; Kurth, *American Cassandra*, 258–259, 517n138; John Chamberlain, "Delilah of the Inkpot," *TNR*, September 27, 1939, 220–221 (second quotation); Margaret Case Harriman, "The It Girl," *New Yorker*, April 20, 1940, 24–30 (quotation, 24), April 27, 1940, 23–29.

46. DS to Leland Stowe, April 20, 1964, Leland Stowe Papers, Box 23, f. 4, WHS.

47. DT, "The Issue," OTR, *NYHT*, May 30, 1936, 13; Sheean correspondence and his Carnegie Hall speech in League of American Writers records, Box 4, Bancroft Library, UC Berkeley; JVS, *Not Peace*, 363; Franklin Folsom, *Days of Anger, Days of Hope: A Memoir of the League of American Writers 1937–42* (Niwot: University of Colorado Press, 1994), 82–85, 58n11; Sam Smiley, "Friends of the Party: The American Writers' Congresses," *Southwest Review* 54, no. 3 (Summer 1969): 8.

48. "To All Active Supporters of Democracy and Peace," released August 14, published in *Soviet Russia Today* 8, no. 5 (September 1939): 24–25, 28, http://www.marxisthistory.org/history/usa/parties/cpusa/1939/0814-openletter.pdf; JVS, "Brumaire: I: The Soviet Union as a Fascist State," *TNR* 101, no. 1301 (November 8, 1939): 7–9; "Brumaire: II," *TNR* 101, no. 1302 (November 15, 1939): 104–106; "Mr. Sheean and His Critics" [letter to editor], *TNR* 101, no. 1306 (December 13, 1939): 232.

49. "Gallup and Fortune Polls," *Public Opinion Quarterly*, March 1940, 102, 108.

50. DT, "Neutrality Today," OTR, *WP*, September 18, 1939, 7. See news articles without byline, "Arms Embargo Viewpoints," *WP*, September 22, 1939, 13; "American Peace Efforts," *WP*, October 11, 1939, 11; "Sheean Favors U.S. Entry into War at Once," *DBG*, October 16, 1939, 11; "Munich Pact Led to War, Says Vincent Sheean," *DBG*, October 20, 1939, 5. Cf. Murray Bloom, "Prophets Not Without Honoraria: The Lecture Business," *NYT*, December 22, 1940, 87.

51. David Reynolds, "1940: Fulcrum of the Twentieth Century?" *International Affairs* 66, no. 2 (1990): 325–350.

52. Reynolds, "1940," 334–335; Stetson Conn and Byron Fairchild, *The Framework of Hemisphere Defense* (Washington, DC: Center of Military History, US Army, 1989), chap. 2, "The Crisis of 1940," https://history.army.mil/books/wwii/Framework/ch02.htm.

53. JVS, "English Villagers on Channel Calm," *NYT*, May 28, 1940, 4; JVS, "Stout British Hearts Seen Best Insurance against Nazi Legions," *DBG*,

August 4, 1940, B9; JVS, "Foreigners See War for U.S. with Dictators," *Atlanta Constitution*, June 16, 1940, 8A (quotation); JVS, "Southeast Towns in England Are Hit," *NYT*, August 17, 1940, 7. He wrote four articles on Britain at war for the *SEP*, published in the issues of December 21, 1940, July 12, August 2, and August 23, 1941; *War Letters from Britain*, ed. Diana Forbes-Robertson and Roger W. Straus Jr. (New York: G. P. Putnam, 1941); "Book Notes," *NYHT*, November 11, 1940, 13. Dinah raised money for war relief in Britain in 1940 and 1941, for example, "British Children's Benefit Planned at York Harbor," *NYHT*, August 18, 1940, D12; "More Nurseries Urged for Defense Areas," *NYT*, November 14, 1941, 20.

54. Edward R. Murrow, *This Is London* (New York: Simon & Schuster, 1941), 158–159; Culbert, *News*, 183–190; JVS, "London Raid Havoc Awes Witnesses," *NYT*, September 9, 1940, 3; JVS, *Between the Thunder and the Sun* (New York: Random House, 1943), 210–236.

55. DT, "The Presidency," OTR, *NYHT*, October 9, 1940, 27; Sanders, *Dorothy Thompson*, 264–271.

56. Gordon, "Why Dorothy Thompson," 282n3; DT, "The Axis and the Campaign," OTR, *WP*, October 14, 1940, 9; DT, "The Axis and the Campaign," OTR, *NYHT*, October 18, 1940, 23A; [editorial] "The Axis and the Campaign," *NYHT*, October 18, 1940, 26; letters to editor, *NYHT*, October 10–18, 1940; Kurth, *American Cassandra*, 324–326.

57. Gordon, "Why Dorothy Thompson," 298, 299n36; Kurth, *American Cassandra*, 331–332. In 1944, she campaigned for FDR again; DT to Robert Sherwood, October 17, October 27, 1944, August 22, 1947, Robert Sherwood Papers, bMS Am 1947 (811), Houghton Library.

58. "Miss Thompson to Post," *NYT*, March 14, 1941, 19; Gordon, "Why Dorothy Thompson," 281–282.

59. For example, DT, "Col. Lindbergh and Propaganda," OTR, *WP*, September 20, 1939, 11; DT, "Col. Lindbergh's Imperialism," OTR, *WP*, October 23, 1939, 7; DT, "Lindbergh and the Nazi Program," OTR, *DBG*, April 25, 1941, 22; DT, "Charles A. Lindbergh, Superman," OTR, *Globe & Mail* (Toronto) [*G&M*], April 30, 1941, 6; DT, "Mr. Lindbergh and the Facts," OTR, *DBG*, September 17, 1941, 16; DT, "Lindbergh's Confession," OTR, *G&M*, November 3, 1941, 15; on Coughlin, DT, "How Long Then, Cataline?" OTR, *WP*, January 17, 1940; DT, "Unpublicized Items in the Dies Report," OTR, *NYHT*, January 24, 1940, 21. See Lynne Olson, *Those Angry Days: Roosevelt, Lindbergh, and America's Fight over World War II, 1939–1941* (New York: Random House, 2013).

60. DT, "On Warmongering," OTR, *DBG*, April 21, 1941, 12. "Effigy of Writer Seized in Capital," *NYT*, February 24, 1941, 7; "Peace Pickets Tie Up Traffic," *LA Times*, March 25, 1941, 2; Frank Lingdon [chairman of the May 6 event] to HFA, April 9, 1941, HFA Papers, Box 62, f. 1; "3000 Hear Dorothy Thompson Ask U.S. Be Put on War Footing," *NYHT*, May 7, 1941, 10 (quotations); "Miss Thompson Honored by N.Y. Gathering," *DBG*, May 7, 1941, 5;

"Dorothy Thompson Asks a New Society," *NYT*, May 7, 1941, 28; Kurth, *American Cassandra*, 328–330; Sanders, *Dorothy Thompson*, 272–274.

61. Kurth, *American Cassandra*, 335–337.

62. JVS, *Between the Thunder*, 401–402. Sheean's reporting from the Far East appeared in the *NYHT*, October 20, 24, November 11, 12, 20, 21, 23, 27, 28, 1941.

63. Kurth, *American Cassandra*, 341; DT, "This War and the Common Sense of Women," *LHJ* 59, no. 4 (February 1942): 6, 129; see DT, "After the President's Speech," OTR, *G&M*, December 12, 1941, 6; DT, January 2, 1942, diary entry quoted in JVS, *D&R*, 317, and see 300–310; Kurth, *American Cassandra*, 337–343.

CHAPTER 10: WAR OUTSIDE AND WAR INSIDE

1. Matthew Sweet, *West End Front: Wartime Secrets of London's Grand Hotels* (London: Faber, 2011), 89–95; Michael Fullilove, *Rendezvous with Destiny* (New York: Penguin, 2013), 171 (Beaton quotation); JG, diary [orig.], October 7, November 7–14, November 27, 1941, Box 19, JG II. Gunther's diaries exist in original form [orig.] and in typed expurgated versions that I am labeling [ts.]. Lee Miller Penrose letters to JG, folder P, Box 35, JG II, and JG to Lee Miller, May 10, 1945, in the Lee Miller Archives, Muddles Green, Chiddingly, E. Sussex, United Kingdom, suggest their relationship began before 1941.

2. JG, ts. diary, April 13, [1936], Box 19, JG II. Given the close timing, he may have literally echoed "Reflective Reporter," *Time* 27, no. 13 (March 30, 1936).

3. JG, *Inside Asia* (New York: Harper, 1939) [henceforth *Asia*], ix; see JG, "Notes on talks with political figures," Box 2, JG II.

4. FFG, Asia trip notes, ts. beginning October 30, [1937], f. 221, FFG-SL. JG, *A Fragment of Autobiography* (New York: Harper & Row, 1962), 24–32, claims twenty-four countries, but his Asia diary 1937–1938, Box 19, JG II, and Frances's Asia trip notes indicate only fourteen or fifteen. JG's Asia diary notes "Total trip cost" for hotels and transportation, $15,605.62. An example of his dozen or more NANA articles is "People of Hankow Take War in Stride," *NYT*, May 5, 1938, 12.

5. FFG, August 31, [1937], diary/daybook for 1937 [a preprinted daybook that FFG used as a diary, ignoring printed dates and entering her own], f. 7, and February 13, [1936], diary of 1935–1936, f. 6, FFG-SL.

6. FFG diaries of mid-1930s, folders 6, 7, and 8, FFG-SL; FFG to JG, September 2, 1936, Box 23, JG II; FFG, "Another Year," *Story* 10 (1937): 74–85; JG, Green notebook II ts., August 1931, Box 2, for "Penelope" comment also in JG, London diary, January 31, 1935, Box 19, JG II. FFG's papers at SL abound with research and drafts.

7. JG to FFG, September 1, 1936, f. 174; postcard postmarked September 7, 1936, f. 173; JG to FFG, September 6, [1936], f. 174, FFG-SL; JG to FFG, scrawled note from Hotel Schloss Velden [September? 1936], Box 23, JG II.

8. FFG, February 13, [1936], diary, 1935–1936 (first quotation, "ridiculous"), f. 6; all others, FFG, August 31, [1937], diary/daybook for 1937, f. 7, FFG-SL.

9. FFG, April 7, [1938], diary/daybook for 1937, for quotations.

10. FFG, November 5, November 10, [1937], FFG diary/daybook for 1937 (quotation); FFG Asia trip notes, ts. beginning October 30, [1937]; see Carolyn Burke, *Lee Miller: A Life* (New York: Knopf, 2005); and Andrew Humphries's blog post, "Lee Miller Invades the Long Bar," Egypt in the Golden Age of Travel, January 29, 2012, http://grandhotelsegypt.com/?p=260.

11. JG, Asia diary, Box 19.

12. FFG, November 15, November 16, [1937], diary/daybook for 1937 (quotations here and in previous paragraphs); FFG, Asia trip notes; JG, *Asia*, 546–559 (quotation, 559); FFG, December 1, December 5, diary/daybook for 1937. Edward Thompson, "Mr. Gunther as Guide," *The Observer*, July 9, 1939, 7, criticized Gunther's treatment of Palestine.

13. FFG, January 26, [1938], diary/daybook for 1937.

14. FFG, April 1, 2, 4, 7, [1938], diary/daybook for 1937; JG, *Asia*, 188, 205.

15. FFG, January 20 [1938], diary/daybook for 1937.

16. See FFG to "my dear Nehru" (apparently not sent), [1939], describing their apartment, f. 318, FFG-SL; JG diary, November 13, 14, 19, 1938, Box 19, JG II; Richard Rovere, "Inside," *New Yorker*, August 23, 1947, 31–32.

17. JG, diary, October 31, November 9, November 13, November 18, [1938].

18. JG, diary, November 10, 1938; see DT, "Women and Freedom in Our Society," *Vital Speeches of the Day* 11, no. 6 (December 16, 1935): 154–155; and "Dorothy Thompson Asks a New Society," *NYT*, May 7, 1941, 28; Peter Kurth, *American Cassandra* (Boston: Little, Brown, 1990), 328–330.

19. JG, diary, November 11, 12, 15 (quotation), 18 (quotation), [1938].

20. JG, diary, November 11, 21, 22, 23, [1938]; *Jo Davidson: Spanish Portraits* [exhibition catalogue] (New York: Georgian Press, [1938]; JG, *Fragment*, 27.

21. JG, *Asia*, 574; JG, Asia diary, lists these "basic questions."

22. JG, *Asia*, 344, 408, 127, 181, 183.

23. JG, *Fragment*, 29–30; JG, *Asia*, 572–575.

24. Charles Poore, "Books of the Times," *NYT*, June 8, 1939, 34; Norman Cousins picked up the word "guntherize" in "The World Today in Books," *Current History*, July 1939, 2. Rodney Gilbert, "Gunther Introduces His Readers to Asia," *NYHT*, June 11, 1939, 11 (quotation); W. A. D., "Political Tour through Asia," *G&M*, June 24, 1939, 11; "Insider: John Gunther Writes of Men and of Masses in Teeming Asia," *Newsweek*, June 12, 1939, 40; Barnet Nover, "The Continent of Complexities," *WP*, June 18, 1939, B8; Wilbur Needham, "Gunther Paints Clear Picture of Asiatic Chaos," *LA Times*, June 25, 1939, C6. Negative reviewers, harsh on Gunther's treatment of India and Palestine, were Edward Thompson, "Mr. Gunther as Guide," *The Observer*, July 9, 1939, 7, and C. I., "Asiatic Panorama: Mr. Gunther Takes a Bird's-Eye View," *Times of India*, August 11, 1939, 4. "Best Non-Fiction of 1939 Selected," *NYT*, January 18,

1940, 21; "39 Key Books Listed, 7 of 10 by Americans," *NYHT*, January 18, 1940, 19. *Inside Asia* stayed on the *NYT* or *Publishers Weekly* best-seller list for a total of fifty-six weeks, while *Inside Europe* had been on one or the other eighty weeks; Keith L. Justice, *Bestseller Index* (Jefferson, NC: McFarland & Co., 1998), 136.

25. JG, diary, November 15, 16, [1938]; Dan Golenpaul, ed., *Information Please!* (New York: Simon & Schuster, 1939), and *Information Please!* (New York: Random House, 1940); Joan Shelley Rubin, "'Information, Please!' Culture and Expertise in the Interwar Period," *American Quarterly* 35 (Winter 1983): 505–517.

26. JG, ts. diary, July 19, 1942, Box 19, JG II; JG to FFG, July 2, July 13, [1939]; JG to FFG, August 8, [1939], f. 174; JG to FFG, September 5, [1939] (quotation), and other letters, f. 173, FFG-SL. Radio listings in daily newspapers, such as the *NYT*'s "Today on the Radio," show Gunther's broadcasts.

27. Ken Cuthbertson, *Inside: The Biography of John Gunther* (Chicago: Bonus Books, 1992), 184–185; JG, "Hitler's Tactics Stiffen British," *NYT*, September 3, 1939, 12; JG, "Finds Neutrals Hard Put and No World War—Yet," *DBG*, September 9, 1939, 8.

28. Cables to JG, September 11, September 14, 1939, and JG to FFG cable, September 19, [1939], f. "summer 1939 Frances-John letters," Box 23; H. R. Knickerbocker to JG, n.d. (quotation), Box 26; JG, Green notebook II, ts., on Knick, JG II.

29. JG to [Dr.] Horsley, February 2, 1945, "Love Affair Crisis" folder, Box 2, JG II, offers his account of the affair; Ronald Steel, *Walter Lippmann and the American Century* (New York: Vintage Books, 1981), 343–367.

30. FFG, December 14, [1937], diary/daybook for 1937; JG, diary, [orig.], November 15, December 11, 1939, Box 19, JG II.

31. JG, ts. diary, October 31, November 15, [1939].

32. JG, ts. diary, fall 1939, passim; JG, 1940 diary [orig.], Box 19, JG II. See Miriam Hopkins correspondence, 1940–1945, Box 22, JG II. Polly Adler wrote a memoir, *A House Is Not a Home* (New York: Rinehart, 1953).

33. JG, 1940 diary [orig.], "Virginia Beach June 1940."

34. JG, *Fragment*, 35–37.

35. JG, diary [orig.], February 17–October 19, 1941, entries for February 25, May 8, 9, 10, 28, June 9, 10, 11, 12, 14, 15, 17. Box 19; and see Leonora Shinasi Hornblower correspondence, 1942–1948, Box 22, JG II.

36. JG, ts. diary, March 29, May 8, July 17, August 7, August 8, August 18, August 29, 1941; diary [orig.] August 22, 1941, regarding Polly's, Box 19, JG II.

37. JG, ts. diary, September 1, 2, 3, 11, 1941.

38. JG, *Inside Latin America* (New York: Harper & Bros., 1941), esp. 5–6, 25–27, 411–422.

39. "Books—Authors," *NYT*, October 3, 1941, 20; Ralph Thompson, "Books of the Times" (first quotation), *NYT*, October 29, 1941, 21; William Lytle Schurz, "Loving Our Neighbors" (second quotation), *WP*, December 7, 1941, L10. See Lewis Gannett, "Books and Things," *NYHT*, October 29, 1941, 23;

Joseph Barnes, "Big League Reporter Covers Latin America," *NYHT*, November 2, 1941, G3; Mercer Cook, "The Whiter Latin-American Countries Are the More Dangerous," *Afro-American*, December 20, 1941, 24; Justice, *Bestseller Index*, 136; "Authorities on Latin America Criticize Book by John Gunther," *Christian Science Monitor*, May 5, 1942, 8, and the statement, ts., in Gunther correspondence, Box 33, HFA Papers. For JG's self-defense against criticism, see JG, *Fragment*, 36–40.

40. JG, diary [orig.], October 7, passim October–November 1941; see Lara Fiegel, *The Love-Charm of Bombs* (London: Bloomsbury, 2013); Carolyn Burke, *Lee Miller: A Life* (New York: Knopf, 2005).

41. JG, London diary, December 1941 [orig.], Box 19, JG II; Ken Cuthbertson, *Inside: The Biography of John Gunther* (Chicago: Bonus Books, 1992), 217, on his passage.

42. JG, ts. diary, January 1, March 6, 1942, Box 19, JG II.

43. JG, ts. diary, February 24, July 19, November 24, [1942] (quotations), and passim; Marion K. Sanders, *Dorothy Thompson: A Legend in Her Time* (Boston: Houghton Mifflin, 1973), 285–288.

44. FFG, "Victory or Victorianism," *Common Sense* 11 (February 1942); "If India Loses, We Lose," *Common Sense* 11 (October 1942), and "England Without India," *Common Sense* 12 (January 1943); she reviewed five books on India in *TNR*, January 10, 1944, 60–61. See FFG to HFA, November 11, 1940, urging American liberals to join British liberals in endorsing Indian independence, in Gunther correspondence, Box 33, HFA Papers; and clippings in FFG f. 229, FFG-SL. Her book *Revolution in India* (New York: Island Press, 1944) highlighted political psychology, an angle she developed while taking classes in international relations at Yale University. On her Irgun work, Alex Rafaeli (also called Hadani), claimed in *Dream and Action: The Story of My Life* (Jerusalem: A. Rafaeli, 1993), 108, 112–113, that he relied greatly on FFG in his work raising funds in the United States 1940–1942. FFG's own autobiographical notes included the line, "Irgun organizes at 300 CPW [the Gunthers' address]—1940"; f. 100, FFG-SL.

45. JG, ts. diary, 1942, passim; quotation, January 14, 1942, said by John Whitaker.

46. JG, ts. diary, April 16 to September 30, 1942, passim; "John Gunther to Sub for Swing for Three Weeks," *Ch T*, March 8, 1942, NW4. Gunther worked closely on "Why We Fight" with Russian-born film director Anatole Litvak, who, coincidentally, had been married briefly to Miriam Hopkins.

47. JG, ts. diary, September 30, [1942]; "Vincent Sheean a Captain," *WP*, May 28, 1942, 2. See JVS, *Between the Thunder and the Sun* (New York: Random House, 1943), 405–422; Capt. J. V. Sheean, AAF, to Hamilton Fish Armstrong, June 4, [1942], Box 57, folder 18, HFA Papers; JVS letters to Dinah Sheean, 1943–1944 (v-mail), Vincent Sheean Papers, WHS, f. 1, Box 1.

48. JG, ts. diary, September 30, October 1, November 4, 6, 7, 18 (Willkie quotation), 1942.

49. Jay Pridmore, *John Gunther: Inside Journalism* [exhibition catalog] (University of Chicago Library, 1990), 33–34; Cuthbertson, *Inside*, 228–241.

50. See DT, "The Problem Child of Europe," *Foreign Affairs* 18, no. 3 (April 1940): 389–412.

51. Kurth, *American Cassandra*, 360–362, including Goebbels quotation; DT, *Listen, Hans* (Boston: Houghton Mifflin, 1942); see DT, "Conditions Existing in Germany Can Start Revolution," *DBG*, December 21, 1942, 10. Reviews included John Chamberlain, "Books of the Times," *NYT*, November 28, 1942, 11; George Shuster, "Listen, Germany! Miss Thompson Speaking," *NYHT*, November 29, 1942, F7; Lewis Gannett, "Books and Things," *NYHT*, November 30, 1942, 11; Malcolm Cowley, "But Listen, Dorothy," *TNR*, December 28, 1942, 861.

52. DT, "Germany Must Be Salvaged," *American Mercury* 56 (June 1943): 647–662; DT, "What Will Happen When Nazism Collapses?" *American Mercury* 57 (September 1943): 263–271; DT, "The Only Road to Peace," *American Mercury* 57, no. 240 (December 1943): 647–656; Kurth, *American Cassandra*, 363–370. Michaela Hoenicke Moore, *Know Your Enemy: The American Debate on Nazism, 1933–1945* (Cambridge: Cambridge University Press, 2010), 177–321, is thorough; see also Marjorie Lamberti, "German Antifascist Refugees in America and the Public Debate on 'What Should Be Done with Germany after Hitler,'" *Central European History* 40 (2007): 279–305, regarding American Friends of German Freedom, in which Thompson served alongside Reinhold Niebuhr.

53. Carey Longmire, "God's Angry Woman," *Collier's* 115 (June 23, 1945): 22, 75; "Dorothy Thompson, Cosmic Force," in Charles Fisher, *The Columnists* (New York: Howell, Soskin, 1944), 16–51 (quotations, 16, 26, 27).

54. DT, "Germany Must Be Salvaged"; Kurth, *American Cassandra*, 369–372, 523–524n31.

55. Kurth, *American Cassandra*, 347–357; Sanders, *Dorothy Thompson*, 295–298, 305–306; DT to HFA, May 24, 1943, September 5, 1958 (quotation), HFA Papers, Box 62, f. 1; DT to Woollcott, June 20, 1942, Alexander Woollcott Papers, f. 1653, Houghton MS Am 1449; DT, "My Husband, Maxim Kopf," *LHJ* 75, no. 10 (October 1958): 11ff.; Sheean, *D&R*, 325.

56. JVS, diary, May 25, 1944, Sheean Papers, Box 1, f. 38, WHS.

57. The Gunthers' divorce was decreed on March 7, 1944; telegram from JG, Las Vegas to FFG, Hotel Taft, New Haven, f. 172, FFG-SL; JG diary, June 6, [1943], Box 19; H. R. Knickerbocker to JG, March 25, 1945, JG to [Dr.] Horsley [Gantt], February 2, 1945, "Love Affair Crisis" folder, Box 2, JG II.

CHAPTER 11: THE AGE OF ADJUSTMENT

1. DT, "From the Holy Land," *LHJ* 62, no. 7 (July 1945): 6; DT, "Self-Destruction," OTR, *G&M*, January 9, 1946, 6; DT, "Return to Principle," *Commonweal*, May 10, 1946, 86; DT, "For a New Foreign Policy," OTR, *G&M*, October 11, 1946, 6; JVS to JG, July 21, [1946,] (describing the previous

summer), Box 35, JG II; Peter Kurth, *American Cassandra: The Life of Dorothy Thompson* (Boston: Little, Brown, 1990), 376–377; Richard Evans, "The Other Horror," *TNR*, June 12, 2007.

2. DT, "The Lesson of Dachau," *LHJ* 62, no. 9 (September 1945): 6.

3. DT, "Mass Murder, Inc.," OTR, *G&M*, September 4, 1944, 6.

4. DT, *I Speak Again as a Christian* (pamphlet published by the Christian Council on Palestine and American Palestine Committee, New York, 1945, reprinting her speech of January 11, 1945); Kurth, *American Cassandra*, 382–385.

5. DT to Ted [Thackrey, the *Post*'s editor], November 3, 1946, Box 36, DT-SYR; JG, diary, October 16, [1939,] for DT's comment about changing one's mind. See DT, "Postwar and the Middle East," OTR, *G&M*, May 14, 1945, 6; "Loss of Dr. Weizman," OTR, *G&M*, January 17, 1947, 6; "Machiavelli Wins," OTR, *G&M*, May 19, 1947, 6; "Who Is Doing It?" OTR, *G&M*, September 12, 1947, 6; Kurth, *American Cassandra*, 422–433; Murray Weisgal, *So Far: An Autobiography* (New York: Random House, 1971), 197–200. Cf. David A. Hollinger, *Protestants Abroad* (Princeton, NJ: Princeton University Press, 2017), 117–138.

6. DT, "Self-Destruction"; "Return to Principle" ("apocalyptic"); "For a New Foreign Policy"; DT, "That They Do Not Die in Vain," *LHJ* 60:1 (January 1943), 6, 83; DT, "If No One Else, We the Mothers," *LHJ* 64, no. 7 (July 1947): 11–12; "We Must Find a Radical Solution for the Abolition of War," *LHJ* 64, no. 9 (September 1947): 11–12.

7. DT, "What the World Needs Most," *LHJ* 55 (November 1938): 4; DT, "Thoughts After Lippmann and Roosevelt," OTR, *NYHT*, January 9, 1939, 13; DT, "Crisis of Christianity," OTR, *G&M*, December 23, 1942, 6 (quotation); DT, "There Is a Tide," OTR, *WP*, December 27, 1939, 7 (quotation); DT, "Recent Conversions," *Commonweal*, March 29, 1946, 197; DT, "The Moral Crisis," OTR, *G&M*, February 26, 1947, 6; DT, "Prayer for Christian Rebirth," *DBG*, December 24, 1952, 10.

8. JVS, journal vol. 1, August 7, [1945], vol. 2, September 10, [1946], Box 1, Vincent Sheean Papers, WHS. (All JVS 1940s journals cited are in this location.) JVS, *This House Against This House* (New York: Random House, 1946), 411–413 ("no time"); see JVS, "Personal Opinion: Journalism Regnant," and "Personal Opinion: Division and Condominium," *United Nations World*, May 1947, 42–43, and November 1947, 49–50; JVS, journal vol. 3, February 19, 1947, notes "USA and USSR, the Gog and Magog of my early novel."

9. JVS to Freda Kirchwey, telegram, April 8, 1946, f. 4103, *Nation* records, Houghton Library; JVS, journal, April 14, 1946; "Movie-Inquiry Witnesses Are Guests at Rally," *NYHT*, November 3, 1947, 9; "10 Movie Figures to Fight Charges," *NYT*, November 3, 1947, 19; DT, "Status of the Communist Party"; DT, "Ike Small Comfort to Admirers of Twenties," *Atlanta Statesman*, January 12, 1954, 4; DT, "What Is Subversion?" OTR, *G&M*, March 10, 1954, 6; DT, "The Other Side of McCarthyism?" OTR, *DBG*, March 23, 1954, 14; Kurth, *American Cassandra*, 391–392.

10. DT, "The Status of the Communist Party," OTR, *G&M*, March 31, 1947, 6; DT, ts. loose diary pages in f. "Diaries 1945–49," Box 59 (quotation); JVS, journal vol. 1, January 10, January 17, February 6, 1946, vol. 3, January–March 1947, passim.

11. JVS, *This House*; Homer Metz, "First-Person Journalism," *Christian Science Monitor*, March 20, 1946, 20 (quotation); Robert Neville, "Mr. Sheean's Opinions," *NYT*, March 31, 1946, 124; Orville Prescott, "Books of the Times," *NYT*, March 27, 1946, 22; Walter Mills, "'Personal History' on Our Recent Battlefields," *NYHT*, March 31, 1946, F1; Lewis Gannett, "Books and Things," *NYHT*, March 27, 1946, 21; John Goodbody, "Sheean's Eye-View of World War II," *DBG*, April 4, 1946, 15; Percy Winner, "No Longer Lost," *TNR*, April 1, 1946, 450–452.

12. JVS, journal vol. 2, September18, [1946]; see Gail Williams O'Brien, *The Color of the Law* (Chapel Hill: University of North Carolina Press, 1999), on the trial.

13. JVS, "Present-Day American Tragedy," *NYHT*, September 27, 1946, 18; JVS, "A Social Question Outlaws Law," *NYHT*, October 1, 1946, 26; JVS, journal, October 22, 1946 (quotations); JVS, "Lawrenceburg Verdict Assessed, Reaffirmation of Americanism," *NYHT*, October 7, 1946, 11. See "Columbia Defense Cries 'Persecution,'" *NYT*, October 4, 1946, 12; Walter White, "People, Politics and Place: Incredible Acquittal," *Chicago Defender*, October 19, 1946, 15.

14. DT to JG, March 28, 1947, Box 35, JG II; see William Shirer to DT, April 9, 1947, Box 28, DT-SYR; JVS, "Personal Opinion: Journalism Regnant."

15. John Gunther Papers 1935–1967 [separate from JG II], Box 30, f. 1, RBSC, University of Chicago, contains a rough outline and table of contents sent to people for comment and forty replies; JG, *A Fragment of Autobiography* (New York: Harper & Row, 1961), 43–60; JG, *Inside U.S.A.* [hereafter *IUSA*] (New York: Harper & Bros., 1947), xiii–xvi.

16. Richard Rovere, "Inside," *New Yorker*, August 23, 1947, 31.

17. JG, *IUSA*, xii–iii, 907, 909. Reviews include Richard Watts Jr., "It's a Big Country, Mister," *TNR*, June 2, 1947, 25–26 (quotation); Ben Ray Redman, "John Gunther's USA," *American Mercury*, August 1947, 238–244; Sterling North, "Gunther's Vast USA Will Rile Whole Regions But Comfort a Nation," *WP*, June 1, 1947, S11; Jonathan Daniels, "The Meaning of America," *Saturday Review*, May 31, 1947, 9; Robert Bendiner, "Report on America," *The Nation*, June 14, 1947, 716–718; Henry Steele Commager, "Mr. Gunther Surveys the USA," *NYT*, June 1, 1947, BR1. See individuals' letters remarking errors, in postpublication correspondence, Subseries 11, Box 32 & 33, John Gunther Papers 1935–1967.

18. JG, diary, November–December 1946; Ken Cuthbertson, *Inside* (Chicago: Bonus Books, 1992), 294–296. Gunther had met Jane when he briefly cohosted a radio program with John Vandercook, her husband then.

19. JG, *Death Be Not Proud* (New York: Harper & Bros., 1949); JG, diary, July 1947, Box 21, JG II.

20. JVS, journal vol. 3, August 13, August 19, August 27, [1947].

21. JG, "Vermont, Wed. July 30–Wed. August 6"; JG, July–September 1947 diary 2, Box 21, JG II; JVS to FFG, August 5, 1947, f. 229, FFG-SL. Just after Maine senator Margaret Chase Smith bravely denounced Joseph McCarthy, Thompson wrote her urging her to run for president, saying, "A little more matriarchy is what the world needs, and I know it. Period." DT to Margaret Chase Smith, June 5, 1950, Box 37; see material about an organization DT favored called W.O.M.A.N., Boxes 37 and 38, DT-SYR. JVS published a little-remarked article, "A Woman for President," *Look*, September 27, 1949, 23–25.

22. JVS, "Victory to Mahatma Gandhi," *Holiday* 3, no. 6 (June 1948): 81–87.

23. DT, "Vincent Sheean Relates Own Spiritual Growth," *DBG*, July 25, 1949, 10; JVS, *This House*, 373–374 (on FDR); JVS to Leigh White, July 20, [1947,] and September 25, [1947] (on Goering), Box 1, Sheean Papers, SYR.

24. JVS, *Lead, Kindly Light* (New York: Random House, 1949), 168–169; JVS, journal vol. 3, November 18–late December, 1947.

25. JVS, "122 Killed as Pakistan Capital Has First Communal Violence," *NYHT*, January 9, 1948, 6; JVS, "The Pakistan Case," *NYHT*, January 16, 1948, 22.

26. JVS, "Prime Minister Nehru," *TNR*, October 10, 1949, 11–13.

27. JVS, journal vol. 3, January 15–19 (quotation, January 19), 1948.

28. JVS, journal vol. 3, January 26, [1948].

29. JVS, journal vol. 3, January 30, 1948; JVS, *Lead, Kindly Light*, 194–195.

30. JVS, journal vol. 3, February 6–14, 1948; Edgar Snow, "The Message of Gandhi," *SEP* 220, no. 39 (March 27, 1948): 24–25; JVS, *Lead, Kindly Light*, 203–208; DT to JVS, February 15, 1948, Box 27, DT-SYR.

31. JVS, "A Disciple from the West Records the Last Lessons Taught by Gandhi," *WP*, February 15, 1949, B2; JVS, "Victory to Mahatma Gandhi," *Holiday*; JVS, "Gandhi: He Obeyed the Inner Voice," *NYT*, September 12, 1948, BR1; JVS, "We Must Find a Faith—or Perish," *Maclean's* [Toronto], October 1, 1948, 12, 57–58.

32. Ralph Thompson, "In and Out of Books," *NYT*, August 14, 1949; see DT, "The Atomic Bomb and God's Peace," OTR, *G&M*, November 28, 1945, 6; Robert Wuthnow, *Inventing American Religion* (New York: Oxford University Press, 2015), and *The Restructuring of American Religion* (Princeton, NJ: Princeton University Press, 1988), 14–20, 35–50; cf. Kevin Kruse, *One Nation Under God* (New York: Basic Books, 2015).

33. Keith Justice, *Bestseller Index* (Jefferson, NC: McFarland, 1998), 136, 277; JG, "This I Believe," *DBG*, July 25, 1954, B2. See items in f. 18, f. 60, f. 67, FFG-SL. Donne wrote, "Death, be not proud, though some have called thee / Mighty and dreadful, for thou art not so. / For those whom thou think'st thou dost overthrow / Die not, poor Death: nor yet canst thou kill me."

34. JG, *Fragment*, 69–95. See his *Behind the Curtain* (1949), *Roosevelt in Retrospect* (1950), *The Riddle of MacArthur* (1951), *Eisenhower: The Man and the Symbol* (1952), *Inside Africa* (1955), *Inside Russia Today* (1958), *Taken at the*

Flood: The Story of Albert D. Lasker (1960), *Inside Europe Today* (1961), all published in New York by Harper & Bros.; on parties, Marcia Davenport, unpublished ts. on John Gunther, Box 9, JG II.

35. DT to JVS, February 28, 1948, Box 27, DT-SYR; DS to Leland Stowe, June 27, August 25, 1949; DS to Leland Stowe and Dolly, October 12, 1949, Leland Stowe Papers, Box 23, f. 4, WHS; "Sheean Re-weds Ex-Wife," *NYT*, December 18, 1949; JVS to HFA, March 30, 1950.

36. See DS to Leland Stowe (and Dollika), letters 1949–1960, Box 23, f. 4, Stowe Papers; JVS to DT, November 22, December 19, 1952; DS to DT, May 27, 1951, January 7, December 29, 1952; JVS, "Memorandum for Dorothy," August 11, 1953, Box 27, DT-SYR; JVS, *The Indigo Bunting: A Memoir of Edna St. Vincent Millay* (New York: Harper & Bros., 1951); JVS, *First and Last Love* (New York: Random House, 1956).

37. JVS to HFA, September 28, [1950], Box 57, f. 17, HFA Papers; JVS, "The People of Ceylon and Their Politics," *Foreign Affairs* 28 (October 1949): 68–74; "The Buddhism That Was India," *Foreign Affairs* 29 (January 1951): 287–299; "The Case for India," *Foreign Affairs* 30 (October 1951): 787–790; JVS to DT, April 30, 1955, Box 27, DT-SYR.

38. JVS to Nehru, April 22, 1948, August 22, 1949, Box 1, Sheean Papers, SYR. See carbons of JVS to Soong Ching-ling, November 7, 1950, and of JVS cablegram to Nehru, December 27, 1953 (beginning "Your insufferable arrogance and bad temper have alienated the whole world from India"); JVS to DT, October 31, [1953], Box 28, DT-SYR; JVS to Adlai Stevenson, June 20, October 24, November 6, 1952 (quotation); Adlai Stevenson to JVS, July 14, 1952, Adlai B. Stevenson Papers, Box 75, f. 5, Princeton University Library.

39. JVS to HFA, September 28, [1950], Box 57, f. 17, HFA Papers; DT, "A Generation of Journalists Passes," ts. draft, May 1958, Box 95, DT-SYR, published as "We Got the News," OTR, *DBG*, May 28, 1958, 22, where "hell" became "heck"; DT to Mr. Dexter, October 25, 1953, carbon copy in Box 62, f. 1, HFA Papers; DT, "The Western Crisis Is Moral," OTR, *G&M*, May 14, 1958, 7; JVS to DT, February 15, 1952, Box 27, DT-SYR.

40. She continued writing for the *Ladies' Home Journal* until her death. See Kurth, *American Cassandra*, 402–468, on her final years; Sheean, *Dorothy and Red* (Boston: Houghton Mifflin, 1963), 326–327.

41. Robert Neville Rome, "A Talk with Vincent Sheean," *NYT*, November 17, 1963, BR32; JVS, *D&R*, 30–31; JVS to JG, May 24, [1963], Sheean correspondence, Houghton Mifflin Papers, bMS Am 2105 (228), f.6, Houghton Library. Reviews include William Shirer, "Marriage Was Quite Another Story," *NYT*, November 17, 1963, BR1; Edmund Fuller, "While Fame Gleamed, Their Marriage Died," *Ch T*, November 17, 1963, M1; Edward Laycock, "Loved Better in Letters" (quotation), *DBG*, November 17, 1963, 79; Edwin Castagna, "Headlong, Full of Flavor," *The Sun*, November 17, 1963, D7; Allen Morse, "Sad Story of a Marriage," *Hartford Courant*, March 8, 1964, 15F; JVS, *D&R*, 255–256.

42. JVS, *Personal History*, with new introduction by the author (Boston: Houghton Mifflin, 1969); JVS to Eric Severeid, June 23, [1968], Box 37, f. 9, Severeid Papers; Nancy F. Cott, "Revisiting the Transatlantic 1920s: Vincent Sheean vs. Malcolm Cowley," *American Historical Review* 118 (February 2013): 46–75.

43. DS to Marshall Best, April 8, 1977 ("honeymoon"); DS drafts, n.d. [1976–1977] (Mortimer quotation), in Jane Morton's possession.

CODA

1. JVS, *This House Against This House* (New York: Random House, 1946), 376–377.

2. JVS, *Between the Thunder and the Sun* (New York: Random House, 1943), 215–216; Malcolm Cowley, "Personal History, Cont'd" [review of *Between the Thunder and the Sun*], *TNR*, April 5, 1943, 450.

3. Henry B. Luce, "The American Century," *Life*, February 1941.

4. Joseph Barnes, quoted in JG diary, October 20, 1942, JG II; DT, "We Got the News," OTR, *DBG*, May 28, 1958, 22.

5. Howard K. Smith, "The Dubious Phoenix," *The Nation*, November 14, 1953, 400.

6. Will Irwin, *Propaganda and the News* (New York: McGraw-Hill, 1936), 10, 226.

Locations of Archives
Cited in Notes

(alphabetical by surname of author)

Edward Scribner Ames Papers 1893–1958, Special Collections Research Center, University of Chicago

Hamilton Fish Armstrong Papers, Public Policy Papers, Rare Books and Special Collections, Princeton University Library

George Pierce Baker Papers, Houghton Library, Harvard University

Joseph Barnes Papers, 1907–1970, Rare Book and Manuscript Library, Columbia University

Milly Bennett Papers, Hoover Institution Archives

Louise Bryant Papers, Sterling Memorial Library, Yale University

Charleston Papers, Kings College, Cambridge University (England)

Henry Wadsworth Longfellow Dana Papers, Longfellow House—Washington's Headquarters National Historic Site, Cambridge, Massachusetts

Louis Fischer Papers, Public Policy Papers, Rare Books and Special Collections, Princeton University Library

Joseph Freeman Papers, Hoover Institution Archives

Lewis Gannett Papers, Houghton Library, Harvard University

Martha Gellhorn Papers, Howard Gotlieb Archival Research Center, Boston University

C. Frank Glass Papers, Hoover Institution Archives

Frances Fineman Gunther Papers, Schlesinger Library, Radcliffe Institute, Harvard University

John Gunther Papers, 1935–1967, Special Collections Research Center, University of Chicago

John Gunther Papers, Addenda II, Special Collections Research Center, University of Chicago

Houghton Mifflin Papers, bMs Am 1925 and bMs Am 2105, Houghton Library, Harvard University

H. R. Knickerbocker Papers, Rare Book and Manuscript Library, Columbia University

Papers of Edna St. Vincent Millay, Special Collections, University of Virginia Library

Fred Millett Papers, Special Collections and Archives, Wesleyan University

Collection of Raymond Mortimer Materials, Rare Books and Special Collections, Princeton University Library

Raymond Mortimer Letters to Edward Sackville-West, Rare Books and Special Collections, Princeton University Library

Harold Nicolson diary, Balliol College, University of Oxford (England)

Radcliffe College Archives, Schlesinger Library, Radcliffe Institute for Advanced Study, Harvard University

Joel Raphaelson, private collection

Samson Raphaelson Papers, Rare Book and Manuscript Library, Columbia University

Samson Raphaelson Papers and Audio Recordings, University of Illinois Archives, University of Illinois at Urbana-Champaign

Rebecca Hourwich Reyher Papers, Schlesinger Library, Radcliffe Institute for Advanced Study, Harvard University

Franklin Delano Roosevelt Papers and Eleanor Roosevelt Papers, Hyde Park, New York

V.[ita] Sackville-West Mss., Lilly Library, Indiana University Libraries

Ellery Sedgwick Papers, Massachusetts Historical Society

Eric Severeid Papers, Library of Congress

Vincent Sheean Papers, Special Collections Research Center, Syracuse University

Vincent Sheean Papers, Division of Library, Archives and Museum Collections, Wisconsin Historical Society

Vincent Sheean–Ruth Falkenau Correspondence, Special Collections Research Center, University of Chicago

Stuart Sherman Papers, University of Illinois Archives, University of Illinois at Urbana-Champaign

Robert Sherwood Papers, Houghton Library, Harvard University

Carol Simons, private collection

Adlai Stevenson Papers, Public Policy Papers, Rare Books and Special Collections, Princeton University Library

Leland Stowe Papers, Division of Library, Archives and Museum Collections, Wisconsin Historical Society

Dorothy Thompson Collection, Special Collections Research Center, Syracuse University

Dorothy Thompson Papers, Special Collections Research Center, Syracuse University

Irita Van Doren Papers, Library of Congress

Rebecca West Papers, Beinecke Library, Yale University

Alexander Woollcott Papers, Houghton Library, Harvard University

Index

INDEX

American Communist Party, 203, 301
CCP, 118–119, 125, 129
Raphaelson, R., and, 203
Communist Party in Russia/Soviet
Union, 147, 152, 161
Sheean and, 256–257
condoms, 79
Cowles, Virginia, 287
Cowley, Malcolm, 205
Crevel, René, 104, 106
Czechoslovakia, 46–47
crisis over Sudetenland, 246–247

Dachau extermination camp, 297–298
Daily Maroon (University of Chicago), 9,
10, 62, 63
Daily Mirror (London), 16
Dana, Henry Wadsworth Longfellow
("Harry"), 78, 153, 170–171
Davidson, Jo, 275
Davis, Elmer, 289
Dawes Plan, 30, 50
Day, Dorothy, 113
De Porte, Barbara, 36–39
Death Be Not Proud (Gunther, J.), 314
Dewey, John, 116, 117
diaphragms, 79
dictatorships, 29–30, 82–86, 185, 193,
219–222, 229–231, 262
Dietrich, Marlene, 288
Dollfus, Engelbert, 194, 213
Dorothy and Red (Sheean), 317–318, 324
Douglas, Paul, 113
Dreiser, Theodore, 11, 62
Dunbar-Nelson, Alice, 11
Duranty, Walter, 155, 168, 206, 283

Edward VIII, 225
Einstein, Sergei, 161
Eisenhower, Dwight D., 290–291, 316
Elliott, Gertrude, 208
Elliott, Maxine, 208
Elmer Gantry (Lewis), 54, 82
Ernst, Morris, 260, 282

Europe, 9, 19, 31, 54–55, 84
authoritarianism in, 3, 6, 45–46,
179 (fig.)
changes from 1914 to 1920, 27 (fig.)
post–World War I, 1–2, 27–28
Sheean on, 28–29
US newspapers in, 3, 22–24, 26
See also specific countries
Evening Graphic, 16
Exile's Return (Cowley), 205

Fadiman, Clifton ("Kip"), 213–214, 281
Farson, Negley, 206
fascism, 3, 9, 24, 196, 197
in Austria, 178
Gunther, J., on, 219, 321
in Italy, 24, 46
Sheean on, 30, 321, 245–246
Thompson on, 234, 241, 321
See also anti-fascism; Nazism
FDR. *See* Roosevelt, Franklin Delano
feminism, 38, 47, 80, 115, 134, 164
Fischer, Louis, 248, 250, 287
Flanner, Janet, 21–22, 107, 281
Fodor, Marcel, 44–45, 48, 178, 186
Forbes-Robertson, Diana ("Dinah"),
209 (photo)
marriage, divorce, and remarriage to
Sheean, 207–210, 301–302,
315, 318
nursing Sheean, 211–212, 248
publication of British letters, 259
relief work by, 244
Ford, Ford Madox, 76–77
Ford, Henry, 185, 215
Foreign Affairs, 216, 250, 273, 315
foreign correspondents, 3, 6, 26, 93, 197,
322–323
censorship of, 193–194
Gunther, F., as, 213, 217
Gunther, J., as, 1, 4, 68, 70–73, 76,
80–84, 169–171, 173, 176–178,
180–181, 188–189, 193–194, 196,
218, 278, 290–291
in Hankou, 137

INDEX

Nancy F. Cott is the Jonathan Trumbull Research Professor of American History at Harvard University. Before moving to Harvard, she was for many years a professor of history and American studies at Yale University. She is the author of several previous books, including *The Grounding of Modern Feminism* and *Public Vows: A History of Marriage and the Nation*. She lives in Cambridge, Massachusetts.